CREATIONS OF THE MIND

Creations of the Mind presents sixteen original essays by theorists from a wide variety of disciplines who have a shared interest in the nature of artifacts and their implications for the human mind. All the papers are written specially for this volume, and they cover a broad range of topics concerned with the metaphysics of artifacts, our concepts of artifacts and the categories that they represent, the emergence of an understanding of artifacts in infants' cognitive development, as well as the evolution of artifacts and the use of tools by non-human animals. This volume will be a fascinating resource for philosophers, cognitive scientists, and psychologists, and the starting point for future research in the study of artifacts and their role in human understanding, development, and behaviour.

Eric Margolis is Professor of Philosophy at the University of Wisconsin-Madison.

Stephen Laurence is Professor of Philosophy at the University of Sheffield.

Creations of the Mind

Theories of Artifacts and Their Representation

edited by
ERIC MARGOLIS
and
STEPHEN LAURENCE

OXFORD
UNIVERSITY PRESS

OXFORD

UNIVERSITY PRESS

Great Clarendon Street, Oxford OX2 6DP

Oxford University Press is a department of the University of Oxford.
It furthers the University's objective of excellence in research, scholarship,
and education by publishing worldwide in

Oxford New York

Auckland Cape Town Dar es Salaam Hong Kong Karachi
Kuala Lumpur Madrid Melbourne Mexico City Nairobi
New Delhi Shanghai Taipei Toronto

With offices in

Argentina Austria Brazil Chile Czech Republic France Greece
Guatemala Hungary Italy Japan Poland Portugal Singapore
South Korea Switzerland Thailand Turkey Ukraine Vietnam

Oxford is a registered trade mark of Oxford University Press
in the UK and in certain other countries

Published in the United States
by Oxford University Press Inc., New York

British Library Cataloguing in Publication Data

Data available

Library of Congress Cataloging in Publication Data

Data available

Typeset by Laserwords Private Limited, Chennai, India
Printed in Great Britain
on acid-free paper by
Biddles Ltd., King's Lynn, Norfolk

ISBN 978–0–19–925098–1
ISBN 978–0–19–925099–8 (Pbk.)

1 3 5 7 9 10 8 6 4 2

Contents

List of Contributors

Paul Bloom, Department of Psychology, Yale University

Alfonso Caramazza, Department of Psychology, Harvard University

Susan Carey, Department of Psychology, Harvard University

Crawford L. Elder, Department of Philosophy, University of Connecticut

James L. Gould, Department of Ecology and Evolutionary Biology, Princeton University

Richard E. Grandy, Department of Philosophy, Rice University

Marissa L. Greif, Department of Psychology and Brain Sciences, Duke University

Marc D. Hauser, Departments of Psychology, Organismic and Evolutionary Biology, and Human Evolutionary Biology, Harvard University

Frank C. Keil, Department of Psychology, Yale University

Deborah Kelemen, Department of Psychology, Boston University

Rebekkah S. Kerner, Department of Psychology, Yale University

Hilary Kornblith, Department of Philosophy, University of Massachusetts

Jerrold Levinson, Department of Philosophy, University of Maryland, College Park

Bradford Z. Mahon, Department of Psychology, Harvard University

Barbara C. Malt, Department of Psychology, Lehigh University

Jean M. Mandler, Department of Cognitive Science, University of California, San Diego

Steven Mithen, Department of Archaeology, University of Reading

Laurie R. Santos, Department of Psychology, Yale University

John R. Searle, Department of Philosophy, University of California, Berkeley

Steven A. Sloman, Department of Cognitive and Linguistic Sciences, Brown University

Dan Sperber, Institut Jean Nicod (CNRS, EHESS, and ENS), Paris

Amie L. Thomasson, Department of Philosophy, University of Miami

Introduction

One of the most striking facts about human beings is that we live in a world that is, to an unprecedented extent, populated by our own creations. We are literally surrounded by artifacts of all shapes and sizes, ranging from simple objects, such as tables and chairs, to vastly complicated feats of technology, including televisions, automobiles, computers, power grids, and water-treatment plants. Given their prevalence, it is only natural that we should take these things for granted. But a moment's reflection reveals the significance of human artifacts for our daily lives. All you have to do is look around you. As Henry Petroski has remarked (1992, p. ix):

Other than the sky and some trees, everything I can see from where I now sit is artificial. The desk, books, and computer before me; the chair, rug, and door behind me; the lamp, ceiling, and roof above me; the roads, cars, and buildings outside my window. If truth be told, even the sky has been colored by pollution, and the stand of the trees has been oddly shaped to conform to the space allotted by development. Virtually all urban sensual experience has been touched by human hands, and thus the vast majority of us experience the physical world, at least, as filtered through the process of design.

Moreover, urban areas aren't the only ones that are populated by human artifacts. Just about everywhere on the planet where humans live, you will find both an abundance of artifacts and a landscape that has been substantially altered to meet human needs—from the roads and fences that cross-cut farmlands to the docks that protrude from small fishing villages.

Many artifacts have clear functional uses. They cook our food, they keep us warm and dry, they take us where we want to go. But human artifacts aren't purely utilitarian objects. They also have enormous cultural value. There is a big difference between driving a Volkswagen Beetle and a Hummer, or between wearing the latest Armani suit and an old pair of ripped, baggy jeans. The artifacts we surround ourselves with speak volumes about what is important to us, what groups we identify with, and who we are as individuals.

Artifacts are also important because of their potential to reveal distinctive features of the human mind. The image of 'man the tool-user' has been complicated by recent discoveries about the ecology of non-human animals (see Gould, this volume), but it is still quite reasonable to point to theoretically significant facts about human artifacts that may distinguish us as a species. Even if non-human animals might be said to produce artifacts of their own—as when chimpanzees employ small branches to collect hard-to-reach termites—it bears explaining why we humans are so much more prolific in the types of artifacts we create and why we are so much more flexible and creative in how we use them.

Humans clearly outstrip all other animals in our technological accomplishments. Why is that? Is it because we have a more powerful general intelligence? Is it owing to our possession of natural language? Is it because we have specialized cognitive systems or a special sort of psychological organization?

These are just a few of the questions that this book aims to address. Our goal has been to bring together theorists from a wide variety of disciplines that have a shared interest in the nature of artifacts and their implications for the human mind. The book is divided into four parts, although we should say at the outset that the divisions are somewhat artificial and that many of the chapters bear heavily on the issues that are featured in other parts of the book. We view this interplay of thought across subject areas and disciplines as a gratifying outcome and as a clear sign that researchers coming from rather different backgrounds and perspectives have a lot to say to one another.

Part I is primarily concerned with the *metaphysics* of artifacts. In one way or another, all of these chapters are concerned with the existence and nature of artifacts, for example, the question of whether artifacts are mind-dependent entities and whether being mind-dependent would make them any less real than other sorts of entities, especially natural kinds. Not all of the authors maintain that artifacts are mind-dependent, but among those who do, there is a further question about *how* artifacts depend on our thoughts about them. For something to be an artifact of a certain type (e.g. a chair) does it have to be the case that its creator had a specific intention in creating that object? And is there a way to distinguish the intention that may be necessary for an ordinary artifact from the intention that may be necessary to render something a work of art? Finally, one further question that is addressed in this section is whether it even makes sense to distinguish artifacts from natural kinds. On views according to which artifacts aren't mind-dependent, the distinction may seem artificial. But there are also numerous examples that challenge the distinction on intuitive grounds.

Part II is primarily concerned with *concepts* of artifacts and the *categories* they represent. Just as artifacts are ubiquitous in human life, so thoughts about artifacts are also ubiquitous—much of our daily thought is concerned with artifacts, making artifact concepts central to the study of concepts in general. Also, irrespective of the metaphysical dispute about the mind-dependence of artifacts, there remains the purely psychological question of how we do in fact think about them. For example, under what conditions would people think or say that something is a boat? Would it affect things to learn that the object lacked the function that is ordinarily associated with standard boats? How about the appearance? Is it possible that our judgments about artifactual identity are highly sensitive to the contextual features of a cognitive task? And what can we learn about artifact concepts by looking at case studies in neuropsychology and in the rapidly developing area of neuroimaging? Finally, Part II takes up the question of whether words for artifacts, and the concepts they express, pick out their referents without embodying a description of what they refer to. This approach to semantics is popular for natural kind terms and concepts but previously has received less support in discussion of artifacts.

Part III is primarily concerned with *cognitive development*. To what extent are infants able to categorize their experience in terms of artifact-related concepts, as opposed to simple low-level perceptual properties? At what point in cognitive development does an understanding of artifacts emerge? Are there important stages that children go through in developing artifact concepts? This part of the book also explores whether there are innate domain-specific systems for representing artifacts or whether the adult competence is based on a confluence of more general systems.

Part IV is primarily concerned with the *evolution* of artifacts and the use of artifacts by non-human animals. One facet of this issue is the widespread use of tools or tool-like entities among non-human animals, from chimpanzees to birds to insects. Another is the dispute about whether the underlying cognitive mechanisms are different for these animals than for humans. Yet another is the fascinating question of what can be said about our hominid ancestors and the role that artifacts play in helping us to determine when and how the modern mind first appeared.

This book has been in the works for a long time. We want to express our deepest gratitude to the authors and thank them for their patience. Thanks also to Peter Momtchiloff of Oxford University Press for his support of this project.

Eric Margolis and *Stephen Laurence*

PART I

METAPHYSICS

1

Social Ontology and the Philosophy of Society[1]

John R. Searle

The argument of this chapter will be a summary of some of the themes in my book *The Construction of Social Reality*[2] and a continuation of the line of argument I presented there. I want to make a plea for a branch of philosophy that in English speaking countries does not yet exist. It is what we might call the 'philosophy of society' and I see this subject as centering essentially around questions of social ontology.

We already have something called 'social and political philosophy' and we have the 'philosophy of social sciences'. But if you look closely at those disciplines you find that social and political philosophy really tends to be political philosophy. And the philosophy of social sciences really tends to be about questions of methodology in the social sciences. What I'm going to urge is that, in the sense in which there is a separate branch of philosophy that we now think of as the philosophy of language, but which didn't exist at the time of Kant and Leibniz, we should think of the philosophy of society as a separate branch of philosophy. And we should think of such topics as the nature of the appropriate methods in the social sciences, which you get in the 'philosophy of the social sciences', or 'the moral implications of social organizations', which you get in 'social and political philosophy', as special topics within the philosophy of society. In this chapter I am going to make a plea for the central branch of the philosophy of society which deals with the question of 'social ontology'.

---

[1] This chapter is based on a lecture originally delivered at The Einstein Forum in Berlin and subsequently published in *Analyse und Kritik*, vol. 20 (1998), copyright John R. Searle. These ideas are developed further and improved in John R. Searle, 'What is an Institution?,' *Journal of Institutional Economics*, vol 1, No. 1, June 2005 and 'Social Ontology: Some basic principles,' *Anthropological Theory*, vol. 6, No. 1, 2006.

[2] John R. Searle, *The Construction of Social Reality*. New York: The Free Press, 1995.

The question is: 'what is the ontology of social reality?' To begin with, I am going to make an assumption which I won't justify in this chapter. The assumption is that we should abandon the traditional Western distinction between mind and body. We have in the Western intellectual tradition been cursed with this dualism, with the idea that there is a fundamental distinction between the mind and the body, between the mental and the physical. And in some respects the situation is made even worse by those philosophers who say that in addition to two worlds, we also live in a third world. Philosophers such as Frege and Popper, and more recently Jürgen Habermas, have said we should think of reality as dividing into three different worlds. My own view is we should never have started counting. Descartes started counting and got up to two, Frege got up to three. I am saying: don't start counting. We live, as my colleague Donald Davidson puts it, in one world at most. That is enough for us. And the basic structure of this world is pretty much as described by physics and chemistry. Ultimate reality consists of entities we find it convenient to call 'particles'. They are organized in systems. These systems are defined by their causal relations, some of those systems are organic systems, some of the organic systems have consciousness. With consciousness comes intentionality, and when we have consciousness and intentionality, we have reached the evolutionary stage of animals, mammals, and especially primates like ourselves, who form social groups.

1. SOME PUZZLING FEATURES OF SOCIAL REALITY

Now with all that by way of introduction, here is my problem. If you look at our social life, it is a remarkable fact that there is a class of entities that have a very important role in our lives, but they only are what they are, because we believe that that is what they are. I will take an obvious economic example: I carry around in my wallet these sordid bits of paper. And they are really not very important as physical objects, but they matter to us. They are examples of 'money'. Now here is my puzzle: It is only money, because we believe that it is money, and yet it is an objective fact that it is money. That is, when I go into a store and I give them one of these, they don't say: 'Well, maybe you think it's money, but why should we care what you think?' They accept it as money. So, here is the initial formulation of my puzzle: How can there be an important and objective class of entities that only exist because we think they exist?

I believe that when you start a philosophical investigation you have to start naively, and I am just going naively to tell you some of the puzzling features about social and institutional reality. After having gone through a stage of naivety we must become immensely sophisticated in giving answers to our puzzles. I have never found the algorithm for deciding when you have to stop being dumb and naive and start being smart and sophisticated. We shall just play it by ear as we go along. Anyway, here goes with half-a-dozen puzzling features of social reality.

Problem number one is that there is a kind of self-referentiality in social concepts. In that it's only money if we believe it's money, and it's only property, marriage, government, a cocktail party, tenure, a summer vacation, if that's what we believe it is. But now, if money is partly defined as that which is believed to be money, then philosophers are going to get worried. If it has to be believed to be money in order to be money, what is the content of the belief? It looks like you are going to have circularity or infinite regress, because if part of the ontology of money is believed to be money, then part of the definition of 'money' is believed to be money, and consequently, the belief that something is money has to be in part the belief that it's believed to be money. And that means you are in trouble, because then the content of that belief is that it is believed to be believed to be money, and so on. So that's the first puzzle: how do we avoid circularity or infinite regress in the definition of 'money' if the concept has this self-referential component? And what goes for money also goes for property, marriage, government, and all sorts of other social and institutional phenomena.

Let me nail down the problem about self-referentiality a little more closely with examples. I said, it's only money, property, marriage, government, etc. if we think that that is what it is. This actually has important consequences. Suppose, we decide we are going to give a cocktail party and we invite the whole population of a town, and we have a hell of a great cocktail party. But suppose things get out of hand and the casualty rate is worse than the battle of Gettysburg. All the same, it's not a war. It's not a war, unless people think it's a war. As long as they think it's a cocktail party, then it's a cocktail party, it's just a hell of a cocktail party. This feature of self-referentiality is actually of some historical importance. I have always wondered, how could Cortez with 150 or so bewildered Spaniards beat the entire Aztec army? Not to mention Toltec, Mixtec, Aranhuac, and other tribes. Well, part of the answer is, they had a different definition of what they were doing. You see, the Aztecs were fighting a war according to their definition. That means you get close enough to an enemy so that you can hold him without bruising him and later on you sacrifice him to the Great God Quetzalcoatl by cutting out his living heart with an obsidian knife on the top of a pyramid. Well, that may be a great definition of warfare for Central American tribes; but it is very ineffective against Europeans on horses with metal weapons. So the sorts of phenomena I'm talking about actually have historical consequences. It isn't just that we are dealing with philosophical puzzles.

Now that leads to a second question, and that is, what is the role of language in the constitution of social and institutional reality? It looks as if in the case of these institutional phenomena, language doesn't just describe a pre-existing reality, but is partly constitutive of the reality that it describes. It looks like the vocabulary of money and government and property and marriage and football games and cocktail parties is partly constitutive of the phenomena. Otherwise, how do we account for the differences between animals that are incapable of language and consequently incapable of this sort of institutional ontology, and language-using animals like ourselves, where the words, in some sense we need to explain, seem to be partly constitutive of the social and institutional reality? Let me nail that down with an example. My dog Ludwig is very intelligent, but there are limits to his intelligence. Suppose I give him a pile of dollar bills and I train him to bring me a dollar bill whenever he wants to be fed. All the same, he is not buying anything, and it's not really money to him. His bringing me the money is not an economic transaction. Why not?

So far I have covered two sources of puzzlement. The constitutive role of language and self-referentiality. A third related source of puzzlement for me (and this has a special interest to me) is the special role of performatives in the creation of social and institutional reality. For a very large number of institutional facts you can create the fact just by saying you are creating it, provided you have the appropriate authority in the appropriate situation and the context is correct. So, you can adjourn the meeting by saying 'I adjourn the meeting'. You can declare war by saying 'We declare war'. You can pronounce somebody husband and wife by saying 'I pronounce you husband and wife', and so on with a large number of cases. Now why is that? How can you create institutional reality just by saying you are creating it? You cannot do it with everything. You cannot score a goal in football by saying 'I score a goal', or even 'We hereby score a goal'. So what is the difference? What is going on here?

I will give you a couple of more of these puzzles and then we will start to try to solve them. A fourth puzzling feature of social reality is the complex interrelations among the elements. They seem to be systematic. So you don't just have money, but in order to have money you have to have a system of exchange, ownership, payment, debts; and in general you have to have a system of rights and obligations. It might seem that games are an exception because games are self-enclosed in a way that money and property and marriage are not. But even in the game you understand the position of a batter and the position of a pitcher only in terms of understanding the notions of rights and obligations. And that already involves you in more general social and institutional notions. So I am struck by the pervasive interlocking character of the kinds of social and institutional phenomena that I'll be talking about.

There is one last puzzle I will mention. We could go on listing puzzles, but let's settle for five. The fifth puzzle that interests me is: though there exists a real institutional reality of elections, wars, property exchanges, stock markets, and so on, nonetheless you can't have an institutional reality without an underlying brute physical reality. Here is an interesting fact. Money can take a very large number of forms. It can be in the form of gold or silver or paper or copper, it can be in the form of credit cards, and some primitive tribes use wampum or seashells. By the way, most of your money underwent a dramatic physical change in the past ten or twenty years that you didn't even notice. It happened in the middle of the night. Most of your money is now represented by magnetic traces on computer discs in banks, and it doesn't make a bit of difference: you didn't lose any sleep at all over this, though there was a revolutionary change in the physical representation of your money. Now, here is the point. Almost anything can be money, but at some point it has to have some physical reality. There has to be something, whether it be gold or magnetic traces, that counts or could count as money or at least as the representation of money. Why is that? Why is the physical necessary, and why is there a primacy of the brute physical fact over the institutional fact?

2. CONCEPTUAL TOOLS NECESSARY TO ACCOUNT FOR SOCIAL REALITY

Now we have a problem. Let's go to work to solve it. In order to solve it, I want to make another distinction that I have been presupposing and that I think is absolutely essential for understanding our position in the world. There are classes of objective facts in the world which have to be distinguished from certain other objective facts in the following regard. Many things that we think of as real nonetheless only exist relative to observers, in the form of reality that they have. We need to distinguish those features of the world that we might call 'observer-independent' from those features that are observer-dependent. Observer-independent features are those that, so to speak, don't give a damn about human observers, and here I am thinking of things like mountains and molecules and galaxies and processes like photosynthesis and mitosis and meiosis. All of those phenomena are observer-independent. But in addition to them, there are lots of other phenomena in the world whose existence depends on being treated or regarded in a certain way by human agents. Observer-dependent phenomena would include such things as chairs and tables and glasses and money and property and marriage. So, we need a general distinction between those phenomena whose existence is observer-independent and those whose existence is observer-relative.

Typically an observer-dependent entity will have both sorts of features. So this object, which I carry around in my pocket, has a certain weight, and that it has the weight that it has is observer-independent. It doesn't depend on me or anyone else, it depends on the gravitational relations between the object and the center of the earth. But this object is also a Swiss army knife, and the feature of being a Swiss army knife is observer-relative. So we need a general distinction between those phenomena that are observer-independent and those that are observer-relative. Typically the natural sciences deal with phenomena that are observer-independent, phenomena like mountains and molecules and tectonic plates. Typically the social sciences, such as economics, sociology, and political science, deal with phenomena that are observer-relative. And here I am thinking of such things as political parties, elections, social classes, and money. We can now specify our topic a little bit more precisely: we are discussing the ontology of a certain class of observer-relative social and institutional reality.

For the analysis of this social reality I need exactly three devices, three tools to try to analyse that ontology.

Here is the first one. We need to call attention to the class of entities to which we have assigned functions. Many of the most common concepts that we use in dealing with the world, for example, concepts like 'cars' and 'bathtubs' and 'tables' and 'chairs' and 'houses', involve the assignment of function. It is a remarkable capacity that humans and certain animals have, that they can assign functions to objects, where the object does not have that function independently of the assignment. And I want to make a strong claim about this assignment of function. I want to say: all functions are observer-relative. It is only relative to agents, only relative to observers, that something can be said to have a certain function.

We are blinded to this fact by the practice in biology of talking about functions interchangeably with talking about causation. But there is a subtle difference. We do indeed discover such facts as the fact that the function of the heart is to pump blood. We do indeed discover that the function of the vestibular ocular reflex is to stabilize the retinal image. But we discover those functions only against the background presupposition of certain norms. We have to assume that life and survival have a value, and it is against the presupposition of the norm, against the assumption that life and survival and reproduction are valuable, that we can say such things as that the function of the heart is to pump blood. If we thought that life and survival were worthless, that the only thing that really mattered was death and extinction, then hearts would be disfunctional, and cancer would have a useful function: it would hasten extinction. We don't think these things, and it is crucial to our assignments of function that we don't. But it is only against the background of the presupposition of normativity that we can discover such facts as the fact that the function of the heart is to pump blood.

One way put to this point is to ask: what is the difference between saying that the heart causes the pumping of blood, on the one hand, and saying that the function of the heart is to pump blood, on the other. And it seems to me there is a crucial distinction, because once you introduce the notion of function you introduce normativity. Once you introduce the notion of function, you can talk about such things as heart disease, malfunctioning hearts, hearts that function better than other hearts. Notice, we don't talk about better and worse stones, unless we assign a function to the stone. If you think this stone will make a good projectile, then you can evaluate it. You can say this one is better than that one. Or if you assign it an esthetic function, you can say this stone is an *objet d'art trouvé*, and with such an assignment of function you may think the stone has some artistic value. So that's the first point, we assign functions and all functions are observer-relative.

The second notion I need is that of collective intentionality. All genuinely social behavior contains collective intentionality on the part of the participants. You can see the centrality of collective intentionality if you contrast genuine cooperative behavior with behavior which merely happens to be coordinated with other behavior. Suppose, for example, that we are playing in a symphony orchestra. Suppose I am playing the violin part and you are singing the soprano part, and together we are part of the performance of Beethoven's Ninth Symphony. We have to be able to make the difference between me sawing away on the violin and you independently but by chance simultaneously singing 'Freude, schöner Götterfunken', and us doing this intentionally together in concert. So a basic ontological fact about social and collective behavior seems to be collective or shared intentionality in the form of collective beliefs, desires, and intentions.

But in my intellectual tradition the existence of collective intentionality creates a real problem. If all the intentionality I have is in my head, and all the intentionality you have is in your head, how can there be such a thing as collective intentionality? There are a lot of ingenious efforts to try to solve this problem in philosophy. Basically they try to do it by reducing collective intentionality to individual or singular intentionality. They try to reduce we-intend, we-believe, etc. to I-intend plus I-believe that you have such and such an intention. And then on your part it is I-intend plus I-believe that you have such and such an intention.

On the view that I am opposed to, the assumption is that We-intentionality must reduce to I-intentionality. Collective intentionality must reduce to individual intentionality. Otherwise you would have violated the 'principle of methodological individualism'. If you say that collective intentionality is primitive, then it seems you are in very bad company. It seems that you are postulating some kind of Hegelian Weltgeist that is floating around overhead, or something like that. Where I live you don't want to be caught doing that, otherwise you'll lose a lot of friends. Given that puzzle—How can there be collective intentionality, when all intentionality is individual?—it looks like we have to reduce collective intentionality to individual intentionality. An enormous amount of intellectual effort has been spent, in my view wasted, trying to do that. The analysis that comes out involves something called 'mutual belief'.

For example, consider a case where we are pushing a car together to try to get it started. Now that is a case of collective intentionality. So how is that supposed to be analyzed? The idea is this. When we are pushing the car together, then I intend to push the car and you intend to push the car. And I believe that you believe that I intend, and I believe that you believe that I believe that you believe that I intend, and so on up in an infinite hierarchy. And for you it is the same. It's 'I believe that you believe', etc., on up. Now I think my poor brain will not carry that many beliefs, and I want to suggest that there is a very simple way out of this puzzle. The puzzle is, assuming that all intentionality is in the heads of individual human and animal agents, how can it be the case that it's all in our individual brains, if some of it is irreducibly collective? And the answer is, that we can have intentionality in your brain and my brain which is in the form of the first person plural as much as we can have it in the form of the first person singular.

On my view there is a trivial notational solution to the puzzle. The irreducible form of the intentionality in my head, when we are doing something collectively, is 'we intend'. And I don't have to reduce that to an 'I intend' and a set of mutual beliefs. On the contrary, I have the 'I-intends' that I do have, precisely because I have an irreducible 'we-intend'. To nail that down to cases, I am indeed playing the violin and you are singing the soprano part, but I am only doing what I am doing and you are doing what you are doing, because we together are collectively playing the chorale movement of Beethoven's Ninth Symphony. I hope everybody sees that point.

As I said, the problem I am discussing has a traditional name. It's called 'the problem of methodological individualism'. And the assumption has always been: either you reduce collective intentionality to the first person singular, to 'I intend', or else you have to postulate a collective world spirit and all sorts of other perfectly dreadful metaphysical excrescences. But I reject the assumption that in order to have all my intentionality in my head, it must be expressible in the first-person-singular form. I have a great deal of intentionality which is in the first person plural.

Nothing comes without a price, and we do pay a price for the solution that I am proposing to this puzzle. The price is this. It turns out that I can be mistaken, not only in what is happening in the world, but I can be mistaken about the very mental state that I have. That violates the Cartesian assumption that we cannot be mistaken about our intentions. But I think that is the right way to think of it. Suppose, in the case where we are pushing the car, I discover that you weren't in fact pushing? You were just going along for a ride, I was doing all the pushing. Well, then I was not only mistaken in one of my beliefs, but it turns out that in a way I also was mistaken about what I was doing. I thought I was pushing as part of our pushing, and in fact that's not what was happening. I was doing all the pushing, you were just pretending. So that is a price that we have to pay. You can be mistaken about the nature of the activity you are engaged in, if you have an assumption about the collective intentionality which is not shared by your apparent cooperators. But that seems to be the situation we are in in real life.

The third tool is this. Years ago, when I first started working on speech acts, I made a distinction between brute facts and institutional facts. Those facts that I said were 'institutional facts' presuppose a human institution for their existence, for example, such facts as that somebody is checkmated in chess, or somebody is elected president of the United States. I wanted to distinguish those facts, which are called institutional facts, from brute facts whose existence does not require a human institution, the fact, for example, that the earth is 93 million miles away from the sun. You need an institution in order to state or describe that brute fact; you need the institution of language and the institution of measurement in mileage to describe it that way, and you could state the same brute fact using different institutions. For example, you could state the same fact in French, using kilometers as units of measurement. But the point I'm making is, the fact of distance between the earth and the sun does not depend on a human institution, though of course you have to have institutions in order to describe or state the fact. Now here is the point. There is a class of facts that are institutional facts and another class of facts that are brute facts, because they do not require human institutions. And then the question is, how are institutional facts possible?

I also made the claim that you need a distinction between two kinds of rule. One sort of rule regulates antecedently existing forms of behavior. Another sort of rule doesn't just regulate antecedently existing forms of behavior, but creates the possibility of new forms of behavior. I call the difference between these two sorts of rule—using a Kantian terminology here—'regulative' rules, that regulate antecedently existing forms of behavior, and 'constitutive' rules, that constitute new forms of behavior. Examples are obvious: the rule 'drive on the right-hand side of the road' doesn't create the possibility of driving. Driving can exist without that rule. That is a rule to regulate the already existing activity of driving. But the rules of chess are not like that. It wasn't the case that there were a lot of people pushing bits of wood around on boards and somebody said: 'Look fellows, we have to get some rules so we don't keep bashing into each other. You stay on the right with your knight and I go on the left with my bishop!' Rather, the rules of chess are constitutive in the sense that they create the possibility of the activity in question. Playing chess is constituted by acting in accordance with at least a certain large subset of the rules of chess.

Now here is the bottom line of this discussion. Those rules have a typical form. The form is 'X counts as Y' or 'X counts as Y in context C'. That is, such and such a move counts as a 'legal knight-move'. Such and such a position counts as 'you being in check'. Such and such a position counts as 'checkmate', and checkmate counts as 'winning' or 'losing' the game. And what goes for chess goes for much more elaborate institutions: such and such noises count as 'making a promise', such and such marks on the paper count as 'voting' in an election, such and such number votes counts as 'winning' an election, and so on with a large number of institutional structures.

3. STATUS FUNCTIONS

We now have three tools to solve our problems. These are, first, the assignment of function, second, collective intentionality, and third, constitutive rules, rules of the form 'X counts as Y'. With all this apparatus assembled, let's go to work. I will now try to put it all together. I want you to imagine a simple community of (let's call them) hominids, beasts more or less like ourselves. Now it's very easy to imagine that such organisms, such primates, can assign functions to objects. It's easy to imagine that they use a stick to dig with, or they use a stump to sit on. They can assign a function of being a digging tool or a stool to sit on. But now it's not a big step to imagine that they do that collectively. That collectively they have a very big stick that they use as a lever, or they have a big log that they use as a bench to sit on collectively. So it's very easy to tie collective intentionality to the assignment of function.

But now I want you to imagine the next step. Imagine—to take an example—our group of hominids live in a series of huts, and they build a wall around the huts. Imagine that they build a wall to keep intruders out and to keep their own members in. And now this is a case of the collective assignment of function, where the function is performed in virtue of the physics of the object on which the function is assigned. We just assume the wall is too big to climb over easily. But now imagine that the wall gradually decays, to the point where it is no longer able to keep the members of the community in, in virtue of its physical structure, nor to keep intruders out, in virtue of its physical structure. But now let's suppose that, out of habit or whatever, the people involved continue to *recognize* the wall as a boundary, that is, they continue to *acknowledge* or *accept* that you are not supposed to cross the boundary. It is important to notice the vocabulary we use of 'acknowledge', 'accept', and 'recognize'. That is, we imagine that the wall continues to serve its function, but no longer in virtue of its physical structure. It serves its function in virtue of the fact that it has a certain recognized status.

Now I wanted that to sound innocent, but I think that the move I just described is the basic move by which we create institutional reality of a specifically human sort. What happened was this. We imagine that an entity is used to perform a function, but it cannot perform the function in virtue of its physical structure. It can only perform the function in virtue of the collective recognition or acceptance of the entity in question as having a status and a function that comes with the status. And I want to say that the underlying idea behind that is 'X counts as Y'. This line of stones, which is all that is left of the wall, now counts as a boundary. It now has a deontic status, it now has a form of power, which it exercises not in virtue of its physical structure, but in virtue of the collective assignment of function.

And I want to introduce a name for this sort of function—let's call these 'status functions'. A status function is a function that an entity or person performs not in virtue of its physical structure alone, but in virtue of the collective imposition or recognition of the entity or person in question as having a certain status, and with that status a function that can only be performed in virtue of the collective recognition of the status. And the structure of that—logically speaking—is the collective imposition of a function of the form 'this entity X counts as having this status and therefore this function as Y in this context C'. Now, I'm making a strong claim: this little device is the foundation stone of all institutional reality. So let's go to work and explain that claim.

I want to extend this account to the case of money. And just to nail it down to historical example, I want to talk briefly about the evolution of paper currency in medieval Europe. (I love the Middle Ages, because it is, in a sense, the childhood of our civilization. In medieval Europe you see institutional forms that are growing and decaying, and the development of paper money is a very good example.) Initially people carried around gold and silver coins and the use of gold and silver was a form of barter. It was a form of barter, because the value of the coin was exactly equal to the value of the gold or silver contained in the coin, and the valuable coin was exchanged for other things. Now, if you look in the textbooks they tell us there are three kinds of money. There is 'commodity money', there is 'contract money', and there is 'fiat money'. But what they don't tell you is, What's the relation between them? The initial case we are talking about, where people actually had gold and silver, is a case of commodity money. Barter in gold and silver is both dangerous and inefficient, so people found they could leave the gold and silver with a group of people who worked on benches, and they were called 'bankers', and the bankers would give them bits of paper on which it was said, 'We will pay the bearer of this note a piece of gold on demand'.

With the introduction of the bits of paper we have now moved from commodity money to contract money, because the bit of paper is a contract to pay in gold or silver on demand. Later some genius discovered that you can actually increase the supply of money in circulation if you give out more bits of paper than you actually have gold in the bank. And as long as not everybody runs to the bank at once, it works. The bits of paper are still as good as gold. Much later on some genius discovered—and it took a long time to make this discovery—you can forget about the gold, and just have the paper. And that's the situation we are in now. We moved from commodity money, which is barter, to contract money, to fiat money. If you look at these bits of paper that I was waving around earlier, they seem to me good examples of the form 'X counts as Y', that is, such and such bits of paper count as 'currency'. As it says on the piece of paper that I'm holding here: 'This note is legal tender for all debts public and private.' It counts as money in the United States. But that it counts as money is a matter of collective acceptance of the status function in accordance with the structure: 'Such and such counts as so and so.' These bits of paper count as legal currency in the United States, just as these other bits of paper count as legal currency in the German Federal Republic.

Now, notice that once you have that structure 'X counts as Y', then automatically certain forms of abuse become possible. If I go into my basement and produce a lot of things that look like these bits of paper, I will be producing counterfeit money. Thus a dollar isn't just anything that looks like this, but it has to be issued by the Bureau of Engraving and Printing under the authority of the Treasury. So one form of abuse is counterfeiting. The structure automatically makes it possible to have abuses, because you can present something as satisfying the X term even if it doesn't in fact, and that's counterfeit. Another form of abuse is if you get too many of the entities in question. Then you have inflation, and in hyper-inflation the entities are no longer able to function as money. And what goes for money goes for other forms of social institutions. You can have counterfeit lawyers and counterfeit doctors, that is, people who don't actually satisfy the conditions, but who masquerade as lawyers and doctors. In the state of California we now have so many lawyers that there is a kind of inflation.

Now here is a puzzling question. If I am correct in describing the logical structure of status functions, if it is just a matter of imposing status and with it a function, then how can the system be so powerful? How can these structures have such an enormous effect on our lives when, as I have described it, it all seems so fragile? There are two parts to the answer to that. One is this: the structure can be iterated indefinitely. Let me give an example. I make noises through my mouth, I just emit this acoustic blast. But these count as sentences of English. And in a certain context making noises of that sort, uttering those sentences of English, counts as making a promise. Making that kind of promise in that kind of context counts as making a contract. Notice how we are going up in the hierarchy. The X-term at one level will have been the Y-term at an earlier level and you keep going with it. Making that sort of contract counts as getting married. And in the State of California, once you get married all kinds of things happen. You are entitled to spousal benefits, income-tax deductions, all sorts of rights concerning property, taxes, and so on. So you get an indefinite iteration.

The second point is that you get interlocking structures. I don't just have money, but I have money in my bank account at the Bank of America, which is put there by my employer, the State of California, and which I use to pay my debts to the Pacific Gas and Electric Company as well as my federal, state, and local taxes and my credit-card debts. Now, just about every phrase I uttered in that litany was an institutional notion. We are talking about interlocking institutional facts. The whole point of the institutional is often to structure the brute. For example, recently I went and stood in front of a woman at a counter. I made noises and she made noises, I gave her a plastic card, she gave me sheets of paper, and the next thing is I was on an airplane on my way to Berlin. The movement of my body was a brute fact. My body moved from California to Berlin. (My body is still complaining about the jetlag.) But the institutional facts made the brute fact possible. We are talking about a structure whose point is not just to empower other institutional structures, but to control brute reality.

However, the structure is also fairly fragile, and the amazing thing is how rapidly it can collapse. I will never forget the moment when I saw the people coming over the Berlin Wall on television. It was an amazing moment, because

I was of a generation that thought the two-power division of the world would go on indefinitely. But there came a point when the system of institutional reality was simply no longer acceptable, and it just collapsed quite suddenly. So you can have a collapse of the institutional structure, if it's no longer accepted, and you can have a decay of the institutional structure of the sort that I have been describing.

4. SOLUTIONS TO THE PUZZLES

Let us turn now to see how we can solve these puzzles I began with. First, how can there be self-referentiality without circularity or infinite regress? Well, the answer is, you don't have to use the word 'money' in order to define money. The word 'money' functions as a summary term or as a placeholder for being a medium of exchange, a store of value, a payment for services rendered, a measure of value of other currencies, and so on. And if something performs all of those functions, then it's money. So we do not have a vicious circularity or infinite regress. If I say that in order for something to be money, people have to believe that it's money, there is no circularity, because they can have that belief without having the word 'money'. The word 'money' here just is a place-holder for a large number of other functional expressions.

Now, what about our second and third points, the role of language and especially performatives? How can performatives create institutional reality? And the answer to that is, that where the X-term is itself a speech act, then typically you can create the reality by performing that speech act. So you can make somebody husband and wife by saying 'I pronounce you husband and wife', or you can find somebody guilty in a court if you are a judge by saying 'I find you guilty as charged'. And the creation of the institutional fact need not even take the performative form. It says on this twenty-dollar bill: 'This note is legal tender for all debts public and private.' Now, I am an epistemologist and my natural worry is, 'How do you know?', and I want to write to the Treasury and say: 'How do you guys really know that it's legal tender? Have you done a survey, have you done an empirical study?' And the answer is, it isn't an empirical claim. They make it legal tender by declaring that it's legal tender.

Our next point—and this is the most important—is the constitutive role of language. Why is language constitutive of institutional reality, in a way that it's not constitutive of other forms of reality? Why is it that money and property and marriage and government require a vocabulary in a way that tectonic plates and gravitational attraction and galaxies do not require vocabulary for their existence? That is in fact a very hard question to answer and I spent a whole chapter on it in *The Construction of Social Reality*, but now I will just summarize the answer in one sentence: for institutional facts there has to be some form of symbolism, because there isn't anything else to mark the transition from X to Y. We just count the X-term as having a Y-status. But if we so count it, there must be some way to represent that counting feature. My dog can see somebody cross the line while carrying a ball, but can't see him score a 'touch-down'. Why not? Because in order to see him score a touch-down you have to have some way to represent the extra status function, and that requires language.

Now you might ask, well, why do you need words? And the answer is in some cases you do not. Suppose we kept score in a soccer match by piling up stones. I score a goal so I get a white stone to put on my side, and you score a goal so you put a white stone on your side, and these are points. I got a point and you got a point. But now here is the 'point': these stones now play a linguistic role. They are now symbolic. They now play the role of symbolizing scoring in the game. So the language or some other symbolism has to be constitutive because there isn't an independent ontology. The move from X to Y is itself a symbolizing linguistic move and there has to be some way for us to represent it, otherwise it doesn't function.

Well, our last questions had to do with systematic relations of institutional reality and also with the priority of the brute over the institutional facts. The answer to the first of these questions is this: the reason we have all this institutional ontology is to organize and regulate our lives. So there has to be a set of interlocking institutions. What I haven't had time to tell you is that all of this at bottom is about power. We are talking about how society creates and organizes power relations. It normally does it through the institution of status functions. Somebody is the boss and somebody else an employee, somebody is an elected president, somebody is defeated, and so on. And all of this is designed precisely to intersect with other elements of the society. So, in order to have money you have to have a system of rights and obligations. You have to have the ability to buy and to sell, to store value in the form of money, to receive money as payment for services rendered. So, that is the reason for the interlocking complexity. That's what we have the system for. It is designed and has developed to enable people to cope in complex social groups, in power relations.

The final question was, why is there this priority of brute facts over institutional facts? And the answer to that is, because the iterated structure of 'X counts as Y' has to bottom-out somewhere. For instance, my making a contract can be derived from my signing my name, and my signing my name can be a matter of certain words being written on a page. But then you reach the point where there isn't any more 'X counts as Y'. You just have the brute fact, for example the signature, as X-term. So institutional reality of ownership and obligation is built on top of physical reality, it has to bottom-out in physical reality.

Now, to conclude, I said I would like us to think of the possibility of creating a philosophy of society, where our first task would be to get an understanding of social ontology. If we got that, then, I think, it would give a different cast to our political and social theories. I think that political philosophy in the West contains a large fantasy element about how we make social contracts with each other, and about when people can violate or not violate the social contract. But in real life it isn't like that, in real life it's a matter of accepting or rejecting, or furthering or fighting against institutional reality. And one way to create institutional reality often is to act as if it already existed. This is how the United States was created. There was no legal way that a group of people could get together in Philadelphia, all of them subjects of the British Crown in a British Crown Colony, and declare themselves to be an independent nation. There was no institutional structure to enable them to do that. But they just did it. They did it and they got away with it. It helped that they had an army and had the support of the French, and so on. But you can do this if you can get away with it. You can create an institutional reality just by acting as if it already existed.

One last thought I want to leave you with is this. In order to articulate this process, I have made it look much more conscious than it really is. Most of these things develop quite unconsciously, and indeed people typically are not even aware of the structure of institutional reality. It often works best when they have false beliefs about it. So there are a lot of people in the United States who still believe that a dollar is only really money because it is backed by all that gold in Fort Knox. It's the gold in Fort Knox that makes the dollar money. This is a total fantasy, of course. The gold has nothing to do with it. And people hold other false beliefs. They believe someone is king only because he is divinely anointed, or they believe that marriages have to be made by God in heaven, and so on. I am not trying to discourage them from these beliefs, because often the institution functions best when people hold false beliefs about it. But I think as philosophers we must, as a first step in understanding social reality, and as our first step in creating a philosophy of society, understand the basic ontology of social reality.

2

Artifacts: Parts and Principles

Richard E. Grandy

1. INTRODUCTION AND A PUZZLE

In thinking about artifacts and concepts of artifacts, it is difficult to know where one should start let alone where one hopes to end. As always, we want to do justice to our intuitions, but there is the question of who the 'we/our' is and whether the intuitions are coherent. For example, there are three metaphysical principles which are widely accepted and which come into conflict. One is that in some sense of basic physical objects, objects are spatially continuous; the second is that objects are temporally continuous; and the third is that when I disassemble a bicycle and reassemble it a week later it is the same bicycle. (I am not here addressing 'ship of Theseus' issues,[1] I am discussing the case in which we reassemble exactly the same pieces.) We are forced in this situation either to accept that:

- the bicycle's existence has a temporal gap, that it does not exist for the week it is disassembled, or
- the bicycle exists as a spatially scattered object for a week, i.e. during that week its location is a discontinuous spatial region, or
- to deny that it is the same bicycle, i.e. the bicycle we assemble a week later is not the same one that we disassembled.

It is easy to multiply examples, but much easier with artifacts such as bicycles, and in addition to the main question about which intuition to sacrifice, I want to explore the question of whether and why this seems special to artifacts.

---

[1] In Greek mythology Theseus replaced various parts of his ship during a journey until none of the original material remained. In 1655 the philosopher Thomas Hobbes (1994: 136–7) embellished the story by imagining someone following Theseus, gathering the discarded planks and re-creating a ship from the original material, posing the question which ship is the original.

2. THE ARTIFACT–NATURAL KIND DICHOTOMY—MUDDYING THE H₂O

Before moving further down that path, I think it will be salutary to examine the range of artifacts. One typically contrasts artifacts with natural kinds, and we usually have in mind as examples of artifacts middle-sized objects associated with sortal predicates: bicycles, cups, clocks. But this represents only a small subset of the kinds of artifacts. For example, there are many kinds of artifacts which are described by sortals but which are somewhat anomalous as 'objects': cities, roads, and lakes; and there are many artifacts which are not objects but substances: polystyrene, decaffeinated coffee, stainless steel. In addition there are also kinds of artifacts that involve a sortal together with a substance term: piece of polystyrene, cup of decaffeinated coffee, sheet of stainless steel.

Prima facie there is a sharp distinction between natural kinds and artifacts, but I think that on reflection this is an illusion due to thinking of natural kinds as biological and chemical kinds and artifacts as medium-sized manufactured objects. If we consider not just items to which sortal predicates apply, but also stuff, then the distinction immediately becomes much more blurred. When I say that the distinction becomes blurred, I don't merely mean that many words have both a natural kind and an artifactual sense. Bloom (this volume) argues that 'water' has two meanings: in one sense it denotes a kind of artifact, in the other a natural kind. I mean that the objects and kinds of objects fall on a continuum. I will argue that while prototypical natural kinds and prototypical artifacts are a considerable distance apart on this continuum, there are no principled points, or reasons, to draw a metaphysical distinction somewhere on this continuum.

For example, consider iron. Iron, as one of the basic chemical elements, would seem to be a prototypical natural kind. Its essence seems to be given by, or determined by, the structure of the relevant atoms, and there are laws about its melting point, conductivity, magnetizability, and so on. But in fact the pure element Fe almost never occurs naturally on Earth, but is almost always found in an iron oxide that has to be chemically purified. Still, the intuition that such a substance is a natural kind is very strong. And while iron oxide may be a natural kind, it is quite a different natural kind from iron. The same is true of most of the metals, and many of the gases. Even hydrogen and oxygen are rare in their elemental form and are much more ubiquitous as components of H₂O. Kornblith (this volume) gives as his example of baptizing a natural kind the creation of a new chemical compound in the laboratory!

The thoughtful reader will already have noticed that none of the substances I mentioned a few paragraphs earlier—polystyrene, decaffeinated coffee, or stainless steel—exist in nature. But they also have essences determined by their molecular structure, and there are laws about their structural strength, conductivity, and so on. In this regard there seems to be no significant difference between natural kinds of stuff and some artifactual kinds of stuff.

It appears that there is a psychological difference in the usual concepts of natural kinds and artifacts, and evidence to support and understand this is adduced by the papers in this volume by Kelemen and Carey, Keil, Greif, and Kerner, and Mandler. In this case there is an objective dichotomous difference in children's concepts or in the 'folk concepts', but in this paper I leave the psychological differences in children's developing concepts and in adult 'folk theories' to the psychologists and the editors. We know there are differences among expert concepts since in this volume Sperber (Ch. 7) questions the dichotomy and Elder, Thomasson, and Kornblith (Chs. 3, 4, and 8) accept it. Bloom (this volume) argues for some recategorization and rethinking, but it seems that he still accepts the basic distinction. My goal is to develop the best understanding I can of artifacts and other related categories and to focus on metaphysical issues, though some issues of semantics cannot be avoided.

On the other side of the alleged dichotomy, natural kinds seem to have three features:

1. they are things, or kinds of things, that occur naturally,
2. they are subject to laws, and
3. they have essences.

That artifacts and natural kinds are disjoint is clear from the definitions. For example, Hilpinen (2004) characterizes an artifact as 'an object that has been intentionally made or produced for a certain purpose', so artifacts violate condition (1). However, if these categories are not exhaustive, then our conception of how different they are may change. For example, if natural kinds and artifacts are not dichotomous, then the question considered by Elder (this volume) of the ontological status of artifacts becomes more complex. While Thomasson and Kornblith (both this volume) are not concerned with the ontological status of artifacts, they address questions about the epistemic and semantic status of artifacts.

It is also important to think about a range of cases, both among artifacts and natural kinds. Artifacts range from slight modifications of naturally occurring objects, for example, stone handaxes which are constructed by chipping away some flakes from a rock, to highly iterative complex objects such as computers and airplanes. By describing some artifacts as iterative, what I mean is that they can only be manufactured using other artifacts, which typically in turn can only be manufactured ... through many iterations. I have no realistic idea, for example, how many layers there are between naturally occurring items and substances and an airplane, but am confident that it is very large. In the other direction, it is also important to have a view of the full range of biological entities. We tend to focus on the familiar middle-sized objects such as dogs and trees, but other examples are amoebas and hives of bees. And it is not only amoebas that can split, many species of plants can be multiplied by judiciously dividing the plant into two portions.

3. WHY ARE ARTIFACTS PROBLEMATIC?

Why do we feel there are philosophical problems specific to artifacts? One reason, which is close to a common-sense philosophical intuition, is that artifacts—their existence and their features—depend on human interests. The second, more technical, is that it seems that if we believe something like the Kripke–Putnam story about kinds, artifacts lack essences and therefore aren't *real kinds*. This is a modern echo of Locke's distinction between *simple modes*, which the mind takes from external sources, and 'mixed modes'. Of the latter he says that 'these Ideas are called Notions: as if they had their Original, and constant Existence, more in the Thoughts of Men, than in the reality of things' (Locke 1690, bk. II, ch. XXII, 1).

3.1. Dependence

There is a crucial distinction to be made with regard to Locke's comment, and that is between 'original existence' and 'constant existence'. There are many artifacts whose continued existence depends on our thoughts and intentions. Money is an excellent example: those little pieces of paper would have no value if they were not embedded within a stable network of social expectations, intentions, and beliefs. Notice that money has evolved from barter, through forms (gold coins) in which the value was independent of the social circumstances, to paper currency whose value was dependent on the social structure, to the electronic forms whose character it is difficult to describe. Chickens and loaves of bread have an intrinsic value to almost everyone, so my accepting chickens and bread does not depend on what I believe anyone else values. Gold coins may be of no use to me, but I may still value them highly if I know that others do and I can exchange them for chickens and bread. At the final stage (so far) my bank doesn't have any physical object or substance which is the money in my checking account (see Searle, this volume).

Thomasson (1999, this volume), in a slightly different context, made the very important distinction between dependence of origin and dependence of continuing existence or properties. The value of my paper dollar bill, both the exact amount and the fact that it has any, depends on the current attitudes of an indeterminately large number of people. On the other hand, my steak-knife owes its origin to a designer and a factory, but its current properties and functioning have been independent of the designer and factory since it left there (except when I send it back for resharpening, but we can ignore that complication).

There are gradations within the blurred region too. It seems natural to say that iron has the chemical properties and some of the physical properties it has independently of our intentions or desires. That this sample of Fe exists depends on human intentions, but not its melting point or solidity. In fact, its existence is due to the human desire to have something that has those properties. Not all physical properties of the sample are independent, of course, since its shape and mass may have been chosen to serve our purposes. On the other hand, a sample of bronze (an alloy of copper and tin), once created, has its properties independently of humans, but to some extent what those properties are depends on human intentions (since the proportion of copper to tin may vary somewhat) in a way that the properties of iron do not.

In some cases at least, the involvement of human intentions in the creation of a sample does not seem to have any effect on its status as an instance of a natural kind. Almost all of us in chemistry class combined hydrogen and oxygen to form water—not artificial water, just plain water. In fact, it is much closer to pure H_2O than what falls from the sky or pours from the faucet. So it appears that for at least some natural kinds, having the same essence is determinative and overrules the condition that the substance be created by a 'natural process'. So, to summarize our conclusion so far in this section, either we recognize that naturalness of origin is not required for something to be a natural kind, or else we give up on most chemical elements and compounds as natural kinds.

3.2. Species

The other standard example of a natural kind is species, and there are three complications of the standard story here. The first is obvious given what was said above, and the point is made in at least two other papers in this volume. Biological entities are often manipulated by humans for human purposes, and so by the definition above these species are artifacts and not natural kinds. Sperber (this volume) cites seedless grapes (and many other examples) and Keil, Greif, and Kerner (this volume) mention square watermelons. From the point of view of a biologist, how a species (or variety) acquired some specific properties is irrelevant for predicting and explaining how the species or variety will function in an ecological niche.

A second complication is that the explanation of how our biological terms refer (independently of the descriptions we may associate with the term) assumes that our biological terms in fact refer to species. For some nouns (e.g. 'tiger') this is true. But for many others it is not. Dictionaries disagree over whether 'elephant' is a name for the pachydermate order (*OED*), the family *Elephantidae*, which includes two living species, commonly referred to as the African elephant and the Asian elephant (Merriam–Webster 2005), or whether it refers to members of those two species (*American Heritage Dictionary*, 423). It is unclear in the last case whether the claim is that the noun is ambiguous or that it expresses a disjunctive concept. All of these definitions are wrong, however, for in 2001 it was discovered that what had been regarded as a single species, the African elephant, is in fact two distinct species (Roca *et al.* 2001).

Other nouns which speakers regard as 'natural-kind' terms do not correspond to genera or families or any other biologically accepted classifications. Two examples are 'grass' and 'tree', both of which are regarded as natural kinds by ordinary speakers, but not by botanists. In these cases, speakers appear to defer to experts who disagree with the classification rather than providing a description of the essence (Atran 1990, 67).

If the Kripke–Putnam story were the correct account of reference, when it was discovered that African and Asian elephants are different species the reaction should have been to find out which species was present when 'elephant', or more accurately 'ἐλέφας', was first used, and to declare the others imposters. And the news story in 2001 should have been that many animals that were thought to be African elephants in fact were not, because they were a different species than the one that was baptized.

How common is this? I haven't carried out a systematic random investigation, but Putnam's favorite examples of 'beech' and 'elm' each refer to a genus, not a single species. There are approximately ten species of beech and twenty of elm. 'Oak' also denotes a genus, one with over 100 species, including both deciduous and evergreen members. 'Crocodile' names a family with about a dozen members.

Part of the Putnam account still seems correct; speakers typically don't know details about the meanings or referents of familiar terms and defer to experts. But the experts don't seem to defer to initial baptizers, perhaps because the latter are so difficult to locate and interrogate concerning their intentions.

The third complication is that, at least according to a large number of philosophers of biology, species don't have essences, so even for those nouns that pick out species rather than a family or genus, the account doesn't work in detail.

In a pre Darwinian age, species essentialism made sense. Such essentialism, however, is out of step with contemporary evolutionary theory. Evolutionary theory provides its own methods for explaining variation within a species. It tells us that the boundaries between species are vague. And it tells us that a number of forces conspire against the existence of a trait in all and only the members of a species. From a biological perspective, species essentialism is no longer a plausible position. (Ereshefsky 2006, sec. 2.1)

There is disagreement among biologists about how to define 'species' and whether species are individuals, sets, or some other kind of entity (see Dupre 1993; Ghiselin 1974; Hull 1965; and Kitcher 1984). The traditional notion that a species is defined by interbreeding conflicts with contemporary notions of species—the African and Asian elephants can interbreed.

3.3. Lack of essence

I suspect that for many philosophers the ontological concern about the status of artifacts is connected with the contrast to natural kinds and what may appear to be a lack of essence in artifacts. On this interpretation, the problem is not with individual artifactual objects, but with kinds of artifacts. (As Elder notes in this volume, however, it may be the predominant philosophical view that no medium-sized objects exist.) I have argued in an earlier section that there seems to be no significant ontological difference between artifactual substances and natural substances. (And I have even suggested there may be no principled difference at all!) But at least some of this point carries over to artifactual objects if we look widely enough. If there is continuity between natural kinds and artifacts, then it doesn't seem that there should be a metaphysical distinction. Dredged lakes seem no less real than natural lakes, and seedless grapes no less real than seeded ones. Two possibilities come readily to mind: one is that there is a threefold metaphysical distinction, there are the truly natural kinds independent of human interests or classification or manufacture, and then there are the conventional kinds dependent on human interests and classifications, but not on human manufacture, and finally there are those that depend on human interests classifications and manufacture.

But again this suggests a trichotomy, where the reality is much more complex. Sperber (this volume) discusses at some length the fact that many species have been shaped by human rather than natural selection, so that current domesticated dogs, cats, and many other domestic species are artifactual, that is they would not exist in their current form without human intervention. These are cases where there was, at a past historical time, a natural kind that has been rendered (at least somewhat) artificial over generations. Even in this genre there are gradations, ranging from the smaller changes in dogs that occurred rather unintentionally when they were accepted as part of the earliest communities, to the quite intentional and highly artificial changes that are produced to create and maintain pure breeds for show. Other kinds of mixed examples can be generated, for example rivers are typically dredged to make them more navigable, natural lakes are often expanded, forests are thinned, and so on. It does not seem plausible that a river changes its ontological status when it is made more navigable!

There are even more extreme consequences of the view that if human intentions are involved in the creation of some entity, then it has a lesser ontological status than otherwise. On this view, among humans there is a distinction between those whose parents intended to procreate and those who did not. Surely there is not an ontological distinction along these lines!

3.4. The causal-historical account revisited

Something like the Kripke–Putnam (Putnam 1975; Kornblith, this volume) account of natural kinds is now part of the general philosophical background, but I believe that some of the subtleties of that account have been insufficiently attended to. This is especially relevant to issues about artifacts, one of them being that the causal-historical account suggests that the intentions of the originator of the artifact should dominate since that seems closer to the account for natural kinds.

So let us review the argument in some detail: We are given, in thought, a twin Earth on which the substance that looks and acts like water has chemical composition XYZ, which has a quite different chemical structure from H_2O. The conclusion of the thought experiment and argument is that on Twin Earth 'water' refers to XYZ. We are given particular inhabitant $Oscar_{TE}$ whose beliefs and language use are the subject of our discussion, and it is postulated that $Oscar_{TE}$ is similar in his qualitative psychological states to his doppelganger Oscar on Earth. (Some less-than-careful statements of the thought experiment say that Oscar and $Oscar_{TE}$ are molecule-for-molecule duplicates, but of course that can't be since most of Oscar's molecules are H_2O while most of $Oscar_{TE}$'s are XYZ, and those are supposed to be chemically very different.)

> *Premise 1.* When the reference of 'water' was fixed on Earth in, say, 1700 speakers referred to a sample of (what turns out to be) H_2O and intended to refer to it and to things that are similar-L to it.
>
> *Premise 2.* When the reference of 'water' was fixed on Twin Earth in, say, 1700 speakers referred to a sample of (what turns out to be) XYZ and intended to refer to it and to things that are similar-L to it.
>
> *Premise 3.* 'Water' on Earth in 2007 has the same referent as it did in 1700.
>
> *Premise 4.* 'Water' on Twin Earth in 2007 has the same referent as it did in 1700.
>
> *Premise 5.* H_2O is not similar-L to XYZ.

From these premises it follows that 'water' refers to H_2O and not XYZ on Earth in 2007, and that 'water' refers to XYZ and not H_2O on Twin Earth in 2007. There is little discussion in Putnam of the similar-L relation. One tempting analysis is that it means 'similar in chemical structure', but of course there are different conceptions of chemical structure at different stages of the development of chemistry. And additionally it would have been anachronistic for someone in 1700 to describe something in terms of 'chemistry', since the subject either did not exist or was not distinguished by that term. Perhaps it should be understood as 'similar in atomic structure according to the natural philosophers', but of course atomic theory was not generally accepted at that time so that would not have been a natural thing for the common speaker to think.

So a better approach might be along the following lines: L is the relation between things when the underlying properties that explain/cause the surface features are the same according to the natural philosophers or the community that takes over from them the concern with explaining surface features on the basis of underlying properties. I have emphasized the problems in how to fill out the L in similar-L because it seems that once we see these complications both Premises 3 and 4 seem less certain. If the linguistic community continues to use as its underlying reference fixing, things similar-L as I am now recommending, the L relation may well change over time as the general linguistic community has differing views about the relevant community of experts. In addition, Premise 5 must be seen as only probable since, although our chemists would regard H_2O and XYZ as chemically different substances, their descendants may discern some similarity we currently do not see. (After all, the apparently disparate underlying structures produce the same density, freezing-point, boiling-point, and interactions with human bodies when ingested.)

One of the weaknesses in most versions of the causal-historical account of reference is that they ignore the social dimension and the other referential intentions that speakers have. The theory is more plausible with respect to proper names, since we very frequently refer to people whom we have never met. In such cases our intention is to refer to the same person as did the person from whom we first heard the name. And in many cases of unfamiliar substances or species, the same may be true. I don't know whether I have ever encountered molybdenum and I know I have never encountered an aardvark.

However, with many other nouns we not only intend to refer as did the person before us, we simultaneously intend to refer to specific things in our vicinity. When I refer to 'water' I intend to use the word the way my mother did (assuming I learned it from her), but I also intend to use it to refer to the stuff in my glass, or your swimming-pool, etc. And it seems to me that in these cases where the uses and substance are widespread, the latter intentions outweigh the former. Imagine that we discover the first user of 'water' was in fact referring to XYZ, the only sample ever on Earth—one which was briefly introduced here and was subsequently removed by the mischievous Twin Earthians! Would we say that we have discovered that water isn't really H_2O or that none of the stuff we have been calling 'water' is water?

Another thought experiment, this one less esoteric, is to consider what we would say if we discovered that the first user of 'water' was actually intending to refer to a cup, not its contents, but was misunderstood by the audience, which then intended both to refer as the baptizer did but also to refer to the familiar stuff. I do not think it is plausible to describe this situation as discovering that 'water' really refers to cups and has all along. A more likely scenario is that we would say that the initial history of 'water' is anomalous, but that 'water' refers to the familiar stuff.

These examples have accepted the idea of a baptizer as unproblematic, but is it? The causal-historical picture of baptism may seem neat and plausible when applied to baptisms of people in Modern English. But the picture becomes somewhat less clear when we discuss an example like 'Aristotle', where the relevant baptism didn't use a token of that type but perhaps ''Aριστοτέλης'. It becomes much less clear if we think seriously about the history of a common noun like 'water'. Either we draw (an apparently arbitrary) line where we determine that was the first use of 'water' or we follow the history further back through the use of the old English '*wæter*', and then we draw an arbitrary line where it was first used, or we look further back at its ancestor … In addition to the arbitrariness, we would face the problem that what we were declaring the first use of the modern 'water' was almost certainly not thought of as a baptism by the person who used the term, but rather he or she was not intending to invent a new word but to continue to refer to what he or she had learned to call '*wæter*'.

We earlier were close to the qua problem (see Thomasson, this volume) of what is being baptized. In the case of water, the baptizer presumably had to intend to be baptizing the stuff in the cup, not the cup, and to either intend that the name apply to all phases of that stuff or that the name apply only to the liquid form of it. (The English word 'water' is ambiguous—in one sense it includes steam and ice, in the other it contrasts with ice and steam.) We saw earlier that while some biologically oriented nouns refer to species, others pick out a genus, order, or family. If the baptizing is to be unique and successful, the baptizer must intend a specific one of these options. And arguably having an intention to specify one of these requires knowing the differences among them, and I find it doubtful that most speakers of most languages know those differences.

4. INTENTIONS OR FUNCTIONS?

I have already argued that artifactual substances, at least many of them, have as essential a nature as most natural substances, and that in many cases the distinction between artifactual and natural substances is artificial and unsubstantial. But that leaves the central problem of kinds of artifactual things. In specifying the L in similar-L for artifacts there are two obvious choices, the function of the thing and the intentions of the manufacturer.

On the first choice, a kind of artifact is identified by taking a particular example and generalizing to objects created with the same intention. On the second choice, a kind of artifact is identified by taking a particular example and generalizing to objects created with the same function. Both raise problems, especially with recursive artifacts that evolve over time. For example, however we identify the inventor of the electronic computer, it is likely that their intention was to solve mathematical equations, probably having to do with artillery trajectories. In this case, it may be that we have to have a finer set of distinctions and not consider 'electronic computer' as a single kind of artifact but instead see a succession of different devices. A similar example is the airplane. (Lest you conclude that this is a special problem for artifact kinds, let me remind you that if evolutionary theory is correct there is a very analogous problem for species, one of our prototypical kinds of natural kind.)

Instead of dealing with that problem (left as an exercise for the reader), I want to address the issue of deciding between our two approaches. In many cases of prototypical artifacts the intentions and the functions will coincide. The two types of cases where it appears that they can diverge is when either the kind of artifact has functions not envisioned by the inventor or when the object fails to serve the intended function. But the first kind is an illusion which disappears if we recognize that if a kind of artifact has a function that was not intended by the original designer, then someone else recognized that possibility and so we should simply broaden our criterion and recognize that in many cases a kind of object has multiple designers/creative users.

There is a familiar difficulty of vagueness, of course, in when some kind of artifact has a new use. A single case of using my desk to open a bottle will not suffice. Something like a broad social recognition of the new possible use, along with questions of what conflicting pressures and alternative language choices are available will enter into the equation. We do know that in other respects the original intentions of baptizers, even when they were very clear and explicit, can gradually lose their force to the repeated intentions of later users. After a while Xerox machines become a subset of xerox machines, and Kleenex suffered a similar fate.

If this line of argument is correct, then setting aside the relatively small and unimportant cases of non-functional artifact kinds, we can let both designers' intention and function play roles in indicating the similar-L relation for artifact object kinds. For artifact substances, invented kinds of stuff, it seems to me that the properties of the stuff should determine the extension of the kind term, just as it does for 'natural' kinds like iron. The designer may have some functions in mind, that is, some kinds of object that are envisioned as being made from that stuff, but new kinds of material often lend themselves to myriad applications that were not envisioned.

On the other hand, artifactual objects appear to be more differentiated by function. One of the better examples may be clocks. Water clocks, sand clocks, mechanical clocks, and digital clocks are physically very different but all provide ways for humans to track the passage of time. Many writers have commented that, aside from problems of whether artifacts can have modal essences, they vary too much within a kind for inductive generalizations. This may well be because we are looking at the wrong level of abstraction. I illustrated earlier that many biological nouns that might be thought to refer to species actually refer to higher-level categories, and thus are going to support fewer inductive generalizations than you might have expected. If we make a similar analysis of artifacts, it may be that the proper level of artifact grain is not 'clock', but 'mechanical clock' and 'water clock'. There are few generalizations you can make about automobiles, but many that can be made about Ford Focuses. (In some ways this point is close to one of Elder's main points (this volume), though I arrive at it from a different direction.)

5. SCATTERED OBJECTS?

5.1. The problem and the positions

The boring, naive, and common-sense solution to my initial puzzle is that some objects, some of the time, are not spatially continuous. This view is subject to criticism from those who think no object is ever scattered, and I recognize that nothing I have said here addresses the concerns of the nihilists who think no macroscopic objects exist. For current purposes, I will be satisfied if I can make out the case that artifacts are not worse off ontologically than other macroscopic objects. The more common criticism of the common-sense view is that it does not go far enough, recognizing only a very small percentage of the scattered objects in the universe. How one goes on to expand the category varies.

For one example, Jubien (1997) opts for the obvious things plus arbitrary parts of them and then allows arbitrary mereological sums of the starting objects and their parts. Note that this brings with it temporal as well as spatial discontinuity since we can take the mereological sum of objects that exist at disparate and non-overlapping times. Quine famously opts for the view on which 'the material content of any region of space-time, however irregular and discontinuous and heterogeneous', constitutes an object (1981, 10). Cartwright (1975) also argues for scattered objects, though he does not provide a characterization of how many or what kinds he thinks exist in any detail.

Jubien uses the example of a bicycle, and Cartwright of his pipe, and in both cases it seems plausible that these constitute scattered objects when disassembled for cleaning or repair. Notice though that both the intent and functioning of these kinds of object foresees their being disassembled and reassembled. We can even think of examples of objects that are, or could be, disassembled more often than not. For example, we might have tables that, instead of folding for storage, easily disassemble and reassemble; they might spend most of their existence disassembled in our storage closet.

So those examples fit ordinary intuitions, and the rub comes in providing principled reasons for rejecting the general extension of these ideas by means of other examples and arguments. Some examples, such as Cartwright's two-volume edition of *The Nature of Existence* and Jubien's three-piece suit, seem easily disqualified as collections of objects whose function involves all of the pieces, but each of which is a separate object. Similar remarks apply to decks

of cards, chess sets, and pairs of shoes. Some of Jubien's other examples are not
designed artifacts, but also do not seem to be compelling as single entities: flocks
of geese, forests, and galaxies.

Cartwright and Jubien also both deploy the argument from atomic theory.
'If natural scientists are to be taken at their word, all the familiar objects of
everyday life are scattered' (Cartwright 1975, 174). An important consequence
(of assuming something approximating atomic theory is correct) is that 'ordinary
things that are large enough to be seen with the naked eye are what philosophers
call scattered (or discontinuous) objects' (Jubien 1997, 155).

There are two ways of responding to these claims. First, there is the somewhat
ad hominem tack that if we take quantum theory seriously then it is not at all clear
that Jubien is entitled to talk of 'things' at the atomic or subatomic level. Early
versions of atomic theory conceived of atoms and electrons as miniature versions
of macroscopic objects, but quantum theory presents a very different picture.
Electrons and other 'particles' at that level don't have locations most of the
time, nor velocities or shapes. Quine's quantification over 'occupied' space-time
regions seems equally implausible—if most electrons don't have locations, which
regions of space-time are occupied? (See Chiara and Di Francia 1995, for further
discussion with respect to Quine.)

5.2. Spelke objects

A more constructive approach is to attempt to provide a principled alternative
that draws a plausible boundary. My own preference is to appeal to the idea
of a maximal dynamically cohesive collection of matter. This conception, or
something close to it, is the notion of object that developmental psychologists are
studying in infants. Xu (1997) argued that this is the (a?) meaning of object in
English, but a number of serious objections were raised (in Ayers 1997; Hirsch
1997; Wiggins 1997), and the idea needs more careful reformulation; also it is
probably advisable to introduce a technical term, such as Spelke object, rather
than make the bold claim Xu did that this concept captures one meaning of
'object' in English. (Elizabeth Spelke was one of the most important researchers
in developing this area; see e.g. Spelke 1990 and Spelke *et al.* 1992.)

There are two parts to the definition: first, a collection of matter is dynamically
cohesive if it moves as a unit. In other words, moving one part of the collection
moves, or tends to move, the other parts. An ice-cube or an iceberg is a Spelke
object; the liquid water in a puddle is not. Each volume of Cartwright's two-
volume *The Nature of Existence* is a Spelke object, the two volumes considered
together are not. A pile of sand is not a Spelke object, but if we saturate it with
enough superglue and let it dry it becomes one. The other important condition is
maximality, the Spelke object consists of all the matter that moves together; the
left half of a Spelke object is not a Spelke object. As Eric Margolis has suggested:
'If you can pick it up with a fork, it is a Spelke object' (personal communication).

A perfectly rigid sphere would be a paradigm example of a Spelke object; a blanket is a poor one. There are problems of vagueness with this definition—however dynamically cohesive some collection of matter is, there is a conceivable force that would rip it asunder. It is unclear whether a soap bubble floating in the air is a Spelke object, nor at what stage in the freezing of an ice-cube it becomes a Spelke object. Some artifacts, for example jars with lids, come apart easily when a very specific force is applied but resist coming apart under considerably greater forces in all other directions. I am attempting to deal with these and other problems elsewhere, but ask your forbearance while I attempt to at least partially unpack some of the desirable consequences of this notion. Let me note in passing that many of these issues of vagueness also afflict paradigmatic natural kinds, like cats (Lewis 1993).

However desirable Jubien objects or Quine objects may be for a nicely rounded-out ontology, there are features of Spelke objects that neither of the others have in general. Given that *a* and *b* are parts of a Spelke object at *t* and that *a* is moving in a particular direction at *t*, it is highly probable that *b* is moving in the same direction at *t*. (A more careful formulation would raise the probability by incorporating a suitable clause for spinning objects.) Given that *a* and *b* are both part of a Quine object or a Jubien object and that *a* is moving in a particular direction, we have no reason to think that *b* is moving in the same direction.

Our interest in such facts depends on—well—on our interests. Sometimes we want to move furniture, avoid oncoming traffic, pick up an (unsliced) loaf of bread, or kick a soccer ball. So how we use the information about Spelke objects depends on us and our aspirations and fears and other sentential attitudes; we care because the information is useful. But it is objective information. In a world without humans there would be fewer Spelke objects, but those that existed would still have the same properties and be subject to the same laws of motion. If a tree falls unseen and unheard in the forest, it falls as a Spelke object.

This suggestion lets us bypass the question of continuity at the atomic level; continuity is not part of the definition. Perhaps, one might argue, the interior of the atom does not truly contain empty spaces because of the fields present there, but I prefer not to tangle with those issues for lack of competence. However, it is a deep physical fact that almost all Spelke objects appear continuous at the macroscopic level, and so it is not surprising that previous definitions that have attempted to capture something like this notion have appealed to continuity.

Given the importance of discerning and tracking what is and is not a Spelke object in the environment, it is not surprising that from a very early stage infants can track a (small) number of Spelke objects both visually and in memory. In one variation of the common experiments, a toy duck or cup is placed on a table in view of the infant, and then a screen is placed to obscure the object. Shortly after, when the screen is removed, very young infants are surprised if there is no object there, or if two objects are there. But they are not surprised if the duck has been replaced by a cup. Similar results can be obtained with up to about four objects. So at this stage children seem to categorize and remember things as Spelke objects and not as items in more specific categories.

To demonstrate the importance of maximal cohesiveness, similar experiments were also carried out by pouring one or more piles of sand on the table, obscuring them from view, and covertly changing the number of piles. Changed numbers of piles of sand did not surprise the infants. On the other hand, when the experiment was done in yet another variation, this time with piles of sand which had been superglued into Spelke objects (i.e. the child saw the object being moved cohesively onto the table), they had the same expectation of numeric constancy as they did with a cup or duck (Huntley-Fenner, Carey, and Solimando 2002).

The ability to discern and remember maximal cohesive objects in the perceptible environment is very basic in humans, as witnessed by the fact that it is present very early in infants. Its roots are undoubtedly older than humans as the ability has been shown to be present in cottontop tamarins and rhesus monkeys (Sulkowski and Hauser 2001; Uller, Hauser and Carey 2001; Hauser *et al.* 2003).

6. CONCLUSION

I have attempted to develop the conceptual machinery of Spelke objects in the hopes of constructing a coherent and persuasive case that we can make sense of the disassembled bicycle as a spatially discontinuous object without being forced to accept all mereological sums of objects as objects. The objects which we naturally regard as maintaining their objecthood while spatially dispersed are those which can be reassembled and resume their function. Indeed, in many cases artifacts are *intended* to be disassembled periodically for maintenance or cleaning. These objects are not Spelke objects while disassembled, but their components are. We can mark out as a significant category the category of Spelke objects plus those entities which are for some part of their existence discontinuous and not Spelke objects if and only if those objects are at an earlier (and later?) stage a Spelke object which was designed to be disassembled and reassembled or whose functioning is facilitated by being disassembled and reassembled (along with some cleaning, sharpening, or whatever). On this criterion, the bicycle of paragraph one of my introduction and Cartwright's pipe are spatially scattered objects for portions of their careers.[2]

---

[2] I am indebted to Eric Margolis, John O'Neal, and Daniel Osherson for helpful discussions of these and related topics. They bear no responsibility for errors, omissions, unclarities, or confusions.

3

On the Place of Artifacts in Ontology

Crawford L. Elder

Suppose that a carpenter shapes pieces of wood and arranges them together so as to compose a desk. In ontological strictness, what has happened? Is it just that certain pieces of wood or bundles of cellulose fibers have gotten arranged differently towards one another, or has some object different in kind from either the pieces or the bundles been created? Suppose that the desk gets crushed, perhaps by a collapsing roof, and no longer can function as a desk. Is this just a matter of certain objects' being set in a new arrangement—perhaps very *small* objects, for example, cellulose *molecules*, if the crushing is severe—or is it a matter of some one object's being destroyed?

Contemporary metaphysicians find it hard enough to believe that even the pieces of wood out of which the carpenter makes the desk really exist, in ontological strictness. Worries about composition (van Inwagen 1990), vagueness (Unger 1979*a*, *b*), and coinciding objects (Zimmerman 1995, 106 ff.) seem to rule out any such claim. Even less easy to believe is it, then, that an assemblage of wood pieces produced by the carpenter's intentional activity is a new object in its own right. The intentions of the artisans among us, and the uses to which the rest of us put their products, simply seem to play too lightly over the surfaces of our material surroundings. It can seem unbelievable that matter upon which such intentions and uses are focused thereby comes to be a material object different in its essential nature from what would exist in its place, in the absence of such focusing.

Thus it is very widely agreed that in the world which serious ontology inventories, there are no artifacts. Artifacts exist only in what Sellars (1963) called 'the manifest image'. Their careers are projected by people onto indifferent materials.

This chapter argues that, to the contrary, an artifact-free ontology is unnecessary and probably incoherent. Artifacts—at least many artifacts—are, in ontological strictness, objects different in kind from whatever composes them. The essential properties which characterize (many) kinds of artifacts hang together in just as mind-independent a way as do the essential properties that characterize members of familiar natural kinds—from argon atoms and H_2O molecules to glaciers and geodes. True, the *reason* for the clustering is different in the case of the kinds to which (many) artifacts belong—I shall call these 'copied kinds'—from what it is in the case of the natural kinds usually discussed. In the case of the natural kinds usually discussed, the characteristic properties accompany one another in instance after instance, sample after sample, because of a common physical composition or microstructure. In the case of copied kinds, the properties essential to the kind accompany one another in instance after instance because of a common history of function (Elder 1995, 1996). The sameness in the instances stems from their surroundings, not from their insides. But the clustering of the properties is just as genuine and just as mind-independent.

This chapter will argue, in sum, that (many) artifacts have no *worse* a claim to being genuine objects than do many familiar medium- and large-sized objects—e.g. glaciers, hailstones, and stars. It will leave largely unaddressed the worries which prevent many contemporary metaphysicians from believing that even *these* objects exist, in ontological strictness. For the position which this chapter opposes is that the careers of artifacts are mere projections by people onto objects that include no artifacts. This position affirms the existence of people. And it is hard—if not altogether impossible (cf. Lowe 1991)—to dispute that people are medium-sized material objects of the familiar sort. People, that is to say, seem to be—if real at all—compositionally vague, mereologically incontinent, coincident with modally different aggregates of matter, etc. Any ontological doubts which these features raise therefore afflict the projectivism which this paper attacks as much as the position for which it argues. Dispelling the doubts is as much the projectivist's assignment as mine, and I will do little to discharge the assignment here—though I will (in section 3) offer a solution to 'the problem of coinciding objects'.

But projectivism faces a problem which my position does not. This problem concerns not the ontological credentials of us projectors, but rather the causes of our alleged projection. To the naive question, 'what gets us to believe that there are artifacts in the world around us?', the naive answer is that our interactions with artifacts themselves do this—we make artifacts, we use them, we observe them. To the less naive question, 'if strictly there are no artifacts in the world, what then causes us to believe in them?', the natural answer would be that our culture or conventions or customs do this; belief in artifacts is instilled by the sentences we hear at our mother's knee. But a true projectivist must be careful, in formulating an answer to this less naive question, to cite as acting upon us only such objects as are recognized by his artifact-free ontology. Quite possibly these objects do *not* include such things as customs or sentences at all. What objects *are* included? For projectivists who are bold, objects eligible to act upon us might include familiar medium-sized objects such as glaciers and geodes; for more cautious projectivists, the objects said to act on us will be very small, for example, 'physical simples' such as leptons and bosons (e.g. van Inwagen 1990, 98–9), or very unfamiliar, such as parcels of primal stuff (e.g. Sidelle 1989, 54–5). In any case there is, as I shall argue, a great gulf fixed between any answer to our less naive question that is available to a true projectivist, and the kind of answer that seems natural. For the realm of our culture, our conventions, and our language is bristling with copied kinds. Thus if the projectivist offers an answer rich enough to depict the action on us of items in this realm, he concedes that members of at least some copied kinds really act and really exist. Then he has no principled way of denying that at least some artifacts exist. If on the other hand the projectivist denies that there are in the world any copied kinds, he denies that there are any objects which might plausibly be said to cause, by their action on us, the projection he believes in.

Strictly speaking, this chapter is an ontological vindication not directly of artifacts, but of copied kinds. Copied kinds *include* many kinds of artifacts, but more besides: kinds of biological devices, kinds of naturally selected behaviors (e.g. mating dances), kinds of customary performances (e.g. rain dances), and kinds of linguistic structure. Kinds of artifacts picked out by the sortals of ordinary language often amount to copied kinds, but not invariably: chairs do not compose a copied kind, and neither do neckties or nose rings (see section 3). I will be content if I have staked out a place in ontology for at least *some* artifacts.

I should add—to clarify the relation between my project and Amie Thomasson's (this volume)—that my aim is to stake out a place for (some) artifacts in a *realist* ontology. Thomasson argues that one can defend the reality of artifacts without assigning to them mind-independence: that artifact-makers and users harbor the right thoughts and intentions, she argues, is constitutive of artifacts' existing, and artifacts do really exist. I aim to establish a stronger position. I cannot shake the misgiving that Thomasson's *defense* of artifacts differs only verbally from the projectivist's *rejection* of artifacts. If the very existence of artifacts consists in the fact that people harbor certain thoughts concerning the material contents of the world, then, I cannot but think, an ontology that posits only those thoughts themselves can explain everything that an ontology also positing artifacts can explain.

1. THE SORTS OF PROPERTIES THAT ESSENTIALLY CHARACTERIZE COPIED KINDS

Artifacts do have a place in ontology if, in fashioning a desk, a carpenter does not merely set pieces of wood or bundles of cellulose into a different arrangement towards one another, but brings a new object into existence. So too do they have a place if, when the desk is crushed by a collapsing roof, what happens is not just that the pieces or the bundles get arranged differently again, but also that something is destroyed. But just how is the question to be decided: just what marks the difference between 'substantial change', that is, change involving creation or destruction, and 'accidental change', change involving mere alteration? The question is most easily addressed, I suggest, by focusing first on destruction. For in that way we can begin by asking what marks the difference between substantial and accidental change where the subject-matter of both is the same. We can ask, that is, what marks the difference between a case in which an object is altered, but continues to exist, and a case in which that same object gets destroyed and exists no more.

Verbally, of course, the answer is obvious: it all depends on whether the object has lost an accidental property or an essential one—a property the object has just contingently, or one it has necessarily. The hard question is what the essentialness of an essential property consists in. In this section I offer a realist answer to this question. I then use the answer to sketch an argument—which the following section will fill in—that artifacts of many kinds possess essential properties which the materials that compose them do not. Thus when a desk is crushed, it is true in ontological strictness that an object is destroyed.

But why not an *antirealist* position on essentialness? Why not the position variously called 'conventionalism' or 'constructivism'? On this position, it is our practices that ultimately fix which sorts of properties are essential to the members of any given kind. On one version the practices come into play when we first introduce our term for the kind in question: we point to a sample, and get the new term to refer to a kind essentially characterized by just those similarities, among members or portions of the sample, that are of the right sorts—similarities with respect to the general sorts of properties that we choose to make crucial (Thomasson, this volume).[1] On non-historical versions, we have conventions of individuation which make certain sorts of properties mark differences in *kind*, among items of the same very general category (e.g. among animals, among minerals), and make certain properties mark out the points at which a individual member of such a kind begins its existence and ends its existence.

So, why not such a position on essentialness? The answer is that a conventionalist stance on the essentialness of a given kind's essential properties is off limits both for my intended opponent and for me. (In fact I consider it off limits for *anyone*, but that is a different story—Elder 2004, ch. 1.) It is off limits for my intended opponent because this is the philosopher who holds that the careers of artifacts are merely projected by us—by our conceptual or linguistic practices—while *our* careers are *not* mere projections, and while the careers of the indifferent material surroundings onto which we do the projecting are likewise not mere projections. For my intended opponent, that is, the facts as to where our existences begin and end, and as to where the existences of leptons or of molecules or of parcels of cellulose begin and end, are fixed independently of us. But the career of any human or any lepton extends just so long as that human

---

[1] This account of what fixes the reference of our terms for natural kinds is sometimes attributed to Putnam and to Kripke. I have argued that it is an untenable account, and not one endorsed by the Kripke of *Naming and Necessity* (Elder 2003). For a better account, see Millikan 2000.

or lepton retains whatever properties are essential to it. If the status of those properties *as* essential were itself but a projection of human custom, the facts as to where those careers begin and end would not after all be fixed independently of us. So my opponent cannot embrace a general conventionalism with respect to essentialness. (Thus Thomasson, who does embrace a general conventionalism about essentialness, is not the sort of 'projectivist' I am targeting in this chapter.) Neither can I embrace across-the-board conventionalism about essentialness. My position is that artifacts have genuine, mind-independent existence—existence *caused* by us, to be sure, but not *constituted* by our believing what we do about where artifacts are to be found. Artifacts trace out mind-independent careers, mind-independent existences. But these existences too continue just so long as artifacts retain their essential properties, and so again the status of those properties *as* essential cannot itself be mind-dependent; otherwise it would after all follow that we carve out or construct the careers of artifacts.

In any case, a realist position on the status, *as* essential, of the properties essential to nature's kinds and stuffs and phenomena is now neither exotic nor unfamiliar. Ever since Kripke's and Putnam's writings in the early 1970s (e.g. Kripke 1972/1980; Putnam 1975), philosophers have been accustomed to the idea that what makes a property essential is not how it figures in our concepts or our conventions, but is rather the way the world works. What makes *being composed of H_2O molecules* an essential property of water is its underlying, not just the surface-level features which the folk have all along associated with 'water'—or perhaps a 'weighted most' of these properties—but its underlying a host of scientifically measurable properties even more crisply distinctive of water. *Being composed of H_2O molecules* underlies water's boiling-point and freezing-point, its index of refraction, and its viscosity. In general, we are accustomed to thinking of essentialness as fixed by the laws of nature. An essential property of a given stuff or kind or phenomenon, on this accustomed way of thinking, is in the first instance one around which a number of other properties lawfully cluster—properties which, either individually or in combination, are distinctive of the stuff or kind in question, are found in no other stuff or kind (see e.g. Elder 1989, 1996). In the second instance, at least for some philosophers, essential properties of the stuff or kind include all those in the cluster (Elder 1994, 1995).

But this familiar realist picture of essential properties may in one way be too restrictive. What, traditionally, is a natural kind? It is a family of instances over which careful inductions will non-accidentally turn out to be true—a family united by possession of a common nature. But this traditional conception provides no reason for supposing that every natural kind will be characterized by some one property that is distinctive of it alone—some one property never found in members of any other kind. So far as the traditional conception goes, a natural kind might be characterized by some distinctive *combination* of properties which individually are undistinctive, even 'run of the mill'. There need be no *one* property responsible, by virtue of the laws of nature, for the presence of others which, singly or in combination, distinguish that kind from all others. Rather, the traditional conception leaves room for this possibility: that properties $p_1, \ldots, p_n$ are essential properties of Xs just in case enough other properties cluster together with $p_1, \ldots, p_n$, by virtue of the laws of nature, that Xs are bound to possess properties or combinations of properties found in members of no other kind. Our realist analysis of essentialness, I maintain, should take exactly this more liberal form. We should not insist that among the properties essential to the members of a given natural kind there need be *any* properties found in that kind alone. We should require only that the essential properties must cluster together non-accidentally, and in a cluster found in no other kind.

The members of what I call 'copied kinds' (Elder 1996) are characterized by three properties which, as I shall argue in the next section, are essential on the more liberal analysis. First, the members of any copied kind are characterized by a particular qualitative make-up or 'shape'. This will *literally* be a shape in the case of artifacts or biological devices, for example the household screwdriver or the double-lensed eye of the eagle; it will be a shape somewhat metaphorically in the case of reproduced behavior, for example the mating dance of the stickleback fish or a ritual rain dance performed by a particular human culture; it will be a 'shape' in a purely metaphorical sense in the case of linguistic forms or constructions, such as the indicative mood in a particular language. Second, the members of any copied kind are characterized by what Ruth Millikan calls a 'proper function' (Millikan 1984, chs. 1 and 2; cf. Millikan 2002). That is, the members are produced by a process or mechanism which copies them from previous members similarly shaped, and does so as a causal consequence of performances, by those previous members, of certain functions—productions by them of certain effects. The process is, in other words, such as to produce more copies of previous items that produced such effects than of previous items that produced *no* such effects, or more copies of items that produced a particular such effect *more often* than of different items that produced it less often, or more copies of items that produced a *more wide-ranging* such effect than of different items that produced one less wide-ranging. In consequence there is, in a historical sense, something which members of a copied kind are 'for' doing, something current members are 'supposed to' do.[2] Third, the members of any copied kind are characterized by what one might

---

[2] Any historical account of proper function, like the one I take over from Millikan, faces a 'poser' concerning the very first item from which a copied kind comes to be copied. An example: didn't the very first telephone, fashioned by Alexander Graham Bell, already have a proper function (Plantinga 1993, 203)? From Millikan's perspective (to which I subscribe) the answer is 'Yes and No'. The first telephone had no direct proper function, but it did have an adapted and derived proper function—that of enabling remote conversation. In just the same way, if a chameleon turns a shade of puce unprecedented in chameleon history, its skin color has an adapted and derived proper function—that of matching its puce surroundings (Millikan 1984, ch. 2). 'Derived' here means that the telephone or the skin color inherits its proper function from that of the program in Bell, or the device in the chameleon, which produced it. In Bell's case, the derivation probably extends further still: beyond the program which underlay production of the telephone, to a program

call a 'historically proper placement'.[3] That is, the operations by past members, on which production of the current ones causally depends, were *co*operations with members of specific *other* copied kinds located alongside those past members. Past double-lensed eyes, in eagles long since dead, did something that causally contributed to the replication of eyes just like them in the eagles of today, but this 'something' would not have helped eagles, nor contributed to the replication, if the eyes had not been accompanied by brains equipped to read the complex neural signals which the eyes sent. Screwdrivers have served to fasten objects together, but only because environed by screws suitably slotted and shaped.

What I shall argue in the next section is that around any actual combination of three such properties—any actual copied 'shape', proper function, and historically proper placement—there cluster other properties, sometimes many and sometimes few, but always enough to constitute a combination that can be found in members of no other kind. Copied kinds truly have essential properties, then, in the same traditional sense as do any other kinds that occur in the world. When a collapsing roof crushes a desk, causing the shape of a desk to be present no longer, an essential rather than accidental property is lost; the collapse involves not just alteration, but the destruction of an object.

This is so, at least, provided the arguments of the next section are successful. But just the identification of *candidate* essential properties, for artifacts and members of other copied kinds, may help dispel some of the scepticism canvassed at the outset of this paper about the place of artifacts in ground-level ontology. When an artisan fashions an artifact, he works on materials such as wood or steel or stone. As stuffs, these materials already have essential natures of their own. It can, as we noted, seem unbelievable—too much like magic—that merely by shaping and joining parcels of such materials in ways that reflect his intentions the artisan brings about the existence of a new object, one possessed of an essential nature not present before. But if the position of this chapter is correct, the creation does not begin with the artisan's intending what he does. Rather the essential properties which his product will inherit stem from a history of function

---

for forming such programs, and perhaps to a capacity for forming programs for forming programs. The derivation ends at a device which operates independently of Bell's conscious intentions, and which has a direct proper function. This brings up the 'poser' concerning the proper function of the first item from which a *biological* copied kind comes to be copied. Suppose the first wings (tokens) arose as a result of a single, massive mutation. Didn't those very first wings already have a proper function? But there is no intuitive pressure upon Millikan to answer yes. The onset of (direct) proper function, she can plausibly reply, depends on the intensity of selectional pressure on the gene pool. It depends on how soon the capacity for flight, bestowed by early wings, conferred replicative advantage on the genes which coded for wings—and replicative disadvantage on the alleles. This is a causal question. The answer to it—and to the question where (direct) proper function begins—may be somewhat vague. But it would be poor practice to throw out causation, or the theory of natural selection, out of preference for a neatly segmented universe.

[3] I say 'historically proper *placement*' rather than 'environment' because the latter suggests a *broad* cross-section of the historical surroundings; placement is a matter of co-location, and consequent cooperation, with tokens of specific other copied kinds.

and of copying that began well before the artisan undertakes his work. This history reaches forward through the artisan's motions—it shapes his shaping. Its existence and its efficacy are independent, largely or even entirely, of the artisan's will. (In other words, artifacts commonly are what Sperber calls 'cultural artifacts'—Ch.7 this volume, sec. 1, esp. Fig. 2.)

For similar reasons we should have no compunctions about terming copied kinds *natural kinds*. It is true that artifacts belong to the kinds they do by virtue of how we shape them—that is, as a reflection of our intelligence and agency. But we ourselves, with our intelligence and agency, are items which nature produced (cf. Sperber, ibid., sec. 2). So the kinds into which we make artifacts fall are kinds which nature fashions through us.

2. FURTHER SORTS OF PROPERTIES ESSENTIAL TO MANY COPIED KINDS

My central contention is that around any actual combination of copied 'shape', proper function, and historically proper placement, a number of other properties will reliably cluster—enough properties, at least, to form a combination found in no other kind in nature. This is so whether the combination characterizes a particular kind of artifact, a kind of biological device, a behavioral routine installed by natural selection, a custom embedded in a human culture, or a linguistic structure. But before beginning to argue for this contention, I must say a few words to justify placing items seemingly so disparate under the common rubric of 'copied kind'. The justification rests on the idea that items of all these disparate sorts are produced by copying processes which, while differing in details, are alike in broad and important respects.

The differences admittedly catch the eye more quickly than do the similarities. The process which copied genes for double-lensed eyes, so effectively that they emerged from lucky mutations in a few proto-eagles to fixation in the gene pool of the eagles of today, was unsupervised and 'blind'—it was natural selection. Natural selection may also be said, as I will presently argue, to have copied the eyes themselves in today's eagles from the eyes of ancestor eagles. But a competent craftsman who fashions a screwdriver, on the model of previous screwdrivers that have proven effective, copies consciously and deliberately. And between these extremes there may seem to be a spectrum of interestingly different copying processes. The current generation of an indigenous people may deliberately copy its ritual rain dance from the dances of previous generations, but with no clear understanding of the benefit to social cohesion which is the real reason for the dance's continued existence. An automobile manufacturer might stay in business only because its automobiles replicate the design of pollution-free prototypes developed by a competitor, but may thus design its automobiles out of concern for profit alone; the replication of a pollution-free design may be not unconscious, but not intentional either. Beavers are not operating *unconsciously* when they replicate, in the dam they build, the design followed by generations of their ancestors, but neither (it seems) are they explicitly *intending* that the weave of the branches should impound water, nor that the underwater supports driven vertically into the stream-bed should keep the woven horizontal branches from washing downstream. (If placed in a room with audio speakers that emit the sound of running water, beavers will pile sticks on the speakers.) A spider spins the web characteristic of its variety, but without intending that that sort of web should entrap prey; caddisfly larvae deploy silken seine nets into the streams where they live, but without intending to catch food (Gould, this volume). And time after time, in building their 'castles of clay', termites place new globs of dirt atop each pillar in a pair, at just the right offset to form at length a perfect arch uniting the pillars (ibid.).

There is a crucial similarity among the copying processes that produce these seemingly disparate items. They are all causally sensitive to the performance, by the past tokens which figure as 'originals' in the copying process, of certain sorts of functions—perceptual or behavioral functions among 'originals' embodied in the physiology of animals, functions of fitting and turning and bending among 'originals' embodied in tools, functions affecting performance and ease of use among commodities. The processes are such as to copy for a longer time, or in greater numbers, previous items which have served some such function than previous items which served none; or previous items which served such a function more often or more effectively than items which served the same function less well; or previous items which served a more urgent such function than items which served one less urgent. The copying processes or mechanisms are not confined by the ways they work to copying items of just *that* qualitative make-up found in the items *currently* produced. They will have copied qualitatively different items, to a lesser degree. Their histories will have warranted the claim that if originals *more* functional than the current products had historically been available for copying, those more functional originals *would have* gotten copied instead.

This is why it is indeed legitimate to speak of natural selection as copying, not just genotypic configurations from generation to generation, but also the phenotypic traits which express those genotypes. Directly, of course, it is only genes that get copied. The offspring of an amputee do not inherit wooden legs. But what causes a particular genotype to get replicated more and more widely, in generation after generation, is often not random genetic drift, but the adaptive (and hence reproductive) success of the phenotypic trait for which it codes. In such circumstances the consequent spread through the gene pool of the underlying genotype in turn causes a spread through the species of that phenotypic trait. Hence often, the successes achieved by earlier tokens of a phenotypic trait cause the production of later tokens. There is a process which produces eyes in present-day eagles that resemble eyes in ancestor eagles, and it is causally sensitive to the successes scored by those ancestor eyes. There is a mechanism responsible for the presence in present-day beavers of dam-building behavior, and it is causally sensitive to the successes achieved by past tokens of just such behaviors. In short, while what *directly* gets copied from generation to generation are genes, it is also true that *indirectly* phenotypic traits get copied across generations, copied as a causal consequence of functions served in the past. It is in this sense that the dams made by present-day beavers can be said to be copies of dams made by ancestor beavers; as Dawkins (1982) points out, the dam is as much a part of the beaver's naturally selected phenotype as is the beaver's tail.

Items produced by such success-sensitive copying processes, then, are the subject of my central contention. (My contention thus concerns not only 'replicators' but 'propagators', in Sperber's terminology—this volume.) The contention is that where a particular copied 'shape', a past performance causally responsible for the copying (i.e. a proper function), and a historically proper placement all come together, further properties will typically cluster with them. Inferences from examined samples will non-accidentally hold true for copied kinds, just as for natural kinds more familiar in philosophical discussions. These further properties fall into three main categories. There are properties connected with material composition; there are functional peculiarities of the design that is copied; and there are specific propensities for historical change when and if the proper placement should alter.

First, then, the members of a given copied kind can warrantedly be expected to be made of the right sort of stuff.[4] This is obviously true for artifacts and kinds of phenotypic hardware; it is true in a transposed sense for even reproduced behaviors. Household screwdrivers, for example, can warrantedly be expected to be made of fairly firm materials. For the screws they turn must be firm enough to penetrate the materials to which they are applied, and the screwdrivers themselves must turn the screws without being bent in the process. The materials composing a beaver dam must be firm enough that, when woven together in the characteristic design, they do not snap or dissolve under the pressure of the impounded water. But they must not be so firm or dense that beavers cannot grasp pieces of them with their teeth. The mating dance of a particular species of fish must not have a choreography so acrobatic that almost no male can dance it, nor so complex that almost no female can recognize it.

Second, the members of any copied kind will embody a particular design solution to what might broadly be termed an engineering problem, and with that solution will go particular excellences and liabilities. The mechanism in humans for localizing sounds has a simple, 'low cost' design, but a recurrent and predictable failing: it commonly fails to differentiate a sound emanating from a source $30°–60°$ removed from 'straight ahead' from a sound emanating

---

[4] Much the same point is made by Ned Block (1997) in his discussion of 'the Disney Principle'.

from 30°–60° removed from 'straight behind'. The stereoscopic visual systems found in mammalian predator species embody a solution to the task of achieving depth perception, but one achieved at the cost of a narrowing of the visual field. Human rituals involving sacrificial offerings embody solutions to the challenge of meeting social and emotional needs, but in times of famine predictably entail suffering and disruption as well.

Finally, the members of at least some copied kinds will have propensities to shift in their qualitative make-up, or a history of having actually done so, in ways that coincide with changes in their historically proper placement. The hunting behaviors in a predator species will alter as the customary prey species acquires new routines of evasion and escape, or dies out and gets replaced by other prey species. New strategies for responding to social defection may develop in a given population as defection comes to be more common. Mating dances or plumage may become more stylized and exaggerated in a given species, when females start favoring by their responses the more colorful of the dances or plumages originally on offer. The syntactically significant suffixes and markers in a language will shift as the phonemes of that language come to be typed differently by its speakers.

The natural kinds most cited in contemporary discussions are chemical kinds, such as water, or physical elements, such as gold. These kinds are characterized by fairly rich clusters of properties which, singly or in combination, distinguish those kinds from other generically similar kinds. It does have to be said that copied kinds, in contrast, may be characterized by relatively thin clusters of properties. There may even be copied kinds characterized *only* by a particular copied 'shape', a particular proper function, and a particular historical placement. Yet even so members of such copied kinds will be characterized by combinations of properties which can be found in members of no other copied kind. (Thus even such copied kinds will satisfy the requirement that an individual belongs to the natural kind it does in virtue of its properties, and no individual can belong to two different same-level kinds.) An example will help make the point clear, and the mating dance of the male stickleback will do as well as any. A dance having just *that* 'shape', *that* choreography, can have gotten replicated on account of its historical successes at causing replication of the dancers' genes only if performed in the presence of females disposed to respond by releasing eggs. Thus *that* shape and *that* proper function can have combined only in *that* historically proper placement; the combination can be found *only* in mating dances of male sticklebacks. Similarly, a dance bearing that choreography can have gotten replicated by a success-sensitive copying mechanism, on account of its historical interactions with females attuned to release eggs, only if *what* the choreography succeeded at was propitious timing of a release of milt. That copied shape can have combined with that historically proper placement only if the success causally responsible for the copying amounted to success at replicating the dancers' genes.

3. CLASSES OF ARTIFACTS WHICH ARE AND ARE NOT COPIED KINDS; COINCIDING OBJECTS

Thus the members of copied kinds are characterized by properties that cluster together in just the way that the essential properties of more familiar natural kinds do. We therefore have at least prima facie reason to judge that when a member of a copied kind is created or destroyed, a genuine substantial change has occurred—that members of copied kinds can be said, in ontological strictness, to exist. But just what does this say about the ontological status of artifacts? Is every kind of artifact for which there is a sortal in common usage—for example, chairs and tables and sweaters—a copied kind in its own right? If not, what marks the division between the artifacts that may be admitted to our ontology and those which must be treated as mere projections of our language and culture?

In this section I defend and refine the position that broad and inclusive kinds of artifacts are less likely to constitute true copied kinds than are kinds more specifically delimited. Chairs are less likely to compose a copied kind than are desk chairs, and desk chairs are less likely than Eames desk chairs of the 1957 design. But this is not to say that where one kind of artifact is a specific version of some broader kind, *only* the more specific can claim to be a true copied kind. Given a modicum of specificity, *both* may be perfectly genuine as copied kinds. The difference may be only that the more specific kind is characterized by a richer, more interesting cluster of properties.

The basic rationale for this position is obvious: kinds as broad as chairs and tables can barely be said to have any one 'shape' or qualitative character in common at all. Moreover, they have no well-defined historically proper placement: there are dining-room chairs, electric chairs, birthing chairs, and camping chairs. The challenge lies not in finding reasons for thinking that artifact kinds must be *fairly specific* to qualify as copied kinds. It lies rather in defending the claim that a fair degree of specificity is *enough*—that where one artifact kind is a specific version of another, the former need not always usurp the latter's claim to being a copied kind. For suppose that one artifact kind is a specific version of some broader artifact kind, that both do amount to copied kinds, and that some one artifact is a member of both. Suppose, to make it concrete, that some one chair is both a desk chair and an Eames 1957 desk chair. Then we seem to be faced with 'the problem of coinciding objects'. Exactly where that chair is located there is an object which essentially has the characteristic Eames shape, and an object which does not essentially have that shape. But if object A differs in its essential properties from object B, A and B are distinct. So in that location there are two objects. Each of them is a chair. Yet if the 30-lb. desk chair and the 30-lb. Eames desk chair are both placed on a scale—which can be done, *mirabile dictu*, in a single motion—the scale reads '30', not '60'.

The problem of coinciding objects has indeed been lurking in the wings since this chapter began. It is a main reason why many contemporary metaphysicians judge that artifacts do not really exist in the world (see Rea 1997). For suppose—to sketch their reasoning—that an artisan fashions a large lump of gold into a statue of Goliath. Then surely the lump still exists, and occupies exactly the boundaries of the statue. But the lump has different essential properties from the statue. The statue has its shape essentially; if flattened, it ceases to exist. Not so the lump of gold. So unless we want to allow that distinct objects may occupy the very same place as one another—and face the embarrassment that two of them together weigh the same as any one singly does—one of these objects must go from our ontology. Many contemporary metaphysicians judge that what must go is the statue (e.g. Zimmerman 1995).

Now the problem of coinciding *artifacts* seems to me genuine, and I will return to it presently. The problem of coincidence between any artifact and a *matter-object* is another matter. Why need we suppose that there is some one matter-y thing, possessed of a spatio-temporal career of its own, which at present composes the statue, but may later not do so? Our ontology must to be sure admit that there is such a stuff or substance as gold; gold, like water and bronze, is what Aristotle called a secondary substance, one which by nature occurs in spatially localized quantities. Our ontology must also recognize the individual atoms which between them compose any localized quantity of gold, and the molecules which compose any sample of water. But why need we say that in addition to the one stuff of which a homogeneous artifact is made, there is some one object which composes that artifact?

What nature are we to think of such a matter-object as having—what features should we think of as marking out its career? One answer is that the object is the *aggregate* of gold atoms now within the statue. *This* matter-object by nature survives just as long as those very individual atoms continue to exist, and just where they come to be; unlike the statue, it can survive radical dismemberment, but also unlike the statue, cannot survive the destruction of even one of those atoms. An alternative answer is that the matter-object in question is a *parcel* of gold, defined by its having exactly that statuesque shape. When even a small chunk is clipped from Goliath's ear, the statue continues to exist, albeit in damaged condition, but the parcel exists no longer.

There is a third answer as well, a more promising answer, and I will consider it in a moment. The problem with these first two matter-objects is that they are said to have, essentially, properties which do not test out *as* essential on any remotely plausible realist test of essentialness (Elder 1998). The test I identified before involved seeing whether a particular essential property of Xs clustered together, by virtue of the laws of nature, with enough other properties to yield a cluster found nowhere else but in Xs. Now an essential property of the *aggregate*-object is (supposedly) that it is composed of exactly, numerically, *those* atoms of gold. But can *being-composed-of-numerically-those-atoms-of-gold* engage the laws of nature in such a way that yet other properties will cluster together with it? No, since the laws of nature are never engaged by bare numerical identity, by haecceities. They apply to things by virtue of the things' properties or circumstances or relations—by virtue of repeatables. (The same reasoning shows that origin, i.e. being-derived-from-numerically-*that*-matter or being-derived-from-numerically-*that*-source, also cannot be essential; I will return to this point presently.) As to the *parcel* of gold coincident with the statue, it is said to have essentially the property of being of exactly *that* extent or size or mass. But, with rare exceptions such as piles of Uranium-235, that a sample of some stuff is of one precise size or another makes no further difference, under the laws of nature, to what other properties it has.

Then might we think of the matter-object with which Goliath appears to coincide in yet a third way—as just *that sample* of gold, that expanse or chunk of gold? The persistence-conditions for this matter-object would be more loosely defined than for either of the first two; they indeed vary with different conversational contexts. Sometimes asking 'where is that sample of gold now? Does it still exist?' will amount to asking whether 90 per cent of the atoms in the original statue are still joined together, sometimes to whether half or more of those atoms are joined together, sometimes just to asking whether some percentage of them still now *exists*. My response is that all such questions are perfectly genuine. But they are questions about many objects, in the plural—many gold atoms—not questions about some one object.

At the same time, the problem of coinciding *artifacts* does seem perfectly genuine. Artifacts belonging to one copied kind often do coincide with artifacts belonging to some other copied kind—typically another kind more specific, or less. An Eames desk chair, 1957 design, occupies exactly the same volume as does some desk chair; and, as in Sidelle's (1998) example, a single long piece of woolen yarn, itself an artifact, might compose the whole of a sweater. How then can two distinct artifacts—which differ, after all, in their essential properties—be wholly present at exactly the same place?

The sting of this question comes from the realist position on essentialness endorsed both by this chapter and by the projectivism which this paper attacks. If essentialness is really *out there in the things*, it may seem, a thing must have essentially those properties that *are* essential to it strictly in virtue of its own material make-up, its being composed of just *those* atoms. And then if thing A and thing B have exactly the same material composition, they cannot differ in respect of their essential properties.

But what I have argued is that, in the case of copied kinds, essentialness can be *out there in the things* in virtue of the histories of function which lie behind the causes that produced the things. The long piece of yarn springs from a copying process long under way, continued over generations because of successes which its earlier products scored at composing primitive socks and mittens and cords as well as sweaters; the 'shape' in virtue of which it figures as product of this process involves its thinness and the criss-crossing of wool fibers within it, not the sweatery form it currently assumes. Eames desk chairs spring from a copying process that began long after the copying of *some* desk chairs *or other*, and that process continued because of special features unique to its products—their exiguous and sinuous shapes, their bright color, and so on.

Because the Eames desk chair and the desk chair possess different essential properties in virtue of their different histories, and not in virtue of any difference in material composition, it is unsurprising that when the two are put on the scale, the scale still reads '30'. The two are composed of exactly the same matter! Now true, this answer would prolong our difficulties about coinciding objects, rather than resolve them, if expressed as the claim that *the parcel* of matter which composes, for example, the Eames desk chair also composes the desk chair, or if expressed as a parallel claim about *the aggregate* of atoms which composes either. But it need not be expressed that way. It can rather be expressed as the claim that every atom found within the boundaries of the Eames desk chair is found in the boundaries of the desk chair, and vice versa. (Refinements may be needed to reflect the fuzziness of the boundaries of either object. But they reflect 'the problem of the many', not the problem of coinciding objects.)

My position, in sum, is this. Commonly recognized kinds of artifacts that are very broad and inclusive are unlikely to constitute copied kinds; fairly specific familiar kinds of artifacts are all likely to do so (more on this in a moment); and among these *fairly* specific kinds the *more* specific will in general be the more interesting copied kinds, the ones which display richer clusters of characteristic properties. Eames 1957 desk chairs are a more interesting copied kind than are desk chairs in general. But now why is that, exactly? Ruth Millikan has argued that for the special sciences, 'historical kinds' are especially likely to sustain a rich range of inductive inferences (Millikan 1999*a*). 'Historical kinds' are defined as ones whose members not only bear qualitative resemblances to one another but derive from numerically the same historical process of copying as one another. Are Eames 1957 desk chairs a richly characterized artifact kind because they all stem from numerically the same originals in the Eames' studios? Is it true in general that the most interesting copied kinds are historical kinds?

Millikan's contention seems to me to give distorted expression to an important truth. By speaking of historical *kinds*, not just *groupings*, she suggests that there would be a difference in essential nature between, say, an Eames 1957 desk chair and another chair qualitatively just like it that were derived from a historical copying process just like the one that produced the Eames chair. But this difference between the genuine Eames chair and its lookalike would be a difference which made no difference, which entrained no further properties in either chair; the laws of nature simply are not sensitive to bare numerical identities. So 'kinds' is an exaggeration.[5] But there is an important truth here. It is that in studying highly specific copied kinds, we should *act as if* part of what constitutes membership in that kind is descent from numerically just *that* historical copying process. For in this way we will focus our study on individual copied items which may bear to one another qualitative similarities we did not originally know to look for. Copied items that stem from numerically the same copying process may resemble each other in *many* details of historically proper placement, or of copied qualitative 'shape', some of which we did not initially recognize.

One last word about certain specifically delimited kinds of artifacts. We copy from one another, half knowingly and half unwittingly, a thousand minor details of personal behavior—turns of phrase, bodily gestures, styles of dress, and articles of personal ornamentation. Much of this copying is entirely uninfluenced by any history of function which the items copied may have. The psychological and social mechanisms which underlie the copying are either sensitive to past functionality only sometimes—perhaps mainly in larger and more consequential aspects of behavior—or are distinct from the mechanisms that underlie function-sensitive copying of cultural items. Or, indeed, the copying may occur because there is a function served by the copying itself—for example, that it affirms group affiliation—rather than by the items copied. In any case familiar artifacts such as neckties, high-heeled shoes, and nose rings are very unlikely to amount to copied kinds. The behaviors of wearing such personal articles may fall into copied kinds, but the articles themselves probably do not.

The main reason for this is that members of true copied kinds have a characteristic shape—in a literal or metaphorical sense—and replication of that shape causally depends on something which previous members of the kind did in consequence of having that shape. Now neckties (for example) do literally have a typical shape: a necktie typically is shaped like two elongated kites joined at the tail. But what causes that shape to get replicated, in one bolt of silk after another, is not some performance which earlier neckties were disposed by their shape to carry out. The causes which produce new neckties have nothing to do with performances which past neckties, as physical objects, effected. That is why neckties can vary widely in width, can have parallel sides, can get fashioned from a wide variety of materials, and why inferences from the shape of this year's neckties

---

[5] My contention is that no copied kind is essentially characterized by descent-from-numerically-just-*that*-historical-process. Millikan's endorsement of historical kinds, however, is not just a comment on the nature of certain *copied* kinds. She also recognizes historical kinds that are not essentially characterized by any proper function at all—notably, biological species. I do now agree with her, contra Elder 1995 and 1996, that (many) biological species are natural kinds. But I deny, for the reasons just identified in the text, that descent-from-numerically-*that*-origin is essential to the members of any biological species. What holds a species together is something distinct from any historical singularity: roughly, it is the capacity of the genes within its gene pool to cooperate, in producing viable organisms, with randomly assembled re-combinations of the other genes (types) in fact present in its gene pool. There are no historical kinds at all.

to the shape of neckties in 2010 will only accidentally be accurate. In contrast, the ways in which neckties get knotted around the neck, and the circumstances in which neckties thus knotted get displayed, actually *are* matters over which we may run inferences that non-accidentally succeed. The reason why is that it is *wearings of* neckties which form a true copied kind. These have a characteristic physical and social 'shape', and get reproduced because, in the historically proper placement of a specific dress code, they have afforded their agents social access or acceptance. Ontologically, there are manufactured materials such as silk and cotton yarn, themselves copied kinds, which are secondary substances in Aristotle's sense (cf. Grandy, and Bloom, both this volume); these materials exist in spatially localized quantities, and of these there are some shaped like two elongated kites joined at the tail; and there are wearings of neckties. That is all. The expanses of silk or of cotton yarn which satisfy the sortal 'neckties' do not have essential properties distinct from those of any other parcels of these materials. Like any such expanses, they are essentially characterized only by the properties essentially characteristic of silk and of cotton. They do not amount to unitary matter-objects which trace out spatio-temporal careers of their own.

4. THE PROBLEM WITH PROJECTIVISM: CUSTOMS AND CONVENTIONS

If there really are in the world instances of copied kinds, there are in the world at least some artifacts. So any philosopher who holds that artifacts do not, in ontological strictness, exist must deny that copied kinds are instanced in the world. At the same time such a philosopher must allow that we *project* onto the world existences of artifacts—creations of artifacts, courses of existence which they trace out, destructions of artifacts. What elements in the world act on us to cause this projection, according to such a philosopher? The only plausible answers must cite our customs or conventions or linguistic practices. But the arena of custom and convention and language is rife with copied kinds, as I now briefly shall argue. If this is correct, an artifact-free ontology is incoherent.

Consider, to begin with, some typical customs. It is customary among many peoples to mark national holidays with public spectacles or the singing of patriotic songs. There are customary ways of preparing meals, there is a custom of taking a siesta, and there is a custom of bringing casseroles to the homes of people recently bereaved. It seems hard to doubt that at least part of what causes such patterns of behavior to get copied from person to person, and from generation to generation, is some function which the patterns have repeatedly, if not invariably, served. Thus such copied patterns have not only a characteristic 'shape' but also, it seems, a proper function. It is no objection to this claim that different patterns or practices could have served the same function as well. So long as we are confident that the mechanisms which copied these behaviors would have copied them (perhaps actually *did* copy them) more widely than behaviors which served no function, or which served the same functions less well, or which served functions less useful, the attribution of proper function is warranted. Moreover, these customary behaviors serve functions only when and as cued to customarily recognized settings—to holidays, to meal-times, to members of the family of the deceased—and can therefore be said to have historically proper placements. At least many customs, it seems, are copied kinds.

To call a copied pattern of behavior a 'convention', in contrast, often is to suggest that it *lacks* a proper function. It is a convention in countries other than England, Australia, and Japan to drive on the right side of the road. But obviously right-side driving is not intrinsically useful, nor is driving on the left intrinsically a poorer practice. It is a convention to say 'hello' when answering the phone, to extend one's right hand when greeting someone, and to call a chair 'a chair'—but in all of these cases the intrinsic content of the act confers by itself no benefit or gain.[6] But coincident with every case of such conventionally copied behavior there is something which does have a proper function, and is a member of a copied kind. It is that same behavior relationally described—that behavior *as* a copying, *as* a replicating of conventional behavior. Replicating right-hand driving, where right-hand driving already has the status of a widespread behavior, copied from person to person over long periods, is indeed extremely useful. Replicating an *expected* sound by saying 'hello'—as opposed to producing just that sound for its own sake—is indeed useful. *Followings of* conventions have specific shapes, they often have proper functions, and they have historically established conventional settings. They too are then copied kinds.

Finally, a word about linguistic practices. There has been considerable debate as to whether, and in what sense, language is governed by conventions (see Millikan 2003). Whatever the outcome of this debate, it seems virtually certain that at least sometimes some linguistic patterns get copied in consequence of functions which earlier tokens of those patterns have served, and that the copying is cued to contexts similar to those of the earlier tokens. If so there are in our linguistic behavior tokens of copied kinds: the current copyings have a characteristic 'shape', a proper function, and a historically proper placement.

5. CONCLUSION

Do the sortals by which common speech picks out artifacts—for example, 'screwdrivers', 'desk chairs'—designate real kinds in nature? I have argued that at least some of them do. They designate copied kinds, the members of which are characterized essentially by a certain qualitative make-up or 'shape', a proper

---

[6] These are examples of the particular kind of convention Ruth Millikan (1998, 2003) calls 'coordination conventions'.

function, and an historically proper placement. To say that these properties are essential to the members of such copied kinds is to say that they cluster together in distinctive packages because of the way the copying processes in the world work. They cluster together mind-independently, and not just because we intend that objects bearing a certain make-up should serve a certain function, or because the concept we wield for a given kind of artifact ties shape and function together. There is no joint in nature between the artifacts copied by intelligent and conscious artisans, such as desk chairs, and the devices produced by naturally selected behaviors, such as beaver dams (cf. Gould, this volume). What is written in the title of this chapter is 'artifacts'. What is written in the book of nature is *copied kinds*.[7]

---

[7] An earlier version of this chapter appeared as chapter 7 of my 2004 book *Real Natures and Familiar Objects*, MIT Press.

4

Artifacts and Human Concepts

Amie L. Thomasson

It is frequently observed that artifacts and other social and cultural objects are in some sense 'creations of the mind', depending in certain ways on human beliefs or activities. But in what sense are such objects and kinds dependent on human concepts and intentions? And what difference does this make to the place of such objects in our philosophical theories?

I have argued elsewhere (2003) that the dependence of institutional objects on the collective acceptance of certain constitutive rules (on a theory like Searle's; 1995 and this volume) entails that we have certain sorts of epistemic privilege with regard to our own institutional kinds that we lack with respect to natural kinds. I have also argued (2001) that the ways in which some social objects and kinds depend on human intentionality have consequences for our capacity to acquire knowledge and make discoveries about social facts.

But the role of human intentions in the creation of artifacts seems rather different from their role in creating social and institutional facts and objects. Unlike social and institutional objects, the existence of artifacts doesn't seem to presuppose any *collective* intentions of any kind—it makes perfect sense to suppose that a solitary human could create a knife, though not a government or money. Thus artifacts don't seem to be essentially *social* objects at all. On the other hand, it seems to be part of the very idea of an artifact that it must be the *product* of human intentions.

At first glance, it might seem that *this* sort of dependence on human intentions has no special consequences for metaphysics, epistemology, or reference, if we think of humans as simply the causal origins of artifacts. After all, many plants and animals are in some sense causally produced by humans in agriculture, without ceasing to be natural objects of natural kinds, and human beings themselves, of course, are the products of other human activities. So having a causal origin in humans does not seem to have any obvious metaphysical or other consequences.

And indeed it has often been argued that the fact that artifacts are the products of human intentions in fact makes no substantial difference to their metaphysical standing as mind-independent kinds, to our epistemic relation to them,[1] or to the way our terms for them refer (Putnam 1975; Kornblith 1980 and this volume). In fact it might seem that one *has to* take this position to defend the view that there really are such things, since it is often thought that any element of mind-dependence or epistemic privilege regarding certain objects or kinds must rule them out of a realist's ontology.

I believe, however, that this is not so. On the contrary, I have argued (2003) that artifacts and artifactual kinds are closely related to human concepts in at least three ways: metaphysically, epistemically, and semantically. First, it is not just a causal fact but a conceptual truth that artifacts must be the products of human intentions, indeed of intentions to produce something of that very kind. As a result, I have argued, the metaphysical natures of artifactual kinds are *constituted by* the concepts and intentions of makers, a feature that sets them crucially apart from natural kinds. I have also argued that the role of makers in establishing the nature of the artifactual kind they create endows them with some protection from certain kinds of ignorance and error about that nature, providing them with a much closer epistemic relationship to their artifactual kinds than anyone has to natural kinds. Finally, I have argued that this even impacts the ways in which the reference of the corresponding general terms is determined, since it turns out that there can be no reference to artifactual kinds without someone having a relevant concept that in turn plays a role in determining the term's extension.

These results are based on analyzing the concepts associated with our artifactual kind terms. It might be thought, though, that conceptual analysis of our artifactual kind terms is simply the wrong way to go, for even if it is part of the ordinary idea of an artifactual kind that its nature bears certain essential relations to human intentions, surely (it might be said) we could all be wrong about that. If our ideas about what sort of nature artifactual kinds have are as open to error as any beliefs about natural kinds, then perhaps human intentions don't *really* play any essential role in the natures of artifactual kinds, with these instead being determined by some mind-independent property such as function, or some mind-independent cluster of properties surrounding a core of properties such as qualitative make-up, proper function, and historically proper placement (Elder, this volume).

Thus in this chapter I will remake the argument from the bottom up, in two steps: first, (sec. 1) by addressing the very idea of artifactual kind concepts and

---

[1] Crawford Elder (this volume) argues that at least *some* kinds of artifacts, namely those he calls 'copied kinds', have essential natures based on properties that cluster together in just as mind-independent a way as those of natural kinds. He also argues (1989) that, for at least some culturally generated kinds (like natural kinds), beliefs even of members of the relevant culture could be massively false for all that is ensured by who they are and the fact that those beliefs are about those kinds.

why we should accept that they refer (if at all) to kinds whose natures are determined by human intentions, and second (sec. 2) by elucidating exactly how human intentions are involved in determining the natures of artifactual kinds, and why that metaphysical difference should have consequences for epistemology (sec. 3) and reference (sec. 4). These points need to be made carefully, however, for (despite their dependence on human intentions) artifactual kinds are certainly not entirely transparent to us. I will thus also discuss the limits of epistemic privilege regarding artifactual kinds, and address a number of objections based in pointing out kinds of error to which people may still be subject (sec. 5). Finally, accepting that the natures of artifactual kinds are mind-dependent, and that humans have certain forms of epistemic privilege regarding them might be thought to undermine the idea that such things really exist. Thus in closing (sec. 6) I will address this worry, arguing that the mind-dependence of artifacts and artifactual kinds should in no way be taken to interfere with accepting that such entities really exist.

1. ARTIFACTUAL KIND CONCEPTS AND NATURAL KIND CONCEPTS

Artifactual kind concepts and terms such as 'table', 'chair', or 'knife' seem to belong to a distinct range of concepts and terms, not (on the whole) reducible to or extensionally equivalent to familiar natural kind concepts and terms such as 'iron', 'maple', or 'aluminum'. The question then arises: how do these general terms acquire reference?[2]

Direct reference theories (Kripke 1980; Putnam 1975) hold that natural kind terms acquire their reference not in virtue of any concepts competent speakers hold about the nature of the kind, but rather in virtue of a causal relationship to a certain sample of entities, so that a term like 'iron' or 'maple' refers to whatever real natural kind all or most of the entities in the sample belong to. The nature of the kind and conditions for kind membership are thus determined by the mind-independent boundaries of the kind, and may be discovered empirically through the work of natural scientists. One heralded result of this view is that it preserves the epistemological independence of such kinds from all human beliefs and concepts: a kind may exist (and we may refer to it) even if everyone is in complete ignorance regarding its nature, and any beliefs anyone may have had about the nature of the kind or specific conditions for kind membership may turn out to be completely in error.

---

[2] Since most of the debate about the reference of artifactual kind terms has focused on the tenability of direct reference versus descriptive (and hybrid) theories, I will limit my discussion here to those theories of reference.

There has been a great deal of discussion about whether or not the same theory of reference can apply to other general terms, especially artifactual kind terms (Putnam 1970, 1975; Schwartz 1978, 1980; Kornblith 1980; Nelson 1982). Much of that discussion has focused on the possibilities for ignorance and error in our artifactual concepts—some of which I will return to below. For now, however, it is enough to notice that (as long as one acknowledges that artifact kind terms are not equivalent to natural kind terms) one cannot hold a *pure* direct reference theory for both natural kind terms and artifactual kind terms. For suppose a speaker is faced with a sample of teak lawn chairs, and attempts to apply a new term to refer to 'that kind of thing'. As those who have drawn out the qua problem have repeatedly argued (e.g. Devitt and Sterelny 1999, 91), the reference of the speaker's term will be radically indeterminate unless she disambiguates the sort or category of kind she means to refer to.[3] For any sample of entities will instantiate many different kinds (chemical, biological, artifactual, cultural, legal, etc.), and so to disambiguate and establish the reference of a kind term, a speaker who seeks to ground that term's reference must have at least a very high-level background conception of what *sorts of* features are relevant to being a member of this sort of kind (i.e. whether it is sameness of underlying causal/explanatory constitution, sameness of legal standing, etc.). This then establishes the category of kind to be referred to (if the term refers at all), by establishing what sorts of features are relevant to unifying the kind.

In sum, then, it seems that we need to accept a hybrid theory of reference for kind terms, acknowledging that grounders of a term's reference must at least intend to refer to a certain *category* of kind, where this is a matter of intending some rather than other *sorts* of common features to be relevant to unifying the kind (Devitt and Sterelny 1999). *Whatever* distinguishes intentions to refer to an artifactual kind from intentions to refer to a natural kind then *determines* what *sorts* of features (though perhaps not what particular features) are relevant to membership in an artifactual kind as opposed to membership in a natural kind. As such, these essential elements of our artifactual kind concepts that distinguish them from natural kind concepts will not be open to revision through future 'discoveries'. Thus, there is a first element of privilege regarding the natures of artifactual kinds (and presumably many other kinds as well): those who ground the reference of any artifactual kind term must themselves have some conception of what general sorts of features are relevant to determining the kind's nature and the term's extension, for it is this that establishes the term as a would-be artifactual kind term. About this, they cannot be proven to be in error through later empirical investigations, since this *establishes* the sort of nature that is relevant to the reference of the term, if it refers at all.

---

[3] In addition, of course, she must disambiguate what *level* of kind of any type she means to refer to, whether e.g. to teak, wood generally; lawn chairs, chairs generally, furniture generally, etc. I will leave that problem to one side here. For further discussion of the need for a hybrid theory of reference sec ch. 2 of my *Ordinary Objects* (2007).

But what is it that distinguishes intentions to refer to a natural kind from intentions to refer to an artifactual kind? Paul Bloom (this volume) reports that psychological evidence suggests that natural kind and artifactual kind concepts are acquired and comprehended differently: 'Natural kinds are understood in terms of internal essences; artifacts are thought of in terms of considerations such as creator's intent, characteristic function, and the social and cultural context of the artifact's creation and use' (p. 154). It seems quite plausible that considerations like these are what distinguish the attempt to ground the reference of a natural kind term from that for an artifactual kind term.

Most attempts to describe the difference between natural kind terms and artifactual kind terms have focused on the second factor mentioned by Bloom, taking *function* rather than *internal essence* to be the distinctive sort of feature appealed to by artifactual concepts. Thus, for instance Hilary Kornblith (1980, 114) draws out an example that seems to be as close as one can get to a 'direct' application of an artifactual kind term that might parallel that for a natural kind term. He asks us to consider a case in which Martian anthropologists are faced with a sample of apparent (Earth) artifacts, whose nature is unknown to them, and coin a term 'glug', declaring 'Let's call the kind of which this is a member "glug" ' (ibid.). But if their term 'glug' is to be grounded as an *artifactual* kind term rather than as a natural kind term, the Martian anthropologists must take, for instance, the exact chemical or physical make-up of members of the sample to be potentially irrelevant to their membership in the kind. What is relevant? Kornblith suggests that—at least for the most part—it is sameness of *function* that is relevant to membership in an artifactual kind (p. 112), and for a time the suggestion was widely followed that artifactual natures are based on *functional* rather than physical, chemical, or biological kinds.

But what sense of function could be relevant here? Sharing *actual* causal powers that enable objects to function in certain ways cannot be sufficient for belonging to a common artifactual kind, since any sample of entities will share a great many causal powers, without belonging to a great many (or even any) common artifactual kinds. Actual causal powers also cannot be necessary for items to be of the same artifactual kind, since our artifactual kind terms such as 'knife' or 'can-opener' generally apply as much to broken or malformed members of the kind as to functioning members. So it has been suggested instead that it is a common *proper* function in something like Ruth Millikan's sense that is appealed to as the general sort of property relevant to delineating artifactual kinds, as opposed to natural kinds.[4]

A thing's proper function, on Millikan's view, may be acquired in either of two ways: either it is some function *past* members of the kind successfully performed, such that *because of* that successful functioning, this reproduction

---

[4] Elder (this volume) takes proper function to be *one of three* essential properties of any 'copied kind', at least some of which are artifactual kinds.

was made (though this particular reproduction may be malformed)—this is a 'direct' proper function—or the thing is the product of some prior device that has the relevant proper function, and normally performs this function by means of producing an item like this—this is a 'derived' proper function (Millikan 1993, 13–14). The latter clause applies to prototype artifacts, which are created by human intentions and behaviors that themselves have the proper functions that are passed on to the artifacts created to help fulfill them. So, for example the proper function of a desire for food might be to gain nourishment for the organism. If, in a particular environment, that desire causes someone to invent a new hunting device, the hunting device inherits the proper function of acquiring nourishment for the person from the intentional state that produced it.

It is important to notice that, where artifacts are concerned, the relevant function (whether it's the derived proper function or direct proper function) must be its *intended* function. This is obvious in the case of derived proper function, since artifacts inherit the proper functions of the intentional states that produce them, and as a result 'artifacts have as derived proper functions the functions intended for them by their makers' (Millikan 1999*b*, 205). It is somewhat less obvious in the case of those artifacts that may plausibly be thought to have direct proper functions. An item acquires a direct proper function F only if it is reproduced from predecessors (in part) *because* those predecessors were able to perform F. But unlike biological creatures, artifacts do not reproduce themselves. A certain kind of artifact is reproduced *because of* the functioning of its predecessors only if human beings believe the predecessors were useful for some purpose, and create the new object with the intention that it also fulfill that function. So if function is what is relevant to membership in an artifactual (rather than natural) kind, it must be *intended* function that is relevant, and when Martian anthropologists coin their term 'glug', they must mean it to refer to whatever has the same intended function as these Earth artifacts.

But while intended function does seem to be a relevant feature for determining membership in a great many of the artifactual kinds picked out by our standard artifactual kind terms, appeal to a common intended function does not seem a sufficiently general way of describing what distinguishes the application of artifactual kind terms (as opposed to natural kind terms or other general terms). For, as Bloom (1996, 5–6) argues, there may be members of various artifactual kinds that are *not* intended to have the function of other members of the kind, for example, something can be a boat or a chair even if its maker desires that it never be placed in water or sat upon (perhaps intending it only 'for show'). Moreover, some artifactual kinds may have no intended function or no *essential* intended function (for example, arguably, it is not *necessary* to have any, or any particular, intended function to be a member of the artifactual kinds *sculpture* or *symphony*), and in many cases sameness of intended function is not *sufficient* for being a member of the same artifactual kind, since other factors such as shape, form, origin, and so on may be held to be necessary as well or instead (Bloom 1996).

Thus, in drawing out what sorts of features artifactual kind terms (as opposed to natural kind terms) appeal to as relevant for determining membership in the kind, we might do better to focus on the first of Bloom's suggestions: the creator's intentions generally (whether or not they specify an intended *function*) are most relevant to determining whether or not her product is in the extension of an artifactual kind term. This fits well with the frequent observation (Bloom, this volume; Hilpinen 1992) that *intentions* play a central role in artifact concepts.

But what sorts of intentions of makers are relevant to determining whether or not their products belong to a given artifactual kind? First and foremost, what seems to be relevant is the intention to create something of that kind. Artifacts, in the strict sense, must be not just the products, but the *intended* products of human activities (Hilpinen 1992, 60); pollution and scrap metal also must be produced by human activities, but these are not artifacts properly so-called. In fact, we can distinguish essentially artifactual concepts (from other concepts such as *gold sphere* that may just *happen* to include only artifacts in their extension) by delineating *essentially* artifactual concepts as those for which any member of the kind must be the product of an intention to create *that very* sort of object (cf. Thomasson 2003). So understood, essentially artifactual concepts, like institutional concepts on Searle's description, exhibit 'self-referentiality', though this self-referentiality here takes a somewhat different form. Whereas for a certain sort of thing to be money, it is necessary (and sufficient) that it be the sort of thing that is collectively regarded as money, for an individual object to be a chair, it must itself have been intended to be a chair.[5]

The proposal, then, is that attempts to ground the reference of an artifactual kind term differ from attempts to ground the reference of a natural kind term by appealing not to a common internal essence in members of the sample as the sort of property relevant for determining what is and is not a member of the kind, but rather to the objects' being the products of intentions that have something in common: namely, the intention to create something of that kind. But how are we to understand the relevant intentions to create something of a given artifactual kind? Bloom has argued that the relevant intention for being of any artifactual kind K is being intended to be of the same kind as 'current and previous' members of the kind (1996, 10). I have argued elsewhere (2003), however, that this intention cannot be understood merely transparently, as a bald intention to make 'one of these' (pointing to a sample). Such an intention could not be necessary, or else we could not accept that prototypes are members of the relevant artifactual kind, nor that people in distinct cultures and traditions could all create the same kind of artifact. Such a transparent intention also could not be sufficient, since an artifact must be the product of a controlled process of

---

[5] On the other hand, kinds such as 'path' and 'village' are not essentially artifactual, since some things in their extension may not be things intentionally created under that description. For discussion see my 2003, and Hilpinen 1992, 66.

making (Hilpinen 1992), involving imposing a number of intended features on the object—so the maker cannot just intend to make 'one of these' without any idea what features are relevant to being one of these. As I have argued (2003), the relevant sort of intention to make a thing of artifactual kind K must thus involve a substantive (and substantively correct) concept of what a K is, including an understanding of what sorts of properties are K-relevant and an intention to realize many of them in the object created.

One other condition is also necessary: for a member of any essentially artifactual kind K to be created, it is also necessary that that intention be at least largely successfully realized. Otherwise the would-be creator may, like so many who sit down with grand intentions at the potter's wheel, have only made a mess, not even a malformed member of the kind.

2. THE NATURES OF ARTIFACTUAL KINDS

We have seen that (in light of the *qua* problem) grounders' concepts of what general *sorts of* features are relevant to being a member of an artifactual (as opposed to chemical, biological, or physical) kind *determine* what sorts of properties are relevant to membership in an artifactual kind and are not themselves open to revision. (It does not, though, mean that those speakers have any detailed knowledge of the specific nature of any particular artifactual kind.) If this is correct, then speakers can't all be wrong about what distinguishes artifactual kind terms and concepts from natural kind terms and concepts, making conceptual analysis an appropriate method for determining what *sorts* of common features must distinguish membership in an artifactual kind. Thus if this analysis is correct, one cannot argue that, although we commonly treat creators' intentions as relevant to membership in an artifactual kind, this is not what is truly relevant (actual causal powers, or a combination of shape, function, and historically proper placement, being the sorts of criteria *really* relevant for membership in an artifactual kind).

The relevant sorts of properties appealed to whenever one attempts to ground the reference of a distinctly *artifactual* kind term, I have argued, are distinct from those appealed to in grounding physical, biological, or chemical kind terms in being fundamentally *intentional.* More specifically, an artifactual kind term will pick out entities that are the products of largely successful intentions to create something of that kind (where that intention must involve a substantive, and substantively correct, conception of what features are relevant to being a member of the kind). It turns out that, as a result of this appeal to intentions, human concepts determine the natures of artifactual kinds on a second level as well: according to the sorts of conditions presupposed by speakers' concepts, *makers'* concepts of what features are relevant to being a member of the kind (whether function, shape, etc.) determine what *specific* features (shape, function, etc.) are relevant to being a member of a particular artifactual kind, and thus collectively determine the boundaries of the kind and the kind's specific 'nature'.[6] And that, in turn, has interesting consequences for the epistemology of artifactual kinds and our reference to them that distinguishes them from paradigmatic natural objects and kinds. But these last two claims need fuller explanation and defense.

To see the ways in which makers' concepts must be definitive of the specific features relevant to membership in artifact kinds and why this has consequences for epistemology and reference, let us begin from an admittedly simplified case. The hope is that there we can see the essential features of the situation clearly, just as botanical drawings and anatomical drawings deliberately simplify the represented subject in order to make the crucial features come to light more clearly. Once the structure is made evident, we can gradually reintroduce the complications of our full real-world situation.

So consider first an individual artisan single-handedly creating a prototype artifact of a kind of her own invention. In order for the artisan to be involved in creating an artifact, her creative activities must be directed and controlled (otherwise she is merely 'messing around'), namely directed to producing an artifact of a certain kind. Since she is producing the prototype, there is no question of her intending merely to produce 'one of these' of an extant kind of artifact; there is no sample of previous members of the kind to refer back to. Yet she must have some goals to direct her activity, including some features she intends to impose on the object created. Thus she must have a substantive idea of what sort of a thing it is she intends to create (say, a K), where that idea incorporates certain features relevant to being a K, so that she can judge her activity's success in terms of the degree to which the product instantiates the relevant features.[7] In this case, clearly, there is no question of the artisan getting it right or wrong about what it would take to be a K, what features are K-relevant. At this stage, what is relevant to being a K is purely a matter for *invention* or stipulation by the artisan based on her goals or intentions; she is not trying to discover what makes something a K (so that she could then be said to get it right or wrong); instead, she is delineating a new kind by establishing success criteria for her activity. Thus she creates not only an artifact, but delineates a new artifactual *kind*, complete with normative success conditions for creating something of that kind.

The artisan can, of course, fail to successfully execute the concept, and can also fail to know whether or not she has successfully executed the concept. But nonetheless, since in order to make an artifact of any properly artifactual kind, the maker must intend to make something of that kind, she can know that *if* she

---

[6] This enables us to get a more *general* view of what is distinctive about artifactual concepts and the *sorts* of features relevant to determining membership in these kinds, while still acknowledging that intended *function* is most often of central importance (though it need not be in all cases).

[7] This, of course, does not preclude the plan beginning quite vaguely, and evolving or changing in the creative process.

has made any kind of artifact, she has made a K, and she can 'know' what it takes to be a K, not in the sense that her beliefs correspond to an independent reality, but rather in the sense that she is the one who stipulates this by establishing success criteria for her activity.

As a result, an artisan constructing a prototype for a new kind of artifact has a very different relation to the artifacts and artifactual kinds she creates than a scientist does to the natural objects she studies. The artisan knows what kind of artifact, if any, she has created; the scientist may not know what kind of natural object (if any) is before her. The criteria the artisan holds as being relevant to whether or not the product is a member of the new artifactual kind also cannot be mistaken (any more than parents can be 'mistaken' when they name their child), for this is a matter of her own stipulation, not (as the case of the scientist investigating the nature of a chemical or biological kind) a matter of discovery of independent facts. Finally, where K is an essentially artifactual concept, if a K *does* exist, it follows from this that someone (namely, at least the maker) has a substantive concept of the nature of Ks that is not subject to massive error, whereas members of natural kinds may well exist without anyone having any concept whatsoever of that kind or its nature.

Now, consider the case of a later artisan in a world containing at least one token of an essentially artifactual kind K. Either that person knows of the extant K or he does not. If he does not, he is in precisely the same position as the original artisan, with the exception that, if his concept largely matches that of the original maker, we may count him (if successful) as independently (and coincidentally) producing things of the same artifactual kind K. Thus members of separate cultures, for example, may all have independently made artifacts under similar concepts (elongated object with a handle and blade, sharp on one edge, to be used for cutting food), and so all be aptly treated as creating knives. They will each share the same forms of privileged knowledge regarding their creations and the nature of the artifactual kind as the inventor described above, although of course none of the knife-makers may use the same word or know of the existence of other knife-making traditions.

If the later artisan does know of the existence of the extant K(s), then he may have the intention to create *one of these*, with an implicit reference back to the earlier K. Yet even so, as I have argued elsewhere (2003), his intention cannot be a mere *transparent* intention to create one of these (with *de re* reference back to the prior K) without any substantive concept of what 'these' are, of what features are relevant to being of artifactual kind K. In order for his making to be controlled and directed, his intention to make a K must be filled out with intentions regarding what features are to be imposed on the object of his creation in order to succeed at realizing his intention to make a K (cf. Hilpinen 1992, 64–5). Here (unlike the prototype-maker) he can get it wrong: if his concept of what features are relevant to creating a K is wildly different from or inconsistent with the inventor's concept, the later maker cannot without reservation be described as intending to make a K, or else we would have to allow that he may succeed at making a K just in virtue of imposing on the object all of the features he *thinks* are relevant. Bloom's own examples (1996, 19–20) nicely illustrate this point: if a madman happily presents a tiny pile of dirt as a chair, or a child happily presents a clay disk as a cup, we will with justice say that they have misunderstood what a chair or cup is, not that they have created a chair or cup just because their product satisfies their own idiosyncratic concept associated with the term.

So a later artisan succeeds at making a K only if he has a substantive, and substantively correct, concept of what a K is and succeeds at imposing on the object all or most of the features relevant to executing that concept. Having a substantively correct concept, in turn, must be a matter of substantially matching the prior concept of Ks, since inventors' concepts were originally definitive of what counts as relevant to kind membership.[8] As a result, if someone is a genuine K-maker, he is guaranteed to have a largely correct concept of what Ks are, and if there are Ks, someone is guaranteed to have a largely correct concept of the nature of Ks. This again differs from the case of natural kinds, since no one's concepts about the specific natures of natural kinds are immune from massive error, and members of the relevant kinds can exist without anyone having any concept whatsoever of their nature.

Hilary Kornblith argues against this that: 'The maker could not insist, "I know what these things are; after all, I made them", since the term is part of a public language which the maker cannot constrain through a sheer act of will; being the maker of an artifact does not provide one with a grant of immunity to error' (this volume, sec. 2). But having the right concept of the artifactual kind in question is one thing; having command of the customary term associated with that concept in a particular natural language is another. While the maker can legitimately insist that he knows what kind of artifact, if any, he has made, this does not mean that he has the right customary term attached to that concept.[9]

As the production of artifacts of kind K continues, things get trickier. Artifactual kinds are notoriously malleable and historical in nature—indeed the possibilities for this are built into our description above. For each subsequent maker needs only have a concept of which features are K-relevant that *largely* matches those of prior makers of Ks (if any there be). Thus, over time, the

---

[8] The requirements that a new maker's concept be only *substantively* correct and *mostly* well executed reflect the fact that some vagueness is essentially built into artifactual kind concepts.

[9] So what have the madman and the child of Bloom's examples made? Assuming that each is satisfied with his product (that it matches certain substantive intentions), it may be that each has made an artifact of a new kind, to which he attaches the wrong public word. It is easy to imagine that if, e.g., the madman made a series of piles of dirt, clearly intending them to belong to some artifactual kind regarding which he was imposing his own success criteria (occasionally sweeping one away in disgust at it's not having succeeded), we might count him as creating things of his own mysterious artifactual kind, and even perhaps even coin a (less misleading) term, like 'dustlets' to refer to members of his obscure kind. ('I see he's made four dustlets today', one employee of the psychiatric institution says to the other.)

concept of Ks, spelling out which features are K-relevant, may gradually change. Note that what is essential (or indeed relevant) to being a K is still determined *stipulatively* by the features makers consider relevant to being a K; it is not a matter of discovery of a mind-independent nature. It is just that the process of stipulation has become much more gradual and diffuse, as it is responsive to the intentions of a great number of makers over an extended period of time. Nonetheless, something is a K only if it largely matches a substantive concept of some group of makers (minimally, its own). And those who successfully make Ks are guaranteed to have a substantially correct concept of what it takes to be a K, at least of that time and tradition.

3. OUR EPISTEMIC RELATION TO ARTIFACTUAL KINDS

The crucial structural point from above is that there are essential connections between artifacts, the nature of artifactual kinds, and human concepts. At the first level, the conceptions of those who ground the reference of artifactual kind terms about what *sort* of features are relevant to distinguishing artifactual kinds are definitive of what sorts of features are relevant. The relevant sort of feature, I have argued, is that the things be the products of successfully executed substantive intentions to create something of the kind.

As a result of this appeal to intentions, it turns out that there is also a second level at which the natures of individual artifactual kinds (unlike those of individual natural kinds) are determined by human concepts: substantive features that determine the boundaries of an artifactual kind are determined (perhaps collectively and diffusely) by the concepts of *makers* regarding what features are relevant to membership in that kind. This fits well with the idea that the methodology of many social sciences, unlike natural sciences, must involve an empathetic understanding of the intentional states of others and their ways of understanding and carving up the world they live in (cf. Hilpinen 1992, 67). If those grounding the reference of the term 'glug' are good Martian *anthropologists*, it seems that what they should take as relevant is the criteria the relevant *earthlings* would have used to categorize things as being or not being in that kind. The categories that are of primary interest to the anthropologist, human geographer, historian, or archeologist are the categories that were used and understood and relevant to the lives of the people studied.

Thus the sense in which these artifacts and artifactual kinds are human creations does have important consequences for their metaphysics, and for our epistemic relation to them—consequences that mark them as importantly different from the objects and kinds of the natural sciences. In the former but not the latter case, the mere existence of objects of that kind entails that there is substantive knowledge of the kind's nature: their existence is not independent of human knowledge of them. And makers of artifacts are (as such) guaranteed certain forms of immunity from massive error about the objects of their creation, whereas scientists are not guaranteed a similar freedom from error about their objects of study.

There has been a great deal of discussion about whether or not there is any sort of epistemic privilege about the nature of artifactual kinds. Against the idea of a built-in epistemic privilege, Kornblith writes: 'To the extent that the makers are in an epistemically privileged position, the privilege is a product of their extensive interaction with the artifacts in question, not a product of any semantic competence' (this volume, sec. 2). But this overlooks the crucial difference I have been drawing out: any epistemic privilege of chemists over laypeople regarding chemical natures is indeed a product of their extensive interaction with the chemicals in question, and the epistemic superiority of botanists over ordinary folk regarding the features of trees is likewise a product of extensive interaction (of a certain kind—different from that of lumberjacks or syrup-makers) with trees. But the sort of epistemic privilege I have been arguing applies to makers is neither the product of their 'extensive interaction' with the artifacts in question, nor a product of semantic competence; it is a consequence of the fact that the concepts and intentions of makers are *constitutive* of the nature of the kind they create, whereas the concepts and intentions of scientists (or anyone else) are not constitutive of the natures of the kinds they study.

4. REFERENCE TO ARTIFACTUAL KINDS

There is a widely accepted view that natural kind terms and indeed most general terms may refer directly to genuine kinds in the world with natural boundaries, so that the term's extension is determined by the nature of the kind, independently of all human beliefs and concepts, thus enabling the term to refer even if everyone is in ignorance or error about the real nature of the kind in question.[10]

If I am correct, there are two ways in which this theory must be modified for the case of artifactual kind terms. At the first level I have argued that, owing to the qua problem, we should accept a hybrid theory of reference acknowledging that would-be grounders of the reference of a general term must have some high-level concept of what category of kind they intend to refer to, thereby establishing the general *sorts* of features relevant to unifying members of that kind. This gives those who ground (and re-ground) the reference of the term some privileged knowledge about what sort of kind (if any) their terms refer to, and what sorts of features unify its members. This much, of course, applies equally to any general term (not just artifactual kind terms).

---

[10] I am not concerned to argue that all of this is part of the essential core of direct reference views (if it is not, so much the better for those views), but merely to point out some interesting differences between the reference of natural kind terms and artifactual kind terms.

Accepting a hybrid view of reference may still leave much of the spirit of the above view intact, for it does not impugn the idea that general terms may pick out their referents independently of any human concepts about the particular nature (though not the category) of the kind involved; regarding that nature, everyone may remain ignorant or in error. Thus, for example Kornblith argues (1980 and this volume) that artifactual kind terms may be introduced, for instance by anthropologists to name a kind of artifact found in a remote culture, in which case the term refers to artifacts of that kind (whatever it is), allowing for everyone *in the anthropologist's language community* to be ignorant or in error about the nature of the artifactual kind in question.

While that much is surely true, it is nonetheless not true that artifactual kind terms could refer to kinds independently of *all* human beliefs and concepts about the nature of the kind. An anthropologist's term for an artifactual kind she discovers in a remote culture has a reference only if there is such a kind to refer to. And there is such an artifactual kind to refer to (and there are artifacts of that kind) only if there are people who intentionally created those artifacts, with some substantive concept in mind of what were to be the relevant features for being of that kind. It is those concepts that not only were behind the creation of members of the kind, but that determine what sorts of features are relevant to being of the kind, and thus determine which things are or are not members of the kind. So, at some level, human concepts (not necessarily those of the language group which coins the term) about the nature of the kind play a crucial role in the reference of artifactual kind terms, whereas this is never the case (on direct reference theories) for natural kind terms.

It should be clear, however, that this is not a matter of accepting a descriptive view of reference for artifactual kind terms—unlike descriptive reference theorists, I have not argued that every competent speaker, just in virtue of being a competent speaker, has knowledge of the essential features of artifactual kinds, nor that the reference of all artifactual kind terms is determined by the sense of the description competent speakers associate with the term. Nor is the resulting immunity from wholesale error a matter of anyone's descriptions being assured of matching the independent natures in the world picked out by them. Instead, it is a result of the fact that, for artifactual kinds, the concepts of those who *create and sustain* the kinds (not of speakers) are *constitutive* of the natures of the kinds available for reference.

5. OBJECTIONS AND REPLIES

I have been arguing that there are close conceptual connections between the idea of a maker, an artifact, and the nature of an artifactual kind, and that in virtue of these connections makers are guaranteed certain forms of epistemic privilege about the natures of the artifactual kinds they create. There has been, however, a great deal of resistance to the idea that anyone has any such privilege, and many cases have been raised in which makers appear to be ignorant about the natures of the artifacts they produce.

One line of objection holds that makers may be completely ignorant of the natures of the artifacts they create, for modern makers may be merely indifferent production-line workers, not artisans creating products of their own design. Thus, for example, Kornblith (this volume) introduces Harry, who works in a factory manufacturing carabiners, with no concept of what these artifacts are, and no intentions beyond earning himself a living (cf. Elder, this volume, sec. 2). Of course such kinds of ignorance (or error) are possible; those working on the production lines may not (individually) have any overall concept of what sort of artifact is supposed to be produced. But properly understood, that observation does not undermine the conceptual connections between makers and artifacts I have elucidated above.

For (as might be expected given the intentionalist approach I defend) the 'makers' in the sense I have been describing them above need not be identified with whoever (or whatever) is *causally* relevant to the physical existence of the object in question. Instead, they are those whose intentions to produce something with certain features enable the production of an *artifact*. For, as I argued above, for something to be an artifact at all (rather than a mere human by-product) and *ipso facto* to be of any essentially artifactual kind, it must be the product of a controlled intention to produce something of that kind—the intention may be that of a designer (or team of designers) who controls execution of the intention by way of the movements of hundreds of other people, or by way of specially designed machinery, rather than by way of the movements of her own limbs and hand-tools. But in any case, whoever it is whose intentions guide the creation of the product is the 'maker' in the sense in which I have been using the term (noting that this may be a collective), and wherever there is a genuine artifact, there must have been a maker in this sense. Makers in this sense retain the sorts of epistemic privilege I am describing, even if others who play a causal role in production may not.

In fact, it is worth noting that, since it is the controlled and detailed intentions that are crucial to 'making' in this sense, the activities of 'making' may also be quite minimal, and involve expropriation of natural objects (for instance, to be paperweights, doorstops, etc.) with little or no physical change imposed on the world. As has often been noted (e.g. Hilpinen 1992), there is a close relation between the concept of artifacts and that of actions, and so just as (on Goldman's view: 1970, 18) refraining from physical motion (e.g. intentionally *not* raising one's hand during a vote) may still count as an action, so may intentionally *not* changing anything about this rock while appropriating it as a doorstop count as a minimal kind of artifact creation, as may appropriating and intentionally *not* changing anything about this piece of plumbing count as creating a work of art (cf. my 2005).[11]

A related line of objection holds that such a close epistemic relation cannot obtain between all artifacts and their makers, since there may be animal artifacts such as beaver dams and anthills, yet we surely cannot ascribe such structured intentions and knowledge of the natures of their kinds to beavers or ants. But again, the sorts of conceptual link I have been describing apply only where we are speaking of artifacts proper—that is, as the *intended* products of human (or other intelligent) activity. I have given reason above for thinking that intentions are at the core of our normal artifact concepts, beginning with the fact that this is essential to distinguish our artifactual kinds (tables, pencils, neckties) from types of unintended by-product of human activity (pollution, scrap metal, footprints). Of course, the term 'artifact' also has a variety of other uses (including uses to describe *unintended* by-products of our conceptual scheme, methodology, or tools) that I make no claim to explicate. As a result, while we might speak of beaver dams or anthills as 'artifacts' in some sense (based on analogy with human dams and homes), they are only artifacts in the core sense I am discussing, and the results about epistemic privilege only apply, if these objects have 'makers' with the kinds of substantive structured intentions I have been describing, in which case the relevant conceptual connections do hold up. Whether or not ants or beavers could be thought to have such intentions (and thus whether they are makers of artifacts in the core sense of each term I am seeking to explicate) I will leave for animal (or insect) psychologists to determine.

Another common line of objection to the idea of epistemic privilege arises from the fact that it is always open to doubt whether any particular individual

---

[11] Jerrold Levinson (this volume) raises the interesting question of whether or not the analysis I provide of artifact concepts also applies to the concept 'artwork': do makers of art need to have a substantive intention of what sort of thing a work of art is (understanding what sorts of properties are relevant to that) and intend to realize many of these features in the object created? The worry about this is that requiring any kind of substantive intention would be too restrictive to account for the varieties of contemporary art and art-making, including Conceptual Art, Found Art, and the like. I am not committed to the idea that the very general term 'artwork' (as opposed to 'sculpture', 'collage', or 'painting') is an artifactual kind term in precisely the sense I seek to explicate above, and the issue deserves more detailed discussion. Nonetheless, I think worries that treating 'artwork' as an artifactual kind term on the above model would be too restrictive to account for much contemporary art can be mitigated in three ways. One is by noting that, on the account I give, the substantive features relevant to being a member of the kind may change over time; e.g. representation may once have been central among the art-relevant features, but plausibly no longer is; a Conceptual artist may adopt certain relevant sorts of features from prior Conceptual Art, rather than considering those appropriate to, e.g., Renaissance painting. The second mitigating factor is that intentions and beliefs about what features are relevant to being of a certain artifactual kind (including work of art) *may* include relational features about the role these objects are to play in human life, vis-á-vis other sorts of artifact and human practice, etc., so that in this sense intending them for certain kinds of treatment or regard may count as one relevant feature. The third mitigating factor is that mentioned above: that intentions, like actions, may be negative, so that (in the case of Found Art), intending *not* to alter various found features may count as part of a structured creative intention (different in degree only from a sculptor intentionally not altering the texture of her stone).

really *is* a maker, or any particular object really *is* an artifact or really does belong to any particular artifactual kind. But these observations do not undermine the idea that there are conceptual connections between genuine makers, artifacts, and artifactual kinds. Kornblith (this volume) writes:

While it is true that the boundaries of natural kinds are determined, in the typical case, by features of the world wholly independent of any individual, and yet the boundaries of artifactual kinds are determined by intentions, which are properties of individuals, the way in which intentions determine artifactual kind boundaries does not provide any individual with privileged access to the essential features of artifactual kinds. (sec. 2)

The truth of this, I would say, is that no individual, qua individual biological person, is guaranteed privileged access to the essential features of artifactual kinds. But this does not count against the point that I am drawing out: that it is necessary that, *if* some individual *is* the maker of a certain kind of artifact, she is (qua maker) guaranteed to have a largely correct conception of the essential features of the artifacts of the kind she is creating (at least of that time and tradition). So similarly, no one (qua biological individual) is guaranteed the right to operate a motor vehicle, but this doesn't count against the claim that all licensed drivers (qua licensed drivers) are guaranteed the right to operate a motor vehicle.

Many of the most prominent objections to the idea that there is any sort of epistemic privilege regarding the natures of artifactual kinds trade on this ambiguity. James Nelson (1982, 362), for example, claimed that we could be wrong about the nature of artifacts like pencils, since pencils could turn out to be alien listening devices. But this does not tell against the view that someone (namely makers) has privileged knowledge regarding the nature of artifactual kinds; it only shows that we can be wrong about who the makers are. Putnam's idea that we could be all wrong about the nature of pencils, since they could turn out to be organisms (1975, 242–3), similarly does not tell against the view that, where there are members of an artifactual kind, there must be some knowledge (among makers) of the nature of the artifactual kind. It only shows that we can be wrong about which objects are artifacts.

So in sum, none of these apparent cases of ignorance undermines the idea that, given the way our core artifactual concepts work, there is a constitutive link between the intentions of makers and the natures of artifactual kinds, in virtue of which genuine makers have certain forms of epistemic privilege about the natures of the artifacts they produce. Nonetheless, while I think it is important to notice the differences between artifactual and natural kinds, it is also important not to exaggerate the sorts of epistemic privilege that result from their metaphysical differences. Those who are guaranteed some knowledge of the nature of the kind are makers, but this is only first-order knowledge by actual makers (considered as such). As the above examples suggest, no one has any higher-order privileged knowledge that he or she really *is* a maker, and thus there is no privileged knowledge that one has such knowledge. The knowledge of any individual maker is also limited to a protection from massive error about what it takes for there to be artifacts of that sort for that time and tradition, but things may gradually change in significant ways.

Finally, the makers' concepts of what features are relevant to membership in that artifactual kind must be considered *intensionally*, and are typically superficial, leaving room for ignorance and error in any beliefs they may have about what, for example, physical conditions are nomologically necessary (or sufficient) for artifacts to possess the surface-level characteristics that are accepted as criterial for membership in the kind. Thus, for example, makers may accept it as a necessary feature of a knife that it be solid enough to cut through many foods, and it may be nomologically necessary that an object have rigid bonds between its constituent atoms to be so solid, without knife-makers having any knowledge of this fact. Makers may also remain ignorant of a great many other facts about artifacts of the kind they create, including causal factors to do with their economic or political role in the relevant society, unintended functions they turn out to serve, and so on. There thus remains much open for discovery by the social sciences even about artifacts of one's own time and tradition—these things and kinds certainly are not completely transparent to anyone.

6. REALISM ABOUT HUMAN CREATIONS

I have argued that artifactual objects and kinds differ metaphysically from natural objects and kinds, and that these particular metaphysical differences also entail that humans are involved in a much closer epistemic relation to these objects and kinds than to natural kinds. I think that these implications have been little noticed, first since the focus in analytic philosophy has lain so heavily on understanding the objects and kinds of the natural sciences, and secondly because (given the way in which that has set the agenda for much of metaphysics, epistemology, and reference) even those who have had interests in the cultural world have had reason to downplay any apparent differences between natural and artifactual kinds if they would have the latter taken seriously, or even accepted ontologically at all.

Indeed, those who seek to defend the existence of artifacts and artifactual kinds sometimes valiantly attempt to do so precisely by accepting criteria for 'real' existence suitable for members of natural kinds, and trying to show that at least certain artifactual kinds meet those criteria and so should be part of our ontological inventory. Thus Crawford Elder defends realism about (at least some) artifacts and artifactual kinds by arguing that at least some artifactual kinds have mind-independent natures just as natural kinds do (this volume), and that at least some culturally generated kinds are like natural kinds in that no one has epistemic privilege regarding the nature of kinds just in virtue of who they are, and what the beliefs are about (1989).

It is easy to see why one might think this is the route one must take. According to some formulations of realism, any metaphysical dependence on human intentionality vitiates a purported entity's claim to reality. Thus George Lakoff takes it to be a central feature of objectivism that: 'No true fact can depend upon people's believing it, on their knowledge of it, on their conceptualization of it, or on any other aspect of cognition. Existence cannot depend in any way in on human cognition' (1987, 164). According to other, related formulations of realism, certain forms of epistemic privilege with regard to a certain (purported) fact or kind may preclude it from being admitted to a realist's ontology. Elder defends such a view when he writes, 'I shall myself construe realism as a denial of epistemic privilege', namely that: '... for any component of the world and any set of beliefs about that component, the mere facts that those beliefs are (i) about that component and (ii) are held by the particular believers, by whom they are held, never by themselves entail that that set of beliefs is free from massive error' (1989, 440–1).

If my arguments above are on track, it is fairly clear that artifacts (and also institutional objects) would fail such a test. For the fact that a particular entity is of a given artifactual kind *does* depend on human cognition in ways we have described. Conversely, beliefs by makers about what sorts of features are relevant to being of a particular artifactual kind must be largely correct about the features relevant to being artifacts of that type (at least in that time and tradition), and so these, too, are assured of being free from massive error, just in virtue of the fact that the beliefs are by makers about their creations. In both cases the relevant beliefs are *constitutive* of the nature of the kind created, and so protected from sorts of error that inevitably threaten beliefs about the mind-independent kinds of nature.

At other times it is assumed that realism about a particular object requires that we have a non-conventional way of tracking its creation and destruction, while realism about a kind requires not just that its nature be opaque to us, but that it involve a mind-independent cluster of essential properties over which one may perform inductions. Thus, for example, Elder (this volume) defends a realism about artifacts and artifactual kinds by arguing that at least some artifactual kinds (those which are 'copied kinds') have a common history of function that leads to a mind-independent cluster of properties surrounding its shape, proper function, and historically proper placement, thus also providing a non-conventional criterion for when an individual artifact has been destroyed. While I applaud the effort to defend a broader ontology including artifacts and artifactual kinds, I think that showing that artifacts and other cultural objects are like natural objects and kinds in ways like these is not necessary to accept that there truly *are* such things, and that they form a genuine part of our world.

Claims that there will be reliably clustering properties for such 'copied kinds' of artifacts, over which we may be able to perform inductions, are surely empirical, and so their fate cannot be settled here. The recent essays on the history of certain artifacts in *The Evolution of Useful Things* (Petroski 1992), however, provides recurrent evidence against the idea that a common function is sufficient to yield a predictable cluster of properties definitive of an artifact type, even for such standard artifacts as paperclips and forks (and other eating utensils). Instead, Petroski details the multitude of contingent historical, aesthetic, and sociological factors that influence the design of our familiar artifacts, noting that: 'Different innovators in different places, starting with rudimentary solutions to the same basic problem, focused on different faults at different times, and so we have inherited culture-specific artifacts that are daily reminders that even so primitive a function as eating imposes no single form on the implements used to effect it' (p. 20). Even Elder notes that such clusters of properties are unlikely to be found for a great number of standard artifactual kinds such as neckties and nose rings, leading to some rather odd results, for instance, that there are bolts of cloth but not neckties. As a result, even if this approach were to ontologically save those kinds that are 'copied kinds', it would not save our ontology of familiar artifacts.

Even where it happens to be true that there are such predictable clusters of properties for an artifact kind, if my earlier arguments are correct, then it is only *accidentally* true. For as we have seen, the defining properties of artifactual kinds are determined by the features makers accept as relevant to something's being of that kind—not necessarily by shape, proper function, historically proper placement, or any other properties that happen to cluster around these. It seems that Elder is providing us with the basis for *replacement* concepts of artifact kinds (which more closely fit the criteria associated with natural kinds) rather than with a justification of claims for the existence of our actual artifactual kinds.

But could we not be mistaken in thinking that makers' concepts are relevant to membership conditions for the kinds of artifacts they create, while our artifactual kind terms *really* pick out whatever shares the properties that more 'naturally' cluster around function, shape, and historically proper placement? Not if the arguments of section 1 were successful, for those showed that, to avoid the *qua* problem, we must accept that speakers' intentions at least regarding the most general *sorts* of features that are relevant for belonging to an artifactual kind (as opposed to a natural kind) are definitive of what sorts of features *are* relevant—about that, at least, we could not be wrong. While Martian anthropologists may be wrong about what the essential features of glugs are (and may discover themselves to have made errors about this, when they discover Earth documents) they cannot be wrong that (assuming the members of their sample do belong to a common Earth artifactual kind) whatever features earthling makers of glugs would take to be relevant to membership in that kind *are* definitive of what features are relevant to kind membership. If our basic idea of what it is for something to be an artifactual kind is not open to revision in this sort of way, then however successful Elder's arguments may be in demonstrating, for example, that there are copied kinds which have properties that cluster in a mind-independent way, this is neither necessary nor sufficient to establish that there are things corresponding to our normal artifactual kind concepts.

But if artifactual kinds as we normally think of them can't be shown to have natures built of properties that mind-independently cluster together in a way that is relevant to inductions, is it so much the worse for artifactual kinds? I suspect that the thought that it *would* be comes from borrowing an idea suitable for realism about natural objects and kinds and assuming it must apply wholesale. But this, I think, misconstrues what it is to be a realist about *cultural* objects and kinds. For if the real ontological question is whether or not we should accept that there are artifacts and artifactual kinds, then the above analyses, if apt, have shown that it is just part of the very *idea* of artifacts and artifactual kinds (suitably explicated) that they lack mind-independence in certain ways. If so, then accepting such criteria for realism does not provide an *argument* against accepting the real existence of artifacts and artifactual kinds, it merely begs the question against them.

Is it at all possible, then, to propose a *non*-question-begging strategy for determining what entities should be accepted into one's ontology? I think it is: for any purported kind of entity, first, determine what it would take for there to be such an entity, then attempt to establish whether those criteria are fulfilled.[12] Then, if natural kinds are *supposed to be* kinds of entities possessing a mind-independent nature involving clusters of properties over which inductions non-accidentally turn out to be true, then anything purporting to be a natural kind had better fulfill those conditions. But our artifact concepts were never designed to pick out mind-independent kinds over which such inductions could be successfully performed, and so the fact that we may have certain forms of epistemic privilege with regard to artifactual kinds (if there are any), and that their natures are at some level constituted by human intentions gives us no reason to conclude that *these* things do not exist.

According to the criteria built into the idea of something being an *artifactual* kind term, what must be the case for there to be artifacts and artifactual kinds? There must, as we have seen earlier, be people with certain intentions to create objects of a given kind, where these intentions are substantive and involve certain success criteria that control their activity, and they must be largely successful in executing their intentions. Do we have reason to think this is ever done? Barring radical conspiracy theories, of course we do.

Such a procedure does not amount to an 'anything goes' ontology, admitting phlogiston and ghosts along with chairs and knives. For, according to the original scientific concept of phlogiston, for there to be phlogiston there would have to be some kind of substance essentially given off during combustion, and we have strong experimental evidence that there is no such substance. According to folk belief, for there to be ghosts, there would have to be dead people who come back in a form that is publicly visible and spatio-temporal, but not material, and who causally interact with the world (affecting the eyes of certain viewers, moving

---

[12] For further discussion and defense of this strategy, see my *Ordinary Objects* (2007).

objects, etc.). And we have pretty good evidence that there are no such things. But what would it take for there to be chairs? That there be objects fashioned by people intending them to be chairs, where they have a substantive concept of what features are relevant to being a chair (e.g. being a solid device for seating one person, with a seat and a back) and are reasonably successful in executing that intention. We have pretty good reason to believe that *those* conditions are sometimes fulfilled. So such a procedure does seem to make appropriate distinctions between what there is and what there isn't, without collapsing criteria for there being things of *diverse* kinds into criteria suitable only for one kind.

7. CONCLUSION

We began by asking in what sense artifacts and artifactual kinds are human creations, and what difference, if any, this makes to their place in our philosophical theories. If it were just that artifacts are brought into existence through human activities, this might aptly be thought to have little impact. But I have argued that not only are artifacts causally produced by humans, but also that, in virtue of the different ways in which our artifactual terms and concepts function (ways that are established definitively by speakers' and thinkers' intentions), the specific natures of artifactual kinds are determined (often gradually and collectively) by makers' concepts about what features are relevant to kind membership. As a result it is not just artifacts, but the natures of artifactual kinds themselves, that are, in some sense, human creations. This metaphysical point in turn has consequences for epistemology and reference—putting at least some humans in a much closer epistemic relation to the artifactual kinds they create and sustain than anyone can be in to the natural kinds they may study, and entailing that the reference of artifactual kind terms must, at some level, be determined by way of human concepts.

These differences, in turn, may make a great deal of difference elsewhere. They help explain why different methods seem to be required for pursuing social sciences such as anthropology and archeology, versus natural sciences such as chemistry and biology, for in the former, though not the latter, case human concepts will play a crucial role in determining the boundaries of many of the concepts central to the scientist's theories. They also make a difference to how we conceive of realism, suggesting that we should not assume that criteria suitable for determining whether or not there is a particular natural kind are suitable across the board, so we are not left in the position of either forcing artifactual kinds into the mold of natural kinds or denying their existence. Although they may be, in various senses, human creations, artifacts are as 'real' a part of our world as most of us ever expected them to be.[13]

[13] I am grateful to Crawford Elder, Hilary Kornblith, and the editors for helpful comments on an earlier version of this chapter.

5

Artworks as Artifacts

Jerrold Levinson

1. THE INTENTIONAL-HISTORICAL CONCEPTION OF ART

What kind of artifact is an artwork? The answer to that question depends, clearly enough, on the conception of art that one is inclined to adopt. Past conceptions of art, according to which art was essentially a mode of representation, or a vehicle of emotional expression, or a display of skill in fashioning, or an exploration of form as such, or the pursuit of the beautiful, no longer seem remotely adequate to the nature and range of what have been accounted artworks in the past hundred years or so. The abstract canvases of Kupka and Kandinsky are almost a century old; John Cage's aleatoric music of the 1960s seems devoid of emotional expression; Robert Rauschenberg's *Erased De Kooning Drawing* displayed no notable skill; Tolstoy's *The Death of Ivan Ilych* does not strike one for its exploration of form; and Francis Bacon's tortured portraits are anything but beautiful. Accommodating art's development since the nineteenth century seems to call for a more circumspect approach, one that is noncommittal as regards medium, style, form, content, and artistic objectives.

I have defended a conception of art of this sort, one along intentional-historical lines, according to which something is art in virtue of being governed by certain intentions with an essential historical, or backward-looking, content. More specifically, what I claim is that an artwork, in the current understanding of the term, is something that has been intended by someone for regard or treatment in some overall way that some earlier or pre-existing artwork or artworks are or were correctly regarded or treated (Levinson 1979, 1983). The art-making intention involved may be either of an opaque sort, having roughly the content just expressed, one that simply references prior art as such, or of a transparent sort, invoking specific ways of regarding or treating objects that, as a matter of fact, and whether known to the agent or not, figure in the set of correct ways of regard or treatment for earlier or pre-existing artworks. In either mode of art-making, the concrete history of art-making up to a given time is thus ineliminably implicated, in whole or in part, in any art-making undertaken at that time.

This conception of arthood has obvious points in common with the art-theoretical and social-institutional conceptions of arthood elaborated earlier by the philosophers Arthur Danto and George Dickie. Like those conceptions, it looks for a relational, situational, or contextual defining feature of art, rather than a formal, intrinsic, or perceivable one. All three conceptions have their roots in the enforced revision of traditional ideas about art that was effected by certain revolutionary ventures in art-making in the early and middle twentieth century, notably those of the Dadaists, Marcel Duchamp, Andy Warhol, Jasper Johns, Robert Rauschenberg, and others. By appropriating, reframing, reconfiguring, and reprojecting as art any number of things theretofore assumed to lie outside of the ambit of art, artists such as the preceding managed to establish—since their ventures must be regarded, at least from our present vantage-point, as undeniably successful—that more or less any object could be made into or could become a work of art, if suitably repositioned, reconceived, or, in Danto's famous term, 'transfigured'. Among the objects that were thus transfigured into art in those years, with little or no physical alteration or manipulation, were the following: a urinal, a snow-shovel, a bottle-rack, a beer can, a coffee cup, a disordered bed, and a postcard reproduction of the *Mona Lisa*. It no longer seemed necessary, then, that an artwork be fashioned by its maker with technical skill, that it make use of traditional materials in its construction, that it display form of any notable complexity, that it have any obvious aesthetic appeal, or that it inevitably reflect in its handling the individual personality of the artist. It is difficult to deny that the concept of art that emerged in the wake of those developments, now almost a century old, was an altered and notably broadened one, covering all that had previously been recognized as art, to be sure, but much that would not have been recognized as art under the traditional concept that had held sway, with only minor modifications, since at least the Renaissance.

The intentional-historical conception of art differs from the art-theoretical and social-institutional ones, though, in positing as the crucial contextual condition of arthood not a relation to some prevailing artistic theory, nor a relation to a surrounding social institution, but a relation to the concrete history of art-making and art-projection into which the candidate object hopes to enter. The intentional-historical conception differs also from its contextualist predecessors in taking its most direct inspiration not so much from the readymade and appropriational modes of art-making that had been established by Duchamp and others, but from the subsequent, more radical activities of Conceptual artists—such as Robert Barry, Robert Morris, John Baldessari, Joseph Kosuth, Sol LeWitt, Vito Acconci—which seemed to establish that art per se had no need even of any concrete object, whether appropriated, readymade, or fashioned from scratch, but could apparently consist merely in concepts, words, statements, gestures, thoughts, and the like, with the apparent consequence that anything, or at least anything thinkable, demonstrable, or designatable, of whatever metaphysical or logical sort, could be, or at least could become, a work of art.[1]

Not surprisingly, the intentional-historical conception of art has elicited a certain number of critiques, turning on such issues as the apparent circularity of such a conception, the status of 'first' (or earliest) art on such a conception, the extendability of the conception to cultures or histories other than our own, and the problematic recursiveness of the procedure for identifying objects as art that the conception appears to entail. I have addressed those critiques elsewhere, if perhaps not to the satisfaction of all, so will not address them again here (Levinson 1988, 2002). I will instead simply assume that the intentional-historical conception is more or less adequate to what it now is to be an artwork, in the most comprehensive sense, in order to ask what that implies for the status of artworks as artifacts, and for the extent to which the artifactuality of artworks differs, if at all, from the artifactuality of artifacts in general.

2. ARTWORKS VERSUS OTHER ARTIFACTS

The cognitive psychologist Paul Bloom has recently extended the intentional-historical theory of artworks so as to cover artifacts of all kinds (Bloom 1996). Bloom proposes that for any artifact kind X, to be an X is to be an object successfully created with the intent that it be an X, where what it is to be an X at a given time is informed inescapably by past instances of X. Bloom's insight is thus that all artifact concepts, and not just that of artwork, have an essential historical component, so that the past deployment of such concepts ineluctably enters into their present and future deployment, through the backward-directed intentions that the makers of such artifacts must of necessity possess. Bloom's explicit statement of his proposal is as follows: 'We construe the extension of an artifact kind X to be those entities that have been successfully created with the intention that they belong to the same kind as current and previous Xs' (1996, 10). Bloom is persuasive in pointing up the superiority of his proposal to existing competitors, those which analyse artifact concepts in terms of necessary-and-sufficient conditions, family resemblances, characteristic functions, or prototypes.

---

[1] The ontology of Conceptual Art, though, is not as simple as it seems. Arguably there is always something concrete involved in the making of a work of Conceptual Art, and in which its identity as that artwork, of that artist, created at that time, is anchored. This applies even to one of the most emblematic of Conceptual Art works, Robert Barry's *All the things I know but of which I am not at the moment thinking: 1:36 p.m., 15 June 1969, New York*. For this work was created by a particular individual at a particular time and place, and was presumably embodied in some particular physical inscription.

But it remains to be seen whether Bloom's own, original and sweeping, proposal is entirely acceptable.

Suppose for the moment that Bloom is right, and that an analysis of the sort that captures what it is to be an artwork also captures what it is to be an artifact of any sort. What, if anything, would remain of the *special* historicality of the concept of artwork, as opposed to those of chair, pencil, house, or other standard artifacts? Two things, it seems.

First, on Bloom's analysis something is an X in virtue of being intentionally related in the right way to preceding X's *generally*. But on the intentional-historical analysis of arthood, something can be an artwork through being intentionally connected in the right manner to a *particular* past artwork or artworks, whether or not intentionally connected to past art invoked generally. For example, someone could make an artwork of a sculptural sort by assembling pieces of wood and plastic with the intention of the assemblage being regarded in an overall manner appropriate to Henry Moore's *Reclining Nude*, but without any intent explicitly invoking the category of art or even the subcategory of sculpture. The history of art, it appears, enters more concretely into what can be art at a given point in time than the history of a given artifact kind enters into what can be an instance of that kind at that time. So to establish that something was an artwork might require tracing intentional relations to a particular item or episode in the history of art, but nothing comparable would seem to be required to establish that a candidate chair, pencil, or house was an instance of those respective kinds.

Second, it is arguable that standard artifact concepts, in contrast to that of artwork, retain at least *some* necessary conditions as regards form or function, whatever the historical dimension of their correct deployment. For instance, a chair must exhibit shape within a given broadly circumscribed range, with certain shapes, such as that of a javelin, being excluded in advance. And a chair must answer to a certain purpose—in the case of chairs, that of being sat upon with some degree of comfort—or at the very least, be aimed at answering to such purpose.

But I maintain that that is not the case with artworks as such, which in contrast to perhaps *every* other sort of artifact, retain only certain purely intentional-historical necessary conditions. In other words, nothing can be declared a failed artwork, in the sense of not succeeding in being an artwork at all, through failing to display a certain broadly specified form or a particular sort of functionality. But something *can* be declared a failed chair, in the sense of not even being a chair, if shaped like a javelin or if incapable of being sat upon at all. Thus even were an intentional-historical account of artifacts in general to be accepted, *artwork* would remain distinctively historical, in contrast with other artifact concepts, in respect of the creation involved requiring *only* the satisfaction of certain intentional-historical conditions.

It is difficult to say whether these differences between artworks and other artifacts, which amount to the latter being less purely intentionally-historically determined, would be contested by Bloom. And that is because of the specific way he formulates his intentional-historical theory of artifacts, in which crucial appeal is made to the action of *successfully creating* an X. What is it, though, to *successfully create* an X? Does *successfully creating* an X differ from simply *creating* an X? If so, it should be possible to create an X, but *unsuccessfully*, which is not, I think, what Bloom is after. So successfully creating an X, it would appear, is just creating an X. What the adverb serves to call attention to, however, is a minimal success condition that Bloom apparently regards as constraining intentional-historical artifact-making in general. This is evident in his illustration of how chair-making, for example, might fail, even though the intentional-historical condition of such making was in place: 'If someone intends to create a chair, but it falls to pieces as soon as it is finished, the person would not view this creation as successfully fulfilling his or her intent, and thus has not created a chair' (1996, 10).

Thus for Bloom, something intended to be a chair but that was merely a heap of materials incapable of being sat upon would not be a chair regardless of how firm the intention involved that it belong to the category of chairs. That seems right, but Bloom's justification of this judgment is rather peculiar. He implies that such an object would fail to be a chair *not* because it could not fulfill the basic function of affording single seating, but rather because its creator would not *recognize* it as the successful product of an intention to create a chair, that is, something effectively affording single seating. This is peculiar, because it seems that whether or not something counts as a chair, though it may depend crucially on the intentions of its maker, should not ultimately depend on whether from the point of view of its *maker* those intentions are fulfilled, but rather on whether, from some *objective* point of view, those intentions really *are* fulfilled. For after all, a would-be chair-maker may be deluded or confused, thinking that a pile of nails or a coiled length of rope for which he is responsible conforms well enough to past chairs to count as a successfully created new one.

It seems that what is relevant to satisfaction of the minimal success condition is not the maker's conception of a chair based on past acquaintance with them, but rather the conception of a chair endorsed by competent users of the term 'chair' in general, one that imports at least some minimal features of form or function. Given satisfaction of that condition, the identity of a candidate thing as a chair may indeed be entirely determined, as Bloom's account would have it, by an appropriate chair-history-invoking intention in its making. But the insistence on a minimal success condition, which rules out piles of nails, lengths of rope, decks of cards, javelin-shaped rods, and so on as chairs, shows that some non-purely-historical conception of chairhood is in play in circumscribing the boundaries of the category. As regards artworks, however, it is far from clear that any such non-purely-historical conception of arthood is in play, or that there is any minimal success condition of a substantive sort on the making involved.

Why is that so? It helps to recall what, in the post-Duchampian era, are two salient features of art-making in contrast to standard artifact-making. First, one can more or less simply *declare* something a work of art, and it becomes such. Or at least one can, in certain contexts, or with a certain standing, do so. Second, *anything*, whatever its material constitution, cultural category, or ontological status, can become, or can be incorporated into, a work of art. These features are arguably enough in themselves to distinguish the concept of artwork from that of other artifacts, even if such artifacts, if Bloom is right, share with artworks the primary determining of their categorial status by a historical, or past-invoking, intention in their making. What is special about the artifact concept *artwork*, one might say, is that it is a *wholly* relational one; it is more like those of *observed thing* or *beloved object* or *prize-winner* than it is like those of standard artifacts, such as *chair* or *cup* or *cabin*, for which there are at least minimal conditions of form as regards finished shape, of constitution as regards material, of making as regards the activity of the maker, or of functional success as regards usability of the final product.

3. ART-MAKING AND SUBSTANTIVE CONCEPTIONS

If the above is correct, then however sound the inspiration of Bloom's intentional-historical theory of artifacts, he errs in blurring the difference between artworks and other artifacts, failing to appreciate that though minimal success conditions, rooted in some not-purely-relational conception of the kind of artifact in question, are ineliminably involved in the making of the latter, that is not the case with the former.

Amie Thomasson, in a careful essay (Thomasson, this volume) highlighting the insufficiently acknowledged role that background conceptions of artifacts play in their creation, holds Bloom's analysis at fault precisely for not sufficiently acknowledging that role, and for thinking that artifact creation can proceed in a more conceptually thin or purely historical way than it in fact can. According to Thomasson, even the intention to create something of a given artifact kind K cannot consist merely in intending the object to belong to the same kind as existing examples of K to which one can point or refer. Thomasson instead maintains, as a completely general principle, that a *substantive* conception of an artifact kind K must be involved in the intentional production of an artifact of that kind: 'the relevant sort of intention to make a thing of artifactual kind K must thus involve a substantive (and substantially correct) concept of what a K is, including an understanding of what sorts of properties are K-relevant and an intention to realize many of them in the object created' (this volume, p. 59).[2]

---

[2] She adds that for an artifact of that kind to be created, the intention in question must be 'largely successfully realized'. This is the minimal success condition implicit also in Bloom's account of artifactuality.

Assuming that Thomasson's principle is true for the making of garden-variety artifacts, is it also true for the making of artworks, that most elusive species of artifact? Can one create an artwork without a 'substantive conception' of what artworks are? More specifically, does art-making on an intentional-historical account of it require that an art-maker have a 'substantive conception' of what he or she is making?

The answer depends, in part, on how 'substantive' is 'substantive'. Can one make an artwork merely by intending something for the sort of regard or treatment appropriate to artworks, but without knowing what artworks are, in any qualitative sense, but only that there are such things, and that they are some sort of artifact, and without knowing what sorts of regards or treatments are appropriate to them, but only that there are such?

I claim one can, and if so, one needn't have a substantive concept of what an artwork is, one implicating characteristic properties or functions. Does one need to possess in any measure a theory of art, *à la* Danto, in order to make art, or need one only know that there are such things as artworks and that there are ways it is correct to approach them? I claim not, and if so, once again an art-maker need not possess a substantive concept of what an artwork is—though of course virtually all art-makers *will* possess such, which concept will vary from artist to artist, and from art-form to art-form.

Elsewhere in her discussion Thomasson offers an argument that could be seen as directly aimed at undermining the possibility just affirmed, one that according to the intentional-historical theory is sometimes realized in the making of art, that an artifact of kind K might be made merely by intending an object to stand in certain relations to existing instances of K:

If the later artisan does know of the existence of extant K(s), then he may have the intention to create *one of these*, with an implicit reference back to the earlier K. Yet even so ... his intention cannot be a mere *transparent* intention to create one of these ... without any substantive concept of what 'these' are, of what features are relevant to being of artifactual kind K. In order for his making to be controlled and directed, his intention to make a K must be filled out with intentions regarding what features are to be imposed on the object of his creation in order to succeed at realizing his intention to make a K. (This volume, p. 61)

But I think it clear that the stricture Thomasson here invokes, of a making filled out with feature-conscious or feature-directed subsidiary intentions, whose satisfaction is necessary for the making to succeed, though applicable to the making of standard non-art artifacts, such as chairs, as well as traditional art artifacts in established media, such as paintings, is inapplicable to art-making in an appropriational or conceptual mode. Arguably nothing more is needed for successful art-making in that mode than the belief that there is a practice of art, that various things are exemplars of it, and that there are correct ways of regarding, treating, or interacting with those things. So far as I can see, this necessarily involves the maker in *some* conceptions about art, to be sure, but not in *substantive* conceptions, in the sense Thomasson seems to have in mind, about the nature of artworks and their characteristic properties.

4. TRADITIONAL ART-MAKING

It would be remiss to end this short essay on the nature of artworks as artifacts without some remarks on the special character of art-making of a traditional sort, that is, all art-making before Duchamp, Warhol, and Conceptual Art, and most art-making after them as well. In art-making as traditionally conceived—and for simplicity I confine my attention to artmaking in the visual arts—there are distinctive raw materials, for instance, paint, clay, charcoal; there are distinctive techniques, for instance, carving, etching, impasto; and there are distinctive aims, such as visual beauty, representational verisimilitude, and emotional expression. But the making of chairs and pencils also involves distinctive materials, distinctive techniques, and distinctive aims, albeit utilitarian ones. So even if art-making in the comprehensive, post-Duchampian sense distinguishes itself from other sorts of artifact-making by its presumed purely intentional-historical character, is art-making of the traditional sort, though issuing in a physical object whose interest is primarily aesthetic rather than utilitarian, fundamentally different from the making of physical artifacts generally, including the making of craft objects such as rugs or pots? To a degree.

Collingwood and Dewey were two philosophers of art who had insightful and consonant things to say on the distinctive character of the making involved in traditional art, especially as in contrast with the making involved in the overtly similar activity of craft (Collingwood 1938; Dewey 1934). What both thinkers stressed is that the making of an artwork is an open-ended, indefinitely extended, creative-critical process, with alternating phases of making and assessing, or 'doing and undergoing', but one not governed by any fixed goal or preconceived idea of what the artwork must be, or how it must turn out. An artist making a sculpture, for example, in contrast with a craftsman making a rug or a pot, need not envisage what its dimensions will be, what it will look like, or what form it will have. This is unsurprising if one recalls that making a traditional artwork is, as much as anything, an expressive activity, but one in which, as Collingwood underlined, the artist does not know precisely what he has expressed until the process is completed. The maker of a craft object, though, must first and foremost assure the creation of a usable object of the craft in question, some of whose features, such as flatness or water-holding capacity, are accordingly non-negotiable, thus enjoining a preconception of some specificity on the craftsman's part of the object to be created.

Granted the above, the upshot for our discussion is this. If, as Thomasson urges, the making of standard artifacts is always governed by a substantive conception of the artifact in question, one that sets clear terms for success and failure in such makings, and if traditional artworks be accounted standard enough in that respect, then what is most noteworthy about the making of such artifacts is that the substantive conceptions involved in their creation are relatively *insubstantial*, that is, not such as to notably constrain them in formal, material, or functional ways. A sculpture, say, needs to be physical, perceivable, and perhaps smaller than the planet, but apart from that, it can be of any size, any composition, any shape, any color, and any subject. The relative insubstantiality of the conceptions governing the making of traditional artworks fits well, of course, with the innovative and exploratory aim often ascribed to art, both traditional and non-traditional.

5. CONCLUSION

So what sort of artifact is an artwork? In the past, and thinking primarily of the visual arts, one might have answered: a physical object, fashioned with skill, involving a recognized medium, designed to be of aesthetic interest, and whose making is governed by a fairly substantive conception of the genre of artwork in question. And such an answer would still be largely adequate to at least traditional art-making today. But at present, and just confining ourselves to the activities of visual artists, such an answer is no longer even remotely adequate. That is because of alternate modes of art-making that have become entrenched in the past hundred years, whereby artworks need not be fashioned by their creators, need not involve recognized artistic media, need not be aimed at satisfying aesthetic interests, and whose making need not be governed by any very substantial conception of a genre in which the artist is working. Those modes of art-making have revolutionized the concept of art, making it the case that the concept-of-art-2005 is something fundamentally, and not just marginally, different from the concept-of-art-1905. Artworks are necessarily artifacts, since they are things intentionally brought into being through human agency. That much remains true. But if I am right, to be an artwork today is simply to be something governed by an intention relating it in a certain way to what have been accounted artworks in the past. By contrast, more is required to be an artifact of a standard sort, such as a chair, even if the intentional-historical connection sufficient for being an artwork plays a crucial role there as well, in the manner that Bloom has underlined.

PART II

CONCEPTS AND CATEGORIES

6

Artifact Categorization: The Good, the Bad, and the Ugly

Barbara C. Malt and Steven A. Sloman

1. INTRODUCTION

A sizeable subfield of cognitive psychology is devoted to how humans categorize entities in their world, yet there has been little explicit consideration of what it means to categorize. One straightforward perspective, the one perhaps held at an intuitive level by most laypeople, is that categories are objectively defined, metaphysically real groupings of entities. The process of categorizing is thus a judgment about which grouping any given entity belongs to, a judgment that is objectively right or wrong. Applied to artifacts, this perspective suggests that when people see an object such as a table or bench, they judge to the best of their ability what metaphysically real category of objects this particular object belongs to.

If pressed, though, most cognitive psychologists would probably claim to be agnostic about whether or not there are objectively defined, metaphysically real groupings of artifacts. Relegating such determinations to the realm of philosophy (see, in this volume, Searle, Elder, and Thomasson, all of whom argue for the metaphysical reality of artifact categories), they would suggest that what they mean by artifact 'kinds' are psychological kinds: groupings recognized by humans that might or might not correspond to the kinds that would be identified by philosophers as metaphysically real (see Medin and Ortony 1989). Given this reformulation, the process of artifact categorization is the process of judging which psychologically real, if not metaphysically real, grouping an object belongs to. This framing would likely be subscribed to by most cognitive psychologists studying artifact categorization (if not by most philosophers; e.g. Thomasson, this volume).

To study how an artifact gets categorized, then, one must choose a task or tasks to reveal how a judgment is made about what grouping it belongs to. And in order to make that choice, one must have an idea of what the relevant psychological groupings are; a task that requires judgments about groupings that are not psychologically meaningful or natural would be of little value. An almost universal assumption is that the psychologically real groupings are stable groupings that map directly onto mental representations constituting 'concepts' (see e.g. Keil, and Mahon and Caramazza, this volume). These concepts in turn map onto names and images, and serve induction, planning, and other higher processes. Under this assumption, nouns provide a convenient entry-point into the system—the words *ball* and *doll* delimit psychologically real groupings of objects, are associated with distinct concepts and images in memory, and so on—and so are frequently used to index the categories of interest, but they do not otherwise have special status. (Hence, for instance, in the developmental literature, word and concept learning are often not distinguished; see e.g. Kelemen and Carey, this volume.) Following from the assumption of stable groupings that map directly onto names, concepts, images, and so on, selecting an appropriate task is relatively simple: one can study categorization through any of a number of tasks, such as naming, sorting, property projection, or clustering in memory. All will tap the same groupings.

But closer examination suggests that both of these assumptions are faulty. Any given artifact can participate in more than one grouping. The same rubber ball may, at different times, be grouped with other spherical, bouncy objects, with other things called *ball* (including non-bouncy beanbag balls and non-spherical footballs), with other toys such as dolls and board games, or with other things to take to the playground such as a tricycle and a snack. What the relevant grouping is depends crucially on the situation at hand (Barsalou 1983, 1991; Ross and Murphy 1999; Sloman and Malt 2003). And different tasks may invoke different processes that operate under different constraints. Naming, for instance, is a task that engages language in order for communication to take place, and it must therefore be sensitive to influences such as a language's history and the particular history of a speaker and addressee. In contrast, tasks such as storing information in memory, projecting properties, or planning in order to achieve goals are not about communication; each has its own unique demands (Malt *et al.* 1999; Malt, Sloman, and Gennari 2003*a*).

Below, we discuss the variety of distinct mental activities that people engage in in daily life that can reasonably be considered 'categorization', and we analyze the cognitive demands of each activity. We consider how these activities relate to tasks used in research on categorization. We discuss the nature of the laboratory tasks involved and how they influence the category judgments that are made, and we argue that the tasks used often do not map well onto the activities of daily life that they are meant to shed light on. We review central findings about how people group artifacts that have accumulated and suggest that some of these are useful with respect to understanding one or more of the mental activities we identify as categorization. We also suggest that some of them are unlikely to contribute usefully, given the discrepancy between the nature of the research tasks used and the nature of the activities of interest. We suggest that given the distinct nature of the activities that involve grouping artifacts, each must be understood on its own terms. To achieve this understanding, researchers must commit explicitly to the type of categorization they are interested in and select methodologies that are appropriate to that type. We argue further that because the term 'categorization' does not carve the space of human endeavors at its joints, no coherent account of artifact categorization is possible, and 'categorization' is not a coherent field of inquiry.

2. CONNECTING OBJECTS TO WORDS

A prominent form of everyday mental activity that involves judging what grouping an artifact belongs to is that of connecting objects with words. In speaking (and writing), people frequently produce names for objects. In almost every utterance, they use nouns, and many of the nouns are intended to refer to artifacts. To produce the utterance, they will usually have an intended referent in mind. They then select a name for the entity: *hat*, *table*, or *ball*, etc. In doing so, they are in effect grouping the object with other objects that have the same name. In comprehension, people hear (or read) artifact names and interpret them by connecting them with objects, real or hypothetical. In some cases—as in hearing 'Hand me that hammer'—potential referents are physically present and the addressee must decide which among them is most likely being called by that name. In other cases, referents are not present—as in discussing needing to buy a hammer—and the addressee must construct in her mind a potential referent. In both cases, the person is, again, in effect grouping the object or objects with other objects that have the same name.

A large proportion of research on artifact categorization uses tasks involving connecting objects with words. The bulk of the research uses a type of task we will call 'name appropriateness judgments'; a smaller portion uses free naming. For each type of task, we first consider its relation to how objects get connected with words in daily life and then review and evaluate findings that have emerged from studies using the task.

2.1. Name appropriateness judgments

In most instances of connecting objects to words in ordinary discourse, there are many options on one end or the other. The speaker chooses among many names; the listener chooses among many possible referents. On relatively rare occasions, a more restricted and explicit form of naming choice is called for.

Such judgments are required in response to questions like 'Is that a telephone?' or 'Is that a telephone or a fax machine?' In such situations, one object and only one or two names are under consideration. Situations of this sort arise mainly when someone sees an object with unfamiliar properties and seeks information about the nature of the object by asking about the appropriateness of a particular name.

Despite the rarity of explicit, constrained name appropriateness judgment in the real world, it is the most common type of problem posed to participants in research on artifact categorization. The task differs from most naming choices in daily life in that it combines elements of both production and comprehension. Names are given (as in comprehension) rather than generated (as in production) but the referent is already known to the respondent, unlike in most comprehension situations, and respondents must decide if the name(s) offered correspond to ones they would produce for the object. Further, laboratory name appropriateness judgments have several distinctive characteristics not shared even by the explicit judgments in real world situations. First, the communication goal for the respondent has little to do with achieving reference. In real-world situations, the goal is to illuminate the puzzled inquirer; in laboratory situations, it is merely to satisfy an experimental requirement for a response. Second, because the primary goal is not to achieve reference, discourse context plays relatively little role in determining appropriateness. In real-world situations, context may have some influence even in explicit name appropriateness judgments in that the respondent may consider whether the names offered would suit the questioner's presumed communication needs. In the laboratory, however, there is little basis for inference about communication needs. Finally, response possibilities in the laboratory task are highly limited. In forced choice versions, one of a fixed number of options, often two, must be selected; there is no option to choose neither or more than one, nor to choose a modified version of a name offered (a respondent cannot say 'it's a cell phone' or 'it's a phone-fax' in answer to 'Is it a telephone?'). Likewise, rarely does the respondent have the option of indicating that a name might be acceptable but only marginally so, or acceptable under some circumstances. In one-option versions, the offered name can be rejected but the respondent still cannot offer alternatives or modifications.

In the forced choice laboratory task, then, the participant must consider the names given and decide which of the alternatives is a better name for the object, with the discourse goal and context providing only weak constraints on the operationalization of 'better'. In the one-option version, the participant must consider the name given and judge its acceptability, again with weak or unclear constraints on what should be acceptable. The key decision on the part of the participant is thus what sort of criterion (or criteria) to use in judging the appropriateness of names offered.

2.1.1. Findings

The goal of studies using name appropriateness judgments is usually, though not exclusively, to determine what type of information is most important in artifact categorization or serves as the 'core' of artifact concepts (e.g. Ahn *et al.*'s 2001 response to Strevens 2000; Kemler Nelson, Russell, *et al.* 2000). Among the bases that have been examined are the form (physical features), current function, original function intended by the creator, category membership intended by the creator, and features having a particular causal status with respect to other features.

2.1.1.1. Form vs. function

The most extensively studied contrast is that of form vs. function. Results of some studies have suggested that form drives naming choices, whereas others have favored function. Some have suggested a developmental trend from form to function, and others have suggested that neither form nor function heavily dominates choices.

In an early study, Gentner (1978) showed children and adults two novel complex objects, named them, and demonstrated their functions. Participants were then shown a test object that had the form of one but the function of the other and asked whether it should be called by the name that had been associated with the same function or the name that had been associated with the same form. Young children and adults both preferred the name associated with the form (though older children tended to make more function-based choices). Rips (1989) presented verbal descriptions of objects created with an intended function associated with one common name (e.g. *lamp*) but an appearance associated with another (e.g. *umbrella*) and asked people to choose between the two names. In contrast to Gentner's results, he found that people preferred the one associated with the intended function.

Several subsequent studies found evidence for variable responses within a single paradigm. Landau, Smith, and Jones (1998; see also 1992) presented novel or familiar objects along with names and, in some conditions, demonstrated the object functions. They then asked children and adults whether objects having either the same function or same shape should be called by the training name. They found that the children tended to accept the name for objects with similar shapes. Adults tended to accept the name for those with similar functions, but they did so more for unfamiliar objects than familiar ones and more when function had been demonstrated during training than when not. Malt and Johnson (1992) used verbal descriptions of objects and varied whether the objects had the physical or functional features normally associated with familiar artifact names. Their participants (adults) judged some objects that had the normal intended function but unusual physical features to be acceptable examples of the name, but not others. At the same time, participants rejected some objects that had the normal physical features associated with a name but an altered intended function, but they accepted others. Malt and Johnson concluded that neither physical features nor intended function alone fully determine whether people would view an object as an acceptable example of an artifact name category.

Kemler Nelson, Frankenfield, *et al.* (2000) suggested that people may reject a name associated with the stated function if that function is not a plausible explanation for the physical properties displayed. They presented 4-year-olds with novel complex objects and taught them a name for the object. In one condition, the object's function was plausibly connected to its physical features; in the other, the function was something that the object could do but did not appear to have been designed for. Participants chose which of two objects—one similar in function but dissimilar in form, and one similar in form but incapable of performing the function—was another example of the name. The children showed a much stronger bias, though not absolute, to choose objects that preserved the function of the training object when the function had been plausibly connected to the physical features.

2.1.1.2. Current function vs. intended function

Another contrast that has been examined is that of the object's current function vs. original intended function, again with conflicting results. Keil (1989) showed kindergarteners through fourth graders pictures of familiar artifacts (e.g. a coffeepot) and then described alterations that gave the object both the appearance and function associated with a different type of object (e.g. birdfeeder). He asked children to choose between the name associated with the original version and the name associated with the new features. In this case, with both appearance and use altered, the children had a strong tendency to prefer the name associated with the current function and appearance. Matan and Carey (2001) presented 4- and 6-year-olds and adults with ambiguous pictures of objects (pictures in which the object was partially hidden) and told them that the object was made for one purpose but was currently being used for another (for instance, an object made to be used as a watering-can was currently being used as a teapot). Participants were asked to judge whether the object belonged to the first category or the second. In contrast to Keil's result, all participants tended to favor the original intended function, with adults doing so more than children.

2.1.1.3. Intended category membership vs. form and function

The intended category membership of an object refers to what category the creator of the object had in mind for it. Motivated in part by several free naming studies examining the impact of intended category membership on naming (see below), Chaigneau (reported in Barsalou, Sloman, and Chaigneau 2004) used scenarios describing familiar objects or variations of them to test the relative impact of several factors including the intended category membership on name judgments. In one type of scenario, the object had the usual properties of an object such as a mop, but it was created accidentally (not intended to be a mop). In another, the object was made by its creator to be a mop but it did not have typical mop features and would not function very effectively as a mop. In others, the object was made by its creator to be a mop but it was used by an agent to perform other actions, or was made by its creator to be a mop but was used to wipe up water only accidentally. Participants judged whether the object was an example of the name associated with target category. Chaigneau found that intended category membership had some influence on judgments but mattered less than the form and use of the object.

2.1.1.4. Causes vs. effects

Several studies have examined the relative impact on name appropriateness judgments of features that serve as causes for other features vs. those that are effects of other features. Ahn (e.g. Ahn 1998; Ahn and Kim 2000) proposed that causes would be treated as more critical to category membership than effects. Ahn *et al.* (2000) gave participants descriptions of named objects, including artifacts, that specified the causal relations among the features (one feature was the underlying cause of the others; another was an intermediate cause, and the third was the effect of the others). Test objects were missing one feature or another, and participants judged how likely the objects were as examples of the named category. Objects missing the most fundamental cause were judged least likely to be an example of the named category, and objects missing the effect were judged most likely. However, Sloman, Love, and Ahn (1998) argued that effects of feature centrality (on naming as well as other tasks) were not due to causal relations per se but rather to dependency relations in general: a feature is central for naming to the degree that other features depend on it. In a similar vein, Rehder and Hastie (2001) suggested that the critical variable may not be depth in a dependency graph, but rather the number of causal relations that a feature participates in. They presented adult participants with information about categories of artifacts (cars and computers) including attribute values and base rates of attribute values in the categories. In some conditions, participants were also given information about causal relations among the attributes, with the attributes being either causes or effects of other attributes. In transfer trials, they were asked if a described object was a member of the learned category or not. Which attribute was weighted most heavily in the decision depended on the number of relations it was involved in, not on whether it was a cause or an effect per se.

2.1.1.5. Influence of background knowledge

Murphy and Medin (1985) suggested that people's background knowledge or naive 'theories' about the world influence how people understand the relation between features of entities and judge their relevance to category membership. A number of studies examining the role of background knowledge in categorization have used other sorts of tasks or stimuli (e.g. Kaplan and Murphy 2000; Spalding and Murphy 1996), but Lin and Murphy (1997) focused on artifacts in a name appropriateness task. They asked participants to learn names for sets of novel objects, giving participants in different conditions different explanations of how the objects were used. They then asked whether test objects missing one feature of the learned set were examples of the name categories. Participants gave different judgments to the same objects depending on how central the missing feature was to the explanation they had been given. For instance, when training objects were long and narrow with a handle on one end and a loop on the other, a test object with a missing loop was less likely to be judged to belong to the training category when participants had been told that the training objects were for catching animals than when they had been told that they were for spraying pesticides.

2.1.2. *Implications of name appropriateness data*

By their nature, the strength of laboratory name appropriateness judgments is in revealing what criteria, of those made available by the stimulus construction, a person uses to decide which of two presented names is better for a test object (in the forced choice version) or whether a presented name is justified (in the one-alternative version). Although experiments using name appropriateness judgments have exploited this strength to try to determine what type of information is most important in artifact categorization or serves as the 'core' of artifact concepts, the results suggest that a number of different types of information can influence name judgments of this sort. Different factors gain importance depending on the information made available by stimulus construction and experimental demands. These factors include the form of the object, its original intended function, its current function, its intended category membership, and the structure of the relations among its features. One factor may dominate another in an experiment in which two are selected to be the main sources of variation in the stimuli, but the aggregate results do not point to one factor as the sole or primary basis for judgments in name appropriateness tasks. The body of research using name appropriateness tasks has thus failed in the attempt to identify specific types of information that are most central to artifact categorization or serve as the core of artifact concepts, although it does offer the conclusion that a variety of different factors may influence judgments.

A second implication that emerges from the data is that people do not treat the manipulated features as independent pieces of information. Instead they often try to understand the causal relations of the features to one another, and they consider how this relation relates to that of typical objects associated with a name (Barsalou, Sloman, and Chaigneau 2004). This suggestion emerges from studies on causal relations among features (Ahn *et al.* 2000; Rehder and Hastie 2001) and those on background knowledge (Lin and Murphy 1997), from Kemler Nelson, Frankenfield, *et al.*'s (2000) manipulation of the relation of intended function to form, and from informal evidence in both Matan and Carey's (2001) and Malt and Johnson's (1992) studies. Matan and Carey noted that adults, and to a lesser extent children, often gave justifications for their decisions that drew not only on the original intended function but on the relation of the functions to possible forms. For instance, a participant might reason that a frisbee can more feasibly be used as a plate than vice versa and so judge that an object that has been used as both is more likely to really be a frisbee. Consistent with Kemler Nelson's suggestion that judgments are influenced by the plausibility of the relation of the physical features to functions, Malt and Johnson noted that their objects with unusual physical features that were most reliably accepted as examples of a name tended to have an interpretation as viable futuristic versions of current objects. Because evidence of this tendency to understand and interpret relations among features emerges from studies that are not designed to make such relations salient as well as from those that are, it appears to be a pervasive feature of how people deal with artifacts rather than one made prominent only by the nature of the experimental tasks.

2.2. Free naming

As already noted, in daily life, people frequently make judgments about artifact groupings in the process of language production. They generate nouns intended to refer to artifacts in many of their utterances. We call the production situation 'free naming' because the names considered and produced for a given object are not restricted to a small set explicitly provided by an external source. In contrast to name appropriateness judgments—rare in the real world but common in the laboratory—free naming is relatively less studied in categorization research despite its ubiquity in daily life.

Free naming has several characteristics that set it apart from name appropriateness judgments. Memory demands are greater because speakers must retrieve potential names from memory. The set of names stored in memory is extremely large, and the subset activated by an object may be more than just one or two, so the choice set at several points in the production process is potentially much larger than in name appropriateness judgments. In addition, because the speaker may choose to name in whatever way he or she finds most useful, a given head noun can be modified in various ways. Finally, in real world discourse, free naming usually has a specific goal—typically, the goal of achieving reference for some intended audience.[1] The context in such situations can help constrain understanding of the intended referent by an addressee and so may influence what name(s) can be used to successfully refer to it. Free naming within the

---

[1] Naming in ordinary discourse may have additional, usually secondary, goals as well, such as conveying attitude (e.g. in calling a dwelling a *hovel* vs. *palace*). In adult speech directed to young children, teaching names may also be a frequent goal.

laboratory shares most of the characteristics of free naming in daily life except, importantly, that (as for laboratory name appropriateness judgments) the goal for the respondent has less to do with achieving reference than with satisfying an experimental requirement for a response, and the context provides little constraint on what name would be a useful choice. However, some studies create semi-natural communication contexts for naming.

2.2.1. Findings

Evidence about artifact categorization from free naming comes both from observations of naming in the real world and from laboratory situations in which participants are presented with stimuli and asked to name them. The data have been used to address a range of issues about how people name artifacts.

2.2.1.1. Form vs. function as a basis for naming

Laboratory free naming data have been used to address the controversy over whether form or function dominates naming choices for artifacts, and they suggest that neither is clearly dominant. Sloman, Malt, and Fridman (2001) examined the ability of three different versions of similarity—physical, functional, and overall—to account for names produced for three sets of sixty objects: bottles, jars, and other small containers for food; boxes, cartons, and other storage containers; and bowls, plates, and dishes. Participants gave judgments of the similarity of the objects to one another (via either sorting or pairwise similarity ratings), judging either similarity of form, of function, or overall similarity. They were then asked what they would call each object in ordinary conversation. A prototype, nearest neighbor, and weighted sum model were applied to the similarity data to predict the names given. Results showed no clear advantage of one type of similarity over any of the other types in predicting names. A small advantage was seen for physical over functional information, but it was not consistent across models. A subsequent study entered features obtained in a feature-listing task into a Bayesian probability model to try to predict names for the same stimuli. No single feature could predict names fully, but the feature with the greatest predictive power for each stimulus set was a physical, not a functional, feature.

These outcomes are compatible with observations of naming in the real world, which suggest that names are sometimes extended based on form, sometimes on function, and sometimes on a substantial or partial match to both (Malt 1991; Malt *et al.* 1999). Table 6.1 provides examples of objects that appear to share a name based primarily on similarity of form, and Table 6.2 provides examples that appear to be based primarily on similarity of function. Table 6.3 provides examples of objects that appear to share a name based on substantial or partial similarity of both form and function. All examples in the tables were observed within discourse contexts (although recorded without details of the contexts). Note that cases of each are rarely pure; for instance, although the

Table 6.1. *Examples of names extended on the basis of form*

Name	Typical example	Form-based extension
blanket	bedroom blanket (keeping warm in bed)	picnic blanket (sitting on)
boat	sailboat (transportation)	jail boat (holding convicts)
bowl	soup bowl (holding and eating liquid)	pasta bowl (holding and eating solids)
		sugar bowl (holding and serving granules)
box	shoe box (holding solids)	juice box (holding liquids)
broomstick	kitchen broomstick (sweeping)	witch's broomstick (flying)
chair	kitchen chair (sitting)	electric chair (killing)
fork	from place setting (bringing food to mouth)	carving fork (holding meat)
		fish fork (serving from platter)
		tuning fork (making sound)
gun	pistol	label gun
		glue gun
		staple gun
knife	kitchen knife	frosting knife (spreading)
paper	note paper (writing on)	waxed paper (covering food)
		tissue paper (wrapping gifts)
		fly paper (catching flies)
		toilet paper (wiping)
spoon	soup spoon (scooping liquids)	pasta spoon (lifting pasta from cooking water)
		grapefruit spoon (serrated edge for cutting)
		slotted spoon (draining)
umbrella	rain umbrella (keeping rain off)	beach umbrella (keeping sun off)
wheel	on auto for tires	steering wheel
		Ferris wheel
		spinning wheel

Note: Functions are provided in parentheses for some examples to highlight contrasts or when function might be unfamiliar.

primary function of an electric chair is quite distinct from the primary function of a kitchen chair, the similarity of form does afford a shared component of function in that one sits in both. Likewise, although shared function seems to be the primary reason that manual razors and electric razors share a name, their shared function leads them to be not entirely dissimilar in form. In general, form and function will tend to be correlated, which may be why Sloman *et al.* found that neither was distinctly superior at predicting the names that artifacts in their sample received. The examples in the tables are categorized according to whether the primary link appears to be one or the other, or whether both appear to contribute about equally to motivating a shared name.

Table 6.2. *Examples of names extended on the basis of function*

Name	Typical example	Function-based extension
auto	Honda Accord	Model T Ford
can opener	manual opener	electric opener
chair	kitchen chair	beanbag chair
computer	Pentium 4 PC	ENIAC (room-sized; vacuum tubes)
corkscrew	with metal spiral	with two prongs
		with propellant cartridge
fan	electric box fan	Japanese paper fan
drill	power drill	dentist drill
		hydraulic drill
key	traditional door key	hotel doorkey (plastic card, magnetic strip)
		electronic car door key (remote control)
razor	manual razor	electric razor

Note: Forms are provided in parentheses for some examples to highlight contrasts or when form might be unfamiliar.

2.2.1.2. Variability in naming patterns across languages

Languages may have different naming patterns for the same sets of artifacts. Kronenfeld, Armstrong, and Wilmoth (1985) found that speakers of English, Hebrew, and Japanese partitioned a set of eleven ordinary drinking vessels by name in different ways. For example, English-speakers asked to name the objects called a paper drinking vessel and one for drinking tea both *cup*, but Israelis labeled them with different names. Japanese participants used three names in partitioning the objects, but they were partitioned by only two different names in English and in Hebrew. Malt *et al.* (1999) asked speakers of American English, Mandarin Chinese, and Argentinean Spanish to name sixty common containers and found substantial differences in the naming patterns across the three languages along with similarities. Malt, Sloman, and Gennari (2003*b*) examined the relation among the linguistic categories of the three languages for the sixty containers in more detail and found a complex pattern. Some of the categories shared prototypes across the three languages but others did not; some cases of nesting occurred (the categories of one language were contained within those of another); and some cases of cross-cutting were found (pairs of objects were put into a single category by one language but into different categories by another language). These divergent patterns have consequences for second-language learners: Malt and Sloman (2003) found that non-native speakers of English failed to match native naming patterns for these same sixty containers and for sixty examples of housewares, and some discrepancies persisted even for non-natives having many years of immersion in an English-speaking environment.

2.2.1.3. Variability in name choices within a language

Even for a given language, artifacts often have more than one acceptable name, both across and within people. Malt *et al.*'s (1999) data showed that although

Table 6.3. *Examples of names extended on the basis of shared form and function or partial overlap of both form and function*

Name	Typical example	Multi-factor extension
bed	in bedroom (sleeping)	sofa bed (sitting and sleeping)
bottle	Coke bottle (holding and drinking liquid)	aspirin bottle (holding solids)
		spray cleaner bottle (holding and spraying liquid; spray top)
box	shoe box	litter box (no lid)
		bread box (metal; curved)
		lunch box (metal; domed top)
		plastic animal-shaped juice box (for liquids; has straw)
camera	film-based	digital camera
chair	kitchen chair	dentist chair (for dental procedures, not just sitting)
		rocking chair (for rocking, not just sitting)
fan	electric box fan	ceiling fan
knife	kitchen knife	butter knife (cutting and spreading)
		paring knife (peeling)
		butcher knife (chopping)
		cheese knife (forked tip for spearing)
ladder	extension ladder (for climbing up to reach)	step ladder (for climbing up to reach)
		rope emergency ladder (for climbing down to escape)
oven	electric oven	Dutch oven
		microwave oven
		toaster oven
phone	touch-tone phone	cell phone
		1920s dial phone
table	kitchen table	drafting table (slanted; for drawing)

Note: Forms or functions are provided in parentheses for some examples to highlight contrasts or when they might be unfamiliar.

consensus among speakers of a given language was very high for some familiar containers (e.g. a glass juice bottle was called *bottle* by all participants), for other members of the set names varied considerably (e.g. a gallon container of milk was called *jug* by some, *container* by some, and *bottle* by others). In a pre-test for a matching task involving artifacts (see below), Malt and Sloman (2004), using free naming followed by name verification, readily identified a number of familiar objects that had two commonly used names. (For example, one object was called a trashcan, a wastebasket, and a trash container, and another was called both a booklet and a pamphlet; individual participants verified that all names were acceptable.)

2.2.1.4. Previous exposure effects

Given the existence of more than one potential name for an artifact, the question arises of what determines choices among them on any given occasion. One factor appears to be the creation of an implicit agreement between participants in a conversation about what name will be used to refer to an object (e.g. Brennan and Clark 1996; Clark and Wilkes-Gibbs 1986). Brennan and Clark (1996) had pairs of participants carry out a matching task in which one participant arranged the pictures in an order described by the other. In the course of the task, participants established tacit agreements about how to refer to the pictures, taking into account the level of specificity needed to discriminate the objects from one another. Brennan and Clark found that these agreements, once established, influenced naming in later discussions even when the context of those discussions would have allowed reference to be achieved with simpler expressions. For instance, if a picture set contained two types of shoes, participants gave them names such as *sneaker* and *high heel*; they continued to use such names later for picture sets in which only one type was present and *shoe* would have been a sufficient label.

Another factor influencing the choice is what names have been recently retrieved from memory and used, regardless of their relation to any previous agreement with a conversational partner. Sloman, Harrison, and Malt (2002) asked participants to name artifact stimuli created by morphing two familiar artifacts (e.g. a pen and a marker). Participants had previously been exposed to other objects that were named with one label or the other. Names given for the target stimuli were influenced by the previous exposures. Malt and Sloman (2004) had pairs of participants discuss artifacts pre-tested as having two acceptable names (e.g. *trashcan* and *wastebasket*) in carrying out a matching task. One participant was a confederate who introduced one of the two names for each object. In subsequent trials, the naive participant performed trials of the same task with another naive participant. Names used with the new partner were influenced by which name was initially used by the confederate, suggesting that a bias toward a particular name, once established, carries over (at least in the short term) beyond conversation with the original partner.

2.2.1.5. Sensitivity to intended category membership

Bloom (1996) suggested that naming is sensitive to the intended category membership of an object's creator: People name artifacts in accordance with the category that they think the creator intended for it. Bloom and Markson (1998) asked 3- and 4-year-old children to draw pictures of a lollipop, a balloon, the experimenter, and themselves, and later asked them to say what the drawing was a picture of. The pictures of lollipops and balloons were generally not distinguishable from one another, nor were pictures of the experimenter and the child, but children of both ages tended to name pictures in accordance with their original intention in producing the drawing. Gelman and Bloom (2000) described objects as either intentionally or accidentally created; for instance, a newspaper was folded into the shape of a hat either by a person or by being run over by a car. Children and adults were asked what the objects were. All age groups gave an object name (e.g. *hat*) more often than a material name (e.g. *newspaper*) when the origin was intentional and vice versa when it was accidental.

2.2.2. Implications of free naming data

The free naming data that exist have been collected under conditions that capture many of the demands and constraints of naming in daily life. A shortcoming of much of the research using free naming tasks is that it does not provide natural discourse contexts and goals for naming, and so outcomes cannot reflect their potential influence. Some exceptions do exist, however (e.g. Brennan and Clark 1996; Malt and Sloman 2004), providing insight into these influences. The aggregate data provide a number of important pieces of information about naming.

The free naming data indicate that there is no unique grouping of artifacts by name, either between languages or within languages. Patterns of naming for the same artifacts differ across languages, and the same artifacts can receive different names from different speakers within a language, and even from a single speaker on different occasions. The variability observed here does not involve labels at different levels of abstraction (e.g. *table* vs. *furniture*), nor does it involve fundamentally different types of groupings such as those invoked in the service of momentary goals (e.g. things to take out of the house in a fire; Barsalou 1983, 1991) vs. those that are taxonomic (e.g. *car*). Rather, the same objects may be grouped by name differently using basic level, taxonomic labels as a function of the individual speaker, the language he or she is speaking, and the circumstances of the utterance.

Some of the variables that affect name choice can be thought of as short-term influences in that they influence the choice made by a speaker on a particular occasion from among those names available in his or her language. The effects of recent retrieval episodes on what is retrieved from memory for a subsequent stimulus is one such factor (Sloman, Harrison, and Malt 2002; Malt and Sloman 2004). The others involve adjusting to the conversational context in ways that are under greater speaker control. These include taking into account the name agreed upon with a conversational partner (Brennan and Clark 1996), and taking into account the presumed intention of the creator (Bloom and Markson 1998; Gelman and Bloom 2000) even when no name has as yet been explicitly offered and accepted.

In contrast, the variability in naming patterns across languages appears to be the consequence of longer-term factors that establish what names are available for objects within a language and what the preferred assignment of names to objects within a domain is. Malt *et al.* (1999, 2003*a*, 2003*b*) suggest that the name for a given object in any particular language is influenced by what names happened to exist in that language at some earlier time and so were available for extending to new objects; what objects happened to exist in the culture at some earlier time and either formed a similarity cluster that was given a name, or extended outward from a cluster and caused a name to be extended to less similar objects by chaining (Brugman 1983; Lakoff 1987; Taylor 1995); what names happened to be bestowed on objects by a manufacturer either from within that culture or from outside for marketing purposes; and what domains were of particular interest to a culture at some point in its history and so required finer linguistic differentiation of the conceptual space. The consequences of each for a given language will vary as a function of the linguistic and cultural history involved, and so languages will diverge to some extent in their naming patterns even when showing commonalities driven by shared perception of the stimulus space.

From the longer-term perspective, perhaps it should not be surprising that languages differ in their naming patterns for the same set of artifacts, nor that names can be shared across objects based on similarity of form, function, or both. Within the domain of artifacts, possibly more than within any other domain, new variations on existing entities are created on a frequent basis. Each new variant is not likely to be given a unique name unless the intention of the maker is to isolate it from its predecessors. Instead, existing words will be extended to cover new cases. Often the variations for each new object, either in form or in function, are relatively minor and so the object retains many of the properties of its predecessor. For users of the language, there is little to impede comprehension if the word is extended to cover such variants.[2] However, the cumulative result of these small steps of extension can be that a word is associated with a set of objects that vary considerably in form, function, or both. For reasons suggested above, languages may follow different paths of extension, with the result that they accumulate different sets of objects sharing a name.

The observed diversity in how objects are grouped by name might seem to work against the usefulness of names for conveying information about objects (that is, allowing the addressee to identify a physically present or hypothetical object and make appropriate inferences about the properties of the object referred to). However, other characteristics of the free naming task in real world

---

[2] Petroski (1993) provides a fascinating example of how the knife and fork evolved in Western culture. In the 1500s table knives were narrow and had a pointed tip, and were used not only for cutting meat but also for spearing food and conveying it to the mouth. Pointed tips later gave way to blunt tips for safety reasons. At that time, forks had only two tines and were used primarily for holding meat steady while it was being cut. Foods that could not be easily speared by the two-tined fork, such as peas, were conveyed to the mouth by piling them on knives, and knives developed a wide blade that was bulbous at the tip to provide a better surface. Later, forks evolved to have three or four tines and became used as the primary means of bringing food to the mouth. The wide, bulbous blade of knives then reverted back to a narrower, straighter style. Each step in this sequence involves a relatively small change, but both the forms and functions of knives and forks changed over the course of the evolution. The names 'knife' and 'fork' (with some variation in spelling) were used in English for these objects throughout this time-period (*Oxford English Dictionary* 1989).

situations may make this diversity unproblematic. The discourse context can greatly constrain interpretation of a noun. If a gallon container is just out of reach of a person wanting to fill it with water, it matters little if the person asks for the *bottle*, *jug*, or *container* to be passed, because any of the names will be sufficient to achieve reference. In addition, the open-endedness of the free naming task allows speakers to use noun-noun or adjective-noun combinations to clarify referents and direct inductions. Someone hearing a noun such as *bottle* or *chair* will look for (if potential referents are physically present) or imagine (if not) different objects and induce a partially different set of properties depending on the modifiers attached. Hearing *electric chair* will lead a person to assume different properties than hearing *kitchen chair*, as will hearing *baby bottle* vs. *aspirin bottle*. Brennan and Clark's (1996) data indicate that speakers adjust the specificity of names as needed to disambiguate intended referents from other potential referents in the discourse context. The open-ended nature of the task also makes it possible for speakers to take into account what name they think their conversational partner intends to be applied to an object or what name they have previous established with the partner for referring to the object, which contribute to the likelihood of successfully achieving reference.

In addition to the specific information provided by the data about how naming choices are made, these data make evident the extent to which naming is an activity that is embedded in a linguistic and communicative context and that reflects the demands and possibilities made available by this context. We suggest that it will be impossible to understand name choices for artifacts without considering communicative issues such as what a particular addressee can understand or will understand most readily (reflecting speaker–addressee naming history and the availability of discourse context to constrain understanding, among other things), and linguistic issues such as the historical linguistic forces that shape the vocabulary available to a speaker of a given language and the language's conventions for applying that vocabulary and the availability of modifying phrases to accomplish goals of naming. Research that has a goal of understanding how people choose names for artifacts but that eliminates most or all of these influences from the judgment process is not likely to substantially advance knowledge about naming.

3. CONCEPTUAL (NON-LINGUISTIC) GROUPING

So far we have been considering forms of categorization that involve connecting objects to words in order to communicate. However, people also group artifacts in other sorts of situations where the primary goal is not to communicate about an object. We now consider a range of other mental activities occurring in daily life that can reasonably be considered 'categorization'. For each, we discuss the laboratory tasks using artifacts that have the greatest resemblance to that particular activity, and we review findings from those tasks and implications of the findings.

3.1. Object recognition: connecting objects with stored knowledge

Perhaps the most frequent form of artifact grouping in daily life is making sense of objects encountered by connecting them with stored knowledge about objects. When someone walks into an office, for instance, and sees an object with a flat wooden surface, four legs, and drawers, he or she recognizes the relation of the object to previously experienced objects (and/or abstractions across them) having similar properties. Doing so allows the person to interpret the visual input in terms of the past experience, yielding an understanding, for instance, that the surface of the perceived object will be rigid and afford writing, that the drawers may contain paper-clips and stationery, etc. This recognition process goes on almost continuously, as people move about the world encountering and making sense of objects. In a familiar environment, much of the time the process will be one of connecting familiar objects with stored knowledge of the same objects (as in recognizing one's own desk, rug, armchair). Sometimes the process will be a matter of connecting a novel object with knowledge of very similar objects (or abstractions)—as for a not-previously-encountered chair of traditional design—and occasionally it will be a matter of connecting an object with more novel features to knowledge about objects that may be less similar—as for example, in an initial encounter with a chair in the shape of a hand or a chair made of rope that is hung from a ceiling.

Notably, this recognition process does not require engaging language. A person can appreciate the relation of a visual stimulus to stored knowledge without needing to retrieve a name for the object. This is amply evident from the fact that such recognition occurs in many situations where a name is not available for an object: an infant who has no word for a bottle nevertheless interprets the bottle offered to it by virtue of previously experienced bottles; a chimpanzee interprets a tree never encountered before by virtue of previously experienced trees (see Hauser and Santos, this volume, for discussion of artifact concepts held by non-linguistic animals); an adult human who is introduced to a novel object will recognize a second object of the same type as such without knowing a name for either. Indeed, even familiar, everyday objects are sometimes appreciated without being named. Many people discriminate several species of birds in their neighborhood without knowing names for them, and Malt *et al.* (1999) found that some participants had no well-established name for certain common objects, such as a plastic container of baby powder with a shaker top. When pressed for a name, participants resorted to phrases such as *a thing* of baby powder. To the extent that encountering a desk may tend to bring to mind the word *desk*, this word retrieval likely occurs as a *result* of having made contact with stored non-linguistic information associated with the word, rather than the word retrieval preceding and enabling contact with the non-linguistic information. Recognizing artifacts in the environment is thus an activity most centrally having to do, not with language, but with the processing of visual input and with memory retrieval and comparison processes.

A second characteristic of this form of grouping is that there are no boundaries to the groupings and hence no discrete categories to which the object belongs or does not (Malt *et al.* 1999; Sloman and Malt 2003). Any given object simply has a resemblance to each previously encountered object to a greater or lesser degree. For instance, a newly encountered wooden object for sitting on that has a round seat, four legs, and a low back will make contact with stored knowledge about various other forms of seating that it resembles, and some of those may have taller backs and arms while some have neither. The former may be called *chair* and the latter *stool*, if naming is required, but coming to understand the new object itself requires no choice between the two. A gradient of relevance to the novel object may exist, but retrieval of stored information across this gradient is not constrained by category boundaries.

3.1.1. Findings

3.1.1.1. Name appropriateness judgments

When psychologists studying artifact categorization talk about a person categorizing an object as a chair, or table, or desk, and so on, they often seem to have in mind the non-linguistic process of connecting an object in the world to stored knowledge of similar objects. However, perhaps because communicating about such processes almost inevitably involves using names—we talk about someone categorizing an object 'as a chair' or 'as a desk'—researchers typically have not discriminated between the non-linguistic process of interest and the process of naming. As a result, studies that may be designed to shed light on non-linguistic categorization often use the choice of a name as the dependent measure. They ask participants whether they would call the object a chair or a stool, a cup or a glass, and so on, and in doing so they conflate the process of selecting a name with the process of object recognition. We have already considered the large literature using name appropriateness judgments from the perspective of how naming choices are made, and have argued that understanding naming as it occurs in daily life requires studying naming as part of a linguistic and communicative system. Because this literature has, as we argued, tended to present naming choices in an impoverished context that does not fully engage this system, might it, in fact, usefully shed light on object recognition instead? Unfortunately, the use of names as a response measure and the failure to discriminate naming from the non-linguistic recognition process has led to a focus on issues that appear to be more relevant to naming than to object recognition. For instance, debates about whether form vs. function or current function vs. original intended function are more influential in determining name choice seem to have little relevance to understanding how an encountered object makes contact with knowledge about objects stored in memory. Furthermore, because the task requirement is to make a choice between discrete categories whereas object recognition requires no such choice, the task itself seems to have little bearing on the recognition process. The primary useful finding from this literature may be the notion we highlighted earlier, that people do not treat object features as independent pieces of information but rather attempt to understand the causal relations among them. This causal analysis is presumably relevant to appreciating the nature of an object non-linguistically, not only to choosing a name.

3.1.1.2. Similarity judgments

A frequent assumption in the literature on artifact categorization is that the task that most directly reflects the representational structure tapped by the object recognition process is similarity judgments. If perceived objects evoke stored knowledge by virtue of their features, then similarity judgments have the potential to reveal the basis on which a gradient of relevance for retrieval of that stored knowledge operates. (Similarity itself, of course, may also play a role in the groupings generated by other mental activities, as we will discuss later.)

When people recognize the relation of objects in their environment to stored knowledge of similar objects, they often do so without conscious awareness, and the end result is simply an understanding of the nature of that object. In laboratory similarity judgments, however, participants usually make deliberate comparisons of presented objects and provide an explicit judgment about their likeness. In some cases, similarity judgments are collected by presenting pairs of objects (usually in the form of pictures) and asking for a numerical similarity rating. In other cases, participants sort objects (again, usually pictured) into piles, and a measure of the similarity between each possible pair of objects is derived from the number of participants who sort them into the same pile. The extent to which making such judgments conscious, requiring an overt response, and having the judgments be entirely among physically present objects (instead of comparing an object at hand to stored knowledge of objects) alters the pattern of grouping indicated is unclear.

Two salient results have been obtained from judgments of artifact similarity. First, perceived similarity is remarkably constant across cultures, despite the variable naming patterns discussed earlier. When Kronenfeld *et al.* (1985) asked the same native speakers of Hebrew, English, and Japanese who produced divergent naming patterns for drinking vessels to sort them into groups according to their similarity, they found that the correlations among interpoint distances in multi-dimensional scaling solutions of the similarity matrices ranged from .81 to .89. Malt *et al.* (1999) had the same speakers of English, Spanish, and Chinese who produced divergent naming patterns for sixty common containers sort the pictures into groups according to their overall similarity. They found correlations among the similarity matrices ranging from .91 to .94. The high degree of consensus across cultures suggests that the featural analysis of artifacts is universal in nature (perhaps based on a universal causal analysis relating form to function, as suggested by the studies discussed earlier) as are comparison processes and will yield a shared understanding of the nature of objects.

Second, despite the consistency of similarity judgments (in parallel neutral contexts) across cultures, perception of similarity for any given population is not fixed across all contexts but rather is influenced by the nature of the comparison at hand. For instance, a given object A may be judged more similar to object B when in the context of object C than when in the context of object D. Medin, Goldstone, and Gentner (1993) found a variety of context effects on similarity judgments for stimulus materials that included some artifacts (see also Barsalou 1983, and Ross and Murphy 1999). Shiftings of perceived similarity based on the comparison objects themselves may be infrequent in actual object recognition, where the perceived object is compared to a relatively stable base of stored knowledge rather than to a small and deliberately varied comparison set, but it does suggest that the broader context in which the perceived object occurs may alter the gradient of relevance.

3.1.1.3. 'Object perception' tasks

A large literature examining how objects are perceived exists outside of that traditionally considered to be categorization research. This literature has addressed a range of topics including how objects are isolated from a complex visual scene, whether recognition is orientation dependent, what the relative roles of parts, outlines, and shading are, the effects of expertise, whether processing occurs at different scales, and whether different brain systems subserve perception of different classes of stimuli such as faces vs. objects. In doing so it has used tasks including word–picture matching, naming, old/new judgments, and familiarity judgments. Reviewing this literature is beyond the scope of this paper, but we note that it does directly examine some of the processes that are central to object recognition. From that perspective, this literature is better focused on issues that are genuinely about recognition. However, as the list of issues above suggests, and as the phrase sometimes used to label this field—'visual object recognition'—implies, the work has focused primarily on lower processes that are part of the initial visual processing that must take place in order for a percept to make contact with stored knowledge. As such it does not directly illuminate how stored knowledge about the properties of objects (beyond their visual features) is brought to bear on understanding the nature of a perceived object.

3.2. Induction

Another form of grouping is induction, in which people use information about one (or more) object(s) to infer properties of others. Induction is not a process that laypeople would be inclined to call 'categorization'. However, it depends crucially on judgments of whether and why entities are alike and as such can be thought of as a form of categorization.

One frequent situation in which induction occurs in daily life is in the recognition process. When someone recognizes the relation of an object with a flat wooden surface, four legs, and drawers to stored knowledge of objects sharing some or all of these properties, that recognition provides the basis for making inferences about properties not readily apparent. When visual input is interpreted in terms of past experience with the same object (e.g. viewing your own desk), and the perceived object is projected to have properties that are not deducible directly from the visual features (e.g. understanding that the surface is rigid and will afford writing, and that the drawers can open and will contain stationery), an inference has been drawn. Likewise, when there is no stored knowledge corresponding directly to the perceived object but it is interpreted by reference to stored knowledge of similar objects (e.g. walking into an unfamiliar room and viewing a desk never seen before), properties of the object are projected from experience with similar known objects. Induction that occurs during the recognition process is typically rapid and non-conscious, and the particular inductions generated are presumably a function of the memory comparison and retrieval processes that take place during recognition.

Induction also occurs in everyday situations in which the inductive process is slower and more deliberate. On a relatively infrequent basis, when recognizing objects, a person may encounter an object with quite novel features and engage in conscious consideration about the nature of unseen features, given knowledge of other objects. For instance, a person viewing an unfamiliar kitchen gadget that fits over the neck of a wine bottle and has a needle may infer that it is made for removing corks, based on familiarity with other forms of corkscrew. More often, the conscious projection of properties occurs within a learning context. When a person learns from external sources or discovers through direct experience with an object that an object has a property previously unknown to him or her, the person may conclude that certain other objects have that same property. For instance, if a person learns that the ink in her ballpoint pen has a certain chemical composition, she may infer that the ink in other similar objects (e.g. other brands of ballpoint pens) probably has the same composition. In such cases, the induction is from a single object to others, but inductions may also be from a group of objects to others. For instance, if a person learns that all waterproof inks have a certain substance in them, she may infer that the ink in her ballpoint pen does. In either case, the person considers what other objects might sensibly be considered to have the same property as the known one(s), given the nature of the known object(s) and other possible ones.

Names can be useful cues to the appropriate projection of properties, since objects that are labeled with the same name tend to share at least some properties in common. Much of the research on induction in the developmental literature has focused on how children make use of category names to guide inductions (e.g. Gelman and Markman 1986; Davidson and Gelman 1990; Gelman and O'Reilly 1988). Nevertheless, as with recognition, induction does not inherently involve language. One can project a property from one object (or a set of objects) to others based on beliefs about the nature of the objects, without reference to their names. Indeed, names are not always reliable cues to properties, especially for artifacts. The fact that baby bottles are made to be unbreakable does not imply that Coke bottles are. (However, it may imply that toddler 'sippy' cups are.) The essential demand in inductive situations is to draw appropriate conclusions about properties of objects that are not readily apparent, regardless of how they are named.

Although induction does not inherently involve language, names are, in fact, present in many inductive situations that involve learning because information transmittal often takes place via language. Rather than discovering new facts about an object through direct observation, people are often told of such facts. In such cases, an added demand to the task of projecting properties is the retrieval from memory of knowledge associated with the words. For instance, if someone is told that 'All carpentry tools are subject to a stiff tariff', in order for her to consider what objects might be subject to a stiff tariff, the phrase 'carpentry tools' must activate information in memory and cause retrieval of knowledge of particular objects or sets of objects. The objects retrieved may or may not be the full set of objects that could reasonably be called 'carpentry tools', and the particular knowledge about the objects that is activated may or may not be the same as the knowledge brought to mind when actually seeing or using such objects. Thus inductive situations that engage language add elements of memory and lexical access to the task.

3.2.1. *Findings*

3.2.1.1. What is the probability that object X has property Y?

A common paradigm in research on induction provides information to participants about the properties of one or more objects and asks them to decide whether another object would have that property, or what the probability is that it would have that property. In most research with adults, the objects are presented by means of words, as just discussed.

Sloman (1998) used this paradigm to investigate whether people would use class-inclusion relations in projecting properties. For instance, given information about a property of electronic equipment, and given agreement that stereos are electronic equipment, will participants agree that the property must be true of stereos? Sloman found, for artifacts as well as natural and social kinds, that people did not consistently follow class inclusion relations in their judgments. Instead, they agreed more often when the objects in question were typical (e.g. stereos) than when they were atypical (e.g. kitchen appliances) of the larger grouping. Sloman found that the effect occurred even when people verified that the named objects were electronic equipment shortly before responding to the induction questions. Although the paradigm in general raises the question of whether the effects obtained are driven by the limitations of memory retrieval in response to the linguistic stimulus, given that this effect occurred even after a recent probe for the information, this particular effect seems less likely to be due to memory retrieval problems upon hearing the phrase 'electronic equipment' than to a reasoning process in which people assess featural (similarity) relations between the set of objects in question and the set encompassed by the superordinate name.

Gelman (1988) used a variant of this paradigm that included pictures to investigate whether pre-schoolers and second-graders were sensitive to differences in the projectibility of properties across different groupings and property types. A child might be shown a picture of a rabbit and told that the rabbit likes to eat alfalfa. The child would then be shown other entities and asked if she thought the others also had the property. The child responded to four test items that varied in their relation to the standard in each case—for instance, another picture of the same rabbit (same name, same appearance), a different-colored rabbit (same name but different appearance), a dog (different basic-level name but same superordinate name—*animal*), and a telephone (different basic level and superordinate name). Half of the standards were artifacts (the remainder were natural kinds). Children showed an almost linear induction gradient across the four test item types, agreeing to the inference less often as degree of relatedness decreased. They also agreed to the property inferences somewhat more often overall for the natural kinds than for the artifacts, but properties concerning function were projected more for artifacts and those concerning substance more for natural kinds. This study provides an important illustration of the fact that induction patterns are not simply a reflection of naming patterns. Children did not consider all and only objects with the same basic-level name to share a property. Rather, children considered the nature of the relation of each entity to the standard and they projected properties based on this relation. They also considered the nature of the property in question along with the nature of the objects in judging whether the property should be projected to the test items. (The same conclusion is suggested by Mandler and McDonough's (1996, 1998*b*) work on induction in children under 2 years old, using an object manipulation paradigm; see also Mandler, this volume.)

3.2.1.2. Forced choice judgments

An induction paradigm used in many developmental studies and in some studies with adults presents a new fact about an object and then presents alternatives, of which one (or more) has one type of relation to the first object and the other(s) have a different type of relation to it. Participants are asked which is more likely to share the property. This paradigm has a similarity to the forced choice naming tasks discussed earlier, in that participants have no option to indicate that both choices might support the specified inference, or that neither does, or that other possibilities not given might be better than either choice offered. These studies can therefore indicate which of two specific options is preferred but do not indicate whether both choices might be acceptable, or what the most likely object to project the property to given free choice would be. Davidson and Gelman (1990), following work by Gelman and Markman (1986) that used only natural kinds, showed children unfamiliar objects, half of which were artifacts, and test objects that either shared a name with the standard or were perceptually similar. They found that the value of names in promoting inferences for children was integrally tied to the conceptual relatedness of the objects associated with the name: if the objects did not share substantial properties in common, children did not prefer inferences based on a shared name. Thus the power of names in these tasks appears to reflect the non-linguistic understanding of relations among objects. Children do not draw inferences based on shared names per se but rather on an assumption that objects sharing multiple observable properties will share unseen properties as well. Farrar, Raney, and Boyer (1992) found similar results using a paradigm more similar to that of Gelman (1988).

Ross and Murphy (1999) used a forced choice task to investigate whether food groupings of different types supported different types of inferences. The new properties they presented were either biochemical or situational, and the choices were between an object with a taxonomic relation to the first or a script-based relation. Thus, for instance, in the biochemical condition they asked: 'Suppose that an enzyme, metacascal, has been found in bagels in the country Quain. What food is more likely to contain metacascal: cracker or egg?' where 'cracker' is the taxonomic choice and 'egg' is the script-based choice. The situational property was that the object is used in an annual initiation ceremony. For the enzyme property, choices were primarily taxonomic, and for the ceremony, they were mostly script-based. Consistent with Gelman's (1988) finding contrasting artifacts and natural kinds, Ross and Murphy suggested that different types of groupings support different types of inferences.

In sum, although induction research using artifacts is limited in quantity, three central points emerge from it. First, people consider the similarity among objects in judging whether a property that holds true of some is likely to be shared by another. Second, they also engage in more sophisticated reasoning that takes into consideration both the nature of the property and the nature of the objects involved. Finally, the patterns of property projection indicate that induction is not constrained by the linguistic categories associated with objects. Instead, it is based on knowledge of the shared properties of objects and beliefs about whether they will share additional, unseen properties. Names are useful as guides to induction only to the extent that they are indicators of such shared properties.

A much larger literature on induction exists that is focused on natural kinds rather than artifacts (for a review, see Sloman and Lagnado 2005). Some of the central findings in this literature concern the role of similarity in driving inferences. For instance, given the premise that robins have sesamoid bones, people find the conclusion that sparrows have sesamoid bones more plausible than that ostriches have sesamoid bones, and they also judge robins and sparrows to be more similar than robins and ostriches. This literature also makes clear that when people reason about familiar objects and properties, they also engage in causal reasoning by attempting to explain the relations between categories and predicates. For instance, when told that a particular type of tree has a disease and asked if another tree will have that disease, people having high familiarity with the forest ecosystem may make a judgment based not on the overall extent of shared properties between the trees but rather on what the likely mechanism of disease transmission would be and whether the mechanism is likely to operate among the trees in question (see Medin *et al.* 2002). The findings discussed above suggest that people engage in a parallel analysis for artifacts.

3.3. Planning and problem-solving

People also frequently create groupings of artifacts in planning and problem-solving in daily life. Some of the groupings are formed in service of temporary goals (Barsalou 1983, 1991). When planning a trip to the beach, people may retrieve from memory knowledge of objects to take to the beach (a towel, a book, sunscreen, a drink); when considering a baby gift for a friend, they may retrieve possible purchases (a receiving blanket, a silver spoon, clothing, a mobile). Other groupings are formed in the service of enduring goals. In order to meet the goal of recycling properly, people may construct a mental grouping of all the types of objects they should not throw in the trash but should save for the recycling bin. In order to eat, people may maintain mental groupings of foods that are appropriate for breakfast, for lunch, and for dinner (Ross and Murphy 1999). Still other groupings may be formed for recurring as opposed to ongoing goals. For instance, people often need objects to contain substances or items. In each episode of need, they will retrieve knowledge of a set of objects that would suit the materials to be contained: round glass containers with wide mouths to hold the firefly their child caught; round and squarish plastic containers with lids to hold their dinner leftovers. Retrieval of appropriate knowledge for enduring and recurring goals may become highly practised and stabilized.

As with recognition and induction, knowing the names of the objects is usually incidental to formulating the thought or solving the problem. Retrieval may activate names associated with objects, and activating the names may be critical to communicating the thought or action plan to someone else, but the central demand of the task is to choose objects that will effectively serve the goal regardless of object names.

3.3.1. *Putting objects together that 'belong together'*

A laboratory task that has been little used in connection with artifacts is asking participants to sort objects according to what objects belong together (rather than on their similarity per se). This task presumably taps the more stable, practised groupings used in planning and problem-solving. Its infrequent use is perhaps because researchers are inclined to think that they already know what stable groupings people use—those labeled by common nouns such as *table* and *ball*. However, the set of objects labeled by a particular noun need not be the grouping used in any given goal-directed task, as our discussion indicates. Some stable groupings may have no single word name, and some single words may label a diverse set of objects only some of which are relevant in the service of any particular goal.

Ross and Murphy (1999) provide one of the few cases of this type of sorting task using artifacts. They asked people to sort foods such as cereal, hamburger, and milk. They found that when instructed to, participants were able to readily form both groupings based on the composition of the foods (e.g. putting dairy products together) and groupings based on the role the foods play in daily life (e.g. putting breakfast foods such as cereal, eggs, and bacon together). When allowed to sort without direction, they spontaneously produced some groupings of each type. This outcome underscores the fact that the same objects can participate in multiple groupings having different bases and indicates that people may maintain such cross-cutting groupings in memory rather than having a strictly taxonomic organization of knowledge.

The sorting task as Ross and Murphy implemented it does differ crucially from natural situations in that there was no task context establishing a particular goal to be served by the groupings. Presumably if specific goals were induced, participants would tend to use whichever type of grouping best served the goal at hand.

3.4. Organizing novel information

Finally, people group objects when they are confronted with an array of novel objects and try to make sense of them by constructing groupings of entities sharing important properties. For adults, this situation arises relatively rarely but may occur when beginning to learn about a new domain. For instance, a person taking a job in an electronics company may need to learn about a large number of different electronic devices, varying in form and function, that she has never encountered before. This person seeks to understand the domain by constructing groupings of the devices sharing one or more properties. For children, being confronted with an array of novel objects in a previously unfamiliar domain may arise more frequently as they explore the world around them.

As with the other tasks we have discussed in this section, knowing or using names is not inherent in the process of organizing novel information. One can appreciate the shared properties among objects and form groupings without having names for them. Indeed, in cases of true discovery—for instance, a scientist exploring a distant land and encountering an array of insects or plants never before known to science—conceptual organization of the new entities must precede generating labels for the groupings. As with induction, though, in many cases language is a medium of input into the formation of groupings. The adult learner who encounters a new domain may not be left to create the groupings entirely on his or her own. He or she receives some input about appropriate groupings from other adults in the form of names for the objects and sometimes explanations of their properties or reasons for being grouped together. For young children, as well, the process of grouping the objects based on shared properties is often guided in part by input from adults in the form of labels and explanations.

3.4.1. 'Category construction'—creating groupings from arrays of novel objects

A number of studies in the general categorization literature have used a task that has been labeled 'category construction'. In this task, participants are given an array of novel objects that they are asked to place into groups in whatever way seems natural. The groupings are examined to determine on what basis they have been formed. This paradigm closely resembles real-world situations in which a child or adult is exposed to a new domain containing many unfamiliar entities and seeks to organize knowledge of them without external input. It differs from those real-world situations in lacking input from others in the form of labels or explanations about useful groupings, and in lacking a task goal to suggest what sorts of groupings might be most useful.

The bulk of studies using this paradigm have not used artifacts as stimuli. Because of the need to provide novel entities to group, many have used highly artificial entities as stimuli such as geometric shapes. In a few cases, the stimuli can be liberally interpreted as artifact-like. Ahn and Medin (1992), using starfish-like shapes that did not necessarily appear animate, found a strong tendency for people to base their groupings primarily on a single dimension (and add in anomalous exemplars at the end). Regehr and Brooks (1995) tested sorting of various shapes under a variety of conditions and found a bias toward one-dimensional sorts but that more sorting based on multiple dimensions occurred when participants did not see all the stimuli at once, and when they did see them all at once but alternated which group they were adding to rather than building one in its entirety and then the other. Wattenmaker (1992) used verbal stimuli consisting of four features, including some describing artifacts, and found a heightened tendency for people to rely on a single dimension when they were making groups based on memorized rather than physically present stimuli. These results are compatible with previous studies using non-artifact stimuli (e.g. Medin, Wattenmaker, and Hampson 1987) demonstrating a bias toward one-dimensional sorts, but they also indicate that the attentional demands under which participants construct the groupings influence whether they attend to multiple dimensions or just one.

Other studies suggest that sorting strategies are influenced by the knowledge base that is engaged by stimuli. Lassaline and Murphy (1996), using stimuli that included artifacts, found that participants were more likely to create multi-dimensional sorts when their attention was first drawn to feature correlations within the stimulus set by answering induction questions (e.g. 'If a vehicle has bench seats, what kind of top does it have?'). Kaplan and Murphy (1999) found that multi-dimensional sorting increased when stimuli could be related to familiar 'themes' (e.g. arctic vehicle vs. tropical vehicle). Ahn (1999) provided background information about stimuli by manipulating whether the features of the prototypes were described as all having the same cause, or all as causing the same effect, or whether the features are related in a causal chain (one causes the second which causes the next, and so on.) Participants were more likely to create multi-dimensional sorts when they had causal knowledge that allowed them to construct explanations of feature variability (i.e. the common cause and common effect conditions; the causal chain provides no explanation for feature variability because each feature predicts a fixed other feature). Category construction tasks thus show that people have a tendency to group objects along a single dimension in laboratory tasks but that they may group based on multiple similarities under some circumstances. They also show that when provided with richer stimuli and information about causal relations among their features, people make use of this information to create groupings that overlap on multiple dimensions.

3.5. Implications of data on conceptual (non-linguistic) categorization

The aggregate data from the laboratory tasks that are not centrally about connecting objects to words, along with our analysis of task demands, highlights several facts about non-linguistic groupings. First, the perception of similarity is an important influence in determining the groupings. The empirical evidence explicitly implicates judgments of similarity in the projection of properties. But our analysis of task demands suggests that it must also be involved in other forms of non-linguistic grouping, influencing what stored knowledge is retrieved in interpreting objects encountered in the environment, what objects will be grouped together in the course of planning and problem-solving, and what objects will be grouped together in making sense of novel domains. Second, analysis of the causal relations among properties of artifacts occurs in these non-linguistic tasks (as it appears to in naming tasks), and, further, in tasks that involve conscious reasoning (as in the more deliberative instances of induction), causal reasoning about the relation of properties of one object to properties of another may take place. Third, despite these common components, the groupings produced in each case are not necessarily the same. This fact derives, in part, directly from the varying demands of each type of mental activity. The previously experienced objects that will be most useful in interpreting an encountered object will not necessarily be the same as the set of objects to which one might project a particular property of the encountered object, nor will it be the same as the set of objects it might be grouped with to serve some temporary goal, or to organize knowledge of the domain if the entire domain is novel. The difference in groupings also derives, more indirectly, from the flexibility of perception of similarity given such differing task demands. The data show that under parallel task demands, people from different cultures speaking different languages nevertheless share perception of commonalities among artifacts, presumably because they all understand the object properties and their causal relations to one another in the same way. However, the data also demonstrate that what properties are most relevant to the judgment of commonalities varies depending on the task demands. As our analysis makes clear, different mental activities that involve grouping artifacts non-linguistically do make distinct demands.

The relative scarcity of data using artifacts in such tasks, though, and the rather loose connection of the tasks to instances of categorization in daily life, indicate that there is much left to learn about the nature of artifact groupings that are formed in the course of the mental activities that can be considered conceptual categorization.

4. GENERAL DISCUSSION

In our analysis so far, we have identified five types of mental activities occurring in daily life that can be thought of as categorization and considered the requirements of these activities. We have reviewed laboratory tasks that have been used to shed light on categorization, discussed the relation of the requirements of these tasks to those of the activities of daily life, and reviewed findings from those tasks. We now consider what has been learned about the nature of artifact categorization from the research reviewed, and we draw out the larger implications from our analyses for what the study of categorization should look like.

4.1. The good

A number of important findings have accumulated from categorization research. We have already summarized the central findings about different forms of artifact categorization and highlighted those we consider most valid. In the case of linguistic categorization, these include that the form of an object, its original intended function, its current function, and its intended category membership may all influence judgments of name appropriateness. In addition, people actively seek to understand the causal relations among features of an object and they consider how the relations relate to that of typical objects associated with a name when they judge name appropriateness. When naming freely, short-term variables influence choices including what names have recently been retrieved from memory and what name for an object has been agreed upon with a conversational partner or appears to be the name the object's creator has in mind. Longer-term historical variables also contribute to naming choices; these establish what names are available for objects and what the preferred pattern of assignment of names to objects within a domain is.

In the case of non-linguistic categorization, several findings also stand out. To the extent that explicit similarity judgments reflect the kind of similarity gradients that must operate in recognition, it can be concluded that what will be perceived as similar in the recognition process is stable across cultures when the context of judgment is similar, but that context may shift what objects are seen as most similar to each other. In induction, the groupings reflected in patterns of property projection are influenced by the similarity among objects and by reasoning processes that take into account the nature of the properties and objects involved; names are a useful guide to appropriate projections but only to the extent that they are understood as indicators of shared properties among the objects. In planning and problem-solving, the same sets of objects may be grouped in different ways depending on the goals and contexts of the situation. In organizing novel information, people draw on their understanding of the causal relations among objects to create groupings of objects that overlap on multiple dimensions.

From these findings, several more general conclusions also emerge. Each has already been noted in the context of non-linguistic grouping tasks; considering them in conjunction with the findings on linguistic categorization makes clear the generality of the phenomena. One general theme is that similarity is a crucial contributor to most or all forms of groupings. We have discussed its involvement in all the variants of non-linguistic grouping. It appears to play a role in determining how perceived objects are connected with stored knowledge, how properties are projected, how novel information is organized, and what groupings are constructed to serve goals in planning and problem-solving. In the case of naming, although cross-linguistic differences in naming patterns are striking, we also noted a degree of cross-linguistic consistency that is presumably driven by a shared perception of similarity among objects.

A second general theme is that the analysis of causal relations among the properties of artifacts occurs spontaneously and is a fundamental part of people's appreciation of the nature of the artifacts. Causal analysis influences people's choice of names and also their grouping behavior in non-linguistic tasks such as property projection and grouping novel stimuli.

Finally, a third theme emerges from contrasting the nature of the groupings that arise in each of the five types of mental activities, and that is that the particular groupings formed vary substantially according to the activity involved. For instance, linguistic categories do not map directly onto the groupings involved in induction. Groupings formed in the service of a particular goal may have little to do with the way that objects from the same domain would be grouped when making sense of them as a novel array.

Can these findings, then, in some way be integrated to begin to provide a truly general and complete theory of artifact categorization? We first review what we consider weaknesses of the research on artifact categorization, and then ask whether a more careful approach will solve the problems and permit development of a unified theory of categorization.

4.2. The bad

Although some useful findings have resulted from the categorization research we have reviewed, we believe that other arenas of investigation have been less fruitful. In particular, findings in some cases have accumulated from paradigms that do not map well onto the nature of the mental activities in which grouping takes place in daily life. If the demands of the research task are substantially different from those of the grouping task in daily life, results from the task are unlikely to be useful in shedding light on the mental activities of interest.

Results from the highly studied forced choice version of name appropriateness judgments are a major case in point. As we have pointed out, explicit name appropriateness judgments are rare in the real world, and so a task that requires this sort of judgment is not likely to capture the nature of most naming. In particular, because of the demands of this task, it is likely that any factor manipulated in controlled contrasts will show an effect. The paradigm requires that participants always choose between two options somehow. Although random responding could occur, a cooperative participant responding to the experimental demand for a judgment is likely to seek some systematic basis for choosing. If an experimenter were to present named objects having particular colors and sizes, and then present test objects having the color associated with one label and the size associated with the other, participants would most likely select either color or size as the basis for their responses rather than respond at random. If a consistent choice emerged across participants, that would suggest that participants see the chosen dimension as more important to naming than the other. However, it would not indicate that the dimension chosen is the sole basis for naming decisions outside of the experimental context. Further, it might not even indicate that one dimension is given more weight outside of the forced choice contrast. For instance, participants may treat function as more important than form in making the explicit judgments because they feel they can justify a judgment based on function more easily than one based on form. In natural naming situations, though, choices may be pushed in one direction or the other by factors outside of the speaker's conscious awareness. Indeed, the free naming observations we have discussed suggest that the preference for function over form that has tended to show up in forced choice data is not mirrored by natural name extension patterns.

Of course, as we pointed out earlier, it is not clear that researchers using name appropriateness judgments are always interested in naming in particular. They do not necessarily talk of 'naming' but rather simply 'categorization'. This raises the question of whether name appropriateness judgments may, instead, be useful as a task for tapping the groupings that are demonstrated in the course of understanding objects encountered in the environment by reference to stored knowledge. As we argued, the task seems poorly suited for studying this form of grouping activity because it requires a choice between names, whereas recognition does not involve choosing between discrete categories. In addition, because the task measure is a name choice, whereas recognition does not inherently involve language, it can at best be a somewhat second-order reflection of the processes involved.

But the tendency of researchers who use name appropriateness judgments to often talk about 'categorization' rather than 'naming' as the issue of interest highlights the somewhat schizophrenic nature of much research on artifact categorization. On the one hand, methodologically, the research treats names as if naming is what categorization is about—that is, the dependent measure is what name an object is judged to have. On the other hand, the discussion that introduces the issues and tasks used is typically not about how objects are named. It is divorced from any considerations of the communicative function of naming, how reference is achieved, how languages evolve patterns of name extension, or the like. Likewise, the tasks themselves rarely are designed to engage naming in any natural sort of discourse context. The primary interest often appears to be something about how objects are grouped non-linguistically: how objects are put into 'categories'. Name choices clearly are attractive as a dependent measure because they provide a tractable overt behavioral response. Nevertheless, we propose that if the issue of interest is not naming, other sorts of measures are necessary. In particular, if the question at hand has to do with how people understand an encountered object by reference to stored knowledge, then the response measures need to be ones that are revealing of how visual input is processed and how memory retrieval and comparison processes operate.

We noted earlier that forced choice judgments about induction—for instance, asking participants whether they prefer to generalize a property to an object that shares a name with the standard or that shares perceptual features with it—have some of the limitations of forced choice naming judgments in that they require the participant to choose one option, when generalizing to neither or both might be reasonable given free choice. Like the naming paradigm, they can reveal the importance only of those options that the experimenter presents, and so run the risk of making especially prominent those factors that current theorizing specifies as of interest but that may not be most central to inductive judgments in general.

Also potentially problematic in the induction arena is the paradigm widely used with natural kinds as well as in some studies involving artifacts in which participants are asked to judge the validity of conclusions given a premise that is introduced verbally. If reasoning as it takes place when mediated by language is the issue of interest, then the paradigm may be well suited to the issue. If the question of central interest is, however, how people understand the nature of some objects by drawing on their knowledge of the properties of others, then introducing information about objects verbally adds demands—in particular, lexical access and retrieving information associated with words from memory—that may alter responses. Indeed, the type of inference about properties that takes place in the rapid, non-conscious appreciation of objects when encountering them in the environment is surely not mediated by language and operates in a distinctly different time-scale than the processes that are engaged when language is involved.

Other tasks that seem of limited value include sorting tasks intended to illuminate the groupings used in planning or problem-solving that do not specify goals or contexts for the sorting, and category construction tasks that do not allow the participant to engage any background knowledge or construct a causal understanding of relations of stimulus properties. Free naming tasks that involve no discourse context or communicative goal will also be less revealing of naming in daily life than those that do.

Finally, there is a large literature that we have not reviewed in this paper in which people are asked to learn to divide abstract patterns into groups and then are tested to see which group they believe a test stimulus belongs with. Because of the need to create novel stimuli to be learned, artifacts are not generally used in such research. However, this literature has the goal of understanding how categorization in general, presumably including artifact categorization, takes place, and so we note our concern with it here. Research in this tradition is not intended to be about naming; category designators are usually arbitrary labels such as '1' and '2'. The main concern in this literature appears to be with how a newly encountered stimulus is associated with stored knowledge; in our terms, with the object recognition process. We have argued that in daily life this process does not involve bounded categories, nor does it involve making any choices between groupings. The relevance of this paradigm to the process of interest thus seems quite limited, in parallel with our comments on the relevance of forced choice name responses for experiments using artifact stimuli.

Given that we have argued that a number of types of task commonly used to study categorization may not be good choices, one might ask whether there is a 'right' task to use. The answer to this must be 'no'. An essential requirement for a good choice of task is that it engages the processes that are normally engaged in the real-world activity it is meant to shed light on. As we have argued repeatedly by now, there is no single real-world activity that constitutes categorization. As a result, there can be no single right task for studying categorization. Many tasks may be appropriate, but their appropriateness can only be judged against a clear specification of what form of categorization is of interest. Is it how people connect objects with words, and if so, in the case of production or comprehension? Or is it how people understand the nature of objects in the world as they encounter them by making contact with stored knowledge and by drawing inferences? If the interest is in inference, is it in those inferences that may be drawn rapidly and non-consciously in the process of recognition, or in those that are drawn in more deliberative situations, perhaps when a new fact has been learned about one object? Or is the activity of interest what groupings people construct or retrieve from memory in the course of planning and problem-solving? Or about how people deal with organizing knowledge of a set of novel objects?

Little progress will be made if researchers treat 'categorization' as a topic of inquiry that needs no further differentiation or analysis. Selecting appropriate methodologies requires identifying what the mental activity of interest is and carefully analyzing the demands and constraints of that activity. Our suggestion is not intended to serve to champion ecological validity in experimentation for its own sake. Indeed, we believe that the purpose of an experiment is not to mimic the world but to explain it. Our point is that in order to explain, one must know what one wants to explain, and one must use methodology that will be revealing of the thing to be explained. In the absence of any common referent in everyday behavior, the class of 'categorization' tasks is itself artifactual.

4.3. The ugly

Thus far, we have been discussing the problems of choosing appropriate tasks to reveal the nature of the categorization activities of interest. But we believe that there is also a more profound problem for categorization research than the need for researchers to make explicit the form of categorization that they are interested in and select research methodologies accordingly. The deeper problem is revealed in the diversity of the groupings resulting from the different types of mental activity, reflecting the different demands and constraints of each type of activity. The problem is that the term 'categorization' does not carve the space of human endeavors at its joints. The sets of mental activities that can reasonably be called 'categorization' are diverse and operate in different ways to accomplish different ends. Indeed, in the traditional terms by which cognitive processes are organized in textbooks and allocated to journals, some of the mental activities we have discussed would be labeled 'higher cognitive processes' or 'thinking' (the conscious induction situations; planning and problem-solving; organizing information in novel domains), some would fall under 'language' (naming), and others would be considered 'lower cognitive processes' and given labels such as 'pattern recognition' or 'object perception' (what we have called 'object recognition' and the associated rapid, automatic inductive processes). These traditional labeling distinctions reflect the differing sets of issues that must be addressed in order to understand the processes involved. Thus we believe that there will not be any useful or coherent account that covers the various forms of mental activity involving grouping artifacts and sets them apart from other components of higher and lower cognitive processes. In other words, 'categorization' is not a coherent field of inquiry. We propose that it will be more fruitful to abandon the goal of having a general theory of artifact categorization and instead focus on understanding, each on its own terms, what people do when they produce and understand names for artifacts, when they recognize artifacts and draw inferences about their properties, when they draw on stored knowledge of artifacts in the service of plans and goals, and when they organize their understanding of a novel domain.

A second consideration also argues against the coherence of 'categorization research' as a field of inquiry. Underlying the notion of categorization research is the assumption that not only stable but bounded categories exist. Categorization researchers talk about objects being members of categories and people putting an object into a category. Such talk may be a result of the fact that both in ordinary discourse and scientific discourse about objects, communication about objects requires using names—we refer to an object as 'a chair' or 'a table'—and names impose discrete structure on continuous conceptual space. But we have argued that much of what researchers are interested in when they talk about 'categorization' does not actually involve bounded groupings. As we have discussed, understanding objects in the world by reference to stored knowledge is what researchers often seem to mean when they talk about categorization. Our analysis of what is involved in making sense of an object by connecting it to stored knowledge indicates there is no need to place the object in any discrete category in doing so. Likewise, there are no discrete boundaries that limit the projection of properties nor the set of objects that may be usefully grouped to meet a goal. Although we have at points followed tradition and talked about the mental activities that yield groupings of artifacts as artifact 'categorization', once the notion of fixed categories, and indeed of bounded categories at all (except in the case of naming), is discarded, then it is not clear that it makes sense to talk about artifact 'categorization'.

Of course, some cognitive processes surely exist that are common to two or more categorization tasks and that map onto some coherent psychological system. The data we have reviewed suggest that a comparison operator that carries out similarity judgments is one, and a causal reasoning system is another. Additional candidates include a perceptual integrator, a decision-making system, and memory storage and retrieval processes. All of these processes are worthy of study. But none of them is unique to grouping activities. Studying them across the different kinds of activities that they participate in may be more useful for the development of cognitive theory than focusing on their operation within only the set of activities that involve grouping.

4.4. Are there such things as artifact kinds?

Finally, we consider two issues that are raised by our arguments about the nature of artifact categorization. First is the question of whether there are such things as artifact kinds.

At the outset of this paper, we noted that psychologists talk of artifacts as coming in 'kinds', where kinds are taken to be stable, psychologically real groupings. We have argued that not only are the psychologically meaningful groupings not stable, but there are no bounded groupings in conceptual space except by virtue of names associated with objects. These arguments suggest that the notion of psychologically real artifact kinds is not viable (Sloman and Malt 2003). The intuition that artifacts do come in kinds, though, remains strong. For instance, in ordinary discourse, it is common to speak of two objects as being the same kind of thing. And such talk is not idle chatter; it usefully serves a speaker's goal of highlighting the existence of commonalities between the objects. Thus some account is needed of why the intuition of kindhood is part of ordinary discourse and what it means for objects to be the same kind of thing in these cases. Notably, however, providing such an account need not require a notion of artifact kinds that are stable and clearly bounded. In ordinary discourse, although it is often relevant to speak of objects as being the same kind of thing, whether any two objects actually are considered the same kind of thing may depend on the context and goal of the particular discourse taking place. A wooden kitchen chair and a beanbag chair may be called the same kind of thing in some circumstances (for example, if being contrasted with tables); on the other hand, the kitchen chair and the beanbag chair may be thought of as different kinds of things in other circumstances (for example, when a wooden desk chair and a wooden rocking chair are also salient in the context). If the goal is to find firewood, the kitchen chair and a broom-handle may be the same kind of thing. Under scrutiny, then, even the lay notion of artifact kindhood is flexible and task-dependent. Thus it may make perfect sense to talk about two objects or a set of objects being the same kind of thing, even while it is impossible to define stable groupings of artifacts that can be identified as the members of an artifact kind.

4.5. Given the considerations about the nature of categorization, what is a concept?

A final issue is what our arguments suggest for thinking about concepts. Much of the goal of research on artifact categorization is to reveal the nature of artifact concepts. That is, the grouping behavior that can be overtly observed is of interest because it is taken as an indication of the contents of a mental representation underlying it. Finding out what type of knowledge determines grouping choices is assumed to directly illuminate the nature of stable, coherent packets of knowledge that reside in memory.

Two aspects of our analysis create problems for this assumption. First, and most important, the fact that there is no unique segregation of artifacts into groups raises a puzzle. If there is no unique segregation of artifacts into groups, what grouping or potential grouping corresponds to something that should be called the concept?

Second, in the case of categorization as naming, factors appear to influence the groupings that names pick out that are not directly represented in individual language users' knowledge base. For instance, speakers of English label a stuffed seat for one person with the same name they use for a wooden seat for one person (calling them both 'chair') but speakers of Mandarin Chinese label the stuffed seat for one person with the same name they use for a stuffed seat for multiple people (although English speakers would call the latter 'sofa'), and the source of the difference may be longer-term historical factors rather than anything having to do with understanding of the properties of the objects by speakers of the two languages. Within a single language, the notion that uses of an artifact name may be extended in various directions on different dimensions also suggests that the knowledge associated with groupings picked out by names does not necessarily form a coherent packet (as in the case of a beanbag chair that is called 'chair' by virtue of a functional relation to kitchen chairs and an electric chair that is called 'chair' more on the basis of its form). The common notion in the literature that artifact concepts are packets of knowledge that map directly onto names, thus, in particular, does not appear to be a useful one.

One way to think about what artifact concepts are, rather than taking them to be stable, pre-packaged sets of knowledge that map onto names, is to consider them to be flexible and situation-dependent (e.g. Barsalou 1987; Barsalou and Medin 1986). That is, each time mental activities take place that result in a grouping of artifacts, one could say that a concept has been formed. This approach captures well the idea that the groupings formed in planning and problem-solving vary from occasion to occasion but constitute coherent packets of knowledge. However, it is less satisfying when thinking about the groupings picked out by names, which we have just suggested may not correspond to coherent sets of knowledge. And conversely, the groupings formed in the recognition or induction process may be coherent but seem not to fit the pre-theoretical notion of 'concept' that implies a packet of knowledge that can be consciously appreciated. It also violates the general intuition that a 'concept' should be something stable and resident in long-term memory.

An alternative is to more explicitly identify concepts with the knowledge retrieved when asked about the knowledge associated with the word. This version corresponds to the lay use of the term and captures the researchers' inclination to associate concepts with words. Thus, for instance, if a person is asked what her concept of chairs is, she will retrieve knowledge associated with the word 'chair', most likely having to do with four legs and a back and arms and being for sitting on. We may consider this knowledge the 'concept' of a chair. This knowledge likely reflects the properties most frequently associated with the word 'chair' and so constitutes a prototype associated with the word. Critically, it does not capture the full set of knowledge that generates the use of the word 'chair' across the full range of potential discourse contexts. Nor does it capture or delimit the range of non-linguistic groupings that may be formed from knowledge of objects that happen to be called 'chair' under other task demands. Thus under this definition of a concept, it is important to remember that 'categorization' is not just about 'concepts', and that an account of 'concepts' will not be derived from studying the range of mental activities we have suggested comprise categorization. By definition, though, it will capture packets of knowledge that are activated in the course of interpreting language and so have some psychological reality. However, it must be noted that the information retrieved by a word may vary according to the discourse context (e.g. Anderson and Ortony 1975; Barsalou 1982; Brauer *et al.* 2003) and so even then, there is no single stable concept associated with the word. And so it may be inevitable that a useful notion of concepts for theorizing about cognitive processes requires discarding the hope of identifying stable packets of knowledge and embracing the construction of concepts in the context of a task.

4.6. Summary and conclusion

We have discussed the variety of distinct mental activities that people engage in in daily life that can reasonably be considered 'categorization'. We have analyzed the cognitive demands of each activity and considered how these activities relate to tasks used in research on categorization. We have argued that the tasks used often do not map well onto the activities of daily life that they are meant to shed light on. As a result, although some of the existing findings from research on categorization are useful for understanding one or more of the mental activities we identify as categorization, others are unlikely to contribute usefully. We suggest that given the distinct nature of the activities that involve grouping artifacts, each must be understood on its own terms. Further, because the term 'categorization' does not carve the space of human endeavors at its joints, we suggest that no coherent account of artifact categorization is possible, and 'categorization' is not a coherent field of inquiry.[3]

---

[3] We thank Debby Kemler Nelson, Art Markman, and Greg Murphy for helpful comments on an earlier version of this chapter.

7

Seedless Grapes: Nature and Culture

Dan Sperber

A fruit is the mature ovary of a plant. Its main biological function is to ensure the protection and dissemination of the seeds it encloses. In the case of fleshy fruits, dissemination is achieved by attracting animals who eat the fruit, digest the sweet softer flesh, and either regurgitate or excrete the harder seeds at some distance from the plant. Humans, however, have evolved, through artificial selection, plants that produce seedless fruits, such as bananas, Thomson grapes, or Arrufatina clementines. Seedless grapes provide an arresting example of the more general issue I want to address in this chapter. Domesticated plants and animals have simultaneously biological, cultural, and artifactual functions. So do also human bodily traits used artifactually, for instance suntans. How should we describe these functions and their articulation? What are the biological and cultural functions of seedless grapes, or of suntans, and how do these functions interact? In trying to answer such questions, we are led to rethink the relationship between nature and culture, and to reappraise the notion of an artifact.

The notion of an artifact commonly used in the social sciences, particularly in archeology and anthropology, is a family resemblance notion, useful for a first-pass description of various objects and for a vague characterization of scholarly, and in particular museographic, interests. It should not be taken for granted that this notion could be defined precisely enough to serve a genuine theoretical purpose (see also Elder's, Grandy's, and Thomasson's contributions to this volume). When definitions are offered, they are based on prototypical cases. This is true of a dictionary definition such as *Webster's*: 'A usually simple object (as a tool or ornament) showing human workmanship or modification, as distinguished from a natural object.' It is also true of a philosopher's definition such as Risto Hilpinen's in his entry on artifact in the *Stanford Encyclopedia of Philosophy*: 'An artifact may be defined as an object that has been intentionally made or produced for a certain purpose. ... Artifacts are contrasted to natural objects; they are products of human actions' (Hilpinen 1999).

Such definitions leave us with a variety of problematic cases, for instance:

1. *Artifacts of which it is not clear to what extent they have been intentionally made.* This includes non-human artifacts such as spiders' webs, beavers' dams, and chimpanzees' termite-fishing sticks. It is of course possible to deny the artifactual character of items that one assumes were not made intentionally, and to say, for instance, that a spider's web is not an artifact whereas a chimp's stick probably is. More difficult are cases of artifacts that resulted from human action without having been clearly foreseen or intended. Consider an old path leading, say, from the village to the river. It started its existence and was maintained by villagers going from the village to the river and back, treading where others have trodden before, thereby marking the path in the landscape and making it easier for others to follow. Individual villagers may never have had any intention other than that of going to, and returning from, the river, but they nevertheless created a path. Is such a path an artifact?[1]

2. *Artifacts that involve no workmanship or modification.* Is a stone used as a paperweight an artifact? Is having been moved sufficient modification? If it is, what about a tree-stump used as a picnic table? If it is not, would, say, cleaning the stone before using it as a paperweight be enough?

3. *Non-standard objects.* Prototypical artifacts are middle-sized, spatially and temporally continuous material objects. Is a multiplication table an artifact, in spite of being an abstract object? Is a word? A queue in front of cinema is made with the intention that people should have access to the theater in the order in which they arrived. Is it an artifact in spite of its being just a temporary spatial configuration of people?

Many organisms, plants or animals, are used by humans for a variety of purposes; they generally show human workmanship and modification; they are artifacts by any reasonable definition, but they are not prototypical ones. Plants and animals used as artifacts provide problematic cases of the three kinds I mentioned. (1) Most of them are the product of artificial selection. Artificial selection, however, is far from being systematically intentional. To quote Darwin (in the first chapter of the *Origin of Species*): 'At the present time, eminent breeders try by methodical selection, with a distinct object in view, to make a new strain or sub-breed … But, for our purpose, a form of selection, which may be called unconscious, and which results from everyone trying to possess and breed from the best individual animals, is more important' (Darwin 1872, 26). Thus, many of the desirable characters of domesticated species were produced by human breeding practices, but were never specifically intended. (2) Some living

---

[1] Thomasson (this volume), argues that paths are not a kind of artifact, since not all of them were intentionally created to be paths. But what kind of artifact (if any) are those paths that were intentionally created as such? And what about (this is my point here) cases where the intention to create or maintain a path as a path played a marginal role in their creation or maintenance?

creatures are used as artifacts without having been domesticated. For instance, live leeches (*Hirudo medicinalis*) have been used in medicine since antiquity to let blood from patients. Being very well suited for this purpose, and being easily found in fresh waters, they were not bred (until very recently) and not modified by humans. (3) Plants and animals are, obviously, not the kinds of object that come to mind as possible artifacts. In particular, unlike prototypical artifacts such as hammers, they can hardly be contrasted to natural objects. In fact, they seem to blur the nature–culture distinction.[2]

Problems arise as soon as we ask of a biological artifact: What is it for? For common sense, the question 'What is it for?'—or, in a more sophisticated form, 'What is its function?'—can properly be asked of two classes of things: biological traits such as wings and thorns, and artifacts such as chairs, violins, and sugar cubes. These two classes of things are seen as disjoint and as having functions in two different senses of the term. They epitomize the contrast between nature and culture. Given that the two classes actually overlap, some conceptual house-cleaning is called for. For this, I outline a framework inspired by Ruth Millikan (1984, 1993), and drawing on earlier work with Gloria Origgi (Origgi and Sperber 2000). (See also Allen, Bekoff, and Lauder 1988; Elder, this volume.)

1. BIOLOGICAL, CULTURAL, AND ARTIFACTUAL FUNCTIONS

When one talks of function, be it that of a biological or that of an artifactual item, one is referring to an effect of this item (Wright 1973). The function of a biological feature is a *selected effect* (Neander 1991). A selected effect of a biological feature is an effect that has contributed to the reproductive success of organisms endowed with the trait and, thereby, to the propagation of the trait itself. Fleshy fruits have many effects: they add weight to the plants that hold them and sometimes break branches, they attract insects, and they attract larger animals that eat them whole and disperse the seeds, contributing to the reproductive success of the plant and, thereby, to the multiplication of the fruits themselves. Fleshy fruits have been selected in biological evolution to recruit animals for the dispersal of the seeds they contain. This effect is their function.

The function of an artifact, on the other hand, is an *intended effect*. Sugar cubes take up space in cupboards, add weight to the drinks in which they are dropped, and sweeten them. Sugar cubes are made and used in order to sweeten the drinks in which they are dropped. This intended effect is their function.

This classical dichotomy between biological vs. artifactual function (see Fig. 7.1) goes well with the common sense nature–culture contrast: on the side

---

[2] See also Bloom's, Elder's, and Grandy's contributions to this volume for similar considerations.

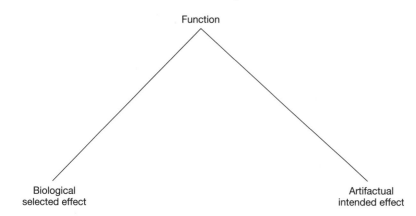

Figure 7.1. A classical dichotomy of functions

of nature, a mindless causality which happens—Darwin explained how—to give the appearance of intentional design; on the side of culture, the causal power of minds and true intentional design. This picture, however, is partial and misleading. Biological artifacts blur the dichotomy. Moreover, as has been argued by Millikan and others, biological functions are a special case of a wider category of 'teleofunctions', which includes not just biological but also cultural cases.

Often, the idea that not only biological traits but also cultural traits have teleofunctions is equated with the idea that Darwinian selection is not confined to the biological sphere and is also found in the cultural sphere. Dawkins in particular has suggested that culture is made of 'memes' and evolves through a process of Darwinian selection among these memes analogous to the selection of genes in biological evolution (1976). I agree that cultural traits have teleofunctions, and I agree that Darwinian selection is not confined to biology, but I don't think the two ideas should be equated. Darwinian selection is only one of the possible mechanisms through which populations of items may propagate and evolve. Darwinian selection operates among items that exhibit descent and heritability, that is, among 'replicators'. However, non-replicating items may also propagate. This is the case, for instance, when a behavior propagates through stimulus enhancement.

The opening of milk bottles by tits in Britain, a famous example of a non-human cultural trait, is now believed to have spread, not by imitation of the whole behavior, but by a disposition of tits to peck at what they see other tits picking at, and by each tit discovering for itself that pecking at the top of milk bottles was rewarded with cream. The spread of addictions among humans provides comparable cases. Tobacco addiction is triggered by the behavior of other smokers but is not inherited from them; rather, it owes many of its crucial features to a susceptibility to nicotine (a susceptibility that is itself biologically rather than culturally inherited, and, of course, inherited from non-smoking as easily as from smoking parents). I have argued in favor of an epidemiological approach to culture where infectious diseases do not provide the sole, and not even the main, analogy for the spread of cultural things: much of culture spreads like addictions rather than like viruses (Sperber 1996, 2000). These considerations are of relevance to an account of the role of biological artifacts (more so than I will be able to show here). This is why I propose a broad definition of teleofunction that applies not just to replicators, but to all 'propagators'.

Let us say that an effect of type F is a *teleofunction* of items of type A just in case the fact that A items have produced F effects helps explain the fact that A items propagate, i.e. keep being re-produced. (I am using 'propagation' as a synonym of repeated re-production, and 're-produce' rather than 'reproduce' to avoid the suggestion that new tokens of a type of items have to inherit all their relevant properties from previous tokens of the type.)

Typically, biological and cultural teleofunctions involve different kinds of items and different propagation mechanisms.

Items capable of having *biological teleofunctions* are phenotypical features of organisms (which may include not just bodily features but also behavioral features such as nest-building behavior in birds and outcomes of these behaviors such as the nests themselves—I am adopting Dawkins's notion of an 'extended phenotype'—see Dawkins 1982). The biological function of a trait helps explain the reproductive success (in the standard biological sense) of organisms endowed with this trait and therefore the propagation of the trait itself. The case of fleshy fruits is an example in point.

Items capable of having *cultural teleofunctions* are of two kinds: mental representations and public productions. Mental representations are constructed within agents by mental processes. By 'public productions', I mean both behaviors (e.g. speech) and traces of behavior (e.g. writings) that can be perceived and therefore serve as input to the mental processes of other agents. Public productions are guided by the mental representations of agents, and in turn may cause the construction of mental representations in other agents. It is through public productions that the mental state of one individual affects the mental state of another. Cultural items propagate through complex causal chains where mental representations and public productions alternate: mental representations of some given tenor favor the production of behaviors and objects of some given form, and these in turn favor the production of more mental representations of the same tenor (Sperber 1996).

Consider, as an illustration, mental representations of suntanned people as attractive and actual suntans (i.e. public productions). These are items of which it may be asked whether they have a cultural function, and if so, which. Before the Industrial Revolution, when poorer people were working outdoors and couldn't help being suntanned, pallor, then a privilege of the middle and upper classes, was seen as more becoming. In contemporary society most work is done indoors, and sporting a suntan is now evidence of leisure and travels, and is evocative of a privileged condition or at least of good times. This induces people to view a suntan as attractive, which encourages them to suntan, and so on, in a self-perpetuating causal loop. The teleofunctions of cultural mental representations (e.g. of suntans as attractive) and of cultural productions (e.g. actual suntans) are those of their effects that help explain the self-perpetuating character of the causal chains that propagate these representations and productions.

Teleofunctions are, by their very definition, effects of items that are produced again and again, the production of later items being caused in part by earlier items. The function of an artifact qua artifact, on the other hand, does not necessarily depend on its being a token of a propagated type. It just depends on its having been intended by whoever devised the artifact. A nonce artifact can be devised for some odd purpose: one might, for instance, fold a tree leaf as a tool for retrieving a ring fallen between two floorboards. Such an artifact could be causally unrelated to any artifact of the same type and nevertheless have a clear function, that of retrieving the ring. Another way of making the same point is to say that an artifactual function is an effect that explains why the artifact is being produced, whereas the teleofunction of an item is an effect that explains why this item is being re-produced.

Still, most artifacts are tokens of a type and are causally related to previous tokens. They are, that is, cultural productions. In other terms, most human artifacts are *cultural artifacts*. This is not surprising. Humans have to perform again and again very similar tasks, and the best way to do so is, quite generally, to take advantage of a type of artifact already devised and produced for this type of task. When an artifact is a cultural production, it has, as such, cultural teleofunctions. Token artifacts of the same type have repeatedly had an effect that explains why they keep being re-produced. What characterizes cultural artifacts is that one of their cultural teleofunctions and their artifactual function, that is, their intended effect, coincide. The fact that artifacts of a given type have in the past produced their intended effect causes people to expect such artifacts to produce these effects in the future, which causes them to make (or have made for them) new artifacts of the same type in order to produce the same effect. Thus new sugar cubes are being produced with the expectation and intention that, by dissolving, they will sweeten hot drinks (this is their intended effect) because sugar cubes have reliably had this effect in the past (and therefore this is also their teleofunction).

In the causal chain that explains the re-production of cultural artifacts, the intention that the artifact should have a specific effect and the mental representations and attitudes that cause people to repeatedly form such intentions play an essential causal role. These mental items may themselves get re-produced by the kind of causal chain I was evoking. In this case, they have a cultural function but, typically, they do not themselves have an intended effect or a purpose: they are not artifacts. Suntans are artifacts. They are produced with the intention of one's being perceived as an attractive person, and in succeeding in doing so, they cause their own propagation. The belief that suntanned people are attractive causes its own propagation through its behavioral effects. However, the belief is just believed. It is not held with the higher-order intention that holding the belief should cause some specific effect. It is a cultural belief with a cultural function, but it is not a cultural artifact.[3]

Ordinary, prototypical cultural artifacts are, I have suggested, characterized by the coincidence of two types of function: an artifactual function and a cultural teleofunction. This coincidence is, of course, found also in cultural artifacts of a biological kind. Leeches, for instance have the artifactual function of letting blood. This is the intended effect for which they are used. This is also the effect the use of leeches has produced in the past and which causes people to go on using them expecting the same effect. In other words, the artifactual and a cultural function of leeches coincide. Biological artifacts, being biological, have, on top of their artifactual and cultural functions, biological teleofunctions. Leeches feed by attaching their suckers onto the skin of other animals, cutting with some 300 teeth into the victim's skin. Their saliva contains substances that anesthetize the wound area, dilate blood-vessels, and prevent coagulation. The effective feeding of leeches by means of these complex effects has contributed to their reproductive success. These effects are biological teleofunctions. It is by performing these biological functions that the leech's feeding mechanism, applied on a patient's skin, performs its cultural/artifactual function of letting blood. So, in the case of a biological cultural artifact, we have not only a coincidence of artifactual functions and cultural teleofunctions, but also of these and biological teleofunctions of the biological item artifactually used.

Suntans are another example. A suntan is, to begin with, a biological adaptation. When the skin is exposed to sunlight, melanocytes found in the epidermis increase the production of melanin, a brown pigment that forms a protective barrier against sunburn and the carcinogenic actions of ultraviolet rays. The artifactual production of a suntan through deliberate exposure to sunlight or to artificial UV light exploits this biological mechanism. The resulting suntan has simultaneously its biological, its cultural, and its artifactual functions.

In general, the use of all artifacts exploits causally potent properties that exist quite independently of their artifactual exploitation. Thus paperweights exploit simple physical properties of heavy materials and sugar cubes exploit physico-chemical properties of crystallized sugar. Similarly, an artifact may exploit the

---

[3] In general, a belief is not an artifact from the point of view of the believers: it is not held for a purpose. From the point of view of suntan-lotion producing companies, however, the perception of suntans as attractive is something that they try to promote through advertising, with the goal of better selling their products. Hence, it would make sense to call the widespread belief in the attractiveness of suntans an artifact partly devised by these companies. More generally, the mental states of some people may be other people's artifacts. My hunch is, however, that pushing this line of thought would just, once again, show how confusing the notion of an artifact can be.

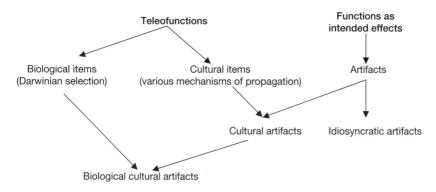

Figure 7.2. Functions and artifacts

biological properties of some biological item. Those which do so I call biological artifacts. Not all properties of a biological item are biological properties. An artifact may exploit just some non-biological properties of some biological material. In this case, it is not a biological artifact in the intended sense. For instance, an ivory paperweight exploits a physical property—the weight—of a biological item—a piece of elephant—but it is not an instance of a biological artifact. Biological artifacts, as I use the expression, perform their artifactual function by performing some of their biological functions.

We have now moved away from the simple dichotomy of functions illustrated in Figure 7.1, and have made and illustrated a number of finer distinctions schematized in Figure 7.2. Biological cultural artifacts are simultaneously artifacts, cultural items, and biological items. As such, they have artifactual functions, that is, intended effects, cultural teleofunctions, and biological teleofunctions. Their intended effect is identical to one of their cultural teleofunctions. That is, their past performance of their intended effect causes them to be culturally re-produced. This is what makes them *cultural* artifacts. Moreover, their artifactual/cultural function is achieved by means of the performance of one of their biological functions. This is what makes them *biological* cultural artifacts.

2. BIOLOGY AND CULTURE

The point of distinguishing different types of functions in biological artifacts and of describing their articulation is not taxonomic or descriptive per se. It is explanatory. The notion of a function is an explanatory one. A teleofunction is an effect that explains the propagation of items having that effect. The propagation of a biological artifact may be both a biological and a cultural phenomenon and it may call for a joint biological and cultural explanation. This goes against standard social science practice. For most social scientists, be they individualists or holists, explanations of social facts are to be given in terms of people's intentions and actions (for individualists) or in terms of social representations, institutions, and forces (for holists). All 'lower lever' causal factors involved, be they physical, chemical, or biological, are considered part of background conditions. Natural ingredients are seen as just part of the material to be taken into account and possibly shaped by psychological and/or social forces.

From the kind of naturalistic point of view I defend, there are only natural causes. Psychological and social causes, if they are genuine, are natural. In particular, intentions and other mental representations are biological phenomena with natural causal powers. They have a role to play in naturalistic explanations, but they hold no particular explanatory privilege. Any state of affairs is brought about by many and sundry causal factors. Which among these causal factors should be highlighted in a given explanation is a pragmatic matter. If, for instance, your ultimate interest is in establishing responsibilities, then, of course, you will give pride of place to intentions among causes. If, however, your interest is more scientific and you want your explanation of a phenomenon to be comprehensive, general, and contributing to a wider, integrated understanding of the world, then the causal factors you will highlight are those which, in the case at hand, best contribute to an explanation having these virtues.

In particular, when you want to explain the cultural character of a biological artifact, then you have from the start at your disposal two types of causal factors: the biological teleofunctions of the artifact, and its cultural teleofunctions. The fact that artifactual/cultural functions involve intentions whereas biological functions do not does not automatically make the former more potent, relevant, or explanatory than the latter. The issue, rather, is in each case to evaluate the causal role played by each type of function. By the definition of a biological artifact, its cultural function exploits its biological function. The issue is whether and to what extent, conversely, the biological function of a biological artifact exploits its cultural function, that is, is causally potent in shaping the propagation process.

Compare, from this point of view, the case of leeches and that of cereal seeds.

Leeches used for letting blood were enjoying their last meal (since once used they were destroyed). While their feeding mechanism performed its proximal teleofunction of feeding the animal, it did so in conditions where more distal functions, such as keeping the leech healthy, and, ultimately, contributing to its reproductive success, were forever thwarted. The artifactual usage of leeches exploited properties of their feeding mechanism that are explained by its biological functions, but it did not serve these biological functions. It did not contribute to a greater reproductive success of leeches particularly well-suited for blood-letting and did not therefore result in the evolution of an artificially selected species of leeches. In the absence of a positive feedback of the artifactual usage of leeches on their reproductive success, there is no co-evolutionary story between the biology of leeches and their cultural usage. In such a case, the biological function is just an opportunity provided by nature and artifactually exploited. It can be treated as a background factor in the explanation of the cultural artifact, just as standard social science would have it. Are leeches, in this respect, typical biological artifacts? Not at all.

One of the biological functions of seeds is the dispersal and reproduction of the plant. Dispersal can be achieved, in different species, by wind, water, or animals. Shape, size, color, smell, placement on the plant, may play a role in animal dispersal of seeds, which is done in a wide variety of ways. Arguably, the best animal agents of dispersal ever recruited by seeds are humans. In the case of cereals, for instance, humans use the seeds primarily as food. When, some 13,000 years ago, humans started cultivating, rather than merely collecting, barley and wheat, they found a second use for seeds, namely the sowing of the plant where and when they wanted. In other terms, humans were starting to use seeds as a biological artifact to perform the seed's main standard biological function: the dispersal and reproduction of the plant. The ancestors of wheat and barley could, at that point, evolve in two directions. They could stay, or become, less attractive as food for humans, hard to collect and to process, less palatable; by so doing they would be spared having most of their seeds eaten by humans (but of course, seeds have other predators) and they would go on reproducing as they had before attracting human attention. Or they could evolve so as to become more attractive to humans, with bigger, more nutritious grains, with more solid stalks to make collecting the grains easier (whereas the easily broken stalks of wild cereals are better for natural dispersal), and so on, and count on humans to make sure that the seeds retained for sowing would be properly protected until the right time, sown in the best possible soil, given the right amount of water, and so on. Cereals that evolved in this second fashion did much better than the wild varieties, by securing human help. Today they cover a significant proportion of fertile lands.

Of course, the story of the evolution of cultivated cereals can be, and generally is, told from the human point of view: by artificial selection, humans engineered the kind of cereals they wanted, and invested in their cultivation the efforts they deemed worthwhile. Seen from this point of view (and, after all, only humans have a point of view, plants don't), the cultivation of cereals is not so different from the fabrication of stone or metal tools: humans take advantage of opportunities provided by nature. There are, however, a number of objections to such an account. Artificial selection is a variety of natural selection: it creates an environment in which evolving traits desirable to humans increases fitness. In particular, it can be quite advantageous for a plant to have a large proportion of its seeds used by humans as food, provided that the remainder of the seeds serves the goal of reproduction and dispersal in a particularly efficient way. When this became the case for various species of cereals, feeding humans became a biological teleofunction of the seeds, that is, an effect that contributed to the greater reproductive success of varieties of cereal providing better food. Both the feeding function and the reproduction function of seeds are simultaneously biological and cultural/artifactual functions of cultivated cereal. The plants take biological advantage of their cultural functions and humans exploit culturally, and more specifically economically, some of the biological functions of the plants. There has been a co-evolution of the plants and of their cultural role. Human culture has adapted to cereal biology just as cereals have adapted to human culture.

Moreover, as Darwin's quote at the beginning of this chapter reminded us, artificial selection has been, for a large part, unconscious. Artificial selection is selection for traits that may turn out to be desirable to humans, whether or not they have actually been foreseen, desired, and planned by humans. Many artificially selected traits have emerged unforeseen and have seduced humans, shaping human taste and guiding human economic behavior. Here are a couple of further illustrations.

Human mental states are altered by the consumption of cannabis because it is the biological function of one of its chemical components, tetrahydrocannabinol (THC), to alter the mental states of animals.[4] This proximal effect has normally the more distal function of protecting the plant from animal consumption. To put it more graphically than accurately (since how this normal function exactly works is a matter of speculation), the animals become quickly too stoned to go on bothering the plant. In the human case, this psychotropic effect actually causes rather than impedes consumption. This, however, contributes to the reproductive success and the evolution of the plant, the propagation of which becomes actively pursued by humans. As a result, THC has now the additional biological function of causing pleasure and addiction in humans, which contributes to explaining the propagation of the plant, and is evolving towards an ever better fulfillment of this function. Of course, here too, it remains possible to tell the story from a human intentional perspective, treating the biological properties of cannabis as mere background: humans stumbled on the psychotropic properties of cannabis, liked them, and started cultivating and modifying the plant to suit their taste. In this story, the taste for cannabis and its motivating power are treated as mere givens. A more comprehensive story would provide a biological explanation of the taste for cannabis and a co-evolutionary account of the biological evolution of cultivated cannabis and of its cultural role. Of course, in this story, only humans have a genuine interest and point of view, but both humans and plants have causal powers and these powers interact with comparable weights.

Domesticated dogs (*Canis familiaris*) may seem to provide a paradigmatic illustration of humans' ability to modify other living kinds and turn them into artifacts.[5] Out of a single species, humans have, to suit a variety of purposes, bred hundreds of quite different breeds: pointers, retrievers, other hunting dogs, terriers initially bred to dig out burrowing rodents, pit-bulls bred to fight each

---

[4] For this example, I am drawing on Pollan 2001.
[5] For this example, I am drawing on Budiansky 2000.

other in pits, shepherds, watchdogs, toy dogs, and so forth. However, this complacent picture of human control of canine nature does not withstand scrutiny. The archeological record and genetic evidence suggest that, many thousands of years before humans began taking advantage of dogs, the ancestors of dogs began taking advantage of humans, hanging around their camps as scavengers (as still do 'village dogs' in many parts of Africa). Dogs' ancestors even began evolving from regular wolves to a new species adapted to life in the vicinity of humans. In particular, they began modifying expressive behaviors involved in their own social life in a way that would elicit sympathetic interpretations on the part of humans. As Budiansky (2000, 29) writes: 'We can't help seeing a humanlike purpose in the things around us. Thanks to the wolf social structure, dogs were prewired in many ways to exploit this foible of ours to a tee.'

Dogs evolved so as to cause their acceptance by humans. Domestication was the crowning of this evolutionary process and started a co-evolutionary process between canine biology and human culture. In this co-evolution, the reproductive success of dogs was extraordinarily well served. There are approximately 100,000 wolves left in the world, while dogs may be a thousand times more numerous. As a result of domestication, some dogs have had to work hard, but many others have enjoyed a life of leisure. In contemporary society in particular, dogs exert a degree of control over the lives of their owners that is comparable to, and often higher than, the control that owners exert on them. Dogs impose their tastes in food, their daily rhythms, their preference for cozy places in the house, their noisy and dirty habits. They are fed, washed, walked, and taken to the vet when needed, and have very little to do in return. Humans may feel that they are getting from their dogs just what they want and that the costs involved are well worth it, and, surely, if they say so, then it is so. However, human wants themselves have been and are manipulated by dogs, or, if 'manipulated' is too intentional, have been altered by the biological evolution of dogs and are stimulated by dog behavior to suit dogs' own wants.

Biological artifacts are cultural things, that is, they propagate in the human environment as an effect of human thought and action. Their propagation, however, is not achieved by a cultural copying process, but by the cultural exploitation of biological reproduction. In other words, their cultural functions are achieved, at least in part, through the achievement of their biological functions. These biological functions are, at least in part, adaptations to the human cultural environment. The seedless grapes of the title illustrate this last point perfectly. They don't serve the standard function of fleshy fruit to recruit animals for the dispersion of seeds, since they are seedless. They might seem, then, to be just artifacts serving the cultural purpose of facilitating the consumption and digestion of table grapes and raisins. However, this would miss the novel biological function that grapes have evolved in the human environment. Just as cereal seeds, grapes have evolved the function of attracting humans as food and thereby securing their involvement in the plant's reproduction. In the case of cereal, this is done by a percentage of the seed being kept and used for sowing. Grapes, however, are generally propagated not by sowing but by means of cuttings or grafts. Their seeds have, on the whole, lost their original biological function. Worse, seeds go against the new biological function of attracting humans. Seedless grapes, then, have a reproductive advantage over seeded varieties of table grapes: they are better at recruiting humans for their own reproduction. Their most cultural trait—their seedlessness—is also an optimal biological adaptation.

3. CONCLUSION

The fact that biological artifacts don't immediately come to mind as instances of the category of artifacts is rather puzzling. Biological artifacts are very common. After the Neolithic revolution some 13,000 years ago, and until the industrial age, they were the most common artifacts in the human environment. Most people had more domesticated plants and animals than tools, clothes, weapons, furniture, and other inert artifacts. Why should, then, the notion of an artifact be psychologically based on a prototype which is not all that representative? Why couldn't we, at least, have two prototypes of artifacts (as we have two prototypes of birds, one sparrow-like, the other eagle-like)? Maybe because, during the long Paleolithic era, simple inert tools were the only artifacts humans had. If there is some innate basis for our notion of an artifact, it probably evolved in an environment where stone tools were indeed prototypical, and a mere 13,000 years with domesticated plants and animals around was not sufficient to displace this mental habit. Moreover, for urban populations, especially after the Industrial Revolution, if not exactly inert, then at least lifeless objects became, for a second time, the most common artifacts.

We are now, however, in the middle of two technological revolutions which will again change the picture. The information technology revolution is progressively furnishing our environment with artifacts that are not only active, like a number of artifacts of the industrial age already were, but that are also interactive and endowed with information-processing capacities. Computers, robots, and their software are no more prototypical artifacts than cannabis and dogs. Their evolution won't be that of human intentions realized in some inert material, they and humans will co-evolve. The biotechnological revolution, with direct manipulation of genes, may, on the other hand, render biological functions of biological artifacts less relevant to their cultural becoming (or differently relevant if genetic engineering ends up having major unforeseen evolutionary consequences). What all this suggest is that, in taking artifacts as a proper category for scientific and philosophical theorizing, we are being deluded by a doubly obsolete industrial-age revival of a Paleolithic categorization.

Here I have tried to cast doubt on the idea that a theoretically useful notion of artifact can be built around its usual prototypes: bracelets, jars, hammers, and other inert objects, or that it can be defined in a more systematic way. There is a continuum of cases between public productions that are well characterized by a specific purpose and others where purpose is unclear. There is also a continuum of cases between public productions that are wholly designed by humans, and others where humans exploit, with little or no modification, a pre-existing structure. Biological artifacts vary in the degree to which they serve a well-defined purpose. Even when they do, this provides at best only a very partial explanation of their complex structure. There is no good reason why a naturalistic social science should treat separately, or even give pride of place to, cultural productions that are both more clearly intended for a purpose and more thoroughly designed by humans, that is, to prototypical artifacts. In fact, I see no reason why a naturalistic social science should categorically distinguish cultural artifacts from other cultural productions.

8

How to Refer to Artifacts

Hilary Kornblith

In the 1970s, a consensus began to emerge about the mechanisms of reference for proper names and natural kind terms. As a result of the work of Donnellan (1966), Kaplan (1979), Kripke (1980), and Putnam (1975), a descriptions-based theory of reference was largely rejected in favor of a causal, historical or direct theory of reference. On a simple descriptions-based account, a speaker uses a name to refer to an individual when that speaker associates a description with that name, where the description uniquely picks out the referent. Thus, for example, if Mary uses the term 'George Washington' to refer to George Washington, she must associate some description with that term—perhaps 'the first President of the United States'—which uniquely picks out George Washington. Similarly, if John uses the term 'water' to refer to water, he must associate some description with that term—perhaps 'clear, colorless, odorless, tasteless liquid typically found in lakes and rivers'—which uniquely picks out water. It is undeniable that speakers often know some such description of the referents of their terms. The descriptions theory explained the ability of individuals to refer to objects by way of this characteristic knowledge.[1]

It is a consequence of the descriptions-based view, and one which was welcomed, that a speaker's semantic competence in using a term gives rise to analytic truths and thus the possibility of a priori knowledge. If Mary's use of the term 'George Washington' refers to whatever individual satisfies the description she associates with the term, and if the description she associates with it is just 'the first President of the United States', then the statement that 'George Washington was the first President of the United States' is a trivial analytic truth—it is just equivalent to 'The first President of the United States was the first President of

[1] This is, in some ways, misleading, for the knowledge that an individual or a kind has a certain property is trivialized by the descriptions-based account of reference in the case of the claims that the individual or kind satisfies the various reference-determining descriptions. What look for all the world like substantive bits of knowledge are, on such a view, turned into knowledge of trivial analytic truths.

the United States'—and it is thus knowable a priori by Mary.[2] Similarly, if John associates the description 'clear, colorless, tasteless liquid typically found in lakes and rivers' with the term 'water', then the statement that 'Water is a clear, colorless liquid typically found in lakes and rivers' is thereby analytic and knowable a priori.

The simple descriptions-based theory came to be rejected because of two problems,[3] which have come to be characterized as the Problem of Ignorance and the Problem of Error.[4] The Problem of Ignorance arises because speakers may succeed in referring to an individual or natural kind even when they do not know any non-trivial description which uniquely picks out the referent of the term. Thus, for example, John may know that Baudelaire was a famous French writer, but know nothing which picks out Baudelaire from Balzac, Dumas, or even Camus. Nonetheless, it seems that John may succeed in referring to Baudelaire when he uses that name. Similarly, Putnam pointed out that he knows nothing about what the difference is between beeches and elms; all he knows is that they are both trees. Nevertheless, when Putnam uses the term 'beech' he refers to beeches, and when he uses the term 'elm' he refers to elms. The fact that a speaker does not know a uniquely individuating description does not seem to prevent the speaker from referring.

Similarly, the Problem of Error arises because speakers may sometimes associate an identifying description with a name or natural kind term, and yet the individual or kind they refer to may not satisfy the associated description. If Jack's sole belief about Kurt Gödel is that Gödel discovered that arithmetic is inconsistent, then Jack has a false belief about Gödel, not a trivially true belief, as the descriptions-based theory would require. If John's sole belief about Camus is that he wrote *No Exit*, then he has a false belief about Camus, not a true belief about Sartre. As Putnam pointed out in great detail, we can only make sense of the history of science by rejecting a descriptions-based account of the reference of natural kind terms, because early on in the scientific understanding of various natural kinds, the descriptions associated with natural kind terms typically fail to be precisely true—in some cases they fail to be even roughly true—of the referents of those terms. Coming up with a true description that uniquely picks out the referent of a natural kind may be a hard-won intellectual achievement; it is not a precondition for a referring use of the term.

---

[2] Strictly speaking, what Mary knows a priori is that *if* Washington exists, he was the first President.

[3] There are other problems which have played a role here as well. For a useful recent overview of the issues, see Devitt and Sterelny (1999).

[4] David Chalmers's two-dimensional account of reference is an attempt to retain a version of a descriptions-based account in the face of the Problems of Ignorance and Error, but it is not at all clear that Chalmers's account is any more successful in dealing with these problems than is the simple account. For a good critical discussion of these issues, see Alex Byrne and James Pryor (2004). Moreover, insofar as the two-dimensional account sees no difference between the semantics for natural kind terms and the semantics for artifactual kind terms, it lies outside the scope of this chapter. The same is true of causal-descriptivist views.

Attempts to weaken the requirements of the descriptions theory seemed not to respond adequately to these problems. Thus, for example, the suggestion that reference is secured by whatever satisfies most, or a weighted sum of most, of the associated descriptions simply does not address the Problem of Ignorance. If an individual does not know any description which uniquely picks out the referent of a term, then *a fortiori* that individual does not associate a set of descriptions with that term such that most, or a weighted sum of most, of the descriptions uniquely pick out the referent of the term. In spite of this, such individuals do, it seems, sometimes succeed in referring in the face of such ignorance. Similarly, the Problem of Error is not adequately addressed by this move either, since virtually all of a subject's beliefs about the referent of a term may be mistaken.

If the reference of names and natural kind terms is not secured in the straightforward way in which descriptions theorists proposed, how then is it secured? The theory which began to emerge as a replacement for the descriptions theory has two parts: a theory of term introduction, or baptism, and a theory of term transmission. Let me begin with the theory of transmission. Once a name has been introduced, a speaker may acquire the term from another competent speaker merely by hearing the term and intending to co-refer with the speaker from whom the term was acquired. Thus, if Mary casually drops the name of Gödel into a conversation with John, then even if John knows nothing whatever about Gödel, he may use that name to refer to whomever Mary was referring to. Similarly, if John hears Mary mention molybdenum, he may succeed in referring to that substance merely by using that term, so long as he uses it with the intention to refer to whatever it is that Mary referred to in her use of the term. The ability to use a term to refer, whether that term be a proper name or a natural kind term, may be transferred from one speaker to another by way of a chain of intentions to co-refer. And it is for precisely this reason that the ability to use a term to refer to an individual or kind is compatible with both ignorance and error.

Such chains of intentions, however, cannot go on forever, and this is where the theory of term introduction comes in. A term is introduced by a speaker as a name for an individual, or of a kind, by way of a 'baptism'. Thus, Mary may name her newborn daughter Emily: perhaps she looks at her newborn daughter and says, 'I hereby name this child Emily'. In this act, the name 'Emily' has been conferred on the child. Other language-users may acquire the use of the name 'Emily' from Mary, or from someone who acquired it from Mary, and so on. But the chain of intentions to co-refer is now anchored in an act of attaching a name to an individual. Similarly, natural kind terms may be introduced into the language by a naming ceremony. Someone may, for example, on first isolating a certain chemical compound, assign a name to it. The term may then be transmitted to other users just as proper names are.

It is important to see that even in the case of the person who introduces a term, that person need not know a description which uniquely picks out the referent of the term. Thus, the person who introduces a name for a newly isolated chemical compound may have many mistaken beliefs about the compound (the Problem of Error) or simply not know enough about it to uniquely describe it (the Problem of Ignorance). The same is true of proper names. Beliefs about an individual to whom a name is assigned may be largely mistaken (the Problem of Error) or insufficiently identifying (the Problem of Ignorance). What then makes the name or term introduced a name for some particular individual or some natural kind? While discussion of examples has made a strong case for the view that descriptions associated by the speaker with the name cannot do all of the work of attaching a name to its referent, a complete account of how names are attached to referents is not currently available, although a good many promising suggestions have been made here. Even without specifying precisely what is required for an act of naming to occur, however, we have enough of a theory sketch here to present an alternative to the simple descriptions theory. (I should mention as well that the account of what is needed for reference transmission given above is also clearly too simple. More work is needed there as well. But, again, enough has been said to indicate that there is a kind of theory under development which provides an alternative to simple descriptions accounts.)

In 'The Meaning of "Meaning"', Hilary Putnam suggested that this kind of account of reference may be extended 'to the great majority of all nouns, and to other parts of speech as well' (1975, 242). In particular, Putnam argued that this kind of account of reference may be extended to the case of artifactual kind terms. But even among those who found the arguments for the new theory of reference persuasive in the case of proper names and natural kind terms, many found this attempt to extend the theory to cover artifactual kind terms unpersuasive. Stephen Schwartz (1977, 1978, 1980, 1983) argued early on that the mechanisms of reference to artifacts are fundamentally different than those involved in the case of proper names and natural kind terms: while something along the lines of the new theory of reference accurately describes how reference is achieved in the latter kind of case, a traditional descriptions-based account is needed for reference to artifacts. A similar view has been defended by Barbara Abbott (1989) and Amie Thomasson (2003; this volume). Michael Devitt and Kim Sterelny (1999) suggest more tentatively that reference to artifacts, or at least some artifacts, may operate in ways quite different from reference to individuals and natural kinds.

In this chapter I explore the suggestion that the mechanisms of reference in the case of artifactual kind terms might be different from those in the case of proper names and natural kind terms. I argue that there is no basis for such a distinction. The very arguments which support the new theory of reference in the case of reference to individuals and natural kinds work equally well for the case of reference to artifacts. While there are, beyond doubt, important metaphysical differences between artifacts and natural kinds, the mechanisms of reference are insensitive to these differences. A single theory of reference works equally well for individuals, natural kinds, and artifactual kinds.

1. REAL VS. NOMINAL KINDS: FROM METAPHYSICS TO SEMANTICS

Following John Locke, Stephen Schwartz draws a distinction between real and nominal kinds. Schwartz argues that artifacts have a nominal essence 'which, unlike real essences, are the workmanship of the understanding rather than nature' (1978, 572, n. 11). More than this: 'Members of a nominal kind do not share a common hidden nature, and we can give an analytical specification in terms of form and function of what it is to be a member of a nominal kind' (1978, 572). The metaphysical difference between natural kinds and artifacts, on Schwartz's view, is thus reflected in a difference in the semantics of natural kind terms and artifactual kind terms: 'It is clear that Putnam is correct about natural kind terms; his error has been in extending his analysis to nominal kind terms. On the other hand, followers of the traditional approach are correct about nominal kind terms, and their error has been in attempting to extend their analysis to natural kind terms' (1978, 574).

Now why should one think that the metaphysical difference between real kinds and nominal kinds—that the essential properties of real kinds are determined by nature, while those of nominal kinds are determined by the understanding—should be reflected in a difference in the semantics of terms referring to these kinds? Schwartz discusses a number of examples of artifactual kinds, and the examples he uses are highly suggestive. Schwartz talks at length about pencils, and he also mentions chairs and lamps. In the case of each of these kinds of objects, it is not implausible to suggest that competent language-users typically do associate a description with each of these terms which is sufficient for picking out the members of the kind. To a first approximation, for example, pencils are a kind of instrument used for writing, and this is something which every competent speaker of English knows. The features which determine kind membership here do not involve some 'hidden structure', but rather certain 'superficial characteristics that all pencils have in common', features having to do with 'form and function' (1978, 572). If all competent speakers of the language know descriptions necessary and sufficient for kind membership, then both the Argument from Ignorance and the Argument from Error are thereby undermined. The principal arguments against a descriptions-based approach to reference which work so well in the cases of names and natural kind terms are apparently ineffective when applied to terms referring to artifacts. Schwartz does not explicitly make this argument, but the examples he discusses are surely suggestive of this line of reasoning.[5] It will thus be worth seeing whether this kind of argument can support Schwartz's view.

---

[5] Abbott (1989) too makes remarks quite suggestive of this line of argument.

The examples of pencils, chairs, and lamps give Schwartz's view a spurious plausibility. It may well be true that competent speakers of English do know descriptions which are necessary and sufficient for picking out the members of these kinds, but it is not at all clear that this ability has much to do with the mechanisms of reference, and, more importantly, it is quite clear that this does not track a distinction between natural kinds and artifacts. Pencils, chairs, and lamps are ubiquitous, and, at least in our society, anyone who is paying attention will have come into contact with numerous examples of these kinds and will be, as a result of that experience, fully aware of what it is that makes something a member of these kinds. But this is not true of artifacts in general. Rheostats, buckboards, spandrels, and Chippendale furniture are all artifacts as well, but knowledge of the defining features of these kinds is not nearly so common. If one allows that, in the case of natural kind terms, reference may be secured merely by learning the word from someone who uses it to refer and then intending to co-refer with that person, it is hard to see why one should say something different in these cases. Thus, if I can succeed in using the term 'molybdenum' to refer to a kind of metal even if I know none of the defining features of the kind, it seems I should be able to do the same with 'rheostat', 'buckboard', 'spandrel', and 'Chippendale' as well. And if one wants to insist that, in the latter cases, one is only mouthing the word and that a certain minimal level of understanding is required if one is even to count as a competent user of the term, then the same claim is equally plausible in the case of natural kind terms. Some items are extremely familiar and others are more recondite; nearly everyone can, with just a little thought, provide at least roughly necessary and sufficient conditions for kind membership for many of the most familiar kinds of item. But the line between the familiar and the recondite is a matter of degree, not a difference in kind, and it cuts across the distinction between nominal and natural kinds rather than marking a difference between them. That many kinds of object are ones which competent speakers can, as a matter of fact, accurately characterize thus seems to tell us nothing about the mechanisms of reference; it is instead a by-product of epistemic capacities exercised in a friendly environment.

The Arguments from Ignorance and Error are successful in the case of names and natural kind terms because of what Putnam refers to as the 'division of linguistic labor':

> ... everyone to whom gold is important for any reason has to *acquire* the word 'gold'; but he does not have to acquire the *method of recognizing* if something is or is not gold. He can rely on a special subclass of speakers. The features that are generally thought to be present in connection with a general name—necessary and sufficient conditions for membership in the extension, ways of recognizing if something is in the extension ('criteria'), etc.—are all present in the linguistic community *considered as a collective body*; but that collective body divides the 'labor' of knowing and employing these various parts of the 'meaning' of 'gold'. (1975, 227–8)

What is clear, however, is that the division of linguistic labor is just as much a part of the world of artifacts as it is a part of the world of natural kinds and individuals. And this point by itself is sufficient to ground Arguments from Ignorance and Error in the case of artifacts which are exactly parallel to those which underwrite the new theory of reference for names and natural kind terms.[6]

2. ARTIFACTS AND HUMAN INTENTION

Amie Thomasson (2003; this volume) attempts to ground the move from distinctive metaphysical features of artifacts to a distinctive semantics in an interesting and subtle way. Drawing on work by Hilpinen (1992, 1993) and Bloom (1996), Thomasson argues that the essential nature of artifacts lies in the intentions of their makers. Thus, for example, if I build a chair, part of what makes it a chair lies in the intentions I have in producing it. Thomasson argues for quite a strong requirement on the intentions of artifact-makers:

Necessarily, for all x and all artifactual kinds K, x is a K *only if* x is the product of a largely successful intention that (Kx), where one intends (Kx) *only if* one has a substantive concept of the nature of Ks that *largely* matches that *of some group* of prior makers of Ks (if there are any) and intends to realize that concept by imposing K-relevant features on the object. (2003, 600)

This requirement that makers have a 'substantive concept' of the artifact they make is used by Thomasson to support certain theses about the semantics of artifact terms. In particular, Thomasson argues that the new theory of reference cannot be correct 'for all cases of reference to artifactual kinds':

It is supposed to be a virtue of causal theories of reference that they enable us to refer to a kind without the need for anyone to have any substantive concept of the nature of the kind, since the term's extension is determined by the natural boundaries of the kind, not by any of our beliefs or concepts regarding those boundaries.... Reference to artifactual kinds, however, cannot proceed without someone (namely, those responsible for the production and reproduction of these artifacts) having a substantive concept of the nature of the kind. (2003, 604)

Thomasson also draws out certain epistemological consequences of her account of the nature of artifacts. While she does not insist that artifact-makers have a

---

[6] Many authors seem to believe that the causal theory of reference requires some sort of robust realist metaphysics for kinds. As Stalnaker (1997) has pointed out, this misconstrues the structure of the argument in 'Naming and Necessity'. Kripke does not argue from a realist metaphysics of kinds to the causal theory of reference. Rather, the causal theory of reference makes room for the possibility of capturing realist intuitions about natural kinds in a straightforward way. The causal theory itself, however, presupposes no metaphysical view about kinds, and thus when we move from consideration of natural kinds to artifactual kinds, there is no reason at all to think that arguments for the causal theory of reference are in any way weakened.

priori knowledge of the nature of the kinds they make (a claim which would parallel standard descriptions-based views about reference), she does insist that artifact-makers occupy a privileged epistemological position:

> For strict kinds, the existence of anything of the kind K entails that there is a unified concept of Ks accepted by the makers. Moreover, that concept is protected from massive error, for [the requirement quoted above] ensures that something can be a K only if the intention to make something that meets the shared concept of K is largely successful, and thus only if the product largely realizes the concept. It should be noted, however, that this privileged epistemic position only applies to makers (conceived broadly); other individuals outside the sphere of production may be entirely ignorant or in error regarding the existence and nature of the artifactual kind. (2003, 602)

Now Thomasson is surely right that what makes an artifactual kind the kind of thing it is has some essential connection to human intention, and this is an interesting point about the metaphysics of artifacts. But this point about the metaphysics of artifacts cannot be used to ground any theses about the semantics of artifactual kind terms or about any sort of epistemological privilege.

First, it is worth pointing out that Thomasson's requirement that the makers of artifacts have a 'substantive concept' of the artifacts they make and that in making the artifacts they intend to impose the kind-relevant features on those objects is surely much too strong. Consider the case of Harry, who works in the Acme Carabiner Factory. Harry stands at his machine, day after day, making carabiners. He is a maker of artifacts if anyone is. But Harry has no substantive concept of carabiners. If asked what it is he makes, Harry will say: 'I don't know what the devil carabiners are for. As far as I'm concerned, they're just something that puts food on the table.' When Harry says that he works at the carabiner factory, or that he makes carabiners, he is saying something that is just plain true; he uses the term 'carabiner' to refer to carabiners. And he is a maker of carabiners. But he has no substantive concept of carabiners. He doesn't know what the kind-relevant features of carabiners are.

Now admittedly, there is very likely to be someone around who knows something about what carabiners are. Saying precisely what the requirement here is, assuming there is such a requirement, will be quite difficult. Note that the person who first made carabiners may have had quite a different intention in making them than the users do in using them, and if the maker, now long gone, is the only one who ever had that intention, and all of the users have a different intention, then arguably the intentions which are connected to making the kind what it is are probably those of the users rather than the maker.[7] The fact that we can concoct such cases will make it extremely difficulty to defend any kind

---

[7] For a comparable example using proper names, see Gareth Evans's discussion of 'Madagascar' in his (1973).

of thesis about epistemic privilege here.[8] The maker could not insist, 'I know what these things are; after all, I made them', since the term is part of a public language which the maker cannot constrain through a sheer act of will; being the maker of an artifact does not provide one with a grant of immunity to error. A similar point applies to each of the users. While it is true that the boundaries of natural kinds are determined, in the typical case, by features of the world wholly independent of any individual, and yet the boundaries of artifactual kinds are determined by intentions, which are properties of individuals, the way in which intentions determine artifactual kind boundaries does not provide any individual with privileged access to the essential features of artifactual kinds.[9] For each speaker, that speaker could be entirely mistaken about what it is that makes a particular artifactual kind the kind of thing it is.[10]

Most importantly, however, the connection, whatever it may be, between human intention and the nature of artifactual kinds has nothing at all to do with the semantics of artifactual kind terms. Notice, for example, that an anthropologist may introduce an artifactual kind term to name a discovered object from a foreign culture (Kornblith 1980; D. Putnam 1982). The term would then be introduced into a language different from that of the makers and users of the artifact; but it would be an artifactual kind term nonetheless. Under these circumstances, no one who uses the artifactual kind term need have a substantive and correct concept of the nature of the artifact named. The epistemological position of users of the artifactual kind term vis-à-vis the artifactual kind would then be precisely like that of the users of natural kind terms vis-à-vis natural kinds. While intentions are relevant in determining the nature of artifacts, the relevant intentions need not be those of the users of the artifactual kind term. And all of this suggests that in those cases where there are makers who do have substantive concepts of the artifacts they make—which is, admittedly, the typical

---

[8] It is worth pointing out as well that any move from claims about an individual's intentions to claims about that individual's knowledge deriving from those intentions seems to presuppose an extremely strong and implausible view about self-knowledge. Individuals do, at times, fail to recognize their own intentions; we often have mistaken beliefs about our intentions. The intentions of makers and users of artifacts are no exception.

[9] Compare e.g. Abbott (1989, 281): 'Artifacts are typically made by humans and are categorized according to their purposes, so we know how they are shaped and what they are used for. When it comes time to name them we have the reference-determining properties there at hand, we know what we are talking about. It is only in the case of nature's species that we have observable kinds whose real essence is mysterious, and so only in that case must we leave the reference-determining properties open.'

[10] Notice that this suggests that even if Thomasson were correct in thinking that some makers or users of the artifact must have true beliefs about it, these beliefs still would not automatically amount to knowledge. Consider an analogy: imagine a very large lottery in which all of the ticket-holders are wide-eyed optimists; each believes that he himself holds the winning ticket. One of these ticket-holders must have a true belief, but none of these beliefs count as knowledge. Thomasson's argument shows, at best, that the way in which artifactual kinds are determined assures that some individual or other must have an accurate concept of the kind; but this tells us nothing about knowledge or epistemic privilege.

case—their ability to produce true descriptions of the objects they are referring to tells us no more about the mechanisms of reference, even of their own terms, than the fact that we can all produce true descriptions of what chairs are tells us anything about the mechanisms of reference to everyday objects. The explanation of the knowledge of makers and users is quite different from the explanation of the reference of their terms. To the extent that the makers are in an epistemically privileged position, the privilege is a product of their extensive interaction with the artifacts in question, not a product of any semantic competence.

Once again, the attempt to ground a distinctive semantics for artifactual kind terms in features of the metaphysics of artifactual kinds proves unsuccessful.

3. HIDDEN NATURES AND COUNTERFACTUAL CASES

Natural kinds have what John Locke called 'hidden natures', essential properties which are not immediately evident. Thus, for example, what makes water the kind of stuff it is lies in its chemical structure rather than its being clear, colorless, odorless, or tasteless. Were we to discover a clear, colorless, odorless, tasteless liquid with a radically different chemical structure than H_2O, then that liquid would not be water. But, as Schwartz argues, artifacts do not have hidden natures: 'What makes something a pencil are superficial characteristics such as a certain form and function. There is nothing underlying about these features. They are analytically associated with the term "pencil", not disclosed by scientific investigation' (1978, 571). Schwartz describes a number of different imaginary cases in which we might discover that the local objects which we had called 'pencils' turn out to be quite different than what we had assumed them to be, and he argues that, unlike natural kind terms, which are attached to the local kind quite independent of our beliefs about its features, artifactual kind terms refer by way of an associated description. Thus, were it to turn out that the objects we had called 'pencils' all along were quite different than what we took them to be, we might well say that these objects turned out not to be pencils. Our intuitions about cases here are quite different from our intuitions about natural kind cases. When the objects we had called 'whales' are discovered not to be fish, we don't say that therefore they turned out not to be whales; instead, we say that whales turned out not to be fish. This asymmetry in what we would say, Schwartz argues, reflects an asymmetry in the semantics of the two kinds of terms: natural kind terms function in the way causal theorists of reference describe, but artifactual kind terms refer by way of associated descriptions.[11]

[11] Devitt and Sterelny (1999, 94–5) are overly impressed by this argument. Putnam (1975) presents an example in which it is discovered that pencils are not artifacts, but organisms; he concludes that the term 'pencil' does not refer by way of an associated description. 'What is wrong with this refutation of the description theory, as Stephen Schwartz points out (1978), is that

Intuitions in these cases may vary somewhat, or be uncertain, but Schwartz presses his case:

> My argument here relies on claims about how we would respond in these situations, but all of the parties to the dispute agree that philosophical claims about the essences of natural and nominal kind terms are to be tested by how the terms function in describing counterfactual situations. If your intuitions are weak about the use of 'pencil,' try 'salt shaker' instead. We discover that all the salt shakers are spying devices sent from Mars (never used for shaking salt). Now we fashion some small cylindrical devices with little holes at the top and use them for dispensing salt at the table. Aren't these salt shakers? (1983, 479, n. 6)

The salt shaker example is, without doubt, a nice one. But it is not, I believe, as telling as Schwartz suggests. Consider, for example, the term 'English horn'. When I discover that the objects we all have been calling English horns are neither English in origin, nor are they horns (they're woodwinds), I don't conclude that these objects aren't English horns. If a British instrument-maker produces a trumpet and, pointing to his new creation, remarks: '*This* is an English horn', then he has made a nice joke, but he hasn't made an English horn. The term 'English horn' is now so well established that its reference is surely fixed to a certain sort of woodwind, and no appeal to analyticity is going to change that. Should we say the same sort of thing about salt shakers in Schwartz's imagined example? It just isn't clear to me that we shouldn't.

What we say about this kind of example, however, simply does not matter for the larger question at issue, because Schwartz's suggestion that the essential properties of artifacts are 'superficial' rather than 'hidden' or 'underlying' is entirely irrelevant to the question of the semantics of artifactual kind terms. Superficial or not, the traits which determine artifactual kind membership need not be known by a speaker in order for reference to succeed, for artifactual kind terms are just as susceptible to the phenomenon of the division of linguistic labor as are natural kind terms. One can simply insist, if one likes, that no one will count as referring in their use of an artifactual kind term unless they know uniquely identifying descriptions which pick out the kind, but this requirement is no better theoretically motivated than a similar requirement for natural kind

---

Putnam has picked the wrong description; artifact is not a description that expresses, even partly, the meaning of "pencil"' (Devitt and Sterelny 1999, 94). But first, it is not clear that an equally convincing counterexample could not be presented whatever description one chooses to identify with the meaning of the term. And second, and more importantly, this simply ignores the issue of the division of linguistic labor: an individual need not possess any identifying description in order to use an artifactual kind term to refer. Devitt and Sterelny do mention that artifactual kind terms 'may' face the Problems of Ignorance and Error (1999, 95), but surely this vastly understates the matter. The case for the Problems of Ignorance and Error is exactly as strong for artifactual kind terms as it is for names and natural kind terms. These issues are discussed further in the text below. While Devitt and Sterelny do not explicitly endorse a different account of reference for artifactual kind terms than for natural kind terms, their entire discussion of the issue (1999, 93–101) leaves such a possibility far more open than, I believe, is warranted.

terms. As far as the actual phenomena of language-use go, there is a continuum in the amount of knowledge speakers possess about the referents of the terms they use. Once a speaker is in a position to use a certain term, the mere ability to use it serves as a conduit for information about its referent: as Richard Boyd (1979) nicely puts it, the use of a term affords 'epistemic access' to the individual or kind to which it refers. Some who acquire the use of a term are, at least initially, ignorant or misinformed about its referent. In the case of more unfamiliar individuals and kinds, ignorance or misinformation may even be the norm. There are also, of course, terms for which the typical user of the term is quite well informed about the term's referent. But, as has already been pointed out, the distinction between the familiar and the recondite does not even approximately mark the distinction between natural and artifactual kinds. Schwartz's thesis about artifactual kind terms can be preserved by making stipulations about what will count as a referring use of an artifactual kind term, but such stipulations do not seem to have any theoretical motivation.

4. CONCLUSION

Descriptions-based theories of reference for names and natural kind terms were defeated by the Problems of Ignorance and Error. These problems arose because of the division of linguistic labor: one need not know a non-trivial description which uniquely identifies the referent of a term in order to succeed in using a term to refer. The division of linguistic labor is a phenomenon which applies just as much to artifactual kind terms as it does to names and natural kind terms. There are interesting metaphysical differences between artifactual and natural kinds, but these metaphysical differences play no role in the semantics for terms which refer to these kinds.[12]

---

[12] Thanks to David Christensen, Amie Thomasson, and the editors of this volume for comments on a draft of this chapter.

9

Water as an Artifact Kind

Paul Bloom

Psychological essentialism is the claim that people tacitly believe that some categories have 'essences' (e.g. Bloom 2000, 2004; Gelman 2003; Gelman and Hirschfeld 1999; Medin and Ortony 1989). These essences determine category membership and are, in the normal course of affairs, causally responsible for observable properties of category members. For instance, people might believe that all tigers share a hidden property that causes them to look and act like tigers. If one took a tiger and altered it so that it looks more like a lion, it would still be considered a tiger, because it still has the right essence. In most cases we do not know precisely what the essences are, although we might have some rough idea as to their nature (a certain atomic structure for chemicals; a certain type of DNA for animals and plants). Most adults know the essence of at least one category, however; we know that the essence of water is H_2O. If something is H_2O, it is water; if something isn't, it isn't.

This seemingly banal claim has proven to be quite controversial. Many scholars have argued that although most of us might *think* that we think water is H_2O, we really do not think water is H_2O.[1] To explore this, Malt (1994) asked people about their intuitions as to the proportion of H_2O present in certain substances. She found that some substances that are called 'water' are seen as having not much H_2O (radiator water and sewer water are judged as having about 67 per cent H_2O) while other substances that are not called 'water' are seen as having a lot of H_2O (tea, saliva, coffee, and tears are judged as having over 88 per cent H_2O). It seems that containing a lot of H_2O is neither necessary nor sufficient for a substance to be called 'water'. Malt takes these results as suggesting that concepts such as water might be quite similar to artifact concepts,

---

[1] Fodor (1998) has a milder attack on psychological essentialism, arguing that a belief in essences holds only for scientifically educated modern adults: '*of course* Homer had no notion that water has a hidden essence, or a characteristic microstructure (or that anything else does) ... he had no notion that the hidden essence of water is causally responsible for its phenomenal properties' (155).

with factors such as source, location, and function determining our intuitions about category membership. Similarly, Chomsky (1995, 22–3) proposes that our understanding of words such as 'water' is affected by 'special human interests and concerns'.

This chapter has four parts. The first is an argument that there is one sense of 'water' that does correspond to H_2O. This will be quick, since I doubt that anyone disputes this claim. The second is a defence of the position that there is a sense of 'water' that does not correspond to H_2O, and here I will respond to Abbott's (1997, 2000) proposal that Malt's data are due to considerations having to do with communication, not with the nature of our categories. The third part outlines the view that we naturally think about many categories, including water, as *both* natural kinds and artifact kinds. The fourth part looks at the problem of concept formation from the standpoint of the developing child, and argues that the existence of such hybrid concepts is a natural solution to a difficult learning problem.

1. WATER IS (SOMETIMES) H_2O

If you ask people whether water is H_2O, they are likely to agree. For familiar reasons, this cannot be taken as proof that this is how 'water' is understood (our conscious notions about word meanings may be inaccurate), but it is surely evidence in its favor. Also, we can make sense of claims such as: 'Earthworms, jellyfish, chickens, and babies are composed mainly of water' (see LaPorte 1998). This use of 'water' has nothing to do with the typical source, location, or function of water, but fits well with the notion that it is a chemical that can be a constituent of certain objects, that it is H_2O (Abbott 2000). Finally, Malt's (1994) data suggest that people would agree to (1).

(1) Tea, coffee, and saliva contain more H_2O than corn syrup and bleach.

Informal observation suggests that people are equally happy agreeing to (2); in fact, (1) and (2) seem synonymous.

(2) Tea, coffee, and saliva contain more water than corn syrup and bleach.

The best explanation for these facts is that people believe that water is H_2O.

2. WATER IS (SOMETIMES) NOT H_2O

As Malt argues, however, if water is H_2O, we should view Sprite and tears as water. After all, it is not as if we only use 'water' to refer to substances which are entirely H_2O, since we describe swamp water and radiator water as 'water', even though we believe that they contain much less H_2O than substances such as Sprite and tears.

Abbott's response is that all of these substances are understood to *be* water. It is just that they are not all *called* 'water'. And this is because of principles that govern language-use: 'What you call something depends not only on what it is, what categories it falls into, but also on why you want to refer to it, what your purposes of the moment are. So we usually ask for a cup of tea rather than asking for a cup of hot water containing an infusion of tea or other herbal matter, because the former turn of phrase is easier for most contexts and purposes' (1997, 315–16).

But this pragmatic explanation has certain problems (see also LaPorte 1998; Strevens 2000). For one thing, the fact that we have a precise term for tea ('tea') does not in itself explain why we do not call it 'water'. Strevens (2000) points out that we have precise terms for rain and ice ('rain' and 'ice'), but this does not stop us from also describing these substances as 'water'. Conversely, some high-H_2O substances are not called 'water' even if no other term is available. In the movie *The Thomas Crown Affair*, the detective played by Renee Russo was shown repeatedly drinking a strange green liquid, presumably a hangover cure. It looked as if the liquid was mostly water, and it was never named. Still, it would be bizarre to say that she was 'drinking water to cure her hangover'.

Finally, Strevens notes that it is not just that people don't normally describe tea as 'water'. It is that when explicitly asked, they will insist that tea *isn't* water. This is an important contrast. I don't normally call my children 'mammals', for reasons of politeness and pragmatics. But if you were to ask me whether they are, in fact, mammals, I would say yes, strictly speaking, they are. In the same vein, I will agree that tea is a beverage, a substance, and even 'hot water containing an infusion of tea or other herbal matter'. But I won't agree that it is water. All of this suggests that there is more going on here than Gricean principles.

It might be true, by the way, that part of the reason we don't think of tea as water is because of what we know about tea. Someone who wasn't aware that tea is created as a distinct beverage might have no reluctance to describe it as 'water'. By the same token, someone who had no inkling that cats were a distinct species might well extend the word 'dog' to refer to them, believing that 'dog' refers to all four-legged domestic animals. In general, information about a category can constrain our understanding about other categories; and the scope of our concept of water is plausibly constrained by the presence of our concept of tea. But this is a fact about concepts, not about communication.

3. BLOOD, SPRITE, AND TEARS

It follows, then, that there are two senses of 'water'. One corresponds to what people think of as the chemical essence of the substance, H_2O. It is this sense that comes into play when we assert that babies are mostly water, and that tea has more water in it than radiator water. But there is another sense of 'water' which refers to substances such as swamp water, but not to tea. In this second sense, 'water' refers to an artifact kind.[2]

As a different example of a hybrid concept, consider Sprite. What sorts of substances do we judge to be Sprite? One answer is: anything that we think of as having the same chemical structure as previously encountered instances of Sprite. Considerations such as function and intent are irrelevant. Although Sprite is typically used as refreshing beverage, you can wash your hair with it, or put out fires with it, and it will still be Sprite. And there is nothing sacred about it being created with a certain intent. Suppose that Sprite turned out to be a miraculous cure for male pattern baldness. I imagine that the Sprite people would be delighted to discover this and would change the marketing on their product accordingly—it would not, for all of this, cease to be Sprite. Finally, an amateur chemist could get hold of the recipe and make Sprite at home and, again, it will still be Sprite.

At this point, the account of Sprite looks much like the traditional essentialist view of water. 'Sprite' refers to those substances that have a particular chemical structure. But such an account would fail to capture certain other facts about our intuitions, facts that correspond to our understanding that Sprite is an artifact, as a commercial product invented by humans for a specific purpose. From this perspective, we find nothing incoherent about the manufacturers of Sprite 'changing their recipe', and producing Sprite out of different chemicals, with somewhat different taste and appearance. Coke might be a better example here, as there have been several versions of this substance over the last decade, one of which involved a radical color change—'Clear Coke'—and others that involved taste changes—'Cherry Coke' and 'Vanilla Coke'.[3]

---

[2] I should respond here to Abbott's argument that 'water' is unlikely to have multiple senses because (a) languages do not exist that have distinct words for different senses of 'water', and (b) unlike words such as 'bat' (baseball bat, flying bat), 'water' fails certain linguistic tests of ambiguity. But the comparison with a word like 'bat' is inappropriate, since nobody would claim that the meanings of 'water' are entirely unrelated. The ambiguity (or better, the polysemy) of 'water' should be viewed as akin to that of a word like 'window', which can refer both to a structure that can contain glass, wood, and metal (which one can buy in a hardware store) and to the spaces that these structures usually occupy (and these might simply be large square holes in the wall, with no glass or frame). I doubt if there are languages that distinguish these two senses, and 'window' would not count as ambiguous by Abbott's stringent tests. The suggestion here is that the two senses of 'water' should be thought of as akin to the two senses of 'window'.

[3] There are similar examples with water. In the 1960s there were reports that chemists had invented something called 'polywater' or 'anomalous water', which was H_8O_4 and was quite viscous. (There were also concerns, reported in the journal *Nature* and elsewhere, that, should this substance make contact with 'normal water', it would lead to the destruction of all life on Earth.) The interest of this story, from our point of view, is that news reports in the scientific and popular press repeatedly described this substance as water (e.g. the *Miami Herald* called it a 'mysterious new form of water'), despite its unusual microstructure, appearance, and properties (Franks 1982).

Tears and blood are also understood in multiple ways. One can focus on the chemical structure of these substances and so, for instance, blood can be created in a laboratory, or can pour out of a shower-head as sometimes depicted in horror movies (see Abbott 1997). But one might also determine category membership in terms of the functional role that substances play within biological systems. From this standpoint, it is perfectly conceivable that the tears/blood of some creature might be made out of an entirely different chemical from our own. (Martians are said to have green blood, after all.) Hence tears and blood are not incompatible. One can imagine a saint with tears of blood—functional role of tears (comes out in droplets from the eye), microstructure of blood (red and gooey). With a bit more of an effort, one can imagine another saint, a very sad one perhaps, who had blood of tears—microstructure of tears (clear and transparent), functional role of blood (pumped by the heart; circulates through the body).

Such cases are, of course, fanciful; in the real world, the multiple construals are typically not in conflict—the very same stuff with the microstructure associated with blood also has the functional role associated with blood. And our intuitions start to fall apart when faced with substances that strongly violate one of the construals (can you make tears in a test tube? If the Sprite people made something that tasted like grape juice, would it still be Sprite?). Nonetheless, these patterns of usages suggest that multiple construals do exist, at least for water, Sprite, blood, and tears.

4. HARD CASES

Why would we come to possess such hybrid concepts?

The answer might lie in the problem faced by children in the course of concept formation and language learning. Many cognitive and developmental psychologists have suggested that the natural kinds and artifacts concepts are represented in different ways. Natural kinds are understood in terms of internal essences; artifacts are thought of in terms of considerations such as creator's intent, characteristic function, and the social and cultural context of the artifact's creation and use.[4] When exposed to a tiger, then, children will form a different sort of category than when exposed to a chair. This intuitive natural kind–artifact contrast is reflected in children's intuitions about the effects of superficial transformations, their categorization of atypical instances,

---

[4] Some researchers, including myself, defend an essentialist theory of artifact concepts where intuitions about creator's intent determine category membership, even for young children (see Bloom 1996, 2000, 2004; Gelman and Bloom 2000; Diesendruck, Markson, and Bloom 2003; see also in this volume, Kelemen and Carey; Keil, Greif, and Kerner; and Thomasson for discussion). But the 'hybrid concept' proposal made here is independent of any specific theory of artifact concepts and can be endorsed even by someone who is unsympathetic to such an intention-based account.

and how they use names for such categories, words such as 'tiger' and 'chair' (see Bloom 2000, 2004; Diesendruck *et al.* 2003; Gelman 2003; Gelman and Bloom 2000; Keil 1989; Keil, Greif, and Kerner this volume; Mandler, this volume).[5]

This approach goes awry, however, if one makes the unnecessary additional assumption that any category must be understood as *either* an artifact kind or a natural kind. This might work for tigers and chairs, but there are many instances where such an either–or categorization is difficult or impossible to make. There are just too many hard cases.

For instance, how are children to categorize milk—is it an artifact or a natural kind? (Does the answer depend on whether the children are breastfed?) What about the distinction between oranges, orange juice, and orange drink, or between cheese, cheese whiz, and cheetos? Are banana and seedless grapes artifacts? (See Sperber, this volume.) What about iron, polystyrene, and stainless steel? (See Grandy, this volume.) How are we to think about 'animal artifacts' such as spider webs and beaver dams? (See Gould, this volume.) Even for animals—presumably prototypical natural kinds—the answer is not so clear-cut. After all, most adults believe that animals are the handiwork of an intentional and purposeful creator—and children appear to be even more prone to such creationist views (Evans 1997; see Bloom 2004 for discussion). If you believe that God created tigers, are tigers then artifacts? For a theist, is *everything* an artifact?

Some readers may have strong opinions on these matters, and many of the philosophers who have contributed to this volume have metaphysical theories that provide answers to these questions. But these are plainly hard questions, and it is not plausible that every normally developing child can answer them. It is more likely that children are never forced to make these choices. They look for cues as to whether something is an artifact or whether it is a natural kind (as discussed in this volume by Keil, Greif, and Kerner, and Mandler)—but they do not treat these as exclusive categories. When faced with cases where both construals seem to fit, children create hybrid concepts.

Such a situation arises with water. There are many cues that it is a natural kind. It falls from the sky, after all, and is found in oceans, rivers, and lakes. But there are also good reasons to take it as an artifact kind. It comes from bottles, cans, taps, hoses, and coolers; it is filtered, processed, carbonated, purified,

---

[5] Note that our categorization might frequently be mistaken. Many of the objects in the world that seem to be natural are in fact just as artificial as anything that comes out of a factory or can be bought in a store. For instance, many people think of categories such as flowers, grass, herbs, weeds, and trees as biological kinds, though (according to biologists) they actually do not share a common microstructure; they are instead groupings of organisms that share certain humanly relevant properties, such as size and taste (see Malt 1991). Wheat and corn are artifacts in a more literal sense; they are new forms of life and need human assistance for their sustenance; corn was carefully bred from wild grass, and if people were to be whisked off the planet for a few thousand years, corn would cease to exist (Hubbell 2001).

and chlorinated; it is advertised on television and sold in stores. The sensible conclusion for children to draw from these facts is that water is both a natural kind and an artifact kind.[6]

[6] I am grateful to Barbara Abbott, Frank Keil, Stephen Laurence, Barbara Malt, Eric Margolis, Karen Wynn, and the participants of my 'Bodies and Souls' seminar for discussion of these matters and for helpful comments on earlier drafts.

10

The Organization and Representation of Conceptual Knowledge in the Brain: Living Kinds and Artifacts

Bradford Z. Mahon and Alfonso Caramazza

1. INTRODUCTION

In this chapter we address some central issues in the organization and represent-ation of conceptual knowledge in the human brain. The focus of our discussion will be on the organization and representation of conceptual knowledge of manip-ulable artifacts. However, the category 'artifacts' is only one semantic domain among others, for instance, 'animals', 'fruit/vegetables', and 'con-specifics'. A discussion of how conceptual knowledge of artifacts is organized and represented will thus require consideration of the same issues with respect to other semantic categories. For this reason we begin with the broader question of how conceptual knowledge of objects in general is organized; a working hypothesis in answer to this question will permit more fine-grained consideration of the questions of how conceptual knowledge of manipulable artifacts is organized and represented.

The principal empirical base we draw upon in evaluating how conceptual knowledge is organized and represented in the brain consists in the patterns of disproportionate impairment and sparing of performance across different tasks, and/or different semantic categories, in brain-damaged patients. The logic behind this method is straightforward: the functional and neural separability of a mechanism can be inferred if it can be damaged independently of other processes. This prioritization of neuropsychological data in evaluating proposals about the organization and representation of conceptual knowledge has potential limitations: the currently available database of patients reported with conceptual deficits spans a wide spectrum of methodological rigor, theoretical evaluation, and statistical reporting. It is thus important to proceed with caution when drawing inferences on the basis of such data. For the same reason, it is also useful to seek a convergence of conclusions through different methods. In this regard, functional neuroimaging provides useful directions for evaluating specific hypotheses about the neuroanatomical implementation of the various functional architectures to be discussed.

Theories of the *organization* of conceptual knowledge in the human brain can be divided into two groups, depending on whether or not they assume the organization of conceptual knowledge is determined by innate representational constraints. One class of theories, based on the Neural Structure Principle, assumes that the organization of information is driven by innate representational constraints. The second class of theories, based on the Correlated Structure Principle, assumes that the organization of conceptual information in the brain is determined by statistical regularities of object properties in the world. Theories of the *representation* of conceptual knowledge can also be divided into two groups. In one group are theories that assume conceptual information and perceptual information are functionally and neuroanatomically separable. A second group of theories assumes that the content of conceptual information is stored in the same cognitive/neural systems that process objects perceptually.

The distinction between the Neural Structure Principle and the Correlated Structure Principle is, at least in principle, orthogonal to the distinction between theories that assume the content of concepts is exhausted by percepts and theories that assume concepts and percepts are functionally independent. Thus, we first develop a working model of the organization of conceptual knowledge, and then return in the second half of the chapter to consider the issue of how conceptual knowledge of manipulable artifacts is represented. The position for which we will argue assumes that the first-order constraint on the organization of conceptual and perceptual processes is object domain, and that the candidate domains are those that could have been evolutionarily salient in our phylogenetic history: living animate, living inanimate, con-specifics, and possibly tools. Throughout the discussion, this Domain-Specific Framework will be contrasted with alternative theoretical positions in the context of data from neuropsychology and functional neuroimaging.

2. CLUES ABOUT THE ORGANIZATION OF CONCEPTUAL KNOWLEDGE[1]

In a seminal series of papers, Warrington and her collaborators (Warrington and McCarthy 1983; Warrington and Shallice 1984) reported several patients

---

[1] In this chapter the terms 'semantic' and 'conceptual' are not theoretically distinguished; thus, 'semantic impairments' and 'conceptual impairments' do not imply deficits at different levels of meaning representation. Following conventions in the literature, we use the term 'category-specific semantic deficits' to refer to disproportionate conceptual impairments to one or more domains of knowledge. We use the term 'domain' to refer to 'living animate', fruit/vegetables', 'con-specifics',

who presented with disproportionate deficits in naming objects from different semantic categories. The clearest dissociations involved either a disproportionate deficit for naming living things compared to non-living things (Warrington and Shallice 1984) or the reverse dissociation: a disproportionate sparing of the category living things compared to other semantic categories (Warrington and McCarthy 1983). Since Warrington and colleagues' initial reports many other case studies have corroborated the double dissociation between living and non-living categories (cases presenting disproportionate impairments for living things: e.g. Barbarotto, Capitani, and Laiacona 1996; Caramazza and Shelton 1998; Dixon, Piskopos, and Schweizer 2000; Hanley, Young, and Pearson 1989; Hart and Gordon 1992; Lambon-Ralph *et al.* 1998; Riddoch and Humphreys 1987*a*, *b*; Samson, Pillon, and De Wilde 1998; Sartori *et al.* 1993; Silveri and Gainotti 1988; cases presenting disproportionate impairments for non-living things: e.g. Breedin, Martin, and Saffran 1994; Gaillard *et al.* 1998; Hillis and Caramazza 1991; Laiacona and Capitani 2001; Lambon-Ralph *et al.* 1998; Sacchett and Humphreys 1992; Silveri *et al.* 1997; Warrington and McCarthy 1983, 1987; for recent reviews see Caramazza and Shelton 1998; Humphreys and Forde 2001; Tyler and Moss 2001; Capitani *et al.* 2003). For instance, Hillis and Caramazza (1991) reported the performance of two patients, JJ and PS, who presented with complementary profiles of impairment/sparing on objects from various categories. In picture naming, PS was impaired for the category 'living things' compared to the category 'non-living', while JJ was severely impaired for all categories except 'animals'. This double dissociation in performance between patients JJ and PS over the category 'animals', compared to other categories, was obtained across the same test materials, ruling out the possibility that the effects might be accounted for in terms of uncontrolled stimulus variables (e.g. Funnell and Sheridan 1992; Stewart, Parkin, and Hunkin 1992).[2]

2.1. The Neural Structure Principle

Along with reporting the first cases of category-specific semantic deficit, Warrington and her collaborators developed a theoretical interpretation of the facts that has until recently been the received view in the field of category-specific semantic deficits: the Sensory/Functional Theory (Warrington and McCarthy 1983; Warrington and Shallice 1984). The Sensory/Functional Theory makes two basic

---

and 'non-living'. We use the term 'semantic category' to refer to groups such as 'vehicles', 'tools', 'insects', 'living things', etc.

[2] Early accounts reporting category-specific deficits should be interpreted with caution. Funnell and Sheridan (1992) and Stewart, Parkin, and Hunkin (1992) have shown that items from different semantic categories can differ significantly along stimulus variables such as familiarity and visual complexity. Because these variables can influence recognition/naming performance, purported dissociations between semantic categories can only be interpreted with confidence if such concomitant variables have been taken into consideration.

assumptions: (1) the semantic system is organized into modality-specific semantic subsystems (e.g. visual/perceptual, functional/associative, etc.); and (2) the ability to recognize/name objects from different categories differentially depends on information internal to different modality-specific semantic subsystems. (We will refer to (1) as the 'modality-specific assumption' and to the conjunction of (1) and (2) as the 'Sensory/Functional Theory'.) The Sensory/Functional Theory proposes that the ability to recognize/name living things differentially depends on visual/perceptual information, while the ability to recognize/name non-living things differentially depends on functional/associative information. The Sensory/Functional Theory explains the existence of category-specific semantic deficits by assuming damage to a type (i.e. modality) of knowledge upon which successful recognition/naming of items from the impaired semantic category differentially depends. The original formulation of the Sensory/Functional Theory has descended into a number of related proposals (e.g. Borgo and Shallice 2001; Cree and McRae 2003; Crutch and Warrington 2003; Humphreys and Forde 2001; Martin, Ungerleider, and Haxby 2000; Vinson *et al.* 2003; for critical discussion of these specific proposals see Laiacona, Capitani, and Caramazza 2003; Mahon and Caramazza 2001; in prep.).

The central assumption of the Domain-Specific Hypothesis (Caramazza and Shelton 1998) is that evolutionary pressures have resulted in specialized (and functionally dissociable) neural circuits dedicated to processing, perceptually and conceptually, different categories of objects. In this way, the Domain-Specific Hypothesis provides a principled way of specifying what constitutes a conceptual domain in the brain, since it is restricted to only those categories for which rapid and efficient identification could have had survival and reproductive advantages. Plausible candidates are the categories 'animals', 'plant life', 'con-specifics', and possibly 'tools'.

Based on these brief outlines of the Sensory/Functional Theory and the Domain-Specific Hypothesis, two types of predictions can be generated. The first type of prediction concerns the grain of deficit that should (or should not) be observed. The original formulation of the Sensory/Functional Theory assumed that the ability to recognize all living things differentially depends on information internal to the same (visual/perceptual) semantic subsystem; this assumption generates the prediction that a dissociation should not be observed *within* the category living things. In contrast, such a dissociation is a fundamental expectation on the Domain-Specific view, since the distinction between living animate and living inanimate is one dimension along which conceptual knowledge is functionally organized.

A recent and nearly exhaustive critical re-analysis of the literature on category-specific semantic deficits (Capitani *et al.* 2003), beginning with Warrington and colleagues' initial reports, establishes several facts.

Fact 1: Disproportionate deficits have been observed for categories more fine-grained than the living/non-living distinction. For instance, patients MD (Hart,

Berndt, and Caramazza 1985), TU (Farah and Wallace 1992), RS (Samson and Pillon 2003), FAV (Crutch and Warrington 2003), and JJ (Hillis and Caramazza 1991) were disproportionately impaired for the category 'inanimate living' but not 'animate living'. In contrast, patients KR (Hart and Gordon 1992) and EW (Caramazza and Shelton 1998) were disproportionately impaired for the category 'animate living' but not for the category 'inanimate living'.

For example, when asked to define the words 'lion' and 'melon', patient JJ provided detailed information about lions, but only sparse information about melons:

Lion: 'A large animal, about four feet tall, maybe taller at the shoulders; it has a long body and very large paws, and stands on all four legs. It has a monstrous head with which it growls: and it has a mane—a large body of hair. It lives in Africa.'

Melon: 'I'm not sure. It's a fruit, a soft material. I don't remember if it is yellow or green or orange. I've forgotten too many things.'

Less anecdotal is the double dissociation between the performance of patients JJ and EW on picture-naming tests. At thirteen months post onset of aphasic symptoms, JJ was at ceiling on a picture-naming test for the category 'animals' but disproportionately impaired for the category 'fruit/vegetables'. In contrast, EW was at ceiling on a picture-naming test for the category 'fruit/vegetables', but only 34 per cent correct for 'animals' (see Fig. 10.1). This double dissociation demonstrates that it can't be the case that the abilities to recognize/name both living animate and living inanimate things depend on the integrity of the same modality-specific semantic subsystem: if that were the case, one would not expect selective impairments to either animate or inanimate living things.

The second type of prediction concerns the profile of knowledge impairment associated with a given pattern of category-specific deficit. Because Sensory/Functional type theories assume that the ability to recognize/name objects from different categories differentially depends on information internal to different modality-specific semantic subsystems, such theories are committed to the prediction that there will be a necessary association between a disproportionate deficit for a type of knowledge (e.g. visual/perceptual) and a disproportionate deficit for the corresponding category of objects (i.e. living). Thus, the status of such theories turns on two observations: first, *patients presenting with a semantic deficit for a category of objects will necessarily be disproportionately impaired for the type of knowledge upon which the ability to recognize/name objects from the impaired category is hypothesized to depend*; and second, *patients with a disproportionate deficit to a type of knowledge must also have a disproportionate deficit for the category of objects that differentially depends on that knowledge*.

In contrast, because the Domain-Specific Hypothesis assumes that object domain is the broadest constraint on the organization of conceptual knowledge,

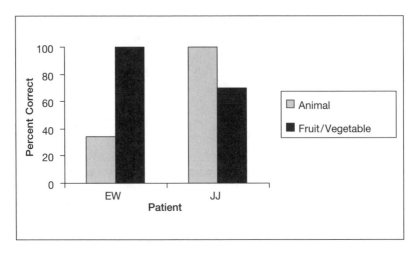

Figure 10.1. Picture-naming performance over 'animals' and fruit/vegetables' for patients EW and JJ

the prediction is made that there will not be a necessary association between a deficit for a type or modality of knowledge and a conceptual deficit for a specific category of objects. Second, because this hypothesis assumes that Domain-Specific constraints operate at a pre-semantic level of object processing, the prediction is made that pre-semantic (i.e. modality-specific input or perceptual) stages of object processing will be functionally organized by domain.

Fact 2: When task difficulty is controlled,[3] almost all cases that presented with a disproportionate deficit for living things also presented with *equivalent* impairments for visual/perceptual and functional/associative knowledge. For instance, cases EA (Barbarotto *et al.* 1996; Laiacona, Capitani, and Barbarotto 1997), EW (Caramazza and Shelton 1998), FM (Laiacona, Barbarotto, and Capitani 1993), Jennifer (Samson *et al.* 1998), and SB (Sheridan and Humphreys 1993) all had disproportionate semantic deficits for the category living things compared to non-living things, but *equivalent* deficits to visual/perceptual and functional/associative knowledge of living things.

This profile of impairment has also been observed in a case of developmental category-specific semantic deficit. Patient Adam, studied by Farah and

[3] Early reports seemed to support predictions derived from the SFT: patients were reported with deficits for living things who were also disproportionately impaired for the visual attributes of objects compared to functional/associative attributes (Basso, Capitani, and Laiacona 1988; Farah *et al.* 1989; Silveri and Gainotti 1988). However, these studies have been criticized methodologically on the grounds that the tasks accessing visual and functional/associative knowledge were not matched for difficulty (see Caramazza and Shelton 1998; for a re-analysis of the published data, see Capitani *et al.* 2003).

Rabinowitz (2003), suffered a bilateral posterior cerebral artery infarction at one day of age. When tested at the age of 16, Adam was disproportionately impaired at naming pictures of living things (40% correct) compared to non-living things (75% correct). The Sensory/Functional Theory predicts that this patient should also have presented with a disproportionate impairment for visual/perceptual knowledge compared to functional/associative knowledge. Contrary to this prediction, when Adam was administered semantic probe questions investigating the integrity of visual/perceptual and functional/associative knowledge, the patient was at chance for both types of knowledge for living things (visual/perceptual = 40%; functional/associative = 45% correct), while performance was within normal limits for both types of knowledge for nonliving things (visual/perceptual = 78%, normal range = 70–90%; functional/associative = 72%, normal range = 73–92%). In other words, the impairment for knowledge of living things observed in Adam is (a) not reducible to an impairment for visual/perceptual knowledge' and (b) concerns all types of knowledge of the impaired semantic domain.

Fact 3: Patients have been reported with disproportionate deficits for visual/perceptual knowledge compared to functional/associative knowledge, but equivalent impairments to living and non-living things (e.g. Lambon-Ralph *et al.* 1998; Miceli *et al.* 2001).

The picture that emerges from this brief review of the empirical evidence is that the basic predictions made by the original formulation of the Sensory/Functional Theory are contrary to the facts. This conclusion implies the rejection of the Sensory/Functional Theory as a viable theoretical framework with which to explain the existence of category-specific semantic deficits. These same data regarding the domains 'living animate' and 'living inanimate' are consistent with the basic expectations of the Domain-Specific Hypothesis.

Rejecting the Sensory/Functional Theory as a causal account of the existence of category-specific semantic deficits does not entail that one must reject all of the individual assumptions that constitute the account. While it is clear that the facts of category-specific semantic deficits are not consistent with the original formulation of the Sensory/Functional Theory, it is an open question as to whether (and if so which) individual assumptions from the theory may prove useful in accounting for a broader range of empirical phenomena. One possibility is that conceptual knowledge is organized by two orthogonal dimensions: Domain and Modality (Caramazza and Mahon 2003).

Is there empirical evidence from category-specific semantic deficits motivating the assumption that conceptual knowledge is organized by type or modality of information as well as Domain? The answer seems to be: perhaps, but the evidence is not very strong. One line of evidence is provided by the performance of patient Michelangelo (Sartori and Job 1988; Sartori, Miozzo, and Job 1993; Sartori *et al.* 1994). Michelangelo was disproportionately impaired for the category 'living things' and was also disproportionately impaired for visual/perceptual knowledge of living things compared to functional/associative knowledge.[4] This pattern of performance could be taken to indicate that there is damage to the category 'living things' within a region of conceptual space specialized for storing/processing information about the visual properties of objects.

Patient Michelangelo also presented with a corresponding category-specific visual agnosia for living things (a deficit in recognizing visually presented objects despite intact elementary visual processing).[5] However, a number of patients who have also been documented with having a category-specific visual agnosia for living things had equivalent impairments to visual/perceptual and functional/associative knowledge of living things (Capitani, Laiacona, and Barbarotto 1993; Laiacona, Barbarotto, and Capitani 1993; Barbarotto *et al.* 1995; Barbarotto, Capitani, and Laiacona 1996; Caramazza and Shelton 1998; Lambon-Ralph *et al.* 1998; but see Capitani *et al.* 2003 for critical review).[6]

This dissociation between a category-specific visual agnosia for living things and a disproportionate impairment for visual knowledge of living things is the basis of the argument from Michelangelo's profile of impairment to the inference that one constraint on the organization of conceptual knowledge may be modality or type of information (see also Lambon-Ralph *et al.* 1998). However, the strength of this inference is mitigated by the lack of an articulated theory of the relationship between the 'structural description system' (generally considered to be a pre-semantic, modality-specific cognitive stage) and stored visual perceptual knowledge, which can be directly accessed through the verbal system. In this situation it is useful to seek convergent lines of inference from different methodologies.

There is a large body of evidence from functional neuroimaging that demonstrates differentiation by semantic domain within cortical regions known to process visual information about object form and motion. Items corresponding to biological categories differentially activate the superior temporal sulcus (right>left) (e.g. Chao, Haxby, and Martin 1999; Chao, Martin, and Haxby

---

[4] This pattern of impairment is in need of confirmation, as there is some question as to whether the materials on which this patient was tested were matched for difficulty. For critical discussion of this case, see Capitani *et al.* 2003.

[5] Michelangelo was disproportionately impaired on an object decision task for living things compared to non-living things. On this task, the patient is presented with a series of pictures, some depicting real objects and some depicting non-existent objects; the patient's task is simply to decide (yes or no) on each trial whether or not the depicted object is real. Performance on an object decision task is usually assumed to reflect whether or not there is damage to the structural description system. The structural description system is a modality-specific input (i.e. pre-semantic) system that stores representations of the visual form of objects (see Riddoch and Humphreys 1987*b*; Riddoch *et al.* 1988).

[6] Note analogous dissociations are observed with respect to con-specifics in face recognition: patients can present with impairments for recognizing faces but not visually presented objects (e.g. Newcombe, Mehta, and De Hann 1994) as well as the reverse: spared face recognition but impaired object recognition (Moscovitch, Winocur, and Behrmann 1997; for discussion of these findings in regard to the Domain-Specific Hypothesis, see Caramazza and Mahon 2006).

1999; Haxby *et al.* 1999; Hoffman and Haxby 2000; Kanwisher, McDermott, and Chun 1997) and the lateral fusiform gyri (Chao, Haxby, and Martin 1999), while items corresponding to non-living things differentially activate the middle temporal gyrus (left > right) (Chao, Haxby, and Martin 1999; Martin *et al.* 1996) and the medial fusiform gyri (Chao, Haxby, and Martin 1999). Furthermore, human face stimuli, in comparison to non-face stimuli (including animals without faces), differentially activate distinct regions of ventral temporal cortex (e.g. Kanwisher, McDermott, and Chun 1997; Kanwisher, Stanley, and Harris 1999; McCarthy *et al.* 1997). For a Domain-Specific interpretation of these findings, see Kanwisher 2000; for an alternative interpretation see Tarr and Gauthier 2000).[7]

In a recent series of studies, Beauchamp and colleagues (Beauchamp *et al.* 2002; 2003) have demonstrated that lateral temporal cortex prefers object associated motion whereas ventral temporal cortex is more sensitive to object associated form and texture. In their 2002 report it was found that the superior temporal sulcus preferred human stimuli moving in an articulated manner (e.g. jumping-jacks) than an unarticulated manner (e.g. rotating about the center of mass). In their 2003 report it was found that ventral temporal cortex preferred videos of humans (lateral) and tools (medial) to point light displays of the same moving stimuli. In contrast, lateral temporal cortex responded either more to point light displays (superior temporal sulcus: humans) or equivalently to videos and point light displays (middle temporal gyrus: tools). The direct contrast of point light displays of moving humans to moving tools led to activation in superior temporal cortex, while the reverse contrast led to activation in middle temporal cortex (see also Grossman *et al.* 2000; Grossman and Blake 2002; Kourtzi and Kanwisher 2000; Senior *et al.* 2000).

Perhaps the most straightforward inference to be extracted from these data is that the ventral object processing stream does seem to exhibit the type of functional architecture that one would expect to observe if the primary constraint on the organization of conceptual and perceptual processing was object domain.

2.2. The Correlated Structure Principle

To this point the focus of the discussion has been on the class of theories based on the Neural Structure Principle, which assume the organization of conceptual information is driven by representational constraints internal to the brain.

---

[7] Not all investigators have been able to obtain reliable category-specific effects with functional neuroimaging. For instance, Devlin *et al.* (2002) did not find reliable category-specific foci of activation for the categories 'animals', 'fruit', 'tools', and 'vehicles' after correcting alpha levels for multiple comparisons (see also Gerlach *et al.* 2000). See Martin and Caramazza (2003) for critical discussion.

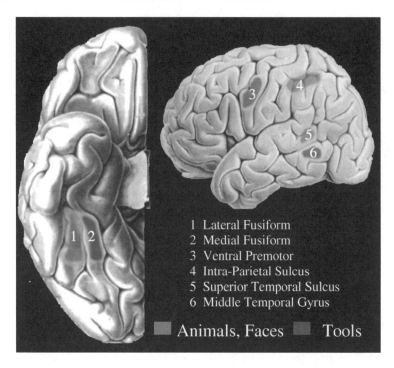

Figure 10.2. Schematic of activation patterns by semantic category in ventral and lateral views of the human brain. Graphics provided by Alex Martin. Figure reproduced from Caramazza and Mahon (2006) with permission from Psychology Press (http://www.psypress.co.uk/journals.asp)

We have argued for a Domain-Specific Framework that admits the possibility of modality or type of information being an independent dimension of organization of object concepts. This framework also assumes that modality-specific input representations are: (a) functionally and neuroanatomically separable from conceptual knowledge, and (b) functionally organized by object domain. Consensus on such a Domain-Specific Framework is still forthcoming; a number of researchers have argued that differential effects of object category (in e.g. ventral temporal cortex) do not reflect domain-specific object processing (e.g. Bookheimer 2002; Gerlach *et al.* 2000; Ishai *et al.* 1999; Martin and Chao 2001; Moor and Price 1999; Mummery *et al.* 1998; Perani *et al.* 1995; Thompson-Schill 2003; but see e.g. Kanwisher 2000). The received interpretation of the functional neuroimaging data reviewed above can be characterized as a hybrid model that combines a variant of the Sensory/Functional Theory with assumptions in the spirit of the Correlated Structure Principle.

Perhaps the most developed account along these lines is the Sensory/Motor Theory of Martin and colleagues (Martin 1998; Martin, Ungerleider, and

Haxby 2000; Martin and Chao 2001). Like the Sensory/Functional Theory, the Sensory/Motor Theory assumes that the only endogenously determined constraint on the organization of conceptual knowledge is modality or type of information.[8] This assumption allows the theory to account for the neuroanatomical localization of the dissociations in activation: in other words, both living and non-living things activate the fusiform gyrus because this area, by hypothesis, is important in visual object processing (i.e. it is part of the neural substrate of the so-called 'visual modality'). However, the observation of a lateral to medial segregation according to living versus non-living things in ventral temporal cortex is left unaccounted for on the original formulation of the Sensory/Functional Theory. On the Sensory/Motor Theory, these patterns of activation are explained by assuming one implementation of the Organized Unitary Content Hypothesis (OUCH) model first proposed by Caramazza *et al.* (1990): the conceptual knowledge corresponding to things with similar shapes, or things that move in similar ways, or things that are used for similar purposes, might cluster together in conceptual space. [9]

One aspect of the functional neuroimaging data that has been argued to support the assumption of 'lumpy' conceptual space is the seemingly arbitrary nature of the patterns of activation. For instance Ishai *et al.* (1999) observed that 'chair' stimuli activated an area in ventral temporal cortex lateral to that elicited by faces. Based on this observation those authors argued that: 'A feature-based model can accommodate the observation that an arbitrary category such as chairs elicited a pattern of neural activity distinct from other object categories (i.e. faces and houses). Clearly, it would be difficult, as well as unwise, to argue that there is a "chair area" in the brain' (p. 196). The premise upon which this argument rests is that a feature-based model *could* accommodate the results reported by Ishai *et al.* (1999). But wouldn't a feature-based model

---

[8] For instance, Martin, Ungerleider, and Haxby (2000) write: '... the features that define an object are stored close to the primary sensory and motor areas that were active when information about that object was acquired. Thus, the organization of semantic information parallels the organization of the sensory and motor systems in the brain' (p. 1023). Note that in this context, 'defining' should be read as both *diagnostic* and *constitutive* (for discussion of this distinction, see e.g. Fodor and Pylyshyn 1988).

[9] Depending on the specific theory, such 'lumpiness' in conceptual/neural space may arise out of the way in which information is processed by the perceptual system (e.g. Levy *et al.* 2001), the way in which the world is structured (e.g. Cree and McRae 2003), or both. Note however that *proximity in conceptual space* and *proximity in neural space* are at least logically independent issues. There are an indefinite number of ways of fleshing out the notion of proximity in conceptual space in the context of accounting for category-specific semantic deficits; for instance, different notions are assumed depending on the way damage to one feature is assumed to affect features that are connected to it, the types of connections that mediate between features, and the types of features themselves that are damaged, etc. Proximity in conceptual space does not in any way entail proximity in neural space; the corollary of course is that observations of *proximity in neural space* can only very loosely (if at all at this point in time) constrain the type of functional model one assumes in order to account for the dynamics of system breakdown. In order to focus in this chapter on the empirical issues, we will set this constellation of issues aside.

face the same dilemma the Domain-Specific Hypothesis purportedly faces? In other words, if conceptual knowledge is organized by the features that define objects, so that the conceptual representations of objects that share features are stored in adjacent neural areas, then why would 'chair' stimuli activate an area next to an area that has previously shown disproportionate activation for 'animal' stimuli? What features are shared between the conceptual representations of exemplars from the categories 'chairs' and 'animals'? Is the claim that animals and chairs share the feature 'legs'? Would this still be the claim if the word referring to the feature $[+\text{LEG}_{[animal]}]$ was not homonymous with the feature $[+\text{LEG}_{[chair]}]$? What about the feature $[+\text{ARM}_{[human]}]$ and $[+\text{ARM}_{[chair]}]$: are these the same feature too because the word referring to each is the same?

This criticism is a species of a more general issue that concerns theories based on the Correlated Structure Principle that have been proposed in order to account for category-specific semantic deficits and category-specific patterns of neural activation. Such proposals have been claimed to be 'more parsimonious' than theories based on the Neural Structure Principle, since a conceptual system is assumed with no internal organization, and all concepts are (putatively) decomposable into a common pool of semantic features.[10]

One of the primary motivations for explaining category-specific semantic deficits and functional neuroimaging data at the level of object specific features[11] is the claim that the empirical phenomena themselves are not truly 'categorical' or 'selective'. For instance, in the ventral object processing stream, the activation elicited by a given object type (e.g. tools) is differential compared to other types of stimuli (e.g. animals); however, in the same area that responds maximally

---

[10] It should be noted that the theoretical framework developed by Tyler, Moss, and colleagues, termed the Conceptual Structure Account, differs greatly from the Sensory/Motor Theory of Martin and colleagues. In particular, the Conceptual Structure Account does not make the assumption that modality or type of information is an organizing parameter of semantic memory. In fact, the Conceptual Structure Account has been developed to the point of predicting that no category-specific patterns of activation should be observed in the brain. The reason for this prediction presumably follows from the way in which the framework accounts for category-specific semantic deficits: not in terms of focal damage to a conceptual system with a 'lumpy' organization, but in terms of the relative susceptibility to random damage of different types of features across different semantic categories. For critical discussion of this proposal see Caramazza and Mahon (2003) and Mahon and Caramazza (in prep.).

[11] See also Martin, Ungerleider, and Haxby (2000, 1032): '... [T]hese [neuroimaging] data suggest that the proper level of analysis for understanding semantic object representations is at the level of features, not at the level of whole-object concepts like animals and tools (for an alternative view, see Caramazza and Shelton, 1998) ...' Note that the Domain-Specific Hypothesis is neutral on the issue of whether the patterns of activation reflect the activation of the 'whole' concept or just one part; as discussed above, this is because the Domain-Specific Hypothesis is not incompatible with the modality-specific assumption. If one assumes that conceptual processing is subject to both domain and modality-specific constraints, the area observed in ventral temporal cortex to be differentially activated for e.g. a picture of a dog would not reflect the activation of the whole concept 'dog' (see also n. 9 above, and discussion in Caramazza et al. 1990).

to tools, animal stimuli may elicit a neural response reliably above baseline.[12] Similarly, it has been pointed out that many patients with category-specific semantic deficits are usually not 'normal' in the spared category, or at floor in the impaired category (Moss and Tyler 2003).

Thus, Correlated Structure proposals developed in an attempt to account for category-specific effects in neuropsychology and functional neuroimaging stress the importance of the types of features that could underlie successful within semantic category discriminations (i.e. features that are 'distinctive', 'distinguishing', 'defining', etc.). Damage to such features could, by hypothesis, underlie the impaired ability of patients with category-specific semantic deficits to distinguish, for instance, a tiger from a lion, and activation of such features could plausibly be what drives the patterns of category-specific activation observed in functional neuroimaging. But such features would also (almost by definition) be those that are not shared among concepts corresponding to objects from different semantic categories. In fact, short of very abstract features, it is not clear that there are *any* features that are shared among concepts corresponding to objects from different domains. The implication of this is that at the level of analysis at which Correlated Structure Theories account for the facts, there is no representational difference between the Domain-Specific Framework and the Correlated Structure Framework. For the same reason, the fact that category-specific deficits and category-specific patterns of activation are observed to be differential and not selective is not evidentially relevant to the status of Correlated Structure Theories.

The observation that so-called category-specific effects are in fact category *differential* effects has also been cast as a negative argument against the Domain-Specific Hypothesis. Proponents of such lines of argument often champion the 'graded' nature of the empirical phenomena as an argument against assuming 'discrete' structure in the conceptual system. For instance, Moss and Tyler (2003) write:

[Caramazza and Mahon] ... cite evidence for category/domain specific activations in a number of imaging studies as further support for the domain-specific account. However, the regions of interest are rarely *selectively* recruited by a specific domain or category; rather different categories produce activation across many of the same regions, but to different degrees [Haxby *et al.*, 2001]. Rather than separate systems dedicated to individual domains, this suggests that concepts within different domains place more or less processing demands on different elements within a single system [Tyler *et al.*, 2003] ...

---

[12] There may be methodological limitations regarding this conclusion: many functional neuroimaging studies first identify Regions of Interest (ROIs) that are activated by objects from all of the categories being investigated. For instance, Chao, Haxby, and Martin (1999) first identified '... brain regions that responded to visually presented objects ...' (p. 918) and then looked within those areas for differential effects of object category, in this case 'animals' vs. 'tools' and 'houses' vs. 'faces'. This methodological approach may be biased against the possibility of observing patterns of activation that are 'selective'. (For further discussion, see Joseph 2001.)

So-called 'graded' or differential effects in experimental psychology are not new, and neither are inferences from 'graded' effects to discrete structure. Consider as an example *all* empirical work based on reaction and response times. So why is functional neuroimaging any different? Without any arguments to the contrary, it is not. Regardless, it is also known that in neuropsychological and functional neuroimaging studies of category-specificity, it is possible to observe 'selective' patterns of impairment or activation. Recall the above discussion of patient EW, who presented with a category-specific semantic deficit for living animate things but normal performance for artifacts and fruit and vegetables. Similarly 'selective' effects have been observed in functional neuroimaging.

In a recent study by Martin and Weisberg (2003) participants viewed three types of computer-animated displays, all consisting of the same geometric shapes, but differing in the type of motion in which the shapes were engaged (for discussion of such stimuli see Heider and Simmel 1944; Scholl and Tremoulet 2000). The geometric shapes could be (a) moving as biological entities (e.g. chasing, playing a game; 'biological motion' condition); (b) moving as mechanical entities (e.g. cue balls, bowling balls; 'mechanical motion' condition); or (c) moving randomly ('random motion' condition). It was observed that superior temporal regions responded more to the 'biological motion' condition, while the middle temporal gyrus responded more to the 'mechanical motion' condition, indicating that the corresponding neural regions for processing motion were engaged by these stimuli. More striking were the findings in ventral temporal cortex: lateral temporal areas responded more to the 'biological motion' condition while medial regions responded more to the 'mechanical motion' condition. Given that ventral temporal regions are most responsive to object form and texture (e.g. Beauchamp *et al.* 2003), and given that object form and texture were exactly the same between the 'biological' and 'mechanical' motion conditions, these data suggest that the activation observed in ventral temporal areas can be driven by higher-order interpretations of the semantic domain to which the geometric shapes belong, and not by object-specific features. Furthermore, the activation observed in lateral and ventral temporal areas by Martin and Weisberg was not only differential for one type of stimulus (e.g. biological) compared to the other (i.e. mechanical): when an area in ventral temporal cortex responded to one type of stimulus (biological or mechanical motion) it did not respond to the other type of stimulus more than to the random-movement baseline.[13]

The weight of the empirical evidence that has been reviewed suggests that the first-order constraint on the organization of conceptual knowledge is object domain. Theories based on the Correlated Structure Principle such as the

---

[13] This was the case bilaterally in ventral temporal cortex, in the right superior temporal sulcus (social>mechanical) and in the left middle temporal gyrus (mechanical>social). Activation associated with social motion was also found in the amygdala and ventromedial prefrontal cortex (Martin and Weisberg 2003; see also Castelli *et al.* 2000; Castelli *et al.* 2002; for discussion, see Caramazza and Mahon 2006).

Sensory/Motor Theory of Martin and colleagues do not necessarily differ from a Domain-Specific Framework in terms of the content of what is represented in a given neural area in the normally functioning brain. However, there is a sharp difference in how that information came to be so organized and represented. Whereas the Sensory/Motor Theory is committed to the view that the resulting organization is not driven by innately determined representational constraints, one of the Domain-Specific Hypothesis' basic assumptions is that innate constraints strongly shape the organization of conceptual knowledge in the brain. Thus, while the Sensory/Motor Theory and the Domain-Specific Hypothesis may be difficult to disentangle in the normally functioning adult system, there are circumstances in which unique predictions can be generated. For instance, the Domain-Specific Hypothesis uniquely predicts that the organization of various higher-order visual areas (e.g. in ventral temporal cortex) will be relatively invariant to the presence or absence of visual input.

Similarly, developmental and comparative work with non-human primates will play an important role in adjudicating between theories. There is some difference, however, in the way in which different authors use the term 'Domain-Specific' (e.g. see discussion in this volume by Mandler and by Hauser and Santos). Not all authors who advocate a Domain-Specific view commit themselves to the assumption that objects must be categorized or assigned to a given domain at a pre-semantic level (e.g. Hauser and Santos, this volume). Furthermore, some authors partial to the Domain-Specific Hypothesis do not commit themselves to the claim that a Domain-Specific organization is innately determined (e.g. Kanwisher 2000). One reason for these differences may have to do with the types of evidential criteria emphasized by various theorists. Our claim is that what makes a given cognitive process Domain-Specific is not so much the content of what is represented, but the types of things in the world by which the process is triggered. Of course, for the most part, the content of what is represented will be congruent with the types of things by which the process is triggered. However, if the criterion for Domain-Specificity is the content of what is represented by a given system, the notion of Domain-Specificity is in risk of being trivialized. For instance, if representational content is the criterion for Domain-Specificity, than one could describe the Sensory/Motor Theory of Martin and colleagues as a 'Domain-Specific' view, since there will be, by hypothesis, areas of conceptual space that represent information about a given 'domain' of objects. On the other hand, if one assumes that pre-semantic object recognition processes are organized by Domain-Specific constraints, the criterion for identifying a given cognitive process as Domain-Specific must be the class of objects that trigger the process in question (see also discussion of 'input analyzers' by Kelemen and Carey, this volume). It seems to us that only on this reading of Domain-Specificity can a coherent story be told of, for instance, the observation that animated geometric shapes can selectively recruit (by hypothesis) Domain-Specific object recognition processes (Martin and Weisberg 2003).

Assumptions must also be made about the type of representational content that is innate, and which allows a given process to become 'locked' to the right category of objects in the world (i.e. a triggering mechanism). The present claim is not that individual object concepts are given innately, but that general properties that are more or less common to exemplars from a given domain are innately represented (see also discussions of 'core knowledge' in Hauser and Santos and Kelemen and Carey, both this volume). For instance, living animate things move in an articulated way, and there may be a triggering mechanism that is initially sensitive to articulated motion (for discussion in the context of the Sensory/Motor Theory, see Beauchamp *et al.* 2003).[14] In other words, stimuli from different domains differ in terms of the computational process that those stimuli require in order to be processed. The present hypothesis is that the conceptual system in humans is innately prepared to carry out such 'eccentric' computations. In this regard, the combination of developmental psychology and neuropsychology offers promising directions for isolating the contribution of experience to the organization of the normally functioning adult system.

3. CLUES ABOUT THE REPRESENTATION OF CONCEPTUAL KNOWLEDGE

One of the issues that could not be resolved above was whether there are in fact category-specific visual agnosias. The resolution of this issue is important because such a pattern of impairment would be predicted by one instantiation of the view that conceptual knowledge is not exhausted by the information represented in perceptual (or modality-specific input) systems. One reason why this issue was not resolvable was because there does not exist an articulated theory of the relation between the structural description system and conceptual knowledge about the visual properties of objects. However, in respect of the category 'manipulable artifacts' there do exist articulated and empirically tractable proposals about the relation between modality-specific representations coding the ways in which objects are manipulated and conceptual knowledge of manipulable objects (e.g. Rothi, Ochipa, and Heilman 1991; Martin *et al.* 2000).

---

[14] The earliest discriminations made by infants concern differences such as 'living animate' versus 'artifact', but not e.g. 'dog' versus 'cat' (Mandler, this volume). It seems that these developmental data suggest that *if* indeed there are Domain-Specific Processes coming on line in the developmental studies reviewed by Mandler (this volume; see also Kelemen and Carey, this volume) these processes, when first observable, cut as fine as superordinate categories (see also Kelemen and Carey, this volume, for discussion). (For discussion of the Domain-Specific Hypothesis in developmental psychology and comparative work with non-human primates, see e.g. Carey 2000; Carey and Markman 1999; Keil 1989; Santos and Caramazza 2002; Santos, Hauser, and Spelke 2002*a*; Spelke 1994.)

A working assumption that we have adopted in this paper is that conceptual knowledge is constituted by that information which mediates between modality-specific input representations and the task-determined modality-specific output representations. With respect to conceptual knowledge of manipulable artifacts, we would assume that conceptual knowledge of manipulable objects is functionally dissociable from representations that encode the motor movements associated with the uses of such objects. For the rest of the chapter we focus on an evaluation of this assumption.

One class of theoretical positions about the representation of conceptual content is based on the assumption that the features over which conceptual knowledge of tools is distributed are the same (modality-specific input/output) features that are active when tools are being used. This assumption has been developed most clearly in the context of the Sensory/Motor Theory of Martin and colleagues (Martin *et al.* 2000; see also Allport 1985).[15] It is important to distinguish the Sensory/Motor Theory of Martin and colleagues from a closely related proposal termed the Simulationist Theory (e.g. Gallese and Goldman, 1998; Barsalou *et al.* 2003). The difference between the Sensory/Motor Theory and the Simulationist Framework is that the Sensory/Motor Theory is not committed to the claim that the same representation underlies production and recognition. Thus, the observation of a dissociation between the ability to use objects and the ability to recognize the correct gestures associated with the use of objects is contrary to the Simulationist Framework, but not the Sensory/Motor Theory (for review of the clinical evidence, see e.g. Rothi, Ochipa, and Heilman 1991; Cubelli *et al.* 2000; Johnson-Frey 2004). Here we review the main empirical findings that have motivated the assumption that conceptual knowledge is grounded in modality-specific input/output representations and generate empirical predictions that are tractable with neuropsychological data.

---

[15] For instance, Martin, Ungerleider, and Haxby (2000, 1028) write: '... [T]he position proposed here is that the information about object function *needed* to support tool recognition and naming is information about the patterns of visual motion and patterns of motor movements associated with the actual use of the object' [emphasis added]. Note the similarity between the Sensory/Motor Theory of object recognition and the Motor Theory of speech perception (e.g. Liberman *et al.* 1967): both theories assume that information required for production (i.e. motor engrams for using tools or producing speech sounds) must be retrieved in the course of successful recognition (of tools or speech sounds, respectively). See also Allport (1985, 53): 'The essential idea is that the *same* neural elements that are involved in coding the sensory attributes of a (possibly unknown) object presented to eye or ear also make up the elements of the auto-associated activity patterns that represent familiar object-concepts in "semantic memory".' Hauser and Santos (this volume) discuss a similar proposal under the heading of the 'affordances perspective'. The basic assumption of this view is that all knowledge of tools is represented in terms of physical features. 'Our representation of a hammer-like object simply consists of a mapping between certain perceptual features (e.g. smoothness, hardness) and certain functional possibilities (e.g. graspability, poundability)' (p. 271). In the context of the Sensory/Motor Theory, it would (presumably) be assumed that such 'functional possibilities' will be represented by modality-specific output representations coding the ways in which objects are manipulated.

The claim that information required to use manipulable objects grounds conceptual knowledge of such objects has been motivated primarily by results from functional neuroimaging. Above we reviewed imaging data indicating that the middle temporal gyrus responds more to artifacts than to living things, and also prefers mechanical motion to biological motion (e.g. Beauchamp *et al.* 2002; 2003; Chao, Haxby, and Martin 1999; Martin *et al.* 1996; Martin and Weisberg 2003; Moore and Price 1999; Mummery *et al.* 1998; Perani *et al.* 1999, Exp. 2). Martin and colleagues point out that this area in the left middle temporal gyrus is at most 8 mm away from an area assumed to store information about object movement (e.g. Corbetta *et al.* 1990).[16]

Another well-documented finding is that left premotor cortex is differentially activated when subjects perform various tasks over tool stimuli compared to non-manipulable stimuli (e.g. animals, houses) (e.g. Chao and Martin, 2000; Chao, Weisberg, and Martin 2002; Gerlach *et al.* 2000; Gerlach *et al.* 2002; Grabowski, Damasio, and Damasio 1998; Martin *et al.* 1996; for review see Grèzes and Decety 2001; Martin and Chao 2001; see Gallese and Goldman (1998) for review of comparative work in the monkey model). The area activated in the left premotor cortex is activated when subjects are asked to imagine grasping objects, but not to actually do so (Decety *et al.* 1994).

However, there are also functional neuroimaging data that would seem to be at variance with the assumption that premotor activation is a necessary step in object recognition. Johnson-Frey *et al.* (2003) found greater activation in inferior frontal regions (precentral and inferior frontal gyri, bilaterally) for photographs of a hand grasping an object compared to photographs of a hand touching the same objects. This activation remained when the objects were non-tools (i.e. novel shapes) and when the hand was grasping the object in a way that would not serve the function of the object (see also recent work by Kellenbach, Brett, and Patterson 2003; Phillips *et al.* 2002).

In order to generate empirical predictions from the Sensory/Motor Theory, we must first be clear about what is meant by 'information about the visual motion and patterns of motor movements associated with the actual use of the object'. We reason as follows: since modality-specific input/output representations and conceptual knowledge are distributed over the same features, this information must be modality-specific. Following conventions in the literature regarding modality-specific representations encoding information about how to use objects, we refer to such representations as 'sensorimotor representations'. Two straightforward empirical predictions follow from the basic assumptions of the Sensory/Motor Theory: (1) *a deficit for conceptual knowledge of manipulable artifacts will be*

---

[16] This area is also just posterior to an area activated when subjects generate action words to pictures of objects (e.g. Martin *et al.* 1995). It should be noted that, in English, tool stimuli differ from animal stimuli in that the names of the former are often homonymous with verbs, whereas the names of the latter are almost never homonymous with verbs. We are not aware of whether or not these two dimensions have been explicitly separated within a single experiment.

associated with damage to modality-specific input/output representations (i.e. sensorimotor knowledge); and (2) *damage to sensorimotor representations will necessarily be associated with a deficit for conceptual knowledge of manipulable artifacts.*[17] Note that the structure of these predictions, and the empirical arguments to be developed below, parallel the above evaluation of the Sensory/Functional Theory.[18]

3.1. Empirical evaluation of prediction 1: a deficit for conceptual knowledge of manipulable artifacts will be associated with damage to modality-specific input/output representations (i.e. sensorimotor knowledge)

Consider the performance of patients FB (Sirigu, Duhamel, and Poncet 1991) and DM (Buxbaum, Schwartz, and Carew 1997), who could indicate the correct use associated with an object despite being impaired for conceptual knowledge of manipulable objects. For example, when FB was asked to verbally provide both functional information (what an object is used for) and manipulation information (how an object is used) in response to a safety pin (presented visually), he responded: 'You open on one side, stick something on it, close it, and it stays in. I can tell you how it works, but I don't see its exact use. I don't think I have seen one like this before, it is not a very common object' (Sirigu *et al.* 1991, 2555). It seems, from this example, that the patient has knowledge of *how* a safety pin is used, but no knowledge of what it might be *used for*.

[17] One question that arises is whether *all* of the motor movements associated with a given tool, in all of the varieties in which that tool can be instantiated, must be activated in order to recognize the tool. For instance, in the course of recognizing a screwdriver, are the motor movements associated with using an electric screwdriver activated as well? If not, then why not? If only the motor movements associated with the particular instantiation of the tool at hand are activated, then this seems to presuppose that the tool has already been identified. Would a patient with a deficit for tools, who cannot recognize or use a manually operated screwdriver, be able to use an electric screwdriver? These considerations cease to be trivial if one is to take seriously the claim that sensorimotor knowledge figures prominently (i.e. necessarily) in the ability to recognize/name manipulable objects.

[18] We have chosen to interpret the Sensory/Motor Theory in its strongest form. The reason for this is straightforward: it is not clear in what ways the theory might be 'weakened' while remaining empirically distinguishable from other theoretical alternatives. For instance, a weaker version of the theory might propose to combine a unitary-amodal account of semantic memory with the assumption that different types of knowledge are differentially important for different categories of objects. (See Plaut 2002 for a computational simulation that can be taken as an existence proof of these assumptions, although the author proposes an interpretation in terms of graded modality-specific specialization of semantic memory; see Caramazza and Mahon (2006) for discussion.) At this point, however, the theory would be indistinguishable from an amodal account of semantic memory in which there is a privileged relationship between the semantic representations of a certain class of objects and the information contained in a certain type of modality-specific input or output representation (for discussion, see Caramazza *et al.* 1990; we thank Laurel Buxbaum (personal communication) for raising this issue).

Similarly, patient DM presented with impaired conceptual knowledge of objects but relatively intact ability to use objects. For instance, on a function matching test, the patient was asked to match two pictures out of three which are used for similar purposes (e.g. given pictures of a 'can opener', a 'hand mixer', and an 'electric mixer', the latter two would be the correct choice). The unrelated foil on this task was always visually similar to one of the two target items, and on many trials all three items were associated (e.g. in the above example, all of the items are found in a kitchen). DM's performance was impaired on this task (61%; 22/36) compared to normal control subjects (94%; 34/36; range: 29–36/36). In contrast, DM's performance was flawless on a task in which real objects were presented in both the visual and tactile modalities and the patient was asked to demonstrate the correct use associated with the object. Crucially, DM's performance was also very good (91%; 10/11) at demonstrating the correct use associated with objects when they were presented only in the visual modality (and the patient was not allowed to touch them). This last result indicates that visual information alone was sufficient to support relatively unimpaired performance on a task requiring objects to be used, but the same information (provided in pictures) was not sufficient to support performance on a function matching task.

The performance of patients FB and DM indicates that (1) there is a dissociation between functional knowledge (what an object is for) and manipulation knowledge (how an object is used); and (2) it is possible to observe, within the same patient, a conceptual impairment for tools without an associated impairment in using tools. These data would seem to indicate that it cannot be the case that conceptual knowledge of tools is distributed over the same features as knowledge of how tools are used, since these patients could access knowledge of how tools are used but were impaired at accessing conceptual knowledge about tools. However, the strength of this conclusion is mitigated by the alternative hypothesis that patients such as FB and DM are succeeding on object-use tests through general mechanical problem-solving abilities and not through accessing stored representations of the correct gestures associated with objects (e.g. Goldenberg and Hagmann 1998; Hodges, Spatt, and Patterson 1999; Hodges et al. 2000).[19] This alternative possibility raises an important theoretical question: on the assumption that part of the conceptual representation of a tool includes knowledge of how to use that tool, a distinction is required between the semantic system *storing* such information and the semantic system *reading*

---

[19] In the case of FB, support for this alternative hypothesis is provided by the fact that on an object decision task, the patient accepted non-objects that were not functionally anomalous as real objects, suggesting that the patient was not accessing stored representations but making judgments based on the extraction of object properties. Furthermore, neither FB nor DM were tested on a novel tool use task, which is generally regarded as informative of a patient's ability to infer the function of a tool from its physical structure. Finally, it could also be noted that neither FB nor DM had lesions extending into the parietal lobes, and that parietal lobe lesions have been associated with impairments in novel tools selection tasks (Goldenberg and Hagmann 1998).

this information from sensorimotor engrams (see e.g. Buxbaum, Veramonti, and Schwartz 2000 and Sirigu *et al.* 1991, for discussion). That is, how might we distinguish between the semantic system storing the information that a hammer is used by swinging the hand in an arc from the semantic system retrieving this information by reading a modality-specific sensorimotor engram? It is the burden of those theories for which knowledge of the ways in which objects are manipulated figures critically in the conceptual representations of those objects to give a principled account of how these two possibilities might be empirically distinguished.

3.2. Empirical evaluation of prediction 2: damage to sensorimotor representations will *necessarily* be associated with a deficit for conceptual knowledge of manipulable artifacts

We turn now to the second, and determining, prediction made by the Sensory/Motor Theory: there cannot be patients who are impaired at using tools but who can access intact conceptual information about tools and/or identify/name tools. If there were to be a patient whose performance was contrary to this prediction, then we could conclude that it is not the case that conceptual knowledge of artifacts is distributed over the same features that constitute sensorimotor knowledge. In fact, there are now a number of reports of patients with impairments for using objects, but spared recognition/identification (Buxbaum, Veramonti, and Schwartz 2000; Buxbaum and Saffran 2002; Buxbaum *et al.* 2003; Cubelli *et al.* 2000; Hodges, Spatt, and Patterson 1999; Montomura and Yamadori 1994; Moreaud, Charnallet, and Pellat 1998; Ochipa, Rothi, and Heilman 1989; Rosci *et al.* 2003; Rumiati *et al.* 2001; for discussion see Dumont, Ska, and Joanette 2000; Hodges *et al.* 2000; for a comprehensive review see Johnson-Frey 2004).

For instance Ochipa, Rothi, and Heilman (1989) report the performance of a patient who was relatively unimpaired at naming tools (17/20 correct) as well as pointing them out when given their name (19/20). However, he was severely impaired at (a) pointing to a correct tool when given its function (7/20); (b) verbally describing the function of a visually presented tool (3/20); (c) pantomiming the use of a tool to a verbal command (0/20); and (d) demonstrating tool use when holding a tool (2/20). Crucially, the same twenty tools were used for all tasks with this patient, and yet the patient was able to name and identify tools but was not able to use them or identify them based on their function.[20]

---

[20] The patient reported by Ochipa, Rothi, and Heilamn (1989) was also impaired at imitating symbolic gestures (4/20); symbolic gestures are learned manual movements, such as making the 'peace sign' or the 'hitch-hiking fist'. Based on this deficit for symbolic gestures, it might be argued that the patient had an uninteresting production deficit which did not compromise sensorimotor representations. However, the patient reported by Montomura and Yamadori (1994) was unimpaired

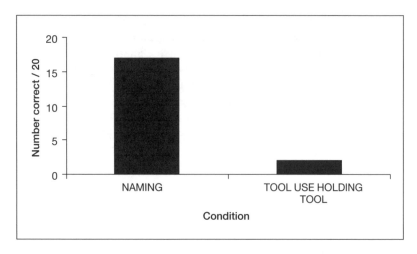

Figure 10.3. Tool use and tool naming data from Ochipa *et al.* 1989

The performance of the patient reported by Ochipa and colleagues (1989) seems to indicate that the ability to recognize/name objects does not require that either functional knowledge (what an object is used for) or manipulation knowledge (how an object is used) must be intact and/or accessible. However, it might be argued that it has not been demonstrated that the patient reported by Ochipa and colleagues (1989) had damage to stored knowledge of how tools are used. Specifically, it might be argued that this patient was impaired at producing the correct actions associated with a tool, but the patient was nevertheless able to access stored knowledge of the movements associated with objects in order to succeed at naming tasks; this position entails the hypothesis that the damage in Ochipa and colleagues' patient was to the *connections* between sensorimotor engrams and the production system. A similar position has been advanced by Buxbaum, Veramonti, and Schwartz (2000) to distinguish between what the authors term 'central' and 'peripheral' apraxics: central apraxics can neither recognize nor produce gestures, while peripheral apraxics are only impaired at producing the correct gestures associated with objects. It is assumed that central apraxics have damage to sensorimotor representations themselves, while peripheral apraxics have damage to the connections between sensorimotor

at making symbolic gestures to command, imitating symbolic gestures, pantomiming tool use to command, and pantomiming tool use to imitation, indicating that the inability of the patient to use the same tools correctly cannot be dismissed in terms of a 'general' motor deficit. This patient was impaired at imitating and pantomiming to command 'meaningless' gestures (i.e. manual gestures that do not have a conventional meaning). This pattern of performance suggests damage to a mechanism for directly converting observed hand movements to motor output, without accessing stored representations of what those movements mean; see Cubelli *et al.* (2000) and Rothi, Ochipa, and Heilman (1991) for discussion.

representations and the production system (but see above distinction between the Sensory/Motor Theory and the Simulationist Framework). The question is: are there patients with impairments in both recognizing and producing gestures who can nevertheless access intact semantic information about objects?

Patient WC (Buxbaum, Veramonte, and Schwartz 2000) presented with an impairment to knowledge of how objects are manipulated but perfect performance on a number of tasks requiring access to conceptual knowledge of objects. For instance, WC was impaired at choosing the correct object out of four to match an observed gesture, indicating an impairment in recognizing gestures (80%; control mean 97%). WC was also impaired in using actual objects presented in the visual and tactile modalities, indicating an impairment in producing the correct gestures associated with an object (73%; control mean 99%). The combination of a deficit in both gesture production and recognition indicates that there is damage to stored sensorimotor representations of the correct gestures associated with objects (Buxbaum, Veramont, and Schwartz 2000). Even more demonstrative that the impairment in WC was to the knowledge (per se) of how to manipulate objects is the patient's contrasting performance on picture-matching tasks requiring objects to be matched based on either their function or their manner of manipulation. In this task, the patient is presented with three pictures and must choose the two that are most similar. In the 'manipulation' condition, all three items on a given trial differ in terms of their function, while two of the three are similar in their manner of manipulation (e.g. given pictures of a 'piano', 'typewriter', and 'stove', the correct response would be to choose 'piano' and 'typewriter'). For this manipulation condition, WC was severely impaired (50%; control mean 96%). Contrastively, for the function condition, all three items on a given trial differ in their manner of manipulation, and the patient must pick the two pictures out of three that have similar functions (e.g. given 'radio', 'record player', and 'telephone', the correct response would be to select 'radio' and 'record player'). WC was at ceiling (100%) on this task. WC was also administered semantic probe questions testing his knowledge of specific conceptual properties of tools. For instance, given a picture of a knife, the patient might be asked: 'Is it used for tightening or for cutting?' WC was at ceiling (100% correct) for answering semantic probe questions about tools.

3.3. Refuting the Sensory/Motor Theory

A final aspect of WC's profile should be noted: WC presented with severe anomia (i.e. an impairment in naming). This aspect of the patient's performance seems to indicate, at least at first glance, that an impairment to knowledge of how to use objects is associated with a naming deficit. However, we know from the performance of the patient reported by Ochipa and colleagues (see Fig. 10.3) that this association of impairments is not necessary. Regardless, even setting aside Ochipa and colleagues' patient, the association of anomia and an impairment for using tools is not relevant to an evaluation of the assumption that conceptual knowledge of tools is distributed over modality-specific sensorimotor representations.[21] It is this assumption that is under evaluation.

Patient WC was at ceiling on several tasks requiring access to conceptual knowledge of tools and at the same time impaired for knowledge of how to use tools. On the assumption that WC had damage to sensorimotor representations that store information about the ways in which objects are used, it would not be possible, given the assumptions of the Sensory/Motor Theory, to account for the ceiling performance of this patient on several tasks requiring access to conceptual knowledge.[22] Furthermore, recall that the Sensory/Motor Theory also appealed to knowledge of the visual movements associated with using tools: the performance of WC speaks to this assumption as well, as the patient was impaired at recognizing the correct gestures associated with the use of tools. The performance of patient WC refutes the hypothesis that conceptual knowledge of manipulable objects is distributed over the same modality-specific representations that are active when such objects are being used. Our conclusion is *not* that conceptual knowledge of artifacts does not include knowledge of the ways in which artifacts are used. Rather, we have been arguing against the claim, in the terms in which it has been proposed, that conceptual knowledge of artifacts is distributed over modality-specific sensorimotor representations.

One possible counterargument to our conclusion is the following: it might be argued that while WC had damage to sensorimotor representations, this damage was not so extensive as to cause a deficit for the conceptual knowledge that is distributed over these representations. There is an empirical argument against this: if there were patients with disproportionate conceptual deficits for artifacts compared to other categories of objects, then we could infer (based on the Sensory/Motor Theory) that these patients must also have presented with disproportionate deficits for the type of conceptual knowledge that is hypothesized to be distributed over sensorimotor representations. Specifically, the prediction is the same as is made by the original formulation of the Sensory/Functional Theory: patients with disproportionate deficits for artifacts will also have disproportionate deficits for functional/associative knowledge

---

[21] Data are not reported on WC's naming performance by semantic category. However, on a triplet matching task, the patient was presented with three words, and had to choose the two that were most semantically similar (e.g. given 'hammer', 'mallet', and 'saw', the correct answer would be 'hammer' and 'mallet'). Contrary to what would be predicted by the Sensory/Motor Theory, WC's performance on this test was actually slightly *better* for tool triplets (94%) than for animal triplets (83%).

[22] Another task administered to WC investigated whether he could choose the correct object corresponding to a given tool. For instance, when presented with a hammer, WC had to choose between a nail and screw as the correct object to use with a hammer. WC was just below ceiling on this task (96%); however, when WC was asked to demonstrate the use of the same tools on the same objects that the patient had just selected, the patient was severely impaired (58%). For instance, on the trial with a hammer and nail, after selecting the nail, WC grasped the hammer at the wrong end and pounded the nail with the hammer's handle.

compared to visual/perceptual knowledge. Contrary to this prediction is the performance of patients PL (Laiacona and Capitani 2001), CN98 (Gaillard *et al.* 1998) and ES (Moss and Tyler 1997; 2000). These patients presented with disproportionate deficits for artifacts, but *equivalent* impairments for perceptual and functional/associative knowledge of artifacts. Furthermore, the structural description system was spared in patient PL, indicating that the impairment to visual/perceptual knowledge of non-living things was not an artifact of having damage to the structural descriptions of those objects. Even more striking is the performance of patient IW (Lambon-Ralph *et al.* 1998), who presented with a disproportionate (albeit small) impairment for non-living things compared to living things (33% and 42% respectively). In direct contrast to what would be expected by the assumption that functional/associative knowledge is needed to support correct recognition/naming of artifacts, this patient was disproportionately impaired for visual/perceptual knowledge compared to functional/associative knowledge for both living and non-living things.

One way in which the Sensory/Motor Theory might be modified in an attempt to account for the neuropsychological evidence that has been reviewed would be to drop the assumption that conceptual knowledge of manipulable artifacts is distributed over the same representations that are active when such objects are being used. In other words, it could be that sensorimotor knowledge is functionally dissociable from conceptual knowledge, but that such knowledge is nevertheless required to perform correctly on naming and recognition tasks. Note that the revised Sensory/Motor Theory *must* assume that knowledge of the ways in which objects are used is required, or at least differentially important, for recognizing tools; if the theory does not assume sensorimotor knowledge is (at least) differentially important for recognizing/naming tools, then it would not have provided an explanatory account of the cause of category-specific semantic deficits for non-living things.

However, even on the basis of the neuropsychological evidence that has already been reviewed, it is clear that revising the Sensory/Motor Theory in this way will not be sufficient to save the theory. For instance, if knowledge of the ways in which objects are manipulated is required (or differentially important) in order to recognize/name objects, then one cannot account for the performance of the patient reported by Ochipa, Rothi, and Heilman (1989). Recall that this patient was relatively unimpaired at naming tools (17/20 correct) but was severely impaired at demonstrating the use of the same tools (2/20 correct) (see Fig. 10.3).

Another version of the Sensory/Motor Theory stresses the contexts in which different types of information are recruited:

Consistent with the notion of 'privileged access' to various kinds of stored information (e.g., sensorimotor versus verbal/propositional) according to the modality of the task (e.g., action versus verbal), it may be that on naturalistic action tasks, manipulation nodes for objects are the most strongly and rapidly activated, whereas on verbal tasks concerned with man-made objects, function nodes receive greater and/or more rapid activation. The hypothesized privileged role of manipulation knowledge in naturalistic action may explain why JD [reported in Buxbaum, Veramanti, and Schwartz 2000] and WC are unable to use their relatively intact function knowledge to prevent object misuse errors in naturalistic action. (Buxbaum, Veramonti, and Schwartz 2000, 94)

It is not clear what work the notion of 'privileged access' could be doing, unless the proposal is that there is an amodal semantic system. In other words, if the semantic system is assumed to be modality-specific, then there would be no need for the assumption of a *privileged* relationship between a certain type of semantic information and a certain type of modality-specific input/output representation, since the semantic representations themselves would already be modality-specific. However, if an amodal semantic system is assumed, then this is not a 'weaker' version of the Sensory/Motor Theory, but rather an amodal account of the organization of semantic knowledge that stresses the importance of different types of semantic information as a function of task demands (see e.g. Caramazza *et al.* 1990).[23]

In this section we have critically evaluated two assumptions: *first*, we have shown that the assumption that conceptual knowledge of manipulable artifacts is distributed over modality-specific sensorimotor representations is contrary to the performance of various apraxic patients. *Second*, we have shown that the (weaker) assumption that in order to identify/name tools information about their use must be accessible is contrary to the performance of patients such as the one reported by Ochipa, Rothi, and Heilman (1989). What we are left with then are data from functional neuroimaging and neuropsychology but no theoretical framework within which to interpret these findings. Specifically, two facts must be explained: (1) the functional autonomy of conceptual knowledge of tools from sensorimotor representations; and (2) the functional autonomy of conceptual knowledge of artifacts from conceptual knowledge of living things. In the next section we consider what a Domain-Specific interpretation of these data might look like.

3.4. The Domain-Specific Hypothesis and the category of tools

The functional neuroimaging data reviewed above demonstrate that 'tool' stimuli compared to 'animal' stimuli differentially activate left premotor cortex, the left middle temporal gyri, and the medial fusiform gyri bilaterally. How does one interpret these findings? Consider the following thought experiment. While subjects are naming pictures of 'tools' and 'animals', the activation of spinal cells is recorded. Specifically, recordings are made of the activation of nerve cells that innervate muscles in the hand and arm, and which are normally activated in the

---

[23] We are grateful to Laurel Buxbaum (personal communication) for bringing these issues to our attention.

course of using a tool. Imagine it is found that these nerve cells are activated when subjects name pictures of 'tools' more so than when they name pictures of 'animals'. Would we want to make the claim that conceptual knowledge of tools is stored (even in part) in spinal nerve cells? Would we even want to argue for the (seemingly weaker) claim that in order to name and/or recognize tools, the 'information' 'represented by' these spinal neurons (be it conceptual or not) must be activated? The thrust of *reductio* arguments of this type is that not everything that is (differentially) activated in the course of completing a conceptual task is conceptual, and not everything that is activated needs to be activated. It seems quite plausible that, while different tasks may *require* access to different types of information, it very well may be the case that in the course of completing different tasks (e.g. sitting on a chair, naming a chair) the same information is activated.

This type of an approach would seem a better fit to otherwise aberrant findings in the functional neuroimaging literature. For instance, Moore and Price (1999) found that fruit and tool stimuli both activated a common area in posterior sensory cortex near the junction of the intraparietal cortex. This area has been shown to be activated in tasks requiring subjects to reach for objects (Binkofski *et al.* 1998; Johnson *et al.* 1996; for review and discussion, see Bookheimer 2002; Johnson-Frey 2004). Thus, we might conclude that information about how to grasp objects is activated when subjects perform naming or matching tasks over graspable objects. However, would we want to conclude that in order to (for instance) name or match pictures of fruit, this information *must* be activated? If we would not want to make the claim for fruit, then why make it for tools?

The thrust of the *reductio* argument outlined above is not intended to be that motor cortex activation in the course of observing manipulable objects is purely ancillary and/or inconsequential. It seems likely that such motor information does play *some* role in how we think about and understand manipulable objects. Our point is rather to highlight the way in which activation evidence can be balanced against evidence from cognitive neuropsychology. Consider what a neuropsychological patient who has an impairment for using objects might be able to understand about those objects. As was reviewed above, such patients can succeed on a range of tasks requiring retrieval of conceptual knowledge (e.g. naming, etc.). This does not mean, however, that future research will not demonstrate that there are fine shades of understanding that are disturbed in such patients. Here we might suggest the possibility that the situation with such apraxic patients is akin to observing a photograph in black and white as opposed to in color. The black-and-white photograph preserves all of the structural and relational information contained in the color photograph. Perhaps the 'conceptual' tasks that have to date been administered to apraxic patients have only queried such 'structural and relational' information.

The functional neuroimaging and neuropsychological data that have been discussed resonate with the view that the organization of conceptual knowledge of tools is determined by Domain-Specific constraints. The neuropsychological data indicate that a deficit for artifacts is not necessarily associated with a disproportionate deficit to a type or modality of knowledge. The data from functional neuroimaging indicate that 'tool' stimuli differentially activate an area in the ventral object processing system, in line with the proposal that conceptual knowledge is organized by object domain within any given neuroanatomically defined modality. Furthermore, the fact that 'tool' stimuli compared to 'animal' stimuli differentially activate left premotor cortex is compatible with the view that information is organized by domain even at a relatively low (i.e. modality-specific) level of representation. In other words, *if* one assumed that conceptual knowledge of tools is subject to Domain-Specific principles, *then* one would also expect that there will be modality-specific representations encoding the motor movements associated with the use of tools, and that these representations will be (perhaps by default) Domain-Specific. An interesting hypothesis for future research is that neural specificity for tools in ventral temporal cortex may be due to input from frontal and parietal brain structures that directly mediate object-directed action.

4. CONCLUSION

The discussion in this chapter has been organized around the issues of how conceptual knowledge is organized and represented. We focused our discussion of the organization of conceptual knowledge on two proposals that have been advanced to account for the performance of patients with category-specific semantic deficits: the Sensory/Functional Theory and the Domain-Specific Hypothesis. It was shown that the basic prediction made by the Sensory/Functional Theory is contrary to the known facts: almost all patients reported with category-specific deficits who have been tested for performance on different types of semantic information presented with equivalent impairments to visual/perceptual and functional/associative knowledge. We concluded that the Sensory/Functional Theory does not provide an explanatory account of the phenomenon of category-specific deficit, and we argued for a Domain-Specific organization of conceptual knowledge. We discussed what it might mean to conjoin the assumption that conceptual knowledge is organized by modality or type of information with the assumption that conceptual knowledge is organized by Domain. This conjunction of assumptions predicts that within (for instance) the visual modality, information will be organized by object Domain. This prediction was found to be consistent with findings in functional neuroimaging demonstrating segregation by semantic category in ventral and lateral temporal cortex.

The functional neuroimaging data that have been reviewed raise more questions than they resolve. If these data are interpreted in the context of a theoretical framework that admits the possibility of two orthogonal dimensions of organization, Domain and Modality, then the question becomes: what is the nature of the information represented in ventral and lateral temporal areas? This question is a species of a broader question that has remained relatively unaddressed since the proposal of modality-specific conceptual subsystems was first proposed in modern times by Lhermitte and Beauvois (1973) and subsequently developed into the Sensory/Functional Theory by Warrington and her collaborators. Originally, 'visual/perceptual' conceptual information was distinguished from 'functional/associative' information. More recently, concerted attempts have been made to establish a more fine-grained taxonomy of knowledge, for instance, distinguishing conceptual information about visual form from information about visual color and visual motion (e.g. Cree and McRae 2003). However, regardless of the grain of the knowledge-type taxonomy adopted, questions remain about what makes a given type of conceptual information the type that it is. In other words: what is visual about 'visual' conceptual knowledge? The answer is not straightforward, as at least three, non-mutually exclusive possibilities could be envisioned. First, it could be argued that what makes 'visual' semantic information visual is that it is stored in a visual format. Second, it could be argued that what makes this information visual is that it is *about* the visual properties of objects. Third, it could be that what is *visual* about 'visual' knowledge is that such knowledge was learned through the visual modality (for discussion, see Caramazza *et al.* 1990). Any theory that seriously pursues knowledge-type taxonomies as a means of functionally carving the conceptual system carries the burden of specifying what aspect of the represented information warrants the applied labels. Furthermore, any positive framework that interprets the patterns of activation observed in ventral and lateral temporal areas must give a principled reason for allocating a given functional role to a given area. Does the differential activation for living and non-living things in ventral temporal regions reflect a dissociation at the conceptual level or at the level of modality-specific input representations? These questions are important challenges faced by all theoretical proposals that invoke either (a) the assumption of modality-specific semantic subsystems, and/or (b) the distinction between modality-specific input/output representations and conceptual knowledge. To our knowledge, all extant theories invoke either one or both of these theoretical distinctions.

One implication of the foregoing discussion is that the assumptions made regarding the representation of conceptual knowledge will influence the possible hypothesis space regarding the assumptions that might be made about the organization of conceptual knowledge. For instance, we have argued that the facts from apraxia compel a model in which it is assumed that conceptual knowledge is not exhausted by the information represented internal to modality-specific input/output systems. *One* way in which such functional independence might be realized is to assume it corresponds to a difference in the format of the representation of conceptual knowledge compared to modality-specific input/output information. For instance, modality-specific input/output representations may be (perhaps by definition) stored in a format congruent with their modality (i.e. motor engrams are stored in a motor format, visual structural descriptions are stored in a visual format). This might in turn constrain the possible formats in which conceptual information could be represented, in that, for instance, conceptual information about the ways in which objects are manipulated could not, by assumption, be stored in a motor format. The speculative nature of such considerations underlines the incredible amount of work that remains to be done in order to flesh out a corroborated model of the organization and representation of conceptual knowledge.

One theme that emerges from this chapter is that the individual assumptions of which different proposals are comprised are not necessarily mutually contrary as hypotheses about the organization and representation of conceptual knowledge. However, theories that conjoin those assumptions may be, and in fact often are, mutually contrary as proposals about the cause of a given empirical phenomenon. It has been our intention to make explicit the levels at which various claims have been made as well as how the different claims succeed or fail to account for the extant facts. Different proposals appeal to different principles of organization, and one way to organize the extant space of hypotheses is to acknowledge where the various proposals fit within a common hierarchy of questions (Caramazza and Mahon 2003).

At the broadest level is the question of whether or not conceptual knowledge is organized by Domain-Specific constraints. We have argued that the facts of category-specific semantic deficits indicate that object domain is one constraint on the organization of conceptual knowledge. The second question is whether modality or type of information is an orthogonal constraint on the organization of conceptual knowledge in the brain. As noted above, before such a hypothesis can be taken seriously, articulated proposals are required as to what it is that makes, for instance, 'visual conceptual knowledge' *visual*. The third level in this hierarchy of questions concerns the organization of conceptual knowledge within any given object domain (and/or modality-specific semantic store): the principles invoked by Correlated Structure Theories may prove useful for articulating answers to this question. Thus, assuming a Domain-Specific Framework in order to account for the facts of category-specific semantic deficits leaves unaddressed important issues about the organization and representation of information within domains.

The combination of neuropsychology and functional neuroimaging is beginning to provide promising grounds for raising theoretically motivated questions concerning the organization and representation of conceptual knowledge in the human brain. At present, however, theories of the organization and representation of conceptual knowledge are to a large extent underdetermined by the data that are often marshaled in support of them. Thus, in conclusion, we highlight the need for patients presenting with conceptual and/or praxis deficits for artifacts to be carefully tested on theoretically motivated conceptual, linguistic, perceptual, and praxis tests.[24]

[24] Preparation of this manuscript was supported in part by an NSF Graduate Research Fellowship to BZM and NIH grant DC 04542 to AC. The authors are grateful to Laurel Buxbaum and Alex Martin for their comments on an earlier version of this manuscript. This chapter is an expanded version of an article that appeared in *Cognitive Neuropsychology* (Mahon and Caramazza 2003).

PART III

COGNITIVE DEVELOPMENT

11

The Conceptual Foundations of Animals and Artifacts[1]

Jean M. Mandler

The thesis of this chapter is that concepts of animals and artifacts begin to be developed in early infancy. Animals and artifacts, of course, represent a distinction between animate and inanimate things. However, although animals are differentiated from other things (including plants) at an early age, virtually all the infant research on inanimates has been confined to artifacts. So we do not know what infants think about other inanimate kinds, such as rocks, shells, pieces of driftwood, or slices of meat. Nevertheless, most inanimate objects other than food that infants deal with are artifacts, and the information infants use to separate animals from artifacts owes a good deal to a few fundamental differences between the animate and inanimate realms. It is these aspects of early learning about animals and artifacts that I emphasize here.

Early concepts of animals and a variety of artifacts form the foundation on which the adult conceptual system of objects rests, and this foundation and the outlines of the system built upon it remain in place throughout life. Because the conceptual system begins to be laid down so early, the first and most deeply rooted conceptions about what is essential to animalness or to inanimate objecthood are constrained by what the preverbal infant mind can conceive. The fundamental notions that organize the developing conceptual system tend to be perceptually based, involving characteristics such as 'moves by itself' and 'moves only when contacted by another object', or 'doesn't move'. Because the overall structure of the conceptual system remains roughly the same throughout life, study of its foundations may provide useful information for understanding differences in how natural kinds and artifacts come to be conceived by adults.

In this chapter I first discuss the experimental evidence for concept formation in infancy. The data show that the earliest object concepts tend to be global in

[1] Portions of section 3 of this chapter are based on chapter 5 of Mandler (2004).

nature and gradually become differentiated with experience. In the next section I discuss what early global concepts of animals and artifacts consist of and how they are learned. I end with a discussion of the relative contributions of innate domain-specific processes and more general learning processes to the formation of concepts of animals and inanimate things (including artifacts). I propose that a mechanism of perceptual meaning analysis accounts for most of the work required to conceptualize objects from these two realms.

1. WHEN CONCEPTUAL LIFE BEGINS

It is a relatively recent discovery that concepts of both animals and artifacts begin to be formed early in infancy. Piaget, who played the dominant role in the study of cognitive development for the past thirty to forty years, believed that nothing even approaching concepts like those of adults is formed until sometime between age 2 and 4 years (Piaget 1951, 1952). He claimed that in the first two years of life infants form increasingly elaborate sensorimotor representations, but only late in this period do they begin to be capable of forming concepts of objects and events that they can use for purposes of thought—whether recall of the past, problem-solving in the present, or anticipation of the future. Even then, he posited that these first concepts are so variable, shifting, and unprincipled as to barely warrant the term—he called them 'preconcepts' (Piaget 1951).

Piaget's hegemony in the field discouraged experimental study of concept formation in infancy. If infants don't have concepts, why look for them in the laboratory? This point of view began to change with studies showing that even preverbal infants are capable of recall of the past (see Carver and Bauer 2001, and Mandler 2004, for discussion), a phenomenon that in adults is considered evidence for explicit conceptual knowledge. Because infants do not yet talk their recall is studied in the laboratory by means of deferred imitation (Mandler 1990; Meltzoff 1990). In this technique an adult models a new event for the infant, using little replicas of animals and artifacts. After a specified delay (up to a year later; McDonough and Mandler 1994), the infant is brought back to the lab and handed the props. Spontaneous imitation of the event that had been modeled is the measure of recall of the episode.

Such data indicated that by the second half of the first year infants have begun to develop conceptual interpretations of the world—otherwise recall would be impossible—and so the question arose as to what these earliest concepts consist of. What properties of objects or events are included? In the past decade a series of studies from my laboratory showed that at least from 7 months of age infants are forming global concepts of animals, vehicles, and furniture, and by 11 months are forming global concepts of plants and kitchen utensils as well (Mandler and McDonough 1993, 1998*a*). (These are the earliest ages for which we have positive evidence; the actual onset of conceptualizing what is being perceived could well begin earlier, in some cases perhaps even from birth.) At the same time, there is no evidence that at these young ages infants conceptualize animals or furniture in a more detailed way.[2] For example, they do not seem to distinguish one land animal from another conceptually, or conceptualize tables and chairs as different kinds, even though 3-month-olds perceive the differences between pictures of individual kinds of animals and furniture and categorize them correctly on perceptual tasks (Behl-Chadha 1996; Quinn, Eimas, and Rosenkrantz 1993). One possible exception to the general finding of global before individual kind concepts is the category of vehicles; even 7-month-olds (in southern California) apparently make some distinctions between different kinds of vehicles, perhaps based on their locations (ground or air) or whether they are enclosed or not (cars and trucks versus motorcycles).

One of the sources of data on conceptualization in the first year of life is the familiarization/preferential-examining task, that uses realistic little models that infants can explore. Infants are familiarized with a number of different examples of a given category and then given a new member from the same category plus a new item from a different category. Longer examination of the new category member is taken as evidence that a categorical distinction between the items has been made. The task does not in itself tell us the basis for distinguishing the categories. It has been suggested that infants' accomplishments on this task do not indicate conceptual functioning but are done solely on a perceptual basis (Quinn and Eimas 1997). For example, if the familiarization category is animals and the contrasting category vehicles, infants might be able to make this discrimination simply because most animals look more like each other than they look like vehicles. However, discrimination between animals and vehicles on the object-examination task occurs even in the face of high perceptual similarity of all the items (e.g. Pauen 2002) and often fails among subclasses of animals that look quite different. For example, 9-month-olds distinguish between little models of birds and airplanes (see Fig. 11.1), all of which have outstretched wings, while failing to distinguish between little models of dogs and rabbits or dogs and fish that are perceptually quite different (Mandler and McDonough 1993).[3]

When infants are somewhat older the sequential touching task can be used. In this task one places haphazardly in front of an infant four objects from each of two categories. One-to 2-year-olds rarely sort objects into piles, but the order in which they touch them tells us if they are sensitive to their relatedness. The measure used is number and length of sequential runs of touches within categories; these runs are assessed against chance levels of responding (Mandler,

[2] It is for this reason that I use the terms global or domain-level, rather than superordinate, to refer to the first conceptual categories, because they tend to have no subdivisions.

[3] Infants as young as 7 months do distinguish dogs and birds, however (Mandler and McDonough 1998*a*). The reason for this difference in response to fish and birds vis-à-vis dogs is not yet known, although it may have to do with familiarity and/or the location and salience of flying animals.

Figure 11.1. The models of birds and planes that 9-month-olds successfully categorize

Fivush, and Reznick 1987). This test is a developmental precursor to the sorting tests used to study classification in older children. Using this task we showed that, from 18 months to 24 months, infants are sensitive to the global categories of animals and vehicles (Mandler, Bauer, and McDonough 1991). Within these broad categories, infants also differentiate land, air, and sea animals, and land and air vehicles (boats were not tested). It appears that there is a relatively early tripartite division among land-, air-, and sea-animals (see also Oakes, Coppage, and Dingel 1997), and at least a division between land and air vehicles. We found little subcategorization within these broad categories (dogs versus horses or rabbits, cars versus trucks or motorcycles) at 18 months, and up to 30 months only about half the children categorized at this 'basic' level. It may be noted that on this task, which is a more stringent test of conceptual categorization than the object-examination task described above, vehicles were not divided into individual kinds earlier than animals.

Other tests using this technique showed that 23-month-olds categorize animals as different from plants, and kitchen utensils from furniture, but do not yet categorize tools and musical instruments (Mandler, Bauer, and McDonough 1991). It is not that infants this age know nothing about the objects in these latter categories—for example, they would hammer with the hammer and toot the horn or 'play' the piano. But they did not react to tools and instruments as categories, choosing instead to do such things as to 'fix' the piano with pliers. This kind of thematic play behavior was different from the systematic within-category touching found with the other global categories studied. So although by age 2 children have learned some appropriate responses to a given musical instrument or tool, they do not seem to see the overall relatedness of one instrument or tool to another; at any rate they do not provide evidence on this test of having formed an overall conception of tools or instruments as forming a common class (see Hauser and Santos, this volume, for comparison with non-human primates, but note that Hauser and Santos discuss the issue of whether non-human primates have a concept of any tool, such as a hammer, whereas the experiment described here concerned a higher-order category of tools that groups hammers and pliers and wrenches together). We also looked at subcategorization within the plant, furniture, kitchen utensil, and musical instrument categories. We contrasted cactus and trees, tables and chairs, spoons and forks, and strings and horns, but found no 'basic-level' categorization at 2 years of age on this task.

We also used the sequential touching task to study the associative categories of kitchen things and bathroom things (Mandler, Fivush, and Reznick 1987). We found that 14-month-olds distinguished these perceptually highly diverse categories. These are not the usual taxonomic categories, of course, but are based on household locations and/or the events that take place therein. Even taxonomic categories may be at least partially based on location, for example, the early division between land and air animals and vehicles. In a similar vein, Bauer and I found that 16-month-olds categorize manipulable household objects as different from vehicles on this task (Mandler 2002). This finding could indicate either a manipulable versus large artifact distinction or an indoor versus outdoor distinction; in either case this contrast has also been found in adults (Warrington and McCarthy 1987).

More recently we confirmed the overall picture of initially global concepts becoming gradually refined by using a third technique that we call generalized imitation (Mandler and McDonough 1996; 1998*b*; 2000). We model a simple event, such as giving a little replica of a dog a drink from a cup. Instead of giving the infants the same objects to use to imitate what they have observed, we vary the choices available to them. For example, along with the cup we do not give the infants the dog but instead we give them different objects, such as a bird and an airplane or a different dog and a cat, and see which (if either) they use to imitate the event they were shown.

The generalized imitation task can be used to assess inductive inferences, by showing how far infants generalize the properties they have observed with specific objects. This in turn gives us information about the breadth of their concepts. In our first experiments using this technique (Mandler and McDonough 1996; McDonough and Mandler 1998) we found that 9- to 14-month-olds generalized the properties of drinking and sleeping across the entire animal domain and the properties of being keyed and giving rides across the entire vehicle domain, regardless of whether the generalization examples were perceptually similar to the modeled exemplar. (It is of interest that some of these generalizations, such as that fish drink or that airplanes are keyed, will eventually have to be revised. It nevertheless seems an efficient way to build a knowledge base—making broad generalizations first, and adding exceptions later.) At the same time infants very rarely generalized animal properties to vehicles or vice versa.

In addition, in Mandler and McDonough (1996) we modeled the incorrect as well as correct behavior (for example, giving both a dog and a car a drink, or keying both a car and a dog). Fourteen-month-olds typically only imitated the correct behavior, ignoring the incorrect behavior. This result shows that the infants use their existing conceptual knowledge when they imitate and are not merely aping whatever the experimenter does. Another illustration showing that infants make use of their conceptual knowledge in their imitations is that if we model something appropriate to both domains (such as washing a car or making a car go into a building), after they imitate this behavior with a different vehicle they often go on to demonstrate it with an animal as well (Mandler and McDonough 1998*b*). It is only behavior that is appropriate solely for one domain that is restricted to that domain. Thus, we see that the kinds of generalizations that infants make are determined by their conceptual categories from an early age. In fact, we have been able to show conceptually based induction with the generalized imitation test as young as 9 months of age (McDonough and Mandler 1998).

Because infants imitate on the basis of what they have understood the model to do, the generalized imitation task is also useful in determining how specifically infants conceptualize what they have seen. In the experiments just described infants generalized to the limits of the domain for both animals and vehicles. But we can also ask how precisely infants conceptualize a dog when they see it being given a drink. Do they construe the event as a *dog* being given a drink? If so, in order to match the model they should choose another dog to use as a substitute in preference to a cat). Or do they construe the event as a *land animal* being given a drink (in which case they might choose a cat or a rabbit as often as another dog)? Or do they construe the event as an *animal* being given a drink (in which case they might choose a bird)?

We have carried out a series of such contrasts (Mandler and McDonough 1998*b*). When we gave a dog a drink or put a dog to bed, and then gave 14-month-olds the prop along with another dog and another land animal, the infants were just as likely to choose the other animal (cat or rabbit) as the dog, indicating that they had not interpreted the animal specifically as a dog. On the other hand, if we gave them another dog with a bird, they were more likely to choose the dog, although they then often went on and gave the bird a drink too. They seemed to be telling us, 'I saw you give a land animal a drink, but birds drink too'. ('Land animal' is my construal—we do not yet know whether infants differentiate land and air animals in terms of where they are found, having legs or wings, or a combination of properties.) With vehicles, on the other hand, infants tended to pick an exemplar from the same subcategory for their imitations. For example, if shown a car being keyed, they were more likely to choose another car than a motorcycle or a plane to demonstrate keying. They also tended to use the other vehicle less often as a second choice for their imitations, especially the airplane. The infants seemed to be telling us, 'I saw you key a car'. Thus, congruent with the data from the object-examination test (although not with the sequential-touching test) at 14 months greater differentiation was exhibited in the vehicle domain than in the animal domain.

Using this technique, we have been mapping out conceptual development within several domains over the first two years. In particular we have been trying to determine when infants differentiate the animal, plant, and artifact domains in terms of assigning different properties to subclasses of these domains. In our first experiment we examined two natural kind and two artifact properties (Mandler and McDonough 1998*b*). For the natural kind properties, we modeled a dog chewing on a bone and tested generalization with a different dog and a goose. We also modeled sniffing a flower and tested generalization with a different flower and a tree. For the artifact properties we modeled drinking with a cup and tested generalization with a mug and a frying pan. We also modeled sleeping in a crib, and tested generalization with a bed and a bathtub. As shown in Fig. 11.2, 14-month-olds did not respond differently to appropriate and inappropriate exemplars for either the natural kinds or the artifacts.

For example, they gave the goose the bone to chew on as often as a dog and were as likely to pick the pan as a mug to drink from. At 20 months infants still generalized the natural kind properties equally often to appropriate and inappropriate objects, but had begun to narrow down their responses in the artifact domains. That is, they still made geese chew on bones and people sniff trees, but now they were more likely to restrict drinking to cups, not pans, and sleeping to beds, not bathtubs. The good performance on household artifacts at 20 months is not merely due to increased ability to imitate, because otherwise the infants should have improved on the natural kind properties as well. Instead it appears to be a function of how much detailed knowledge about artifacts and natural kinds infants (in our culture) have.

We have replicated this result with other household artifacts, to see when infants have learned that you wash dishes in a sink, not a bathtub, that you sit at table on a chair, not a toilet, that you brush hair with a hairbrush, not a toothbrush, and that you hammer with a hammer, not a wrench (Mandler and McDonough 2000). At 14 months most infants did not significantly distinguish among these alternative possibilities (although they were somewhat more successful with the chair–toilet contrast than the others), but by 19 months they did. In this series of experiments we also again checked for differences in rate of learning about animal and vehicle properties. We asked when infants know that birds, not rabbits, go in nests and that rabbits, not birds, eat carrots.

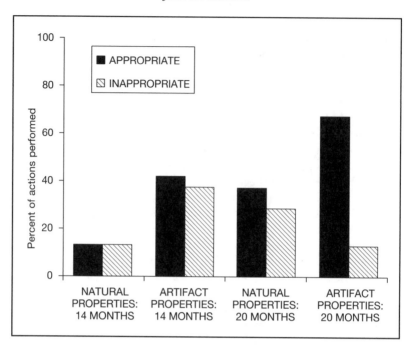

Figure 11.2. Generalization of properties to appropriate and inappropriate objects by 14- and 20-month-olds. Adapted from Mandler and McDonough (1998*b*) with permission from Elsevier

We also asked when infants know that you wear a helmet on a motorcycle but not in a car, and that you put gasoline into a car but not into a child's wagon.[4] Again, we found that at 14 months infants did not make these discriminations. At 19 months they showed learning of the vehicle properties, but still were poor at the animal properties. By 24 months they were knowledgeable on all.

Even though 14-month-olds were not good at differentiating artifacts, it is not the case that they know nothing about them or that they are simply responding to the affordances that objects provide (see Keil, Greif, and Kerner this volume). When we provided choices for the imitations that were conceptually less related than the examples just described, even 14-month-olds were successful. For example, although they imitated washing plates in both a tub and a sink they did not wash plates in a bed, in spite of its end pieces and sides making a container like the sink, and although they used a toothbrush to groom hair, they did not use a spoon to do so. In these cases, by 14 months infants have gone beyond responding to mere affordances. At the same time, it appears

---

[4] It is state law in California that everyone, including children, must wear a helmet when riding a motorcycle or a tricycle.

that there is gradual, and sometimes haphazard, differentiation from very global characterizations of objects to increasingly more specific characterizations. Thus, although 14-month-olds distinguished between beds and sinks as places to wash dishes, in one of our experiments they did not distinguish between beds and tubs as places to sleep. Differentiation of the functions of various household objects may be learned in a piecemeal fashion, so that anomalous assignments exist along with correct ones. Children might first learn that certain kinds of objects can be used to hold things (Baillargeon, Kotovsky, and Needham 1995), then that small containers with handles are used for drinking (whether they be cups or pans) and large containers are used for washing and sleeping, then that some large containers are used only for sleeping and others only for washing, and finally the specifics that differentiate tubs from sinks. During the course of this learning, however, the overarching global concepts control the associations that get formed. The control of associations by conceptual meaning (rather than spatiotemporal contiguity or physical similarity) means that infants can and do make extensive conceptual generalizations beyond what they actually experience.

Although our data suggest that at the end of the first year understanding the functions of familiar artifacts is still not very precise, recent work indicates that if given a brief training session even 11- to 12-month-olds can appreciate artifacts' functions in a more detailed way. Träuble and Pauen (in press) showed infants novel objects and found that they categorized them by overall similarity without paying any particular attention to the parts. But if shown how the parts performed different functions (a T-bar that could pull a pair of hooks out of an object, and an inverted T-bar that could poke into a hole and make a sound), the infants then categorized the objects according to these parts rather than by overall similarity. Such data indicate that learning artifacts' functions requires closer attention to detail than infants often give to objects, but is well within the capabilities of 1-year-olds.

Combining the results across these various experiments, we can conclude that in the second half of the first year a number of global conceptual distinctions are made that differentiate animals, vehicles, furniture, utensils, and plants. In addition, infants in this age range distinguish several kinds of vehicles (cars, motorcycles, and airplanes but not cars from trucks) and land versus air animals (or at least dogs versus birds). Near the end of this period they also distinguish between classes of varied land and sea animals (Oakes, Coppage, and Dingel 1997). However, aside from differentiating cars and motorcycles (both road vehicles), there is as yet no evidence that individual kinds within global domains (or at least within broad divisions of them such as land, sea, and air animals or vehicles) have been conceptualized as distinct from others.

By the first half of the second year infants begin to make conceptual distinctions *within* the global categories of vehicles and household artifacts, but lag behind on differentiation of the natural kinds of animals and plants. Overall, in the first year we found few if any differences in performance on various global concepts. However, as infants begin to make finer differentiations within these concepts in the second year, differences in rate of learning about natural kinds and artifacts become apparent. In contrast to the speculations of Keil, Greif, and Kerner (this volume) about older children, in the beginning artifacts are categorized more easily than are natural kinds, even if their exact function is still not well understood. Needless to say, the findings reported here do not imply that this difference is a universal characteristic of development. It is more likely due to the emphasis our culture places on artifacts. Infants in southern California have much more daily interaction with a variety of artifacts than they do with animals or plants. Greater experience and opportunities for learning seem the most likely cause for these differences. However, cross-cultural studies would be useful to test this view.

A reasonable question is whether early conceptions of animals are generalized from conceptions of people, or even if people and animals are distinguished. At this point we do not have a great deal of evidence about how infants conceive of humans versus other animals. What evidence there is suggests that humans and other animals may not at first be well differentiated from each other (Quinn and Eimas 1998), but become so by about 7 months (Pauen 2000). There is also some indication that humans are categorized in a different way than are other animals (Quinn and Eimas 1998). It would not be surprising if the course of learning about people differs from all other categories, and whatever human bias exists might affect the way in which other animal categories are learned as well, but as yet there are few direct comparisons that might answer this question. Overall, these data from the infancy period dovetail nicely with the work of Keil (1979), who found that older children's development of ontological knowledge also proceeds in a downward direction, consisting of the gradual differentiation of broad, higher-level categories into increasingly narrow subclasses. One of the last divisions to be made is that between human psychological characteristics and those of other animals.

The data are also consistent with neuropsychological data on breakdown of the conceptual system under brain damage in adulthood (Mandler 1998, 2002; Patterson and Hodges 1995; see also Mahon and Caramazza, this volume). The neuropsychological data indicate a hierarchical system of superordinate concepts with various subclasses nested within them. The broad outlines of these superordinate concepts seem quite similar to the global concepts formed in infancy, and the major subdivisions of these concepts are those found slightly later in infancy. Because of the nature of the learning process, in which individual kinds are learned as a subdivision of global conceptual divisions, the global (superordinate) conceptions should be the most firmly established. That is, every time one learns a differentiation in the animal domain—for example, differentiating sheep and goats—it is done in the context of their animal membership, which itself is not in doubt. Therefore one might predict a pattern of 'first in, last out' if the system begins to fall apart (Mandler 1998). The available literature indicates exactly that pattern (Patterson and Hodges 1995; Warrington 1975). For example, in their systematic study of the loss of knowledge in a patient with semantic dementia who was particularly impaired in the animal domain, Hodges, Graham, and Patterson (1995) found that at first distinctions between individual kinds such as eagles and robins or horses and cows were lost, then higher levels such as the division of animals into land and air creatures, and only very late in the course of degeneration was the notion of animal itself sometimes misattributed to an inanimate object.

Thus, the breakdown data are consistent with the acquisition data, showing a conceptual system organized from the top down. Interestingly, language appears to be relatively unimportant in constructing these object domains in the sense that the outlines of the adult system are in place before language begins. Naming 'basic-level' categories has been shown to facilitate differentiation of animal kinds (Balaban and Waxman 1997), but there is no evidence that it reorganizes the overall outlines of the domain. It should be noted, however, that the conclusion of a relatively small organizing role for language concerns object concepts. Language may be more important in structuring conceptual systems of relational concepts, such as spatial relations (Gentner 1982; McDonough, Choi, and Mandler 2003).

The neuropsychological data on breakdown of the conceptual system are also consistent with the notion that infants carve out a number of domains early in infancy that do not necessarily reflect an animate–inanimate distinction (Mandler 2002; see also Santos and Caramazza 2002). Infants clearly distinguish animals from plants, but we have no evidence that they see any relation between them or that they contrast plants with inanimate objects. Indeed, given that they don't move, it is more likely that plants are treated as inanimates. The category of food is undoubtedly another early categorization (unfortunately one we cannot study by our methods because infants tend to dwell on it to the exclusion of everything else—which, of course, is evidence in its own right). Although still unstudied, buildings are highly apt to form still another early category. At this point we do not know how, or if, these various inanimate categories are related to each other. They may be unrelated for infants, but it is equally possible that there is a broad category of non-animals, divided into movable and unmoving things. The role of motion in identifying objects as animate or inanimate is discussed in the next section.

One consequence of the outlines of conceptual knowledge of animals and various artifacts being laid down so early in life may be a persistent tendency to think about such objects in a rather primitive way, even when schooling and other experience teach us differently. Infants have not yet learned about the biological nature of animals (Carey 1985) and often very little about the function of artifacts. Nevertheless they appear to have some firmly rooted conceptions, such as that animals are things that move themselves. It seems likely to me that even as adults our most basic view of what animals are is that they are things that can move themselves and that inanimate objects are things that cannot. I suspect most adults could tolerate the news that tiger DNA can transmute into shark DNA more easily than that a stone can move by itself.

2. HOW THE FIRST CONCEPTS OF ANIMALS AND ARTIFACTS ARE LEARNED

The previous section showed that the earliest object concepts tend to be broad and relatively undifferentiated, but did not address the issue of how they are defined and learned. In the past the most common view of concept formation was that infants learn to categorize objects such as dogs on the basis of the physical similarity of one dog to another (e.g. Quine 1969). Concept formation was said to consist of categorizing dogs as alike and then associating various behaviors and other properties to them. Thus a concept equaled a set of physical properties plus various associations. For example, Quine posited that infants and young children use an innate animal-like sense of similarity to make their first generalizations because they do not yet have any concepts at their disposal. In this view, upon seeing the family dog eat, the infant generalizes that other dogs eat as well. With experience the infant observes cats eat, birds eat, and various other animals eat, and eventually (perhaps with the help of language) makes the more difficult inference that all animals, even though they don't look alike, nevertheless all eat.

As we have seen this view does not hold. As far as learning concepts are concerned there appears to be no elementary law of association that operates independently of meaning. The early concepts are much broader than dog or chair, and inferences and associations are made at this broader conceptual level as well. Our data show that infants generalize behavior characteristic of animals and vehicles to instances they have never seen before, such as aardvarks and forklifts, and even overextend characteristic behavior, such as making a fish drink or an airplane give a bird a ride. Differentiation, not synthesis, is the rule of concept formation in infancy. Nevertheless, infants must be able to identify class membership or else they could not make conceptual generalizations at all. Because they do not seem to make much use of perceptual similarity in early concept formation, it is a fair question to ask how they identify any animal as a member of the animal class. There must be *some* basis of similarity for them to identify an animal as an animal.

Our understanding of the exact nature of the earliest global concepts such as animal is still tentative. However, we do know that infants are highly responsive to motion. Moving objects engage their attention much more than stationary objects, and various categorical achievements appear earlier when objects are moving (Spelke 1985), presumably because the information carried by motion specifies object properties better than does static information (Kellman 1993).

Furthermore, because of poor acuity in the first few weeks of life the main source of perceptual information for infants is more likely to consist of the paths that objects take than their physical appearance.

There are a number of characteristics of object motion that give adults an impression of animacy (Stewart 1984).[5] Important ones that have been studied for infancy are contingent interaction with objects from a distance, self movement, and the rhythmical character of biological movement (see Wilson 1986, for a description of variables involved in animal motion). For example, 3-month-olds perceptually differentiate the motion of people from similar but biologically incorrect motion (Bertenthal 1993). One of the most powerful of the factors influencing infant perception appears to be sensitivity to whether objects interact contingently with the infant, which has been shown to be operative as early as 2 to 3 months (Frye *et al.* 1983; Watson 1972). Infants this age give what appears to be a social response to objects that interact contingently with them, regardless of what the objects look like. By seven months or so infants have also learned that people start motion on their own, whereas inanimate objects either do not move at all or move only if contacted by another object (Poulin-Dubois, Lepage, and Ferland 1996; Spelke, Phillips, and Woodward 1995). Infants also learn at an early age the difference between biological and mechanical motion. For example, as young as 3 months they can identify animals and vehicles simply by seeing point-light displays of the motion trajectories these objects take (Arterberry and Bornstein 2001).

I have suggested that infants redescribe their perceptions of animals, so that their parameters become reduced to highly simplified descriptions such as 'rhythmic motion', 'self-motion', or 'interacts from a distance' (Mandler 1992; 2004). These redescriptions characterize events; that is, they give a very abstract description of what animals do (or in the case of objects what is done to them). A combination of several such redescriptions is sufficient to establish a primitive concept of animal; it creates a non-perceptual description (or very abstract perceptual description) of the sort of thing an animal is. Thus, a likely first concept of animal is a thing that moves by itself and interacts with other objects from a distance. This concept does not include information about physical features. Of course, various features, such as legs, wings, and fins, gradually become associated with the concept, enabling infants to identify new exemplars even when they are not moving, but these features need not be part of the concept's core meaning. Similarly, a likely first concept of inanimate thing is something that either does not move at all, or if it moves it does so only when another object comes in contact with it, and does not by itself interact contingently with the infant.

---

[5] Technically, we should say 'animalness', because these characteristics do not apply to plants, but the distinction between animate and inanimate motion in the literature usually refers to animal versus mechanical motion.

A mechanism is needed to create such redescriptions. I posited a mechanism, called perceptual analysis, to fulfill this requirement (Mandler 1992), defined as an attentive process that analyzes perceptual input and recodes it into a reduced and more abstract format. Because this terminology suggested to some a purely perceptual process, I have renamed it perceptual meaning analysis, a term I hope better conveys its function (see Mandler 2004). It is a central process and so differs from the usual perceptual processing, which occurs automatically and is typically not under the attentive control of the perceiver. It is the kind of process we engage in when we study what we are looking at or make a concerted effort to encode it in such a way that we will be able to recall it later. Of course, adults have a conceptual system available in which to couch the results of such an analysis, whereas infants have to build that system in the first place. In both cases, however, selective attention is used to enable analysis and redescription of visual information into a simpler and explicitly realized form. In both cases it is this process that creates the concepts that enable one to describe, recall, or think about something in its absence.

Karmiloff-Smith (1992) described a similar process with her notion of representational redescription, which enables procedural information to be brought to awareness. Our views are related, but perceptual meaning analysis acts on-line and does not require a well-established body of knowledge to operate. An example that illustrates on-line analysis was given by Piaget (1951) when he described his infants' attempts to imitate his blinking his eyes. Before they got the action right they tried out on-line various examples of opening and closing, such as opening and closing their hands or their mouths while he blinked his eyes. This behavior evinced an understanding of opening and closing that was more abstract than the specific gesture he was performing, an understanding that needed to be hooked up to the right body part if imitation was to occur.

I have suggested that the redescriptions that result from this kind of perceptual meaning analysis are in the form of image-schemas—in this case, a schema of opening and closing that is related to containment (Mandler 1992). Image-schemas are abstract, rather topological-like, spatial representations of the paths that objects take, their onsets and end-points, and contingent relations with other paths, as well as spatial relations such as containment, contact, and verticality. They have been extensively described by cognitive linguists as the basis on which understanding of language takes place (Johnson 1987; Lakoff 1987). These researchers use image-schemas to represent the underlying meaning of relational terms and the grammatical structuring of event descriptions (Langacker 1987; Talmy 1988). In so doing they have described a rich form of representation that is well suited for preverbal concept formation, and is appropriate as a conceptual base onto which language can be mapped (Mandler 1994, 1996, 2006).

Some mechanism such as perceptual meaning analysis is required for any theory of the origins of concept formation. Piaget (1951) proposed that concepts develop from sensorimotor schemas, but he did not specify a mechanism that would accomplish this transformation. He emphasized the importance of motor learning in this process, and in part for that reason thought that concept formation was a late development in infancy. (Piaget appears to have confused the motor ineptness of infants with conceptual ineptness. It takes infants six to eight months to gain control over their hands, so any theory that depends on object manipulation to enable concept formation is forced to make concepts rather late in appearance.) There are undoubtedly other mechanisms that could effect the transformation of perceptual information into conceptual interpretation of what is seen, but some method is required. I stress this point because psychologists sometimes seem to assume that interpretation is given by perception. It is not. Seeing is not the same as conceiving. Whatever the mechanism is, it almost certainly must be an innate characteristic of human mental functioning. This discussion raises the issue of what if any other innate mechanisms are required for concept formation in infancy and whether dedicated learning processes are required to form concepts of animals and artifacts.

3. DOMAIN-SPECIFIC VERSUS DOMAIN-GENERAL LEARNING

The data we have collected to date indicate very similar learning patterns for both natural kinds and artifacts. Although, as discussed earlier, artifacts become differentiated more rapidly, that is more likely due to the greater amount of exposure infants have to them than to any fundamental differences in learning about these domains. Insofar as early learning is concerned, there does not seem to be a need for domain-specific processing. The notion of domain-specific processing varies from writer to writer, but two prominent proponents are Carey and Spelke (1994; see also Carey 2000), who have said it is necessary to build into the organism a set of core beliefs that differ for animate and inanimate realms (and therefore between animals and artifacts). As Carey (2000) put it, core conceptual knowledge derives from innate learning mechanisms that differ for animate and inanimate objects. For understanding animals there is intuitive psychology, with the concept of an agent and intentional causality at its core, or as Carey and Spelke (1994) put it, the notion that people are sentient beings who choose their actions. For understanding inanimate objects (including artifacts) there is intuitive mechanics, which has the concept of an object and physical contact causality at its core. Although full understanding of artifacts may require understanding of the animate user's intentions and the development of a design stance (Keleman and Carey, this volume), as we have seen, even 1-year-olds can appreciate an object's function without such knowledge.

In contrast to the view that learning about animate and inanimate realms rests on different core notions, I believe we do not yet know whether it is necessary to build in concepts of causality versus intentional causality that innately separate these realms. It is possible that the work required to distinguish animals from artifacts and other inanimates can be done by the perceptual system in conjunction with the common mechanism of perceptual meaning analysis. It may be that many of our innate proclivities are those associated with the perceptual system rather than with concepts per se. For example, the perceptual system itself supplies the information that specifies three-dimensional objects (Kellman 1993). As discussed in the previous section, it also delivers adequate information to distinguish animate and inanimate objects in terms of self starting motion versus motion following contact, biological versus mechanical motion, and contingent interactions from a distance versus contact interactions. Consider also causality. There is a good deal of evidence that infants from a few months of age distinguish contact causal relations between objects from very similar but non-causal spatiotemporal relations (Leslie 1988). To account for this ability, Leslie (1994) posited that infants come equipped with a domain-specific module that computes mechanical properties of objects (Theory of Body Mechanism or ToBy). (He also posited two other innate modules that interpret goal-directed action and the states of mind of agents.) ToBy receives inputs from vision and includes a device that analyzes motion with respect to force dynamics. For this purpose ToBy is equipped with an innate concept of force, which it 'paints' onto the object and kinetic information provided by the perceptual system, leading to the perception of causality in infancy. (The relationship between causal perception and causal concepts is not entirely clear in this formulation.)

This kind of view is a legacy of the philosophical arguments of Kant and Hume about causality. My impression is that many psychologists (including Leslie 1994) assume that Kant won: we can't actually perceive a causal relation, only constant conjunction, so it must be an innate characteristic of the human mind to interpret certain conjunctions as causal in nature. But what if Hume and Kant were both wrong and we *can* perceive causality? That we may actually be able to see contact causality has been proposed by White (1988). He suggested that the powerful sense of causality perceived in launching displays (such as those studied by Michotte 1963, using films of billiard balls hitting each other) comes from several aspects of iconic storage, but mainly its short duration (about 250 msec). The iconic store is a large-capacity sensory store that holds visual information prior to attentive processing. The store is continuously refreshed, and this is what enables the temporal integration by which we see motion as continuous. If this temporal integration function is present in early infancy (and it would seem to be, given that even young infants can track continuously moving objects and are disrupted if discontinuities occur; Mullen and Aslin 1978), it can account for their causal perception, rather than causal perception being a special innate module such as proposed by Leslie.

Michotte (1963) reported that the timing of the launching events in which one billiard ball hits another is crucial for our illusion that we see one ball 'make' the other move. When there is a delay of more than 100 to 150 msec between the first ball contacting the second and the second ball moving, the impression of causation is lost and people see two independent movements. The hit ball also has to be present for at least 100 msec before the first ball contacts it if a causal impression is to occur; at shorter intervals, the impression is that there is only one object that is in continuous movement. When there is actually only a single ball and it pauses briefly, motion is not perceived as discontinuous until the pause is almost 100 msec. Thus, when there is one object and a pause of less than 100 msec, continuity of motion is seen. When there are two objects and the pause at contact is less than 100 to 150 msec, a causal relation is seen. White (1988) concluded that we see a causal relation when a conflict exists between two types of continuity cues. Spatial discontinuity between the two objects says there are two objects, whereas continuous motion suggests there is only one. The conflict is resolved by perceiving the sequence as involving two objects and the transfer of motion from one to the other (Michotte called this 'ampliation'). The causal perception disappears when the temporal parameters of the movement do not fall within the time frame of temporal integration.

This view, which to my mind is persuasive, says that the innate temporal integration function of the eye makes us perceive transfer of motion from one object to another. The account does not say anything about force, but it seems to me that perceiving transfer of motion from one object to another takes us a large part of the way toward an account in which we actually *see* contact causality at work. There is not space in this chapter to cover the further issue of force in detail (see Mandler 2004, 2006 for discussion), but I suggest that it takes the experience of pushing, pulling, and other resistance activities associated with moving bodies to cause infants to begin to think of transfer of motion in terms of force or a sense of pressure. This analysis casts doubt on the necessity of building in innate core knowledge about mechanics as a requirement for the development of a concept of causality. If I am correct in my approach to deriving concepts from perception, a mechanism like perceptual meaning analysis is needed to extract a spatial motion description from causal displays, derived from what the infant perceives as transfer of motion from one object to another. The redescription (e.g. an image-schema of motion transfer) gradually becomes associated with the bodily feelings of force or pressure that arise from pushing and being pushed, resulting in a complex amalgam of spatial and kinesthetic information. In this view the concept of physical causality consists of a spatial analysis that has become coupled with an unanalyzed feeling of 'umph' (Mandler 2006).

There remains the more problematic question of agency. We can perceive contact causality in a way that lays the foundation for its conceptualization, but is there any possible way we can *perceive* goals, and if not, on what kind of information does the concept rest? Perhaps we don't need innate core knowledge of mechanics or a dedicated processor to interpret certain interactions as causal.

But do we need instead innate core knowledge of psychological goals or intentions in order to understand animate behavior?

I have already mentioned infants' sensitivity to contingent responding and to the kinds of paths that animate objects take. Another, much less studied characteristic of animate objects (and, crucially, perhaps objects in general) is that when going from point A to point B they typically take the most direct (shortest) route. For example, infants see balls roll in a straight line and come to rest when they hit an object. Similarly, infants may see various household members take a direct path to the telephone when it rings and generalize that people tend to take direct paths to the telephone from wherever they are located. These descriptions, although not mentioning goals, can be considered primitive goal statements involving a hit object or the telephone as an 'end of path' (part of the path image-schema; Mandler 1992). Lakoff (1987) discusses how a source-path-goal image-schema can be derived from the experience of following or watching objects move along paths and observing what happens at their ends (coming to rest, hitting or picking up an object, and so forth). In this view the notion of destination or goal is derived as an abstract generalization from characteristics of objects' spatial behavior. It also appears to be independent of animacy. The end of path of a rolling ball that knocks over an object can be generalized as a destination just as much as the end of path of a person picking up an object. The crucial generalization in both cases is the analysis of the end of a path as the place where the object is 'going to' or 'headed for'.

An interesting series of experiments by Gergely and Csibra and their colleagues suggests that by 9 months infants have made some abstract generalizations about objects taking direct rather than circuitous paths (Csibra *et al.* 1999; Gergely *et al.* 1995). In the first of their experiments, Gergely *et al.* habituated 12-month-olds to computer displays showing two circles, separated by a bar. One circle, A, approached the bar, paused, returned to its original position, and then approached the bar at a faster speed, jumped over it, and ended in contact with the other circle, B. A control group was habituated to the same display except that the bar was placed at one side of the display rather than between the two circles, thus making A's jumping action unmotivated. Test displays consisted of the same display as seen by the control group during habituation (i.e. jumping but no bar) and also a novel action in which the first circle went in a direct line to the second one. Experimental subjects dishabituated to the same action they had seen before (A jumping, although now not in the context of a bar) but not to the new action in which, in the absence of the bar, A immediately moved in a direct line to B. Csibra *et al.* (1999) replicated this finding with 9-month-olds, but not with 6-month-olds.

In the first experiments, A showed various signs of animacy (for example, it pulsated when it contacted B). In a second set of experiments, all indications of animacy were eliminated, including self-starting motion. In these experiments, infants were habituated to A coming from off screen, sailing over a bar, and coming to rest by B. The height of the bar varied from trial to trial, and in each case A just cleared it. The same kind of result as in the previous experiments was found: when the bar was removed, infants dishabituated to the movement to which they had been habituated, but did not dishabituate when A took a straight path to B. These data imply that toward the end of the first year infants have learned something abstract about the kind of route that an object traveling along a path to another object will take. Of course, in these experiments infants were habituated to an object A taking the most direct path to another object B. The generalization the infants made appears to be that A, having repeatedly taken a direct route to B, would do so again even though the physical situation was changed. The end of path or 'goal' in these experiments was demonstrated to the infants by repeatedly showing A following a direct path to B.

In more recent work Csibra *et al.* (2003) expanded this work to include scenes of a large circle A 'chasing' a smaller circle B. B went through a small hole in a bar, too small to accommodate A, which proceeded around the end of the bar instead. After being habituated to this display infants were shown test scenes that were the same except that the hole in the bar was now large enough to let either circle pass. At 12 months (but not at 9 months) infants dishabituated to the test scene in which A still went around the bar rather than through the large hole. Csibra *et al.* (2003) suggest that these displays are more difficult than the previous one because the end-point of the path was not shown (only the chase). Perhaps not seeing a destination (end of path) makes it less likely that a 9-month-old would interpret the scene in a goal-oriented fashion. Csibra *et al.* (2003) suggest that the ability to infer an unseen goal, such as shown by the 12-month-olds in this experiment, is a step along the way to attributing 'unseen' goals to other actors.

Gergely, Csibra, and their colleagues ascribe infants' responses to these kinds of displays to a teleological bias, by which they mean a tendency to interpret events in terms of goals and 'rational' ways to achieve them, given the constraints various situations impose. Thus, the repetition of A going to B by the shortest available route, given the constraint of the bar, made the infants interpret the events as A trying to reach B. If the bar is no longer there, the jumping route is no longer the rational (most direct) way to reach B. Similarly, for the chase scene: if the large circle cannot follow the small circle through the hole in the bar, then the rational (most direct) route is to go around the bar. If the hole is large enough to let the large circle through, it is not rational to go around.

There is nothing in these descriptions that says that this teleological stance should be restricted to animate agents (nor do Csibra and colleagues say so). Perhaps infants' first assumption is of 'rational' behavior for *all* objects that move on direct paths to other objects or continuously track them. Experience with both animate and inanimate objects moving along such trajectories could lead to the kinds of expectations Gergely and Csibra's infants evidenced, rather than their expectations being due to core knowledge that animates, in contrast to inanimate objects, are goal-directed. Learning to limit a teleological stance to animates may take developmental time.

A crucial point is that contingent interaction with another object and following a goal-directed path to (or from) an object are not coterminous. Goal-directed paths are only an intersecting set with contingent interactions from a distance. In the case of a ball moving over a bar, following a direct path repeatedly to an object on the other side may evince goal-seeking but not necessarily contingent interaction. Conversely, various conditioning phenomena involve contingent interaction but do not involve goal-seeking. Rochat, Morgan, and Carpenter (1997) showed that even 3-month-olds distinguish one object 'chasing' another in continuously varying paths from independently moving objects, but we do not know whether they did so on the basis of goal-directed behavior or contingent interaction. In either case contingent responding to the infants themselves was not involved. Recognizing goal-directed behavior is not the same as recognizing contingent behavior, or contingent responding to oneself. For example, adults smiling at infants when they coo are not engaged in goal-directed behavior, but are responding contingently to the infant from a distance. It seems clear that to untangle early learning about animals we need to distinguish among contingent interactions from a distance, contingent interactions to the infant's own actions, and goal-directed behavior.

Csibra and Gergely (1998) make a good case for the teleological stance as underlying the development of a theory of other minds. Their work suggests that a teleological stance precedes mentalistic interpretations of goals. They propose that mentalistic explanations are theoretical extensions of the teleological (goal-driven) stance to fictional states. The goal-based nature of a teleological analysis could well provide a primitive basis for the later understanding of goals in terms of mental states. From this point of view, a goal-based analysis of events is innate, but it may be an indiscriminate analysis to begin with, and only become narrowed down to animates via accumulated experience with the classes of objects most reliably apt to behave in goal-directed ways.

I conclude from these considerations that at present there is insufficient evidence for domain-specific learning in the sense of there being innate processors strictly devoted to the activities of animate versus inanimate objects. Such a division of labor may not be necessary. Of course, we do end up by assuming that goal-directed behavior (mostly) characterizes animals rather than artifacts, and we do learn that artifacts are designed by people to satisfy goals. However, domain-general mechanisms may suffice for such learning. I have posited an innate mechanism (perceptual meaning analysis) for analyzing spatial information, a mechanism that can be used to start conceptualization of and theorizing about any kind of object, not just those of a particular onto-logical category. That this analyzer concentrates on the paths that objects take and emphasizes their beginnings and ends as well as contingent interactions among them is undoubtedly also innate, and it surely has a long evolutionary history involving the visual perception of space and the kinds of events that are crucial to our survival. We are spatial creatures par excellence, but we are also analyzers of events; these predominantly involve objects following intersecting paths.

As for the concept of a goal, it is uncertain whether this notion can be derived as a generalization from analyzing objects moving on paths and what happens at their ends, or whether the notion of goal-directed behavior (independent of object paths) must be built in. Even if the notion of goal-directed behavior is innate, however, there is at present no evidence that it is applied only to animals. It seems to me this is an empirical matter, and that we should not take it for granted that there is innate core knowledge that animals are intentional agents (Carey and Spelke 1994). If the attribution of agency is an innate response to an object following certain kinds of contingent paths with respect to another object, it seems more like a domain-general assumption that with experience becomes narrowed down (although never completely) to animates. It may be that the domain-general kinds of learning described in this chapter are sufficient to conceptualize animals as different from artifacts.

12

The Essence of Artifacts: Developing the Design Stance

Deborah Kelemen and Susan Carey

1. THE THEORY-THEORY OF CONCEPTS

First some terminology: by 'concept', we simply mean a mental representation. We endorse a 'two factor' theory of conceptual content: concepts are individuated both by causal processes that relate mental symbols to their referents and also by internal inferential role. Philosophers sometimes treat these two factors as determining distinct kinds of content (wide and narrow), but we will not take a stance on this issue here. We assume that the meanings of terms in natural language are fixed in the same way, and thus we will sometimes speak of the meaning of a word such as 'accordion' and sometimes speak of the concept *accordion*.

According to the 'theory-theory' of concepts, concepts are analogous to theoretical terms in the following straightforward sense: whatever determines the content of a theoretical term such as 'gene' also determines the content of at least some ordinary concepts, such as *dog* or *think*. Of course, so described, the theory-theory places almost no constraints on conceptual representation. The theory-theory merely posits a continuity in the content determining mechanisms in the two cases—whether these turn out to be classical definitions, patterns of use, conceptual/inferential role, socially based causal connections, or something else.

Most psychologists, including ourselves, who endorse the theory-theory are committed to some particular aspects of conceptual role being central to concept individuation. They hold that the causal-explanatory principles embodied in intuitive and scientific theories provide the most important inferential machinery for determining the content of both scientific theoretical terms and of concepts that articulate intuitive theories (e.g. Carey 1991; Gelman, 2003; Keil 1989; Murphy and Medin 1985). Work in this tradition has uncovered the phenomenon of 'psychological essentialism' (e.g. Gelman 2003; Gelman, Coley, and Gottfried 1994; Keil 1989; Medin and Ortony 1989), and has demonstrated that causal-explanatory features of objects are indeed the most heavily weighted in category membership decisions (e.g. Ahn 1998; Ahn and Kim 2001). Work in this tradition has also analyzed conceptual change in childhood on analogy with conceptual change in the history of science (Carey 1985, 1991; Chi, Glaser, and Rees 1982; Thagard 1992).

As indicated above, we endorse a dual theory of conceptual content, believing in both a wide determining factor (Burge 1979; Fodor 1998; Kripke 1972/1980; Putnam 1975) and narrow determining factor (see Block's 1986 argument for a dual theory). One way of reconciling arguments for both wide and narrow content is to assume that internal conceptual role will turn out to be part of the causal link between entities in the world and mental representations (see Harman 1987; also Margolis 1998, on 'sustaining conditions'). Like others, we have no psychologically adequate analysis of the causal connections between entities in the world and the symbols that refer to them, but we do believe that a full theory of conceptual content will detail these causal connections. We focus here on internal conceptual role, for this is where psychological methods can shed light.

2. ARE ARTIFACT CONCEPTS IN THE DOMAIN OF THE THEORY-THEORY?

What is the domain of the theory-theory? Nobody would expect the theory-theory to provide an analysis of the concepts *over* or *of* or *seven*. These concepts are not embedded in intuitive theories, and do not engender the assumptions of psychological essentialism. Convergent evidence from many sources suggests that natural kind concepts such as *tiger*, *gold*, and *star* fall under the theory-theory. That is, adults adopt an essentialist stance when reasoning about natural kinds (Gelman, Coley, and Gottfried 1994; Keil 1989; Medin and Ortony 1989), assuming they have causally deep, hidden properties (i.e. their essence) which explain the existence of individual members of the kind, determine their surface properties and their behavior in causal interactions with other entities in the world. Since essences determine kind membership for natural kinds (a metaphysical assumption), the representations of essences or of essence placeholders are also at the core of the meaning of natural kind terms (a psychological fact).

Lexical categorization practices have provided one source of data in support of psychological essentialism. For example, Keil (1989) showed that adults are sensitive to the origin of surface properties in deciding animal kind: an animal that looks identical to a skunk and acts like a skunk, spraying smelly stuff at enemies, is not judged a 'skunk' if these features are the result of plastic surgery or a mistaken injection of some mystery chemical during the life of the animal.

Moreover, if this animal's parents and babies are not skunks, it is not judged to be a 'skunk'.

But while theory-theory adherents are in broad agreement that natural kinds fall within the purview of theory-theory, many have been at pains to show that it does not apply to artifacts (Gelman 1988; Keil 1989; Keil, Greif, and Kerner, this volume; Wellman and Gelman 1992; see also Schwartz 1979, for an argument that the causal theory of reference applies only to natural kinds and that artifacts are not natural kinds). For instance, a point often made is that while theoretical developments (e.g. the discovery of genes) are highly relevant to understanding the true nature of natural kinds such as tigers, such developments are irrelevant to the understanding of the true nature of artifacts such as baseball bats (although theoretical developments may allow the successful design of a more ergonomic bat). This absence of a science illuminating the underlying nature of artifacts along with the relative irrelevance of an artifact's underlying material constitution to its identity, has thus led many writers to treat natural kinds alone as falling under the assumptions of psychological essentialism (e.g. Gelman 1988; Keil 1989; Schwartz 1979).

In spite of these considerations, in this chapter we argue that artifact concepts can be readily analyzed within the framework of the theory-theory and, contrary to the emphases on their distinctiveness, that artifact concepts function in everyday life very much as do natural kind concepts. A causal-explanatory structure, with some similarity to what Dennett (1987, 1990) calls 'the design stance', underlies adult concepts of artifacts much as the causal structure of a theory of mind ('the intentional stance') underlies concepts of belief, knowledge, and perception, and much as an intuitive vitalist biology underlies concepts of living things. (Although we are using Dennett's terminology, we do not go along with his view that there is no fact of the matter as to whether an intentional system has intentionality—we do not think that attributions of intentionality are a mere 'stance'.)

3. THE DESIGN STANCE AND EVIDENCE THAT IT STRUCTURES ADULT ARTIFACT CONCEPTS

According to our version of the design stance, an artifact is intentionally created by a designer to fulfill some function. The intended function is the factor which determines the artifact's surface properties, the actual uses it can serve (the intended function as well as others), and its kind. In that sense, the original intended function is the artifact's essence (Bloom 1996, 1998, 2000; Keil 1989; Putnam 1973). Thus, a coffee mug is capable of containing liquids because that is what its designer intended. This intended function in turn constrains its form (it must be closed at the bottom, open at the top, graspable when filled with hot liquids, and so on) and also constrains the material from which it can be made (e.g. not ice). Note that the properties which make it function as a coffee mug also allow it to be used as a pencil holder. Nevertheless, the ability to hold pencils is not the reason the mug came into existence. The cause of its coming into existence is the intention of its designer that it function as a coffee mug.

If it is correct that adults reason about artifacts in terms of the design stance, then just as essential properties are weighted over more superficial properties in judgments of natural kind categories, information about original intended function should be weighted more heavily than superficial properties in judgments of an artifact's kind or purpose. And, indeed, research indicates that adults do just that. Rips (1989) showed that adults weight the original function of an artifact over its form in kind judgments. For example, adults judged an object that had the features of an umbrella but whose creator had intended it to be a lampshade to be a lampshade. Richards *et al.* (1989) found that adults exclude objects from familiar artifact categories if, despite appropriate overall form, a central feature suggests an alternative intended function. Thus, adults judge that an object that looks like a shower cap but is made of paper is not a shower cap (also Kemler Nelson, Herron, and Morris 2002). Kelemen (1999*a*) and German and Johnson (2002) have both shown that adults weigh intended function over current function in judging a novel artifact's purpose. For example, adults judge that an object that was made for one activity (e.g. exercising backs) but used everyday to perform another (e.g. stretching clothes) is 'for' the design function (i.e. back exercising). This same weighting has also been observed by Hall (1995) and Matan and Carey (2001) in adults' kind judgments: an object used for watering flowers but made for making tea is judged a 'teapot'. In short, when making kind and purpose decisions, adults weight the intended function of an artifact over both a current function (Hall 1995; Kelemen 1999*a*; Matan and Carey 2001; German and Johnson 2002) and other properties such as its form (Rips 1989; Richards *et al.* 1989).

Despite this body of research, some researchers have failed to find the expected salience of causally deeper features over more superficial ones in kind determination. For example, Malt and Johnson (1992) argue that both the intended function and the physical properties of the artifact are important features that influence kind decisions, but that neither absolutely pre-empts the other. Consistent with this, they found that a 'thing manufactured and sold to carry one or more people over a body of water for the purposes of work or recreation' (the function associated with boats) but which is 'spherical and made of rubber, is hitched to a team of dolphins, and has a large suction cup that can keep it in one place' (physical features not typically associated with boats) was not judged to be a boat, despite the clearly stated intended function.

Our response to this is that reasoning in terms of the design-stance schema, like all causal reasoning, is a form of inference to the best explanation. People infer function from form, and intended function from possible function, and draw inferences in the other direction too. According to the theory-theory of concepts, intended function is not the most heavily weighted feature because it provides a definition of artifact kind, or because it is the most reliable feature in a prototype structure, but rather because people try to rationalize all they know about an artifact, and knowledge of the intended function constrains this process. It is likely that in the Malt and Johnson (1992) boat example participants did not accept that somebody would design something to carry people over water in such a manner, given that they know that better boat designs are available (see also Bloom 1996, 1998).

In sum, there is considerable evidence that adults reason about artifacts in terms of the design stance, and that intended function plays the same role in reasoning about artifact kinds as representations of essences play in reasoning about natural kinds. This is not to deny important differences between artifact kinds and natural kinds. For example, natural kinds have true essences that are the object of scientific endeavors that do not apply to artifacts: there is no need to study what causes a telephone's surface properties in the same way as one might study what causes an animal's surface features. Furthermore, despite people's commitment to the existence of hidden causes to the surface properties of entities such as gold and tigers, adults' representations of natural kind essences are often under-determined in ways that representations for artifacts are not. That is, people allow that they lack accurate or any ideas concerning what causes a tiger or gold to look as it does—indeed, until relatively recent history they could not know that atomic and genetic structure held the key to each respectively. By contrast placeholders do not play much role in adults' artifact concepts since adults have explicit representations of the causal-explanatory structure underlying chairs and cups. They understand intended function, hence, the design stance.

This noted, our contention is that these differences are less important than they seem and that one need only look to development for evidence that this is the case. Developmental parallels exist to indicate that just as children have to construct a vitalist understanding of living things (Hatano and Inagaki 1999), along with an understanding of species based on reproductive transmission (Solomon *et al.* 1996), so too children must construct the design stance—the intentional-historical scheme that makes full sense of artifact kinds in terms of their intended function. In other words, full insight into artifact kinds is not a given. Early in childhood, all essences are placeholder essences, including those for artifacts.

4. DEVELOPMENT OF A DESIGN STANCE ABOUT ARTIFACTS: CONSTRUCTED OR CORE KNOWLEDGE?

When in development does the design stance become available to organize children's understanding of artifacts and to provide the core of the meaning of artifact terms? There is a natural alternative to the proposal that the intentional-historical understanding of artifact kinds is not constructed until well into childhood—namely that it is one of the domains of innate core knowledge. It may be available early in development, perhaps even in late infancy, as are the physical stance toward inanimate objects and the intentional stance towards agents (Baillargeon 1993; Baron-Cohen 1995; Gergely *et al.* 1995; Leslie 1994; Spelke 1991).

What is core knowledge? Baillargeon, Carey, Leslie, Spelke, and colleagues have made an empirical claim that there are systems of core knowledge with the following properties: core knowledge is articulated in terms of conceptual representations, some of which are innate. The identification of entities in the world that fall in a domain of core knowledge is supported by innate perceptual input analyzers. Core knowledge systems are learning mechanisms, they support learning about the entities in their domain. Finally, core knowledge continues to articulate our representations of the perceived world throughout development. It is never overturned (e.g. see Carey and Spelke 1994, and Hauser and Santos, this volume, for further characterization of core knowledge, and see Mandler, this volume, for a critical perspective on the existence of systems of knowledge that meet the specification of core knowledge).

Although our concern in this chapter is mainly the narrow determiner of content, it is worth noting that core knowledge systems provide a partial account of the causal connections between the entities in their domain and the symbols for them. There are dedicated perceptual input analyzers for the entities in the extension of core knowledge which take specific kinds of spatio-temporal information as input and yield specific representations as output (e.g. representations of objects (Baillargeon 1993; Carey and Spelke 1994; Spelke 1991), goal-directed action (Csibra and Gergely 1998; Gergely *et al.* 1995; Johnson 2000; Watson 1979), contact causality (Leslie and Keeble 1987; Oakes and Cohen 1990)). We look to evolution to explain how these perceptual analyzers came to be, but their operation satisfies Fodor's explication of asymmetric dependency (Fodor 1998). That is, these analyzers may be fooled into outputting a representation *object* when there is no object present (perhaps just a pattern on a computer monitor), but this mistake depends upon the relations between the spatio-temporal specification of ordinary 3D objects and the processes that build representations of them.

Consider Michotte launching causality as a specific example of a piece of core knowledge. Michotte (1963) carried out elegant psychophysical studies that specified the spatio-temporal properties of events that led to the perception of causality as one object hits a stationary one, leading the latter to go into motion. These events can be described entirely in spatio-temporal terms, but the mind provides a causal interpretation. In addition, elegant studies by Leslie and Keeble (1987), and by Oakes and Cohen (1990), suggest that young infants make this causal attribution, which is supported by the same perceptual analyzers of the spatio-temporal relations among events throughout life.

Or consider representations of intentional agents. Infants analyze patterns of motion (again specifiable in spatio-temporal terms), especially contingency among moving entities and contingency between moving entities and stationary objects in their environments, and attribute goals and attentional/perceptual states to agents or agentive action from this information (e.g. Gergely *et al.* 1995; Johnson 2000; Johnson, Booth, and O'Hearn 2001; Spelke, Phillips, and Woodward 1995; Watson 1979, 1985). As Heider and Simmel (1944) and Durgin and Gelman (see Gelman, Durgin, and Kaufman 1995) elegantly showed, adults also create representations of intentional agents from such displays.

Evolutionary considerations would justify the hypothesis that an intentional-historical understanding of artifact kinds might be part of core knowledge. Human beings, alone among animals, are prolific tool-makers and users. Just as natural selection endowed us with an innate language-acquisition device, and with an innate intentional stance, so too she may have endowed us with core knowledge of artifacts. Such a system of knowledge would enable infants to identify artifacts, guide them in inferring their functions from the uses to which adults intentionally put them, guide them in explaining their properties in terms of those functions, and explain all of this in terms of intentional design. It might be so, but is it?

5. DEVELOPMENTAL DATA FROM STUDIES OF CHILDREN'S ARTIFACT UNDERSTANDING

Developmental research certainly suggests that several prerequisites to a design stance are present from early in development. That is, even if the design stance itself is not innate, components of it probably are, and may form parts of other systems of core knowledge, for example the physical stance (e.g. sensitivity to the structural properties of physical objects) and the intentional stance (e.g. the ability to attribute goals).

With respect to the physical stance, toddlers (Brown 1990; DiYanni and Kelemen 2006; also McCarell and Callanan 1995) and even infants (Caron, Caron, and Antell 1988; Hespos and Baillargeon 2001; Mandler and McDonough 1998*b*; Mandler, this volume) can analyze the functional affordances of objects, recognizing those structural properties that make objects appropriate means to ends. For example, 8-month-olds consider physical width and contact relations when reasoning about containment and pulling events (Aguiar and Baillargeon 1998; Willatts 1999) and 1–3-year-olds are sensitive to shape, rigidity, and length requirements when selecting tools for pushing, pulling, and crushing (Brown 1990; Casler and Kelemen 2005, 2006; DiYanni and Kelemen 2006). With respect to the intentional stance, research focused on early theory of mind suggests that children between 1 and 2 years of age recognize the relevance of monitoring intentional cues from others as the basis for figuring out how to make an artifact work or what an artifact does (e.g. Carpenter, Nagell, and Tomasello 1998; Carpenter, Call, and Tomasello 2002; Gergely, Bekkering, and Király 2002; Hanna and Meltzoff 1993; Meltzoff 1995 for work focused on theory of mind; see Casler and Kelemen 2005; DiYanni and Kelemen 2006; Tomasello 1999 for work focused on artifacts). Finally, by at least 2 years children have built on their intentional stance such that their behavior towards objects reflects a functional construal in which children presume that novel artifacts are 'for' a single, privileged purpose. For example, after only one exposure to an adult intentionally using a novel tool, children will fast map this goal-directed action as the tool's enduring function, consistently returning to the same kind of artifact as the 'tool' for the task and avoiding use of it for any other activity (Casler and Kelemen 2005, 2006; also Markson 2001).

However, while this initial functional construal provides a substantial basis for explanation and inference about objects (e.g. Kelemen *et al.* 2003; Kelemen 2006), it is still not equivalent to the causally rich explanatory structure represented by a fully fledged, intentional-historical design stance based on intended function. Indeed, for a long time it seemed unlikely that any evidence of a design sensitivity would be found until late childhood. This was because of the much-replicated finding that, until at least 6 or 7 years of age, children do not attend to shared function but rather shared shape when lexically categorizing artifacts. Thus, it was repeatedly found that on being shown an exemplar artifact and told its category name, children would extend that name to other artifacts that looked alike but did not serve the same function, eschewing dissimilar objects that could actually do the same thing (e.g. Gentner 1978; Graham, Williams, and Huber 1999; Landau, Smith, and Jones 1998; Merriman, Scott, and Marazita 1993; Smith, Jones, and Landau 1996; Tomikawa and Dodd 1980). Although adult subjects in these studies sometimes demonstrated the same pattern (e.g. Gentner 1978), children's apparent indifference to what artifacts did in these tasks seemed to render it unlikely that the deeper principle of intended function could play much of a role, let alone a core role, in their artifact concepts.

Recent work demonstrates, however, that these experiments underestimated the weighting children give to functional considerations when classifying artifacts into kinds. This was because, in many such studies, form was, unnaturally, treated as dissociable from function, and this frequently led to comparison stimuli whose functions were arbitrary with respect to shape and were, instead, tied to material or other properties—an approach giving rise to somewhat uncompelling 'functions' (e.g. the capacity to rattle, roll, absorb, and be stickable by pins). In contrast, more recent research finds that when studies use comparison artifacts whose structural properties clearly relate to their functions, children can generalize labels on the basis of function rather than shape similarity as early as 2 years of age (e.g. Kemler Nelson 1999; Kemler Nelson, Russell, *et al.* 2000; Kemler Nelson, Frankenfield, *et al.* 2000). For example, when they are allowed to briefly explore a toy-like artifact called a 'gidget' (e.g. a rectangular object with a hinged flap that slots into the base like a puzzle piece) and are then asked to find another gidget out of a pair of objects, 2-year-olds will select a less similar but functional object (e.g. differently shaped base and flap) rather than a similar object with a dissimilar function (e.g. same shape as exemplar but with a flap that slides into a base like a drawer) (Kemler Nelson, Russell, *et al.* 2000). Three-year-olds will perform in this manner even when the object functions are never directly observed and therefore have to be inferred (also Kemler Nelson and students 1995).

Young children can, then, categorize artifacts on the basis of functional properties from quite early on, as long as the perceptual information is clearly consistent with a specific function. Moreover, recent work suggests that other precursory components to an adult-like design stance are also available quite early. Several studies now reveal that in addition to knowing that artifacts—rather than natural kinds—are made by people (Gelman 1988; Gelman and Kremer 1991; Keil 1989; Petrovich 1997; Kelemen and DiYanni 2005), pre-schoolers recognize the special role that a designer's intention plays in designating an artifact's category and name. Some indication of this first came from studies exploring children's naming of representational artifacts like drawings. Bloom and Markson (1998) found that 3- and 4-year-olds named pictures whose referent was objectively ambiguous (potentially lollipop or balloon) based on what the creator (themselves) intended the picture to depict. Similarly, Gelman and Ebeling (1998) found that 2- and 3-year-olds were only likely to label familiarly shaped drawings with familiar object names when they were told that the pictures were the products of intentional creation as opposed to accidental action (e.g. someone spilling paint). Importantly, this finding has now also been extended to non-representational artifacts with Gelman and Bloom's (2000) finding that, from 3 years of age, children are more likely to generate an artifact term (e.g. 'belt', 'hat') for familiarly shaped objects described as purposefully created, but more likely to generate a material composition term (e.g. 'paint', 'clay') for the same objects if told that they were accidentally originated. However, while these results reveal significant competence relevant to the design stance, they provide direct evidence only of young children's knowledge that (i) artifacts are created by people, (ii) it is appropriate to extend a familiar artifact category label to an intentionally created object, (iii) the intentional designer has the right to designate the name and category membership of their creation, in other words, the designer possesses 'baptism rights' (see German and Johnson 2002, for discussion). This still stops short of evidence for the full adult design stance, which requires that the above elements are drawn together and given cohesion by a notion that subsumes them—the idea that the designer creates an artifact category member with the intention that it perform a particular function. Children who have this insight should consequently weight the design function over any non-designed, salient current use in their artifact reasoning. So, when exactly do children demonstrate this level of understanding?

As with most developmental research, a precise answer to this kind of question is up for debate, because different methods have produced slightly different findings for different researchers. Nonetheless, current evidence converges to suggest that a full understanding of the design stance does not emerge until late in the pre-school years, somewhere in the 4- to 6-year age range. For example, on the older side of this range, Matan and Carey (2001) and German and colleagues (e.g. German and Johnson 2002; Defeyter and German 2003) both find evidence that the design stance is not constructed until close to 6 years of age. Matan and Carey (2001) presented children with scenarios in which one character made an artifact for a particular purpose (e.g. to eat dinner on), but before it was ever used for that purpose, another character used it for another purpose (e.g. to play a game throwing it to other people in the park). When asked what the object was—a plate or a frisbee—the 4-year-olds were at chance in one study and just above chance in selecting the intended function in another. Few 4-year-olds appealed to intended function when justifying their judgments and, while they were not tested unless they did, many had difficulty remembering who made the object and for what purpose, as if this information was not naturally relevant to organizing their representations. Indeed, Matan and Carey suspected that the apparent design-based responding of some of their 4-year-old children may have only reflected shallower knowledge of a creator's 'baptism rights' rather than any understanding of the design stance. Six-year-olds, in contrast, differed from the 4-year-olds in each of these respects, resembling adults in being able to remember the information upon first being told it, in categorizing the artifact on the basis of original intent of the designer, and justifying their responses in terms of the design stance.

The question of whether those of Matan and Carey's younger children who did categorize consistent with intended function were solely responding on the basis of a creator's right to name their creations rather than insight into the significance of intended function remains open, in part because, beyond the function information presented in the stories, half of Matan and Carey's trials involved items with function-based names (e.g. shopping cart vs. stroller, baseball bat vs. rolling pin) (see Kelemen 2004 for additional discussion). Nevertheless, findings by German and Johnson (2002) accord with Matan and Carey's conclusion that a design stance based on intended function is not present until quite late. In one condition of German and Johnson's studies, 5-year-old children were told stories about an object that was made for one purpose, given away, and then intentionally used by a new owner for something else. German and Johnson found that while 5-year-olds showed a sensitivity to baptism rights by weighing a designer's label over another agent's label when deciding what the novel artifact's category name was, they did not reliably use designer intent over current intentional use when judging what a novel object was 'really for'.

German and Defeyter (German and Defeyter 2000; Defeyter and German 2003; Defeyter 2003) have gone on to argue that further evidence of pre-school children's lack of a design-based construal is also provided both by 5-year-olds' performance on tests of functional fixedness and by their approach to functional fluency tasks. For example, in context of functional fixedness, German and Defeyter (2000) have found that while 6- and 7-year-olds have difficulty disregarding an artifact's design function when asked to creatively problem-solve with it (e.g. figure out how to use a box to reach a shelf), 5-year-olds have far less problem-solving difficulty, more readily seeing an artifact as 'for' whatever someone wants it to be 'for' (i.e. seeing the box as a mounting block, not as a container). They suggest that this immunity to functional fixedness occurs because design function is not yet core to pre-schooler's artifact conception. Similarly, in functional fluency tasks in which children are asked to generate possible uses for familiar artifacts (e.g. bricks), Defeyter (2003) has found that while both 5- and 7-year-old children are uniformly relatively poor at the task, 7-year-olds are more likely to remain fixed on conventional 'design' functions than 5-year-olds, who are more likely to generate entirely novel uses—a tendency that, again, seems to indirectly suggest that intended function is less central to their artifact thinking. German and Johnson (2002) point out that results suggesting that 5-year-olds do not have a design stance are potentially unsurprising if the computations involved in reasoning about design intentions are actually considered. Specifically, they argue that design attributions involve recursive reasoning about second-order mental states (e.g. 'the maker intends (that the user intends) that X will perform Y'), something regarded as difficult for young children (e.g. Perner and Wimmer 1985; but see Sullivan, Zaitchik, and Tager-Flusberg 1994).

However, the involvement of second-order mental state reasoning in design attributions is challengeable. Computationally, design intentions may reduce to 'the maker intends that the user does X with Y' or 'the maker intends that X does Y', and children's ability to manipulate embedded mental state content of a more opaque, complex form than the goal state content of design intentions has been documented as early as 3 and 4 years of age (e.g. Chandler, Fritz, and Hala 1989; Siegal and Beattie 1991) and even, perhaps, infancy (Onishi and Baillargeon 2005). In principle then, it is not clear that there is any computational barrier to children representing and reasoning about intended function earlier than 6 or 7 years of age. Additionally, with regard to German and Defeyter's functional fixedness and functional fluency results, there are reasons to suspect that factors independent of children's artifact concepts underlie the findings. For example, other studies by Kelemen and colleagues (Kelemen 2001, 2006*b*) have directly explored whether there is any correlation between 3- to 5-year-olds children's susceptibility to functional fixedness during problem-solving tasks and their tendency to construe artifacts in terms of original design (as assessed by a task described below). These studies find none of the expected negative correlations between the two tendencies. Furthermore, follow-up work by Defeyter (2003) on functional fluency has revealed that when children are given instructions highlighting the acceptability of generating entirely novel functions, developmental differences between 5- and 7-year-olds are eliminated. Both these patterns of results therefore strongly suggest that something other than children's immature artifact concepts (e.g. age- or education-related increases in conventionality) might account for 5-year-olds' relative advantage in both German and Defeyter's functional fixedness and functional fluency findings. Finally, questions also occur regarding German and Johnson's (2002) function judgment results, for two reasons. First, aside from children's performance, even adults' tendency to judge that the novel artifacts were 'really for' the designed function rather than the intentional use was low—initially more than half of the adults made design-based judgments on 50 per cent or less of the trials suggesting possible issues with stimulus items (see Kelemen 2004). Second, using the same kind of function-judgment method, earlier work by Kelemen (1999) had already found evidence of a design stance understanding in children as young as 4 to 5 years of age.

Specifically, in Kelemen's (1999) study, adults and a mixed group of 4- and 5-year-old children were told about depicted novel artifacts that were successfully intentionally designed for one purpose (e.g. squeezing lemons) then immediately given to someone else who, depending on the experimental condition, accidentally or intentionally used the artifact for another activity on either one or many occasions (e.g. picking up snails once or repeatedly). Children were reminded about both functional activities after hearing the story and all alternative uses, whether accidental or intentional, were explicitly described as positive outcomes. Nevertheless, when asked to judge what the objects were 'for', children and adults had no overall differences from each other and showed a significant tendency to say the artifacts were 'for' their intended function in each condition. A subsequent study then replicated this effect using actual, manipulable novel artifacts (Kelemen 2001). In contrast to 3-year-olds, who were at chance, separate groups of 4- and 5-year-olds not only judged the objects as 'for' their design function rather than their everyday intentional use, but also favored design function when judging what kinds of other items the novel artifacts would belong with (i.e. in a house). The tendency to favor intended function in this latter study was most marked in the 5-year-old group who averaged doing so 72 per cent of the time.

Kelemen's (1999) finding of a sensitivity to design in younger pre-schoolers does not stand in isolation. Kemler Nelson, Herron, and Morris (2002) recently found that 4-year-olds are more likely to extend familiar category names to unfamiliar non-functional artifacts by making inferences about intended function rather than by attending to the objects' superficial appearance (see also Richards *et al.* 1989). Indeed, newer evidence indicates that, under certain conditions, even 3-year-olds know to weigh intended function when deciding how to categorize an artifact. For instance, Jaswal (2005) found that 3- and 4-year-old children are more likely to assign 'label-consistent' functions to hybrid artifacts resembling members of one familiar artifact category but labeled as another (e.g. a hat-like object labeled 'cup') if told that the labeler 'made' the object rather than 'found' it. Furthermore, DiYanni and Kelemen (2006; see also DiYanni 2006) found that 3-year-olds demonstrate a tool preference across contexts and users if shown two equally affordant tools successfully performing a task (e.g. ringing a bell in a cage) but hear one tool described as 'made for' the purpose and the other's intended function described as unknown. Finally, DiYanni and Kelemen (2006; see also DiYanni 2006) also found that unlike 2-year-olds, 3-year-old children can be induced to select a physically inappropriate novel tool for a task (e.g. a fluffy object for cookie-crushing) over a highly appropriate novel tool (e.g. a pestle) but only if (misleadingly) told that the inappropriate tool is 'made for' for the purpose (for related research see Diesendruck, Markson, and Bloom 2003, but also see Truxaw *et al.* 2006).

In summary, minor age differences aside, the body of contemporary research converges on 4 to 6 years as the age range when an explicit understanding of design becomes progressively more evident, with studies also beginning to find that, under certain conditions, design-stance insights can be elicited from children during the early pre-school years. Nevertheless, despite these findings of earlier competence, even the most sympathetic interpretation of the current evidence indicates that the answer to the question of whether humans are innately endowed with the design stance as an aspect of core knowledge is 'no'. Instead, using the innate building blocks that core knowledge provides them, children's design stance seems to be gradually constructed. The developmental progression can be crudely characterized (Casler and Kelemen 2005, 2006; Kelemen 2004*a*) as one in which children move from understanding an artifact as a means to an intentional end (thus 'for' a user's current goal), to viewing it as the embodiment of a goal (thus 'for' a privileged, intrinsic, enduring, function), to finally understanding it in terms of a full-blown design stance—an explanatory structure that is anchored by an understanding of intended function and supports rich inferences about the artifact's *raison d'être*, kind, properties, and future activity.

6. CAUSES AND IMPLICATIONS OF THE DEVELOPMENTAL CHANGE

The evidence surveyed above suggests that young toddlers attend to artifact function and conceptualize artifacts in terms of an explanatory structure that is derived from their understanding of goal-directed action and supports function-based reasoning and inference about objects. Nonetheless, it is not until several years later in development that children draw together various elements of their understanding to construct a fully elaborated design stance.

This brief summary of the current state of the art regarding children's conceptions of artifacts raises several questions. First, how should we understand the transition from artifact concepts not rooted in the design stance to artifact concepts that are so rooted? In descriptive terms, does this transition involve a conceptual change in artifact concepts? Second, how does the child construct the design stance? What contributes to such a transition? Third, how does this transition relate to developmental transitions within representations of essentialized natural kinds? Are there parallels, or perhaps even direct influences of one on the other?

6.1. Conceptual change in artifact concepts?

Whether the transition we have argued for constitutes a conceptual change depends, of course, on one's analysis of concepts and of conceptual change. As we use the term, concepts are representations, and representations persist through time (one thinks thoughts about the same entities on different occasions). Conceptual change, then, occurs when whatever determines the content of a given representation changes. On many analyses of concepts, as different from one another as the classical empiricist view and Fodor's atomistic view (e.g. Fodor 1990, 1991), the very notion of conceptual change is incoherent. On the classical view, in which concepts are individuated by definitions that provide necessary and sufficient conditions for category membership, it is more natural to think of concept replacement than conceptual change (i.e. a change in a definition results in a new concept; see Katz 1972). Similarly, on the atomistic view, if the causal laws that relate a symbol to entities in the world change such that a new set of entities is picked out by a given symbol, it may seem more natural to think of concept replacement rather than conceptual change. It should be noted, however, that this assumption of conceptual replacement depends upon the way the concept-to-world causal laws are characterized. If the extensions of successive concepts overlap and if the processes leading to the change of extension involve some transformation of those very causal connections, then it makes sense to talk of conceptual change.

At any rate, the current work is placed in a theory-theory framework that endorses a place for conceptual role in determining conceptual content. Indisputably, theories change, and the most deeply entrenched causal schemata that structure theories change. Indeed, it is this fact that has led students of conceptual development from Piaget on to look to historical theory change for insights into the process of conceptual development in childhood, and parallels between historical theory change and conceptual development motivate the theory-theory of conceptual development, as well as the theory-theory of concepts. The theory-theory of concepts speaks of conceptual change rather than replacement because much of the inferential role that partly determines conceptual content remains constant over the change; as Kuhn (1983) puts it, incommensurability is always local.

Returning to the specific case of artifact kinds, according to the present analysis, the identification of something as a member of an artifact category (e.g. a chair) is not a process of applying a classical definition but one rooted in inferences to best explanation based on the deepest causally relevant features known. Conceptual change can be said to take place to the extent that these causally deepest structures—those used to explain an entity's existence, properties, and activities—undergo modification. This is because, on the theory-theory view (with its emphasis on internal conceptual role), such structures are central to the concept-to-world sustaining mechanisms determining reference and, as such, re-analyses may cause changes in the extension of the concept (see Kitcher 1988, on mismatch of referential potential across episodes of conceptual change).

Pre-school developments in the artifact concepts between 3 to 6 years reviewed earlier satisfy this analysis of conceptual change. For sure, the explanatorily deepest features change: artifacts move from being explained in terms of an intentional stance (how a person might use an object), to a deeper functional stance (what the object itself is for), to an even deeper design stance (what it is made for). A consequence of this change is that the referential potential of the term changes throughout these years. For a 2-year-old, an object that someone drinks out of, but which was made as a flower vase, might fall in the extension of the concept *glass*. Of course, the child also defers to experts, and a correction that it is a vase not a glass might be part of the input that leads to a change in the core of the concept. These changes would be expected to reflect in children's categorization decisions, and such changes are the primary evidence of the transition under discussion.

This is not to deny that theories change in many ways, and conceptual change can be a matter of degree—there will be a continuum of changes between mere changes in beliefs about the entities in some domain and changes in the very concepts of those entities. Thus, while we argue that the construction of the design stance does entail conceptual change within artifact concepts, we also importantly note that it provides a relatively weak case. It does not involve the multiple interdependent differentiations and coalescences that constitute conceptual change accompanying radical theory changes (e.g. Carey 1985, 1988, 1991; Kitcher 1988; Kuhn 1962).

6.2. Where does the design stance come from?

Let us turn now to the second question. Whether or not the creation of the design stance contributes to conceptual change within artifact concepts, how does the child manage it? Our answer appeals to two very different types of influences. First, we must account for the origin of conceptual components of the design stance, the conceptual stuff from which it is constructed. And second, we appeal to domain general factors that enable children to construct kind representations overall, both natural kinds as well as artifact kinds.

As we indicated in the above review, we trace the ultimate origin of the components of the design stance to two innate systems of core knowledge—the system that provides representations of intentionality and the system that provides representations of objects and their causal potentials. It is because humans are innately endowed with the capacity to analyze their own and others' actions in terms of goals, as well as with the capacity to analyze events in terms of the causal relations among objects, that they can also analyze the role and properties of external objects in terms of human goals. It is these abilities that get artifact representations off on the right foot, so to speak.

Several domain general tools that support concept acquisition also play a role in the process. First and foremost, children have the capacity to distinguish kinds from other types of categories (e.g. those united by properties), and they are sensitive to several types of information in establishing whether a given term refers to a kind or not. One type of information is linguistic—kinds are lexicalized as nouns and properties typically by adjectives, and children as young as 13 months are sensitive to this contrast (Waxman and Markow 1995; we speak of 'spoons', not 'spoonish things'). Also, kinds are referred to by generics (e.g. 'cars need gasoline, the radio is a wonderful invention'), and children as young as age 2 take generics to refer to kinds (Gelman 2003). Other information is conceptual—kinds have more inductive potential and are more causally potent, on average, than are properties (Gelman, Collman, and Maccoby 1986). Evidence of this sort helps the child establish that *cup* is a kind concept and *red* is not. These assumptions lead children to weight causal explanatory features most heavily in their representations of concepts such as *cup*, which is why functional features are weighted more heavily than purely perceptual features by children as young as 2.

Once the child has evidence that a given concept is a kind concept, the child's first assumption is that it is a basic level substance sortal (e.g. Carey 1994; Hall 1993; Macnamara 1986; Xu and Carey 1996). Substance sortals are contrasted with phase sortals (e.g. passen*ger*) or stage sortals (e.g. *puppy*) because, unlike these other sortal types, substance sortals trace identity throughout an entity's entire existence. As a result of this identity-tracking property, children's assumption that the kind concept is a substance sortal may lead them to focus their attention on origin, which may be why the child begins to attribute the maker with baptism rights. That is, if a cup is a cup throughout its whole existence (if *cup* is a substance sortal), any explanation of how it comes into existence that coheres with other, already analyzed, explanatory features will become entrenched. Certainly, the child must learn about manufacture, but he or she has ample opportunity to do so from very early in development—the child creates drawings and participates in making meals, creating towers with sticks, blocks, and so forth. Children's participation in the kinds of easily observable 'manufacturing' activities that pervade all human cultures (e.g. cooking, building) readily provide information about the relevant aspects of origin tied to intention. Indeed, a prediction can be made that, among children who are equivalent with respect to meta-cognitive skill (thus equivalent in their abilities to reflect on their own and others' creative actions), children from more 'self-reliant' (do-it-yourself) rather than 'consumerist' (just buy it) social/cultural backgrounds may show precocious development of a design stance.

In sum, we offer two types of answers to the question of the origin of the design stance: we appeal to the systems of core knowledge that provide part of the material from which it is constructed, and we appeal to domain general theory-building processes that guide the child toward essentializing and theorizing about artifacts in terms of their origins.

6.3. Artifact concepts and natural kind concepts: relations in development

We turn now to the third question raised by our brief review, namely, how the construction of the design stance relates to developments within natural kind categories. Structurally, there is a close analogy between the changes within artifact concepts sketched here and some of the conceptual changes within concepts of animal kinds that have been described in the literature. Studies of switched-at-birth animal adoption show that by age 4 children know that cats give birth to cats, and that even if a baby born to a cat mother is raised by dogs, it will grow up to be a cat (Wellman and Gelman 1992; Johnson and Solomon 1997; Lopez, Atran, and Coley 1997). However, this origins knowledge is only gradually elaborated into a causal schema of inherited essences, as the mechanisms of biological transmission of traits are differentiated from social transmission, and the traits that fall under each type are differentiated from each other. This process takes place, in Western culture, over the years of 4 to 7, as shown by Keil's transformation task and discovery tasks (Keil 1989) and in inheritance tasks (Johnson and Solomon 1997; see also Solomon *et al.* 1996; and Springer and Keil 1989).

Insofar as this process reflects a gradually deepening understanding of the relevance of origin to explaining object properties and kind, this is the same kind of conceptual change as that described for artifact terms, and it may not be coincidental that it is taking place at roughly the same time. Analogical transfer of knowledge derived from developments in the domain of intuitive biology might contribute to developments in the artifact domain—increasing weighting of details of origin in determining species kind may reinforce increasing weighting of details of origin in determining artifact kinds. For example, as 5- to 8-year-old children increasingly reorganize their understanding of the identity of living things in terms of reproduction and birth (e.g. Solomon *et al.* 1996; Johnson and Solomon 1997), their attention to origins in the biological realm may inform their attention to origins in the artifact realm (Matan and Carey 2001).

Alternatively, the direction of analogical transfer might be the reverse. Children have an early toehold into understanding the artifact domain, given their precocious abilities in relation to the intentional stance. Perhaps it is unsurprising then that Mandler (this volume) finds that 19-month-olds have greater expertise identifying the specific properties of artifact categories versus biological kinds, and as we reviewed above, there is some evidence for the beginnings of the construction of the design stance as early as 3 years. These data suggest that insights into artifacts and artifact origins are developmentally antecedent to insights into the domains of biology and other natural phenomena (see Keil, Greif, and Kerner, this volume for a proposal why this should not be the case). Indeed, artifact knowledge may not only help to facilitate children's understanding of the biological and natural world but also potentially obfuscate it. Specifically, it may be via the influence of their privileged sensitivity to intentionality and hence their deepening artifact knowledge that children become prone to develop a 'promiscuous teleology'—the tendency to treat natural objects of all kinds as occurring for a purpose; a cross-culturally documented bias that impacts the ease with which scientific ideas, such as those inherent to evolutionary theory, are ever truly acquired (Kelemen 1999*b*, *c*, *d*, 2003, 2004; see also Evans 2000, 2001; but see Greif *et al.* 2006; and Keil 1992).

Evidence of the influence of artifact knowledge on reasoning about natural kinds is further provided by findings that children both endorse and spontaneously generate artifact-like, other-serving functional explanations for natural objects and their properties (e.g. animals have wide backs so that they can be physically sturdy *and* so that other animals can ride around on them) (Kelemen 1999*b*, 2003, Kelemen and DiYanni 2005; but see Kerner and Keil cited by Keil, Greif, and Kerner, this volume, for possible conflicting evidence) and regard natural entities that cannot perform other-serving activities (e.g. a mountain that can no longer be climbed) as 'broken' and in need of being fixed or replaced (DiYanni and Kelemen 2005). Finally, elementary-school children's tendency to ascribe purpose to nature is significantly correlated with their tendency to view natural phenomena as being 'made by someone' (Kelemen and DiYanni 2005). In short, at developmental points when children's design stance on artifacts seems well established, there are results suggesting that children are using artifact knowledge to make sense of domains where they have less expertise.

Of course, ultimately the question of whether biological knowledge influences artifact knowledge, or whether the reverse is true, may never be decided, since both possibilities could be accurate—analogies of this sort may serve to reinforce explanatory schemata back and forth across both domains.

In considering these similarities between the biological and artifact domains, it is important to note how the kinds of conceptual changes involved in each of these domains are also different in degree, if not in kind. We have argued that changes in the core of a specific artifact concept (e.g. *broom*, *cup*) parallel those that take place in the core of a living thing concept (e.g. *baby*, *dog*), insofar as, in both cases, the child constructs an explanatory schema that privileges origin at the core of the kinds in the domain. However, it is also true that the biological case involves much deeper and far-reaching conceptual change, such that in some cultural contexts it is not complete until adolescence or even adulthood (Astuti 2001; Astuti, Solomon, and Carey 2004; Bloch, Solomon, and Carey 2001). On Carey's analysis (1985, 1995), this is due to the fact that a vitalist biology, as well as biological understanding of naturalized kind essences, has no direct precursors in core knowledge. In contrast, as we have argued here, the infant's understanding of intentionality places artifact concepts in an inferential structure that maintains some fundamental continuities throughout development, and this has implications for the degree of incommensurability between child and adult artifact representations and talk. In sum, while acknowledging their differences, an analysis of artifact concepts in terms of the design stance has many deep parallels with the analysis of natural kind concepts in terms of psychological essentialism and the theory-theory of concepts. These analyses place an explanatory schema at the core of each type of concept, and pose parallel questions for development. From the point of view of development, they yield many parallel answers.

13

A World Apart: How Concepts of the Constructed World Are Different in Representation and in Development

Frank C. Keil, Marissa L. Greif, and Rebekkah S. Kerner

Most children are surrounded, from birth, by a world of things created by the people who live around them and by those who came before them. The very first act that infants perform on another object, that of nursing, is often on a bottle designed for that specific purpose. In the months and years that follow, the world of artifacts will envelop the child. In this chapter, we contrast the development of children's understanding of artifacts with patterns of cognitive development in other domains, most notably that of living kinds and non-living natural kinds. We will focus on children who are no longer infants, although some discussion of artifact notions in infancy will frame what follows. The principal themes of this essay are the following: (1) there is far more variability in the patterns of development of children's intuitions about artifacts than about living kinds; (2) because many insights about artifacts' origins and identity are likely to be 'non-natural', initial conceptualizations of artifacts should be more difficult to acquire than those of most natural kinds; (3) as artifacts evolve and classes and subclasses of artifacts expand, associated patterns of concept acquisition may change quite radically; (4) despite this diversity, the course of acquisition of the artifact concept may have some overarching developmental characteristics that are quite distinct from those of other kind domains; and, finally (5) understanding people's intentions may be very important to our concepts of artifacts, but initially at least, perhaps not in the ways we might think.

1. THE VARIETIES OF ARTIFACT KINDS

The literature in cognitive science often contrasts artifacts and natural kinds as though they were comparable levels in a standardized hierarchy of objects in the world. Although this distinction has featured prominently in many studies of cognition and cognitive development (e.g. Keil 1989; Simons and Keil 1995; Rips 1989, 2001), it has the potential to mislead. Consider those frequent cases in which non-living and living natural kinds are associated with each other but are contrasted altogether with artifacts. Do the entire classes of living kinds and artifacts sit at roughly equivalent levels of generality in this putative hierarchy? It is clear that they do not. The domain of artifacts is much more varied and much less predictable in form and function than the domain of living kinds. Because of the heterogeneity of artifacts, the more appropriate contrast with living kinds would be an artifact subclass such as hand-tools or furniture (Rosch *et al.* 1976). Indeed, this issue of generality is more than a quibble. There is also the distinct risk of retreating to a very minimal characterization of what such a diverse set of entities shares in common, and thus the possibility of under-representing the extensive diversity of the artifact class. A closer examination of the nature of artifacts reveals a vast domain with subdomains that may differ at least as dramatically from each other as they do from the entire domain of living kinds. These differences have consequences not only for how adults represent and think about artifacts, but also for how children acquire artifact concepts.

This claim for greater diversity for artifacts is borne out empirically. In a series of studies by Keil and Smith (1996), for example, adults were asked to rate how much the category integrity of various kinds was disrupted by counterfactualizing typical properties (e.g. 'To what extent is something that seemed to be a catapult still a catapult if it was twice as long and half as high as most other catapults?'). People's responses indicated that separate subclasses of artifacts seemed to group together each in their own discrete clusters. Unlike artifacts, living kinds all tended to cluster together. In other words, changing typical color, size, or shape had roughly the same impact on all living kinds, whether they were ants or antelopes. By contrast, comparable changes on artifact categories, such as vehicles and hand tools, yielded tight clusters within those two domains and large differences between them in terms of the properties that mattered the most and least to their category membership.

Similarly, patterns of developmental change in word meaning can vary considerably as a function of artifact subdomains but not for living kinds (Keil 1989). For instance, a young child might put excessive weight on a number of characteristic features at roughly the same time in conceptualizing hand-tools but consider the same features at either younger or older ages for other artifact subdomains. With living kinds, however, once a child overrides typical features of a subdomain, say lions, for an appreciation of deeper properties defining category membership, she is likely to do the same for most other living kinds. That is, unlike for artifacts, for most living kinds there is a relatively uniform shift in understanding that the underlying fundamental properties of one living kind apply to other living kinds as well.

There are other groups of artifacts that seem even more conceptually distant from the subclasses of artifacts considered so far. A piece of art is clearly an artifact, but once art is included in the domain of artifacts, intangible artifacts such as performances, poems, and stories enter as well. Computer software, recipes, dollar bills, and exercise routines would also seem to clearly be artifacts, as would social conventions such as giving silver gifts for a twenty-fifth anniversary, or driving on the right side of the road. As Searle suggests (this volume), the functions of many artifacts are established by collective agreement and the norms of the society in which they exist. For example, paper money has no real physical representation in modern-day banking. Instead of gold and silver, paper notes are simply tied to computer transactions between financial institutions. We all agree, however, that paper notes signify value of a certain kind. Indeed, to try to mark a clear boundary between the physical and non-physical seems hopeless. Because of the physical and functional diversity of items in the grand domain of artifacts, perhaps the best characterization of the commonalities of artifacts is that they are simply things that were intentionally created to help achieve some sort of goal. The goals in question vary considerably and include everything from communicating information, to surprising and delighting, and even to traumatizing and terrorizing.

Intuitively, however, one could argue that the entire class of natural kinds is also immense. After all, we need to consider instances of *both* living and non-living natural kinds. In addition to living kinds, there are elements such as gold, molecular compounds such as water, and even particular configurations of these molecules, such as carbon that can be formed into diamonds or into coal. For all of these there is a common story focusing on microstructural elements and relations; but the details of that story—how such entities and substances come to exist—may vary considerably across those kinds. To make matters even more complicated, many other things have been called natural kinds for which an appeal to microstructures does not necessarily hold. These include volcanoes, glaciers, stars, and planets. Instead of being strictly defined by their molecular make-up, these things seem to be the result of complex processes and laws that are often external to members of that kind.

There is no denying that the natural world consists of a diverse set of entities. However, it may indeed be the case that for any one type of artifact, there exist an almost infinite number of variations in ontogeny, form, and function. This is not the case for natural kinds. To make any progress in highlighting the important differences in conceptualizing artifacts and natural kinds, we need to assess artifacts against a comparable standard. For the remainder of this chapter we will often contrast the class of living kinds, the most discussed case of natural kinds, with artifact subcategories such as tools or furniture that correspond to bounded and enduring physical objects and will consider some of the patterns that emerge from such contrasts.

2. CUES TO 'ARTIFACTHOOD'

Long before they can speak, children may sense that the world of artifacts is different from the natural world. There is a huge array of perceptual patterns that set most physical artifacts apart from items in the natural world. For example, many classes of artifacts are much more rectilinear than most natural kinds. Their junctions are often at right angles and are signaled by dramatic color shifts as well protrusions or indents (Levin *et al.* 2001). Straight lines and equal-interval spacings of components are comparable cues. Texture is also often a cue, with many artifacts having smooth surfaces in contrast to the fractal character of many natural surfaces. Artifacts tend to have striking uniformity of size for members of local categories while natural kinds usually do not. While a group of the same kind of chairs or spoons will often be physically identical because of the nature of mass production, even those most closely related members of a subspecies will usually show considerable variation in size, coloring, and even shape. Non-living natural kinds, such as glaciers, stars, and diamonds, often show even more physical variation. Thus, long before they understand much about the use or origins of artifacts, children may see them as somehow different and distinct from the natural world. They may not necessarily know that artifacts are created by other humans and that natural kinds are created by natural processes, but they are likely to see that they are different domains of things (e.g. Simons and Keil 1995; Mandler 2002, and this volume; Mandler and McDonough 1993, 1996, 2000).

Other differences are evident over time. Artifacts do not grow or have periods of fragile infancy (Hatano and Inagaki 1996). They are also not usually functional until they are complete. A half-built car doesn't run, and a half-made shirt might not be wearable. Most living kinds, in contrast, must function in some crude way from the moment of their conception, one of the great organizing principles of developmental biology (Gilbert 2000). An infant animal is just as much a complete and functional animal as is an adult and, similarly, an ailing adult is still as much an animal as a healthy one. The basic mechanics of life must be sustained throughout development for that living organism to continue to exist as a living organism. Children surely witness this difference on many occasions. A related difference is that the path of creation of an artifact is largely arbitrary as long as the end-state is the same. A chair made with the legs attached to the seat first is the same chair as another made from the same parts but with the back attached to the seat before the legs. Living kinds, even those that undergo dramatic metamorphoses, always follow the same path of creation, which indeed helps to define the final state. This difference is one that is sensed by quite young children (Keil 1989).

The large range of cues that correlate with artifacts may therefore enable very young children to see this hugely diverse class as somehow different from the biological world. The key question is, what follows from such an awareness? Do young children explore artifacts differently from natural kinds? For example, are their manual explorations and their questions about artifacts different than they are for living kinds? Do they sometimes seem to ask more 'What is that for?' kind of questions about artifacts than about various natural kinds? As adults, we tend to treat whole artifacts as having purposes (hence the sensible nature of questions such as 'What is a protractor for?'), but not infer or enquire about general purposes for whole natural kinds (e.g. 'What is a tiger for?', 'What is a planet for?'). Similarly, children's patterns of visual or tactile exploration might be different for artifacts and natural kinds. For example, a 3-year-old, on encountering a strange, small, detached artifact, may pick it up and try to use it on yet a third object through pounding or pushing. That tendency may be less common when picking up a strange, detached, living kind such as an unusual fruit. These patterns, however, must remain speculations until further studies are conducted.

Another important area of research on children's understanding of artifacts involves the degree to which children can understand the link between different types of teleological causation and different kinds of object. There is some evidence that young children have difficulty judging whether whole object statements of function apply solely to artifacts but not to natural kinds. For example, they will sometimes argue that both tigers and rocks have overall purposes (Kelemen 1999*a*; Kelemen and Carey, this volume). However, ongoing work (Greif, Kemler Nelson, and Keil, in preparation) suggests that children as young as 3 years of age may actually seek out quite different information about artifacts and living kinds. For example, if they ask ambiguous questions such as 'What is it?' about a living kind, they are often satisfied with its name. By contrast, for artifacts they will ask further questions until they are given functional information about the object as a whole.

There are other patterns at the conceptual level that may be used to distinguish artifacts and natural kinds. One conceptual difference revolves around the causal centrality of typical salient features (Ahn *et al.* 2000). It can be difficult to define a 'feature' in the first place, as one could think of myriad ways to divide up a toaster or a tiger into parts, and also continuously redefine which features they want to include in a set belonging to an entity. But by any reasonable notion of feature, those of artifacts are often seen as causally irrelevant to being that artifact, whereas comparable features for natural kinds are seen as central to their existence. We tend to assume that most features of natural kinds play causal roles for them, some of moderate importance, some of great importance, but few that are irrelevant. Thus, for tigers, surface markings and shape are both assumed to be important to tigerhood, but the color and surface markings of most vehicles or most items of furniture are considered unimportant, when judging the status of such artifacts as members of that kind (Keil 1989). We assume that there are no accidents for features of natural kinds, but freely accept the idea that some features of artifacts may be accidents or merely conventions. Indeed the tendency to assume that there are important causal roles for virtually all features of living kinds has been deemed a misleading cognitive bias (Gould and Lewontin 1979), and the assumption that most or all traits are naturally selected-for adaptations is an idea of much contention among evolutionary biologists and psychologists (Gould 1997). Interestingly, this pattern of assumptions seems to be pretty much the same in children as young as 5 years of age, who tend to think that, for natural kinds, almost all features matter, while for artifacts only a small subset of features are critical (Keil *et al.* 1998).

It seems, therefore, that there are many distinctive patterns to most artifacts that occur at both perceptual and conceptual levels that set them apart from natural kinds. Children as young as 5 years of age are very much aware of these patterns and use them to reason about category membership, property induction, and other concept-related tasks. More importantly, for artifacts, these different patterns can arise without invoking intentions of the artifacts' creators at all.

3. CONCEPTUAL COMPLEXITY AND NATURALNESS OF ARTIFACTS

One of the consequences of artifact diversity is that some artifacts are conceptually difficult to apprehend. This is, generally speaking, not the case for most living kinds. If you teach a person about a new living kind at the species level by pointing to a few exemplars, that person will usually have pretty good success at subsequent classifications (Keil 1994; Atran 1998). The same may be true for many simple hand-tools or items of furniture, but other classes of artifacts have purposes embedded in highly technological and/or cultural niches that make them meaningless unless an individual has a real understanding of that context. A good example of this is a class of devices known as differential Global Positioning System (GPS) receivers. Normal GPS receivers receive data about the location of GPS satellites at any given time, and the time it takes for the signals from the satellites to travel to the Earth. With just three signals, the receiver can calculate the coordinates of your position on the ground. This device was originally designed by the military; as the technology was released to the civilian public, the capacity for accurate calculations of location was made less precise. A new generation of machines, differential GPS receivers, were created as correction devices to give more accurate readings of coordinates. To correctly classify such a device requires knowledge of how GPS receivers generally work, knowledge of the military's strategy to downgrade civilian versions of the signals, and the relation between the two. Countless other examples exist.

Even where the structural complexity of an entity is not readily observable, the functional complexity requires a great deal of knowledge of social and cultural scripts for the object's use. For instance, the ATM Debit/Check card functions as a form of payment and is often seen being swiped through some sort of detection device. How the card works and by what mechanism are not visually obvious. Knowledge of its membership in a category requires reasonably advanced knowledge of trade and commerce in modern Western society, as well as some comprehension of the technology of data storage. There seems to be no upward limit on the potential complexity of artifact categories and levels of knowledge required to be able to successfully identify members of such a category. There are, of course, arcane cases in biology where species are confused, but rarely if nowhere in the domain of living things will you find whole classes of physical entities that cannot be categorized at the basic level upon visual inspection. There are some conceptually awkward living kinds (Hull 1965; Sperber, this volume), but it is rare to stumble into an environment and be as clueless about the identity and function of biological entities and their parts as we can be for many artifacts.

There are, of course, conceptually deep issues in the natural sciences that can be extremely difficult to grasp. These may involve categorizing entities based on deep theoretical principles rather than more physically obvious traits. Examples include classification of a compound as a superconductor, or a molecular structure as a transcription factor, both of which require a great deal of specialized knowledge unavailable to all children and most adults. But again, these exceptions are beyond the parameters for comparison that we set out for ourselves at the beginning of this chapter—that we consider bounded enduring objects. There is usually at least one inductively rich way to categorize a group of natural kinds that is available to most people. Walking through a strange ecosystem, one may group new kinds of animals and plants quite easily and without any sort of explicit instruction. To be sure, there can be confusions between legless lizards and snakes, or aquatic mammals and fish, but for the most part the entities in the domain of biology are easily categorized (Atran 1998). There is a grain of an analysis for almost all samples of the *macroscopic* living world that is easy to grasp. In contrast, if one enters a strange laboratory or manufacturing facility, one may be completely at sea with respect to categorizing the objects one encounters. In this way, despite being created by human minds, some artifacts are conceptually quite non-natural and require detailed local knowledge.[1] For living kinds, such as for various animal species and their subordinates and superordinates, such difficulties seem to be far less common.

Why should we expect this divergence between artifacts and living kinds in terms of ease of early categorization by young children? One answer might lie in the ways in which instances of the category are related in a hierarchy or taxonomy. There is an immediate and compelling sense that living kinds are embedded in a unique taxonomy that is not arbitrary (Atran 1998). For most artifacts, however,

---

[1] More intuitively, it seems obvious that some classes of artifacts, such as basic hand-tools like scissors or hammers, might be easy for a pre-schooler to learn well enough to categorize fairly successfully; while others, such as diagnostic tools used by a computer-repair technician, might not be accurately conceptualized until many years later.

it seems that many alternative hierarchies are possible for the same kinds. Indeed, some artifacts do not seem to fit easily into any hierarchies at all. For example, a fancy stereo system can be placed in a hierarchy of furniture, of electronic devices, or of toys. An intricately carved knife may be categorized as art to hang on one's wall, as a kitchen utensil, as a digging tool for use in the garden, or as a weapon. Similar problems are obvious when one tries to come up with a definition of even simple artifacts like chairs. There are no obvious physical characteristics that are shared by all chairs, and there is great flexibility in what physical characteristics any one chair can possess. To complicate matters further, some artifacts do not seem to fit any organized hierarchy or conceptual structure whatsoever. Is a handkerchief a piece of clothing? Is a lamp a piece of furniture? Unlike natural kinds, for artifacts there is no strong sense of a unique solution to the hierarchy issue. It may be that artifacts are more easily and more consistently categorized by thematic rather than taxonomic relations (Lin and Murphy 2001). Because artifacts can be assigned a variety of purposes or functions, a binding theme or context may be just the factor that can provide cues to a particular artifact's identity as a member of a particular category. This allows artifacts to adopt multiple identities as the context demands, and potentially avoids the difficulty of assigning any one artifact to an immutable singular position in any one hierarchy. In this way, a sword can be both a work of art and a weapon; the primacy of any one identity would depend heavily on other cues in the context in which the object exists and the other objects it is related to in that context (Barsalou 1983).

Thus, even when the class of artifacts is restricted to physically bounded objects, they can vary greatly in their conceptual naturalness as individuals and in the extent to which they systematically relate to other kinds. The dilemma for conceptualizing artifacts is deciding their memberships in multiple categories governed by ad hoc rules. The dilemma for living kinds, conversely, lies in placing each kind in a hierarchy whose taxonomy is restricted by laws of genetics, speciation, and evolution.

4. HOW CHILDREN LEARN ABOUT ARTIFACTS

In conversations with children, adults are unlikely to provide definitions about the meanings of words or discuss an object's membership in a category. That is, they often label objects but rarely define them or explain their nature to children (Gelman *et al.* 1998). With this dearth of direct semantic instruction, what information do young children use to learn about artifacts? Two forms of information may dominate conceptualization early on: direct perception of an object's affordances, and attention to contexts surrounding goal satisfaction. Both factors may influence children's notions of artifacts, though in very different proportions depending on the particular artifact in question.

Most objects have been said to have 'affordances', ways in which the layout and material properties of substances provide potentials for action by and interaction with an agent (Gibson and Adolph 1999). By this theory, affordances are invariant and 'directly perceived' features of objects that relate information about the utility of various surfaces and objects for behavior. They are not constructed via inference mechanisms. That is, one should immediately see an object as a container, a barrier, a supporter, or a handle and act on it in an appropriate manner, even when it is a highly novel object. We might conclude, then, that one of the earliest ways in which artifacts are distinguished is in terms of their different affordances. A pre-verbal infant, for instance, may see some surfaces as excellent for walking or sitting on (Gibson *et al.* 1987). Investigations into early notions of physics suggests that infants as young as 4 months can recognize that falling objects cannot pass through a solid horizontal barrier (Spelke *et al.* 1992). Hence, an object, a horizontal plane made of a particular material, may be perceived as providing support for performing a particular action—traversing. In this sense, an artifact is understood as part of a direct interaction between agent and object.

A second sense of affordance may involve the perception of an object as a causal mediator between an agent and another object. This intuition is more likely to be distinctively associated with artifacts. Hand-tools such as hammers and knives are just two examples. Not only are they directly perceived as graspable, they contain their own surface and material properties that can aid agents in transforming and acting on objects in particular ways. For instance, hammers generally have solid, heavy parts that can pound other objects. Likewise, knives have thin, sharp edges appropriate for cutting. Large containers generally have cavities in which other smaller objects can be placed.

This second sense of affordance has been studied less directly, although some work does suggest some emerging understanding of objects' roles as containers by 17 months of age (Baillargeon 1998; Caron, Caron, and Antell 1988) and as pulling devices by 9 and 12 months of age (Schlesinger and Langer 1999). Others have claimed that infants demonstrate some understanding of the link between form and function by 18 months of age (Madole and Cohen 1995; Madole, Oakes, and Cohen 1993). Further, in work with older children, Kemler Nelson *et al.* (1995) found that 3-, 4-, and 5-year-olds categorized artifacts as either painting devices or musical instruments based on the functional affordances that particular crucial features specified.

Despite its clear phenomenological appeal, the notion of affordances remains frustratingly vague. Even under the most optimistic and charitable interpretations of affordances, it is clear that many artifacts do not offer their functions up so easily to direct perception. For example, without any other information, no amount of visual inspection of an antibiotic pill or credit card will reveal its function. There is, however, an alternative way to learn about artifacts that, like affordances, does not involve any explicit instruction by adults. Imagine a child watching an adult using a key for the first time. Inspection of the key itself is unlikely to yield insight into its function, since its most important functional parts, its serrations, interact with the parts of a lock that are not visible from the outside. Yet very young children come to learn what keys are for and what they do—and usually without being told. They do so by watching an actor with a goal perform an action, such as opening a door, and observe the key being central to goal satisfaction, the opened door. Whether it be keys, television remote controls, glue-sticks, or metal-detectors, an artifact's global function can be understood without knowing how its form is related to its function and, it would seem, without explicitly knowing that someone made it for a particular purpose.

Inferring function from an actor's intentions, however, is a more subtle process than it first appears. A basic problem of inference lies in the mapping of an object's function to the relevant goal in a sequence of actions. It is necessary to decide which of the many actions involved in satisfying a goal are linked to the function of the artifact the agent is using. A child should not infer, for example, that a person uses a key because they like the sensation it creates in their hands, or because it is useful for making a nice sound when jangled against other keys. The determination of the relevant function of the object lies in noticing the way in which it is used to create an end-state that matches a person's initial intentions.

Another challenge for inferences about function is to decide how general any one object's function is in relation to the other objects with which it interacts. A person's immediate goals may be highly specific (e.g. 'I want to attach together these particular pieces of paper'), but the inference of, in this case, the tool's function may not be as distinctly mapped to the object upon which it is first used. Thus, a significant question for further distinguishing the properties of artifacts is to ask at what level of generality do children and adults internalize their inferences about function? Is a glue-stick understood as effective for those two particular pieces of paper, or just for pieces of paper of that size, shape, and color? Or is it conceived as able to glue together wood, metal, glass, and fabric? Is there a happy medium between the tool satisfying a global goal and performing a specific operation on a specific material? That is, is a glue-stick a global 'attacher', a local 'paper gluer', or something in-between? For inference to have any value the child must abstract away the appropriate function at a sufficient level of generality to be of some use in other contexts. If not, we would need an infinite number of tools to solve an infinite number of problems.

Experimental work is just beginning to address this conceptual problem (Greif 2004; Greif, Keil, and Gutierrez 2003). In one paradigm, children watch a video of an actor trying to achieve a goal, such as opening a wooden box, joining two pipes, or cleaning off a pile of dirt from a table. The actors display frustration at not being able to perform the task with their bare hands and then search for a tool to solve their problem. After finding a tool that will help them, their moods shift and they are subsequently shown with their initial goals satisfied (for instance, with an opened box, or with a clean table). The videos never show the tool itself, its manner of use, or make statements referring to the function of the tool; rather, the scenarios imply its role through goal satisfaction. Finally, the children are shown photographs of objects that vary from the object in the initial scenario on dimensions of color and size, on their material and form, and the appropriate function or action required to fulfill the actor's goal. Children are asked to decide which of these variations can be solved by the tool from the target video.

There are two key questions to this work: (1) are children able to infer function from the goals set up in videos?; and (2) at what level of abstraction do they make such inferences? The research is still under way but it is already clear that children at least as young as 5 years easily infer functions from goal-satisfaction episodes, and that they do so in roughly the right conceptual space. That is, they infer some subclass of opening devices for situations where adults judge that the goal is opening.

With respect to the second question, young children were not completely specific (for example, assuming the tool is only for opening red wooden boxes), but seemed to be considerably more narrow in their generalizations of tool function than older children. This result may have been driven by an effort to think of a known tool (for instance, a screwdriver to pry open stuck edges of a wooden box), and to assume that the tool the actor uses is a member of that category. By positing a familiar tool, young children may use whatever they know about that tool's mechanism to reason about its utility on other objects. Because their knowledge of tool mechanism is necessarily limited compared to that of an older child or adult, their abstraction of function may thus be similarly restricted. With novel tools whose mechanisms are unfamiliar both to children and adults, young children may be just as, or even far more, abstract than older children in terms of generalizing function. In a second study using similar video stimuli (Greif 2004), asking children to make inferences about novel tools led to just this pattern of results. Ultimately, the rationale underlying this line of research illuminates the notion that young children are quite adept at making inferences about tool categories on the basis of goal states of others, while apparently not having to know that the tools themselves were intentionally designed for a specific purpose.

Within this account, there should be a critical distinction between differentiating artifacts from natural kinds and thinking about what it means for something to *be* an artifact (that is, to come to understand what properties and characteristics define artifacts in and of themselves). It may be that these two facets of cognition about artifacts develop quite independently of each other. It may seem at first that the core that distinguishes between artifacts and natural kinds is to know that artifacts were made by agents with goals and intentions and that the intention of the creator is paramount (Bloom 1996, 1998; Thomasson, this volume). Because children very rarely see people actually *create* the artifacts common in daily life, but very often see people *use* such objects, it is reasonable that this second kind of information is especially informative early on before children understand all of the intricacies of designer intent. For instance, assessing real-time goal fulfillment requires the ability to infer current intent of a physically present entity. This is a somewhat different, and seemingly simpler, cognitive task than formulating hypotheses about the beliefs and desires of a frequently absent individual who performed a creative act some time in the past.

We do know that young children, well before the first year of life, are quite sensitive to a person's intentions and will imitate an action they believed an agent wanted to engage in rather than the one they actually performed (cf. Meltzoff 1995). They also demonstrate surprise at actions that fail to reflect the intentions of an agent even when those actions might be physically identical to ones performed earlier (Woodward 1998; Gergely *et al.* 1995). All of this suggests that current goal fulfillment may be an important way that very young children account for artifact function and categorization.

5. WHAT CHANGES WITH DEVELOPMENT?

What is different about the young child's concept of artifacts in comparison to an older child or an adult's concept of artifacts? One major change may be an increasing appreciation of intended function in contrast to salient current function. Though the two usually coincide, it seems to become more obvious with time that the intended function should trump all else in assigning membership to artifact categories. One elegant demonstration of this pattern occurs in work on children's drawings. Three- and 4-year-olds labeled pictures they had drawn themselves according to their own intent to create a representation of an item such as a lollipop or balloon; this was despite the indistinguishable appearance of their renditions of the two objects (Bloom and Markson 1998). Children were also able to determine the appropriate labels for pictures that others had drawn, given information about the artist's intent. Gelman and Bloom (2000) also found that 3-year-olds were more likely to provide artifact names for objects that an experimenter indicated had been intentionally created.

Other evidence suggests, however, that a comprehensive understanding of the role an intentional designer plays in determining the identity of an artifact does not emerge until around 6 years of age. Matan and Carey (2001) found that children as old as 4 years have difficulty understanding the notion of designer intent as the determinant of artifact identity. In functional fixedness tasks, German and Deyfeyter (2000) also noted that 5-year-olds' responses were not influenced by notions of 'proper' or original function. It is possible that, as children get older, they are more likely to explicitly think about how the artifact might have been created and if that manner of creation is consistent with the function they have inferred through observation (see also Kelemen and Carey, this volume). However, the first pass at determining artifact identity may indeed be by observation of how an actor currently uses an artifact to fulfill particular goals. This perspective is supported by work done by Mandler and McDonough (1996, 1998*b*) and again by Matan and Carey (2001), and German and Defeyter (2000). Just by way of example, Mandler (this volume) outlines a vast program of research that has demonstrated that infants between 14 and 24 months begin to interact appropriately with artifacts in classification and imitation tasks. Moreover, children's artifact classification is remarkably more refined for artifacts than for animals, suggesting that young children have rather early understanding that the way an artifact is used may be an important conceptual marker that distinguishes it from other kinds of artifacts.

Another type of knowledge that should be implicated in a developmental account of a concept of artifacts is the ever-increasing database of information about the mechanisms involved in any artifact's function. Children may often get the only the highest level of functional gloss for any artifact and then only gradually fill in the detailed knowledge about the more precise mechanisms that subserve that larger function. Thus, they might know that a camera is for taking pictures, but have no idea of how images are captured, processed, and represented. This understanding should grow over time as children are exposed to more and more technological minutiae through experience and formal instruction. The consequence of this increasing mechanistic knowledge may be to yield better insights into how such a device was originally designed and created, thus bringing together both the intuitions of intentions of users with those of creators.

Third, we should expect that, as artifact concepts develop, children and adults should come to understand that the identity of artifacts might easily jump across category hierarchies in ways not possible for living kinds. Something that might have been initially identified as a piece of jewelry may later be categorized as a time-telling device. Something that was initially understood to be a toy may later be conceptualized as a word-processor. Not only can these artifacts be re-categorized, they can maintain membership in concurrent categories quite easily. These kinds of dramatic leaps are far less common for the living world. A member of a living kind might be categorized as both a basic-level and superordinate-level kind—an animal categorized as a cat might also be categorized as a mammal. It is less likely that a species of cat would concurrently be categorized as a dog; this would clearly be an assignment error. Again, an increasing tendency to view artifacts as flexibly belonging to more than one category would rely heavily on a growing understanding of intended design, use, and mechanism.

Finally, one of the most subtle and latest emerging insights concerning artifacts may be to understand the ways in which they are often co-mingled with natural kinds (see also, in this volume, chapters by Bloom, Grandy, and Sperber for extensive discussion of this possibility). Hunting-dogs, racehorses, and dairy cows are artifacts created by intense breeding practices. Human actions and intended function have transformed many of the salient properties of these animals. Similar phenomena can be found across many species of animals and plants, and can be quite dramatic with modern technology. Researchers have, for example, discovered ways to express genes for spinning spider's silk in bovine cells in order to produce the silk more economically (Lazaris *et al.* 2002). Similarly, farmers in Japan have produced square watermelons in order to optimize shipping and storage density. Perhaps one of the factors prohibiting easy re-categorization of such cases is the level of salience of the essences of natural kinds. Not only does one need a somewhat broad knowledge base of technological advances that permit transformations between natural kinds and artifacts (and the ill-defined line that divides them), the driving intuition that natural kinds have particular steadfast essences prevents a full understanding of how natural kinds can become artifactualized. This might be the case for children, in particular, whose exposure to information about scientific advances, or the history of agriculture and animal husbandry for that matter, is understandably limited. For instance, knowing something is a living kind permits a number of inferences about its properties—that it reproduces, respires, that members of a category share internal parts and a similar path of development (Gelman and O'Reilly 1988; Hatano and Inagaki 1996; Keil 1989, 1992; Simons and Keil 1995). When artifactualizing a living kind, a serious cognitive conflict arises. These types of essential properties are hard to remove from a living kind and still deem it living, and they are almost impossible to bestow upon artifacts without a miraculous act or an incredible feat of science. In the cases of entities like square watermelons and hunting-dogs, just looking at them provides many cues to their living status. Clearly, the essential characteristics of living kinds are maintained, and given all we know about watermelons and dogs, the intuition that these beings are living kinds is just too compelling to ignore in favor of less obvious cues to artifacthood. Not only should the ability to transcend this conflict be late-developing, some adults may never fully understand the dual status of these entities.

Note that this argument does not make claims about whether there is a clear line between artifact and natural kinds as actual extant categories out there in the world. There might very well be biological artifacts (Sperber, this volume), water might be properly classified as both an artifact and natural kind (Bloom, this volume), the distinction between the two kinds might be illusory (Grandy, this volume), and they might also follow the same laws of reproduction (Elder, this volume). The questions central to cognitive development ask how children themselves come to carve up the world of objects into systematic groups and which underlying principles guide such divisions. Empirically, fuzzy categories like biological artifacts could provide a fascinating test of the limits of children's concepts of living and artifact kinds. Quite simply, we do not yet know if or when young children blend kinds in the face of knowledge about biological and cultural functions (Sperber, this volume). Though it might be sensible for children to adopt multiple modes of construal to consider biological artifacts, as Bloom (this volume) suggests, they may not actually do this in practice, or they may come to do this in a predictable and systematic way throughout development.

6. CONCLUSIONS

Humans show an extraordinary ability relative to all other species to create and learn about artifacts. Some of this special ability may revolve around a more sophisticated ability to see affordances. We may even perceive affordances on a relational level; that is, not only do we see the structural/functional capacity of an object itself, we see the ways in which it can be used on other objects. However, we also have a more sophisticated ability for reasoning about the features of artifacts that is less relevant for understanding aspects of living kinds. Our ability to infer the intentions and goals of others helps us to identify and refine our categorization of a seemingly infinite class of artifacts. While this ability could play an obvious role in thinking about how an artifact was originally created, it may figure in an equally if not more important role early on in determining the functions of artifacts in real time through looking at goal satisfaction in others. With development, a greater appreciation of all of these factors may help us to distinguish artifacts and natural kinds in much deeper and more elaborate ways. Thus, even though very young children have some sense that artifacts and other kinds are worlds apart, a complete grasp of the full depth and extent of the contrast may take many years to acquire.[2]

[2] Preparation of this paper, and some of the research reported on therein, was supported by National Institutes of Health grant R01-HD23922 to Frank Keil and by Natural Sciences and Engineering Research Council of Canada Postgraduate Scholarship (NSERC PGSB-243737–2001) to Marissa Greif.

PART IV

EVOLUTION

14

Animal Artifacts

James L. Gould

1. INTRODUCTION

What is an animal artifact? The first definition of 'artifact' in my dictionary reads 'a simple object (as a tool or ornament) showing human workmanship or modification' (Merriam 1981). The next two definitions are of equally little help in providing a guide to the meaning of animal artifact: 'a product of civilization', and 'a product of artistic endeavor'.

For the purposes of this review, I will take an artifact to be any creation on the part of an animal, using and/or modifying available materials, which is useful to it or its offspring. This definition is consistent with the more philosophical formulation by Elder (this volume).

Less formally, I think this boils down to things animals make or use that most humans find impressive. Because the number of examples of animal artifacts easily runs into the tens or hundreds of thousands, only a very personal set of biases can permit the kind of broad but selective survey needed here. All are, technically, creations of the mind: instinct—the most common basis for artifact construction—is 'implemented' through neural circuits necessarily located in the brain. In addition to this view of the brain as a processing engine, I will look at the extent to which the 'mind' in its more romantic sense—as an organ of thought—may be involved in specific cases.

Broadly considered, animal artifacts fall into three main categories: artifacts used for hunting, foraging, or processing food; artifacts employed for protection or as homes (perhaps just for the offspring); and artifacts used to attract members of the opposite sex. Some artifacts serve more than one of these purposes; the vast majority are, at least in part, homes for their builders (Gould and Gould 1999).

Lacking any better organizational rationale, I will look at examples phylogenetically, beginning with arthropods and moving ever closer to our own species.

Animal building behavior, and its cognitive implications, are treated in far more detail elsewhere (Gould and Gould 2007).

2. HUNTING AND FORAGING

Most species on our planet are insects; they are part of the phylum known as the arthropods—animals with an external skeleton. This body armor includes many ingenious tools, many of which are essential for creating artifacts. I will begin with cases in which the animals use one of their own body products (silk) to generate artifacts, and then look at instances in which external material is employed.

2.1. Silk

Silk is typically spun by insect larvae to make the cocoons in which they pupate. But insects can use silk in a number of other ways (the majority of which, as we will see, come under the heading of homes). The most spectacular example to my eye is the silken seine net that certain species of caddisfly larvae create in the streams where they grow and mature. These funnel-shaped structures are kept open by the flowing current; potential food is filtered out by the silk mesh and collects at the base of the funnel, where the larva can eat what it likes. A typical 1 cm-long larva will build a net with a roughly square opening of perhaps 3 cm on a side and a length of about 10 cm (Wallace and Sherberger 1975).

In spiders (arthropods, but not insects), silk is inevitably used to enclose egg masses. The majority of spiders also use silk to build traps, of which the classic (and stunningly beautiful) orb web is the most familiar. The web is, of course, a hunting tool, and requires various gauges of silk (heavy-duty threads for supports and radii, lighter ones for intermediate threads that must sag under the spider's weight to help create some of the early design, sticky ones for the spiral catching threads, and so on). There are a number of variations on this theme, but my favorite is the more recently evolved group that makes a small, elaborately woven, sticky net which is held between two very long front legs. Upon encountering prey, the net is cast over the victim, trapping it (Comstock 1940).

The trap-door spider uses its silk in a different way: it digs a tunnel into the earth, which it lines with silk. It then selects a stone of the appropriate size to cover the tunnel. One edge of the stone is woven to the silk of the tunnel to provide a hinge for this lid. The spider then waits for night. When the world turns dark, the lid is opened slightly; the spider waits just at the surface under the lid listening (with organs in its legs) for the tell-tale vibrations produced by potential prey passing nearby. Upon hearing the footfalls of a possible victim, the spider tosses the lid back on its hinge and springs out upon the prey (Comstock 1940).

There is no evidence of mental intervention in these behaviors beyond instinct and learning—and learning (or rather conditioning, the most common form of learning) is itself an innate process, well endowed with tell-tale species-specific biases (Gould and Gould 1999). But the absence of any obvious mental activity does not mean there is none. Coughing, sneezing, and vomiting (to name just three behaviors) are innate in humans, and yet we can think while performing these essential responses. In salticid spiders there is clear evidence of route planning (Tarsitano and Jackson 1994); it hardly makes sense to rule out similar cognitive activity in other members of the group simply because we may not have had the wit or luck to observe or recognize it yet.

2.2. Stones and shells

Desert spiders construct burrows much like those of trap-door spiders, but use their silk and the stones available to them in quite a different way. The spiders select a set of flat stones (usually high in quartz) to surround their burrow entrance. The stones taper in width toward the entrance, creating a more-or-less continuous circle, rather like a patio decoration around a specimen tree. This array is used for detecting passing prey. The spider employs silk to bind the stones together and then to the burrow entrance, where it waits just below the surface. The spider's vibration-sensitive legs are positioned on the silk which is connected to the stones, so that the circle serves as a large detection array (Henschel 1995). The context-specific choice and use of the available stones may suggest a degree of cognitive activity.

Some species of jawfish excavate vertical burrows, which, as with human wells, are prevented from collapsing by pressing stones (and shells) into the sides of the cylinder. The reinforcement layer is often two shells/stones thick. These masonry wells provide a secure spot from which to ambush passing prey (Frisch 1974). Like many of the artifacts discussed in this section, these creations also serve as homes for their builders. And again, the degree of flexibility in executing the species-specific plan is striking.

2.3. Tools

At first glance, tools would seem automatically to qualify as artifacts. But in fact, a tool is technically defined as an instrument used or worked by hand, or less specifically as something used in performing an operation or necessary in the practice of a vocation or profession (Merriam and Merriam 1981). Viewed in this light, eyes, fingernails, teeth, and Wernike's area in the brain qualify as tools; and, of course, animals have an astonishing array of such specialized bodily and mental paraphernalia. Thus to be both a tool *and* an artifact, we must at the very least demand that the animal should be highly selective in its choice of external objects (as in the case of the desert spider described above), or (preferably) modify the object to its own ends.

Perhaps the most famous animal tool is the cactus spine employed by the woodpecker finches on the Galapagos Islands; these tools are used to remove insects from branches and trunks, thus compensating for the birds' length-challenged beak (Grant 1986). The list of animals using naturally occurring objects as tools—objects chosen with some apparent care—is astonishingly long. Griffin (1992) describes how animals of one species will use individuals of other species as defensive weapons; in other cases, leaves and bits of bark are used as sponges or bowls for transporting liquids, and stones or bark are employed for tamping down soil. (All of these examples are drawn from invertebrates.)

Among birds there is apparent learning or insight involved in some tool-use cases, as with crows, ravens, Egyptian vultures (which hurl rocks at ostrich eggs to break them), and herons (which use—and reuse—artificial bait to attract fish). Sea otters, of course, use stones to break or pry molluscs from the ocean bottom, and then employ the very same rocks as anvils for hammering the prey open at the surface. And then there is the frequently photographed termite-fishing by chimpanzees using grass stems, and the less-often-observed practice of using stones on wooden anvils (depressions in fallen trees) to crack open nuts (Griffin 1992). The original example of tool-use by chimps, of course, was reported by Köhler (1927): the animals, kept in a large outdoor enclosure in the Canary Islands (waiting for the end of World War I, which had interrupted this collection expedition of the Berlin Zoo on its way home from Africa), solved a variety of food-acquisition problems with boxes, poles, and sticks.

In retrospect, there is something slightly unsatisfying about considering even carefully chosen objects as artifacts—even though anthropologists might have little hesitation in considering such ad hoc tools as genuine artifacts if they bear signs of wear as a consequence of human use. But if we hold tool artifacts to a stricter standard for animals (the usual trick we use to relegate non-human species to a suitably low status), and require that the tools be modified in some non-trivial way (so that wear and tear, or cutting a grass stem to a better length, or breaking a twig to create a more realistic piece of bait do not count), then the list becomes dramatically shorter. Except for the seine net and other creations described above, which are constructed from body secretions, I know of only one clear case: the hook and the step-cut tools carefully crafted by the crows on New Caledonia for removing insect larvae from branches (Hunt 1996).

The implements made by these birds are essentially harpoons, fashioned either from twigs or painstakingly cut leaves with back-curved barbs. They are used to remove insect larvae from trees. Field observation of birds making and using these tools suggests an unusual degree of understanding about both construction and use. This impression is reinforced by laboratory tests of New Caledonian crows. Weir, Chappel, and Kacelnik (2002) showed that a year after a casual (one hour unreinforced) experience with a wire pipe-cleaner, a bird could successfully and spontaneously bend a thin wire into a hook and use it to retrieve a small metal bucket containing meat, placed at the bottom of a tube. In formal tests on two birds, one (but not the other) enjoyed significant success: in nine of ten trials she successfully bent the wire and used the resulting tool to lift the pail. Like the beaver discussed below, this bird seemed to have some sense of the goal, and adjusted her behavior accordingly. Hence she was able to solve a wholly unnatural problem using material not found in nature, and employ a construction behavior which is unnecessary in the wild. It is difficult (but not impossible) to account for the crows' tools as something other than creations of the mind.

3. PROTECTION AND HOMES

Homes and shelters constitute by far the largest category of animal artifacts. The use of silk is again a good starting point.

3.1. Silk

All insects with a larval stage (a grub or caterpillar) must undergo metamorphosis through a pupal state to assume an adult form (Gould and Keeton 1996). (A variety of insects, such as termites and grasshoppers, hatch from the egg as miniature adults, and grow through several molts until they achieve mature size; insects that metamorphize in the complete sense—ants, bees, wasps, flies, beetles, butterflies and moths, and so on—emerge from the pupal case as full-sized mature adults.) The larvae spin a tough cocoon of silk as they enter the pupal phase; it is from the cocoons of silkworm moths that commercial silk is produced. (The pupal cocoon may be surrounded by yet another structure to provide additional protection to the maturing insect.)

Some species also employ silk either before or after metamorphosis. The caddisfly larvae of the species mentioned earlier created a seine net; the larvae of other species of caddisflies instead spin a hollow tube of silk and adorn it with shells and/or stones, for (depending on the species) protection, camouflage, or ballast (Wiggins 1977). Other species of insects build silken tubes on or near their food supplies; the tubes serve as refuges to which the builder can return between foraging bouts. The homes of clothes moths and grain moths are perhaps the most depressingly familiar of these constructions; the largest examples are the cooperatively built homes of 'bag worms'. These leaf-eating caterpillars generally remain within the safety of their waterproof homes during the day, then venture out to forage at night (Fabre 1916).

Perhaps the most imaginative direct use of silk is by weaver ants. This tropical species differs from most ants in that it nests in the leaves of trees rather than in the ground. The nests are created by pulling leaves together and then binding them with silk. The source of silk is the larvae of the ants, which are used like shuttles: while other workers hold the leaves together, an adult moves a larva first to one leaf edge, and then back to the other, over and over again. The silk glues the two edges together (Hölldobler and Wilson 1990).

Most species of hummingbirds make some secondhand use of spider silk as a binding agent to hold together the primary materials employed in nest construction; bird nests fabricated out of vegetation are described in a later section. The long-tailed hummingbird of Venezuela, however, uses almost nothing but stolen silk. It chooses a slightly folded hanging leaf and weaves a nest from silk at the bottom (Attenborough 1998). (The nest is finished with a thin lining of plant fibers, and a few are mixed in with the silk itself.) I will return later to the possible cognitive contribution in nest-building by birds.

3.2. Wax

Another body product used in creating a home is the wax secreted by the abdominal glands of some species of bees. The most famous example of a wax artifact is the honeycomb of honey bees, a geometrically precise array of hexagonal tubes two cells thick. The junction of any three adjacent cells on one side of the comb is the center of a cell on the opposite side, an arrangement that is sufficiently strong that the structure can hold a thousand times its own weight in nectar, ripe honey, pollen, water, larvae, and pupae. The honeycomb of the temperate-zone honey bee is constructed inside cavities as a series of parallel sheets two bee diameters apart; some species of tropical honey bees (from which region our honey bees evolved) build a single exposed sheet of honeycomb (Frisch 1967; Gould and Gould 1995).

3.3. Other secretions

A few species of swiftlets in South-East Asia and Indonesia build nests on cliff faces out of their own saliva. After one layer of saliva hardens, the birds add more until the nest cup is complete (Frisch 1974). It is these remarkable structures that are the key ingredient of authentic bird's-nest soup. (The majority of swiftlets use their sticky, fast-drying saliva simply as a glue to bind vegetation and other building materials together into a nest—though in some species the nests are more saliva than vegetation.) An analogous strategy is seen in stickleback fish, the freshwater species made famous by the studies of Niko Tinbergen (1952). The males of the three-spined species create a trench in the substrate, gather vegetation (particularly filamentous algae), glue it together with a sticky substance from the kidneys, and fashion a tunnel in which females are induced to lay their eggs (Frisch 1974).

3.4. Excavation

One good place to build a home is underground or in a tree. An excavated burrow or nest may be inconspicuous, protected from predators or parasites, and insulated from unwanted variations in surface-air temperature and humidity. I find it somewhat problematic to argue that a hole can be an artifact. But consider the precisely 'excavated' 1.2 cm-wide tunnels that female carpenter bees create every spring in posts and wooden walls: few uninitiated observers fail to conclude that these perfectly circular and straight holes are the products of power drills wielded in accord with some inexplicable plan of a handyman run amok. But beyond the obvious craftsmanship, the tunnel is more than a pointless exercise in digging: it is soon lined with leaves, packed with pollen, endowed with an egg, and closed—at which it point it becomes a nursery.

Countless thousands of species of solitary bees and wasps create variants on this theme (Spradbery 1973). My favorite is the edifice erected (and then partially dismantled) by a species of Australian hunting wasp. The female begins, as do her counterparts in many species, by excavating a tunnel in the earth. She then reinforces this nursery-to-be by collecting mud, and lining the tunnel in a circular motion with a mixture that dries nearly to the hardness of concrete (Smith 1978). (An idea of this process is readily visible by watching the construction of exposed nests on walls by organ-pipe wasps: the females return again and again with a ball of mud and work it into successive 1 mm ring-shaped additions to the growing tube. The species common in the northeastern United States fills these nests with paralyzed spiders, lays an egg, seals the compartment, and then lengthens the tunnel to add other chambers. The work is rough on the outside, but smooth—almost slippery—on the interior surface.)

After excavating and lining the burrow, the Australian species then constructs an impressive funnel atop the tunnel entrance; the funnel consists of a straight cylindrical stem at least 2 cm long rising perpendicularly from the soil, a curved neck, and then a bell-like structure which points about 30° away from straight down—enough of an angle so that the bell does not touch the stem. This bit of exterior work is a defensive device: it is too large for parasites to hold onto the rough lower edge of the bell with the rear legs while reaching up to gain purchase on the neck with the front legs so they can haul themselves in—just the procedure the builder must undergo to gain admission to her own nest. The wasp then captures and paralyzes caterpillars, stores them in the tunnel, lays an egg, seals the chamber, and so forth until the tunnel is full of developing young, one to a compartment. Then she demolishes the funnel, conceals the opening, and moves on to excavate another burrow.

The inability of these wasps to repair even (to our eye) trivial but unnatural damage during construction, or compensate for human-generated changes that defeat the purpose of the funnel, argue that the wasp's behavior is wholly innate.

Indeed, it is the key example in our understanding of how building behavior is programmed: the wasp cycles endlessly through a specific sequence of behaviors until a criterion is met—a tube of the appropriate height having been built, say—and then enters another cycle dedicated to generating the next component of the edifice.

Other groups that depend on excavation include nearly all species of ants and termites, as well as such familiar rodents as beaver, prairie dogs, and woodchucks. The formless mounds of excavated dirt belie the intricate subterranean complexity of the nests of ants, with their specialized chambers for the queen, brood (often segregated by age), food stores (sometimes separated by type), refuse, and provisions for drainage, ventilation, heating, and cooling (Wilson 1971).

The homes of termites and beaver will be discussed at greater length later. However, as examples of tireless and impressive excavation, both beaver and termites deserve special mention here. Many termites (as we will see) have an enormous cooling problem to deal with. In warm arid regions the solution often lies in digging a well down to the water table and ferrying water up to the nest proper, where it is used for evaporative cooling. It is not unusual for these wells to reach distances of 30–50 m (Wilson 1971; Frisch 1974). At the scale of a worker termite, this is the equivalent of a human well 50–100 km deep; the deepest hole drilled by our species (to date) goes down only 20 km.

Beaver make their living consuming the living parts of trees (the leaves, and the cambium at the tips of twigs and just under the bark); much of what they cut is stored underwater to provide food for the winter. Once they have felled the trees at the edge of the stream or pond they inhabit, they must either move on or find another way to bring freshly cut branches to their larder. In suitable locations, they excavate canals up to 0.5 km long into the surrounding forest, and float their woody booty back home (Morgan 1886; Sparks 1982). The sight of these elaborate fingers of water extending across marshes into the forest, being navigated by beaver transporting freshly harvested branches, is quite unforgettable.

3.5. Building in adobe (dried mud/clay)

The use of hardened mud (often rich in clay) by wasps has already been mentioned. Potter wasps (a fairly common North American species) construct spherical vessels about 2 cm in diameter (generally in pine trees), complete with a short neck and opening at the top. These miniature pieces of pottery are filled with paralyzed caterpillars, an egg is added, and then the vessel is sealed with a final ball of mud (Spradbery 1973). More impressive structures are built by several species of social wasps, in which an entire free-hanging nest containing hundreds or thousands of cells is enclosed by an incredibly tough wall constructed of clay and 'straw' (mostly grass). In some species these artifacts are quite smooth on the outside, suggesting that they are defenses against large predators unable to gain much purchase on a slippery surface (Spradbery 1973; Frisch 1974).

Easily the most impressive mud-built structures created by animals are the nests of termites. The tiny workers (typically 1–2 mm long) are sightless, and yet some species construct an internal array of perfect arches, along with external walls, chimneys, or pagoda-like roofs that can rise many meters into the air (Wilson 1971; Frisch 1974). The main building materials are mud and feces, sometimes reinforced with sand and straw. Again, scaling these edifices to human dimensions, our tallest buildings are but a fraction of the height. Despite their astonishing size, these artifacts are mostly uninhabited (at least by termites; a motley collection of uninvited tenants occupy various bits of the superstructure).

The key to understanding the logic of termite 'mounds' is the need for ample ventilation. Cellulose is the most common organic compound on earth, and though it is a polymer of energy-rich glucose, the sugars are joined by an almost indigestible bond. Only certain species of anaerobic bacteria (bacteria unable to function in the presence of air), as well as many fungi, are able to feed directly on wood. (Fungi can also digest the other major component of wood, lignin.) Termites have two strategies for making a living off cellulose (Wilson 1971). Many species (including the termites common in the temperate zone, which live inside dead trunks and branches—and lumber) maintain a flourishing fauna of symbiotic bacteria in the gut; under these internal anaerobic conditions, the bacteria are able to digest the cellulose, and the termites digest the excess bacteria.

The other, more interesting, strategy involves bringing (usually dead) vegetation back to the nest and inoculating it with fungi adapted to grow in termite nests (Wilson 1971). The termites eat the excess fungi. (Leaf-cutter ants use a fresh-food variant of this approach: they cut green leaves from trees, carry them back to their immense underground nests, chew the edges, infect them with bits of fungi, and later consume the fungi and feed it to their larvae.) Termites (and ants) that depend on fungal gardens live in some of the numerically largest colonies found on earth (human cities not excepted). The heat generated by the metabolism of millions of termites, plus the fungi upon which they feed, is enormous—and can be a particularly serious problem, since many of these species live in the tropics where the outside air temperature can be close to the limit for unaided survival.

The internal design of these nests varies greatly between species, but in general there is a free-standing, heavily armored chamber for the king and the enormous queen termite, which is located below ground level. Higher in the nest are the vast fungus gardens, where mature workers process the incoming vegetation while managing and weeding the fungus (upon which the tiny young termites graze). The heat and carbon dioxide generated in these chambers rises into species-specific air-exchange structures, which vary from simple chimneys to largely hollow buttresses heavily perforated with minute holes.

The height of the tallest of these artifacts reflects the reality that on still days the only chance of a breeze is high above the ground; moreover, air several meters up is often cooler by virtue of being farther from the baked, heat-radiating earth below. Thus, with the gas-exchange devices elevated as far as necessary, the metabolic heat and waste gasses are drawn up and away from the royal bunker. Channels are usually excavated into the nest near the bottom, and angle down to a point below the queen's chamber; oxygen-rich outside air is thereby drawn into the 'cellar' and then is pulled up through the nest. When the outside temperature is too high, water must be brought up from the well described previously and spread on the nest surfaces to provide evaporative cooling (Wilson 1971; Frisch 1974; Gould and Gould 1999).

The 'castles of clay' built by termites reward more detailed study. The behavior of individuals, while apparently coordinated in some global way, looks quite independent in detail. The structure is built as a set of arches, each different yet generally symmetrical, each built in the dark. An arch begins with two separate pillars. A termite with a pellet of building material will typically climb one of the two growing verticals, descend, climb another (not necessarily the only plausible alternative in the vicinity), and then place the pellet. If the pillar is high enough, the material is placed on top but slightly toward the other pillar; if the bias in the pillar toward the other side of the arch is already there, the pellet is added with the same directional bias, but with some attention to the degree of curvature. To be strong, arches connecting pillars must be built according to the distance between the two bases, so that curvature and height differ between arches. In short, arch-building is not highly stereotyped, and would in humans require forming a mental picture of the pillars and their relative location. Responses to damage, human interference (placing a tarp over the mound), and differences in design strategies between colonies of the same species in contrasting habitats all argue for more flexibility than is generally conceded to insects.

The building feats of vertebrates in this medium are less impressive. One species of South American tree frog uses clay-rich mud as a means of protecting offspring. As amphibians, frog eggs must develop in water, where they hatch into tadpoles. The tadpoles grow slowly, finally metamorphosing by reabsorbing the tail and assuming an adult form. The eggs and tadpoles are at particular risk from predators. A parent in a number of species guards the eggs or early tadpoles in one way or another, but one species has a remarkable solution to the problem: before courting females, the male piles up mud in a wide circle to create a relatively safe swimming pool for the tadpoles. The mud is then shaped and smoothed with the male's webbed feet into an impressive state of perfection, and may well be one component of the decision-making process that females use to choose between males (Gould and Gould 1997). After mating, the males abandon the eggs to the relative safety of this private pond (Frisch 1974).

Several species of bird make nests out of clay-rich mud. To my mind the most impressive is the smooth, spherical structure crafted by the ovenbirds of Central and South America. The clay is mixed with straw and other vegetation, and the edifice is normally erected atop a branch. In cross-section there is an inner sphere for the nest, and an outer sphere on one side which provides an indirect and narrow access to the enclosed opening of the interior chamber. Far less impressive are the mud-based nests of swallows. These structures, which are typically built against walls under overhangs, are constructed of hundreds of mud pellets, which may be mixed with vegetation to add strength. Since the builders make no effort to 'finish' the nest, the individual lumps of hardened mud are readily evident (Goodfellow 1977). There are no experiments on this building process, so we know nothing of what might be going on in the mind of the birds.

3.6. Vegetation

A number of insects build nests from leaves, pine needles, strands of grass, or bits of bark. In some cases the vegetation has been chewed, roughly shaped, and left to dry, creating a crude structure called a 'carton nest'. A much more elegant use of vegetation is seen in many species of wasp. These insects scrape wood fibers from trees, chew them with water to create a damp mash, and then spread this pulp in thin, narrow layers to create cells and (in some social species) surrounding sheets of rough paper which serve as both insulation and protection. The underground nests of yellow-jackets and their aerial counterparts built by hornets are familiar examples, but the exposed combs of paper wasps are an even more common sight, located under porches and eaves, and behind shutters. In cross-section, a hornet or yellow-jacket nest consists of several concentric layers of paper with a circular opening at the bottom. Within the inner layer are numerous horizontal tiers of paper comb connected by thick buttresses (Wilson 1971). Bald-faced hornets regularly create nests 0.5–1 m in diameter.

3.6.1. *The nests of birds*

The vast majority of vegetation-based artifacts used as homes by vertebrates are, of course, bird nests (Frisch 1974; Goodfellow 1977; Attenborough 1998; Hansell 2000). There are literally thousands of species-specific designs, ranging from simple scrapes in the ground (many terns) to enormous enclosed communal nests (the sociable weaverbird). A few generalizations are possible: the designs and general choices of materials (and the order of their use—and even in some cases the way they are carried to the nest site) are innate; the quality and speed of nest-building, as well as some aspects of nest-location choice, improve with experience; all building is done with the beak and feet; and most nests are built with the bird serving as the 'last' (the form around which the edifice is constructed). Most birds build some sort of cup nest, and this is a good place to start our look at these artifacts.

A few familiar cup nests illustrate the generalizations outlined above. House wrens, for instance, always choose enclosed cavities with openings 2.5–3.5 cm in diameter. They begin with a base of small sticks arranged tangentially. (Larger sticks are stuffed into alternative cavities, presumably to discourage other wrens from building nearby.) Next comes a layer of thin twigs (again mostly arranged tangentially), and finally a circularly woven layer of thin fibers. The rather shallow nest is a fairly exact fit for an adult wren. The twig and grass stages are performed with a wren in the nest cup; each new piece of material is inserted with a highly stereotyped quivering motion of the beak, which serves to insinuate the new element into gaps in the existing material. (This striking quivering, which seems to shut off all other behaviors, is observed in most species of birds as they add material to their nests.) First-time nesters regularly misjudge stick sizes, choose cavities with openings too wide or with perches for nest predators, and take many extra days to complete the interior arrangements. Other species of wren (the Carolina and European wrens, for instance) weave a spherical nest with a small opening.

Robins select a tree fork, and begin weaving a lattice of sticks; to this base they next apply mud, followed by a layer of twigs and mud, and finally they add an elaborate lining of grass. These relatively deep nests are, again, just the size of an adult robin. First-time nesters often select branches that are too low, move wildly in the wind, or whose forks provide little support. Many of these initial nests come crashing down before the eggs are laid.

Herring gulls inevitably nest on the shore, scraping a hollow and lining it with grasses. But individual pairs differ greatly in the details of their location preferences and the amount of material deemed suitable for a nest (varying from little more than a scrape to a huge mound of vegetation); whether this variation reflects genetic factors, experience, or the immediate contingencies at the time of building is not known, but doubtless all three are involved to some extent. Any gull with nesting material settles into the nest before tucking the newly gathered vegetation into its abode. The closely related kittiwake gull always nests on narrow ledges on cliffs next to the ocean—or a human analogue such as windowsills on the upper floors of a building-wall that rises from the water in a harbor. First-time nesters frequently fail to use enough mud to hold the nest to the cliff during the high winds that accompany storms.

The variations on cup nests are endless. Blue grosbeaks usually finish the outside of their multilayered nests with a skin shed by a snake; some hummingbirds complete their nests with a layer of lichen. Indian tailorbirds begin their homes by first finding two suitable leaves, punching matching holes in the edges of each, weaving the leaves together with spider silk, and then constructing the nest inside.

The nests that most impress humans are the woven ones. The northern oriole in the eastern United States, the oropendula of Central America, the penduline titmouse of Europe, and the many species of weaverbird of Africa and southern Asia are among the most famous. Perhaps the best-studied is the nest of the village weaverbird (Collias and Collias 1984). The males begin with long strips of vegetation which, if too wide, they first tear to make the material suitably narrow. Construction starts at a downward fork in a branch, and the first step is to tie a very strong knot at each end of the strip. The technique at this stage, and in most subsequent steps, is to hold the strip near its end, move it to a visual gap, and quiver until the end goes through the opening; the bird then reaches around and grasps the end of the strip and pulls it tight; it repeats the process until that end of the strip is used up, and then turns its attention to the other end. As is easily imagined, tying the first knot can be very time-consuming, since there is no true gap to begin with, and the eventual success looks fairly accidental; once that first knot is tied, however, the probe–quiver–pull technique proves rapid and effective in subsequent tying and weaving.

The male starts off building a highly reinforced circular perch hanging down from the fork; the size of this circle is the distance from his feet to his beak when the neck is stretched. Dozens of strips may go into completing this step. Since the fork is rarely pointed directly down, and parts of the diverging branches are (quite sensibly) woven into the top of the perch, this initial structure is at some angle from the vertical; this angle determines the direction of subsequent building. The male stands on the perch with the fork just above and *behind* his head, and begins to build outwards; the result is (depending on the angle of the forked branch) something between a quarter-sphere and a hemisphere, whose diameter is again the distance from the male's feet to his outstretched beak. This will become the roof of the nest. The spherical building, still centered on the bottom of the perch, is continued; the lower half of this sphere will be fitted out later as the nest cup. The male next reverses position on the perch and builds out the other direction to create the top of the entrance. Then the male thatches the roof with coarser material to make it waterproof (and opaque). Finally, he displays to attract a mate.

If he is successful in securing a female, he will begin building a long, vertical entrance tube from the opening he left on the side of the circular perch away from the nest cup; this tunnel, which can be more than 0.5 m long, is an anti-predator device. The female, for her part, will finish the nest cup with fine grass, then softer material, including downy plant seeds and feathers. To contemplate one of these finished nests, and attempt to replicate it by hand, even with the soft basket-weaving materials available ready-made from craft shops, is a humbling experience.

The first attempts by weaverbird males are loosely woven and crude. Nevertheless, they are built according the elaborate species-specific design, constructed from the correct materials, and located at plausible (though not necessarily ideal) places. Like most birds, the nests improve with experience, suggesting either learning or maturation; the former is far more likely. But the extent to which the learning is merely conditioning, or instead involves some understanding of the shortcomings of nest construction and situation (and the ways to improve on subsequent attempts), is not at all obvious. The initial building follows the general pattern of the funnel-wasp programming strategy, but the often dramatic improvement suggests that these creations become increasingly products of the mind.

3.6.2. The nests of mammals

After the nests of birds, the homes of most mammals seem quite amateurish in comparison. The sleeping nests of chimpanzees, for instance, consist of some broken leafy branches wedged together high in trees; though surprisingly sturdy, the workmanship looks quite shoddy. Fieldmice are one exception to the generally low regard in which mammalian nests are held: their homes bear an uncanny resemblance to the abodes of European wrens (Frisch 1974). But the mice take a distant second place to another non-human mammal: the beaver (Morgan 1886; Frisch 1974; Griffin 1992; Gould and Gould 1999).

The generic picture of beaver is that of a family group of these large aquatic rodents, with a lodge as a 'nest' and a dam across a stream to create a pond. However, unlike most animals, the degree of flexibility and adaptation to local contingencies displayed by beaver is enormous. The classic beaver artifacts—lodge and dam—are in fact just means to an end: maintaining a burrow entrance safely under water (even when water levels are low, or an ice-layer forms). Thus, along rivers with fairly steep banks and ample water, the burrows are hollowed out of the bank, with an entrance safely below the waterline and the living area well above it; no dam is built, and nothing like a lodge is to be seen. When an abandoned shed is available at the edge of a pond, beaver are content to tunnel into it. But, to be sure, the most common first step in colonizing a new area is to create a burrow opening below the waterline, tunnel up toward the surface, create a comfortable living space above the waterline, and cover this nest with a huge pile of sticks. In fact, the heap of sticks in the most-usual-case scenario is begun before the burrow is fully excavated, so that the beaver must estimate early on the eventual point at which the tunnel will break through the ground. (A beaver colony may eventually relocate to an even safer position, as we will see presently.)

This goal-directed behavior is equally obvious in the construction of dams. The object is to keep the water level above that of the burrow entrance, and thus make the nest inaccessible to predators. If the locale provides a stable minimum water level of sufficient depth, the beaver generally omit to build a dam. (When the habitat is, in fact, a pond created by humans, there is a tendency to add to and renovate the existing dam; one reason for this tampering with human workmanship will become obvious presently, but there seems to be a Puritanical inability to accept such a gift wholly gratis.) When the water level is not stable, or not deep enough so that if the pond freezes over the burrow entrance will still be accessible (that is, not be blocked by the ice), then a dam is attempted. The initial stages of the construction of this artifact—which can be up to 0.7 km long—are the ones that show the most flexibility of engineering.

The underlying structure of beaver dams typically consists of a number of tree-trunks which lie across the flow of water, and which are held in place by large limbs sharpened at each end and driven vertically into the stream bed; none of this is normally visible under the veneer of the finished dam. The basic framework is then filled in with smaller branches, leaves, stones, and mud to create a sturdy water-control artifact. Leaks are systematically plugged, in part on the basis of hearing: beaver seem to home in on the tell-tale sounds of water flow, although they can discover and plug soundless leaks as well.

Though the trunks are ultimately held by the vertical branches, this is not the way they are supported initially. The two most common contingencies at the outset of building differ in the availability of on-shore supports. In the simplest case, the beaver are able to fell a tree along the bank so that it falls across the stream. If there is a nearby stump or boulder both close to the bank and downstream of the felled first tree, this may prevent the fallen trunk from slowly washing away: the base of the trunk lodges against the stump. Ideally a similar operation can be carried out from the other bank. Next, vertical branches are driven into the stream bed both upstream and downstream of the fallen trees. The downstream supports prevent the trees from washing away; the upstream verticals prevent rotation into a skewed orientation. Now the beaver can remove the side branches from the fallen trees, and wedge these pieces between the vertical supports. Along with other large and medium-sized branches brought to the site, the beaver weave a porous, fence-like structure across the stream.

To deal with the other frequent contingency—the absence of convenient onshore braces—the beaver use large rocks in the streambed (or move stones weighing up to 10 kg into position) as supports. In these cases some of the vertical supports may be installed first, followed by cross-stream trunks, after which long braces (made of branches with forked ends) are wedged between the trunks and the rocks and boulders downstream. With the trunks now in no danger of washing away, more verticals can be added, and the branches woven in. The 'fence' which results in either case is then used as the framework for the sticks, mud, leaves, and stones that will make the dam watertight.

Beaver dams are high-maintenance artifacts. By its nature, mud (no matter how rich in clay) slowly dissolves and washes away. Leaves and branches rot fairly quickly, and even the major structural elements have only a limited lifespan. Periods of flood, with their fast-moving, scouring currents, can be a particular danger. It is not unusual for beaver to react to the threat posed by floodwaters by disassembling some of the dam to create a spillway. Another instance of deliberate 'damage' to this largest of all animal artifacts is sometimes seen in the winter: after a thick layer of ice has formed, the beaver may cut an opening in the dam just under the ice, and thereby lower the water level. This creates a air-filled gap between the water and ice, so that the beaver no longer need to seek out ice-holes for breathing while they forage.

With a large, stable pond, and a sufficient workforce, there comes the opportunity to build a bigger and safer lodge. The most impressive version of these up-scale structures is created by first bringing stones to the center of the pond to create a base, followed by piling up sticks and branches to create a structure many meters in diameter and up to 2 m high. This new lodge, surrounded as it is by a moat created by the dam, is much less vulnerable to potential predators.

As with the New Caledonian crows and the termites, I am surprised at the degree of flexibility and goal-oriented problem-solving apparent in this behavior. There are numerous instances of clear or possible planning in non-human animals (Gould and Gould 1999), but building (because of its inherent difficulty, and thus the near-impossibility of learning the task) is very often innate—at least in its essentials. The tool-use of crows and the behavior of beaver suggest a combination of innate urges, pre-existing behavioral components to make use of, and an ability to plan that might make restrained flexibility a plausible alternative strategy.

4. MATE ATTRACTION

While beaver create the largest and, in some ways, the most challenging of animal artifacts, the award for the most exotic must go to the many species of bowerbirds found in New Guinea and northern Australia (Marshall 1954; Gilliard 1969; Griffin 1992; Attenborough 1998; Gould and Gould 1999). The generic bower consists of an 'avenue' between two walls of sticks; the surrounding arena serves as a display area, while mating takes place within the bower itself. (Females go elsewhere to build nests, and rear their brood as single parents.)

The preparation that goes into even this simplest of bowers is astonishing. First, the male defoliates the trees that would otherwise shade his arena. Then he removes the vegetation growing on the ground. Next he weaves an arena floor of sticks and other vegetation, into which the sticks or stems that define the bower will be thrust; so strong is this platform that it can be picked up, bower and all, and carried off (by researchers). The avenue which is created by the two parallel walls of sticks is oriented north–south in most species. Finally, the area around the bower is decorated with colorful objects.

More is known about the satin bowerbird than any other species, because it nests near human settlements in Australia; the majority of other species are found in the remote highlands of New Guinea. Satin bowerbirds build a conventional arena and avenue bower, and decorate the platform at one end (the one facing the noon sun) or one side with yellow and blue objects. Prior to the arrival of our own species, the yellow decorations were flowers and blue ones were generally feathers. Apparently blue objects were in short supply, because the males would regularly rob the bowers of lower-ranking birds to increase the magnificence of their own display. Now, however, there is a surfeit of blue material, including plastic clothes-pins, cigarette packages, and other human detritus.

Like all bowerbirds, the male satin bowerbird is very particular about the bower and its decorations. When experimenters put out a full range of poker chips for the males to harvest, only the blue ones (and a few yellow chips) were taken. If the arena is lifted and the bower rotated by a few degrees, the returning male will tear the walls down and rebuild them north–south. If the blue decorations, which seem randomly distributed at the sunlit end or side, are moved about, the male will painstakingly return them to their original locations. Presumably the male 'cares' because these things matter to the females. When a female visits, the male picks up a blue ornament and begins his courtship display.

Though young males can build species-specific bowers without previous exposure or experience, the initial structures are flimsy and crude. Young males often build in groups, and visit the bowers of older males. The gradual improvement in the quality of their edifices is generally (and plausibly) attributed to learning rather than simple maturation. If so, it is possible that cultural traditions could arise in subgroups of these species, and there are some hints that such is the case.

Variations on the basic bower include species that paint the inside walls with berry juice or charcoal, decoration patterns involving not only different species-specific colors but unusual array patterns—separate piles of red berries and green berries, fan-shaped arrays of bleached shells, a scattering of brightly colored beetles, and so on. One species creates a bower with two parallel lanes. Others opt for a kind of circular bower: they construct a maypole in the center of the platform and cover it with moss; fresh flowers may be inserted into this layer of vegetation, and the other decorations are laid out around the pole.

The various species of gardener bowerbirds build an elaborate hemispherical hut with an opening on the sunlit side; so perfect are these structures that at least one early explorer deduced that a race of pygmies inhabited the region. The huts also have color-specific sets of decorations, some in piles and others spread out in a single layer. The most elaborate huts are built around a decorated maypole, and the male is careful to replace any flower that wilts. Bowers are at once absurd and aesthetically appealing; while they might seem to be the least utilitarian of all animal artifacts, as mate-attraction devices they are at least as important to reproductive success (the wholly unromantic bottom line of natural selection) as any nest or prey-capture device. The seeming aesthetic factor in bower construction and choice hints at a role for 'mind' in these species.

5. CONCLUSION

The artifacts created by the animals with whom we have the undeserved good fortune to share this planet mirror in many ways the artifacts created by our own species: tools for hunting and foraging, homes and other constructs used for ensuring the safety and comfort of ourselves and our offspring, and 'decorative' objects used in mate-attraction rituals. A clear difference is that in animals the vast majority of these artifacts are built according to innate specifications using a set of inborn instructions.

But in some species we see a more flexible, goal-oriented system, in which urges rather than detailed instructions seem to motivate the creation of the tools, homes, and decorative devices—sometimes with apparently traditional group-specific designs. Thus we sense some similarity in the creation of flint tools by early humans on the one hand and the fashioning of beak prostheses by crows on the other. Both seem to reflect a goal-oriented problem-solving, in which some idea of the object of the behavior must be borne in mind while manufacturing the tool.

Presumably analogous inborn urges account for some of the cross-cultural patterns of artifact production in humans, though obviously the role of tradition and innovation is enormously (if not pathologically) greater. Language is an intangible artifact in its own right, and enormously facilitates the spread (both horizontally and vertically) of information and tradition. As Hauser and Santos (this volume) point out, language also makes the use of concepts easier. Animals, from honey bees on up, spontaneously form concepts, though there is an obvious species-specific bias in the process. Language allows this innate facility at categorization to be used with devastating effectiveness.

Whether any non-human animal might possess what Mithen (this volume) calls 'cognitive fluidity'—the ability to combine knowledge from different mental domains—is hard to say. Nearly all of animal behavior (including conditioning) is triggered by context-specific cues. From the first, then, a behavior is restricted to a particular class of challenges—a domain. Even given the apparent ability of many species to form and use concepts, as well as to create plans ('cognitive maps'), there may be relatively few circumstances in which cognitive fluidity would be useful (or even not be actively dangerous). For instance, in the lives of species that (like the vast majority) must grow to maturity and reproduce in a very few years at most, where can knowledge of predators and prey usefully inform nest design (and vice versa)? And what would the relative costs and benefits be of pausing to think about something that needs to be done quickly and accurately the first time? A more serious problem, however, is that this is the kind of question that is almost never asked by those of us studying building behavior.

As a student of animal behavior, who necessarily supposes that humans are part of the evolutionary continuum, I automatically assume that methods of artifact production in animals and in humans are to some degree linked, rather than a result of a separate creation. If so, then perhaps beyond simply admiring these non-human products of natural selection and attributing them to clever programming, we should consider the possible (if highly restricted) role of planning and cross-domain learning. We may thereby perhaps catch a glimpse of the hidden origins of our own aesthetic and utilitarian compulsions and abilities to modify the world around us.

15

The Evolutionary Ancestry of Our Knowledge of Tools: From Percepts To Concepts

Marc D. Hauser and Laurie R. Santos

To primitive man each thing says what it is and what he ought to do with it... a fruit says 'Eat me'; water says 'Drink me'; thunder says 'Fear me'.

(Koffka 1935, 7)

A lot of stuff that's domain specific or species specific or both has to be innate in order that we should come to have the concept DOORKNOB (or for that matter, the concept RED)... The issue is whether it requires a lot of innate intentional stuff, a lot of innate stuff that has content.

(Fodor 1998, 143)

It is hard to imagine two more polar extremes than Koffka and Fodor. An attempt to unite them would surely create one of the most heinous intellectual marriages of all time. Koffka, a leading proponent of Gestalt psychology, suggested that when an organism perceives the world, the world spits back affordances, properties of the environment that tell the organism what to do. Under this view, there are no mental representations, no concepts. Fodor, on the other hand, one of the central architects of the representational theory of the mind, has argued that concepts do all the interesting work. In fact, for Fodor, all concepts are innate and without them organisms wouldn't be able to learn. This is Fodor's strongest challenge to those interested in concept acquisition.

Our goal in this chapter is not to arbitrate between these views. Rather, we explore one particular corner of our conceptual world—the domain of tools—and assess how such knowledge developed both phylogenetically and ontogenetically. In particular, we hope to convince the reader of three things. First, the comparative approach to conceptual representation is crucial to any theory of concepts as it forces one to entertain how concepts are acquired and managed in the absence of language. Second, although a number of animals naturally manufacture and use tools, such behavior does not entail evidence for a concept of tool or artifact more generally. Rather, tool-use may grow out of a particularly good sense of the functionally relevant features *associated* with tools, a sense driven by affordances or perceptual categories as opposed to conceptual knowledge. This claim does not deny the possibility of concepts in animals. It does, however, raise the criterial bar used by many researchers to assess conceptual representations in animals, as well as in human infants and toddlers. Third, there are serious methodological problems underlying most current attempts to uncover the content of animal representations and concepts more specifically. Some studies use training approaches, while others explore spontaneous abilities; some test animals in the wild, some in captivity; some use tasks which require action, while others require only perception; some consider discrimination among category exemplars sufficient, while others demand evidence for theory-like organization of knowledge that is separate from the perceptual input that might be used for discrimination. Given such variation, it is not always easy to draw straightforward conclusions about what any particular animal does or does not know. We hope to clarify some of these general problems by assessing what animals know about tools, and in particular, whether there is any evidence that animals have a concept of tool; this specific discussion should have significant implications for how we evaluate the evidence for concepts in non- or pre-linguistic creatures more generally.

1. CARVING UP OBJECT KNOWLEDGE

The world is filled with objects. All animals make discriminations among some of them. The kinds of discriminations they make, and the sensory resources they recruit, are often different. Sometimes, differences in discrimination are due to the kinds of selection pressures that have operated to favor either coarse- or fine-grained analyses of object categories. For example, animals in the wild are frequently concerned with the threat of predation. At the simplest level, prey must discriminate between predators and non-predators. In some species, however, there has been strong selection for individuals to make even more fine-grained discriminations among different types of predators, a situation that has been carefully described in vervet monkeys living on the savannas of Kenya (Cheney and Seyfarth 1990; Struhsaker 1967). Because vervets are preyed upon by a wide variety of predatory species, each with a unique hunting style, they have evolved a predator-specific alarm response, including acoustically distinctive calls and escape responses. Thus, seeing a leopard (often) causes vervet monkeys to give a call that is different from the one they give to eagles and, respectively, causes them to run up into a tree as opposed to running under a bush. For vervets, therefore, there is both the superordinate category of PREDATOR and the subordinate-level categories of LEOPARD, EAGLE, and SNAKE.

Differences in discrimination are also mediated by the kinds of perceptual and cognitive abilities that each organism brings to the task of categorizing objects in the world. Dogs make distinctions between the urine markings of other dogs, while humans do not. Humans draw distinctions between filet mignon, sirloin, and hamburger, while dogs do not. These are descriptions of performance, of recognizing objects as members of particular categories. But what do they reveal about either the perceptual or conceptual capacities of these species? On the one hand, we know that at both central and peripheral levels, the olfactory system of a dog is able to make finer discriminations than the olfactory system of a human. Differences in performance are not due to differences in one species being smarter than the other, at least not in any interesting sense of the word 'smarter'. It also says nothing at all about conceptual organization. When it comes to pieces of beef, dogs may well be able to discriminate between filet mignon, sirloin, and hamburger, but it is unlikely that they have a conceptual representation like ours that places beef as one of several food categories of meats, that rank-orders each type of meat in terms of quality, that places different cuts of beef in relationship to other kinds of food with different values, that sees these as the kinds of distinctions a meat-eater would make but that a vegetarian would care little about, and so on. For dogs, we presume that beef is beef is beef. It is an object that, in Koffka's phrasing, cries out 'Eat me' without playing any significant role in the animal's conceptual representations. Dogs may prefer filet mignon over sirloin and sirloin over hamburger, showing the same kinds of preferences as a human connoisseur of beef. And they might make these distinctions by attending to particular features of each cut of beef, using both smell and sight. But using particular perceptual features to make such distinctions is not sufficient to show that an organism, human or non-human, has a concept. Concepts are not mere collections of features, although featural distinctions certainly play a role. What makes the conceptual distinction more interesting, at least from our perspective, is that particular tokens of a class are situated *in relationship* to other tokens, and the organization of tokens is mediated by a particular theory of how they cohere. Given this perspective, it therefore becomes imperative to assess both how concepts are acquired and how they are modified.

With respect to conceptual acquisition, we see the field dividing into three core groups (see Fig. 15.1), with lots of bleeding at the edges. Group 1, championed by Fodor, posits that concepts are largely innate, and that without this starting point there would be no learning. On this view, there is massive continuity between the concepts of a child and those of an adult. Note, importantly, that Fodor's view does not deny learning. Rather, his point is that core concepts are already part of the mind's system of core knowledge and that our experience with the world can shape how this core knowledge is reorganized. Group 2 posits few or no innate representations, and sees concept acquisition as tapping quite domain-general learning mechanisms (for reviews of the latest thinking, see Mandler, this volume). Quine (1960), as one proponent of this view, argues that children acquire concepts such as DOG and HAMMER by simply building up a set of associations based on relevant features. What makes the varieties of DOG tokens cohere is that individual learners build up a similarity space of features based on associations. A different view, which also denies the significance of mental representations, is represented by the Gestalt psychologists such as Koffka, as well as their successors such as the ecological psychologist Gibson (Gibson 1979; 1950). On this view, as discussed above, organisms make distinctions between objects based on the perceptual properties that they afford. Perceptual features of an object are therefore like instructions for action. A HAMMER cries out 'Pick me up, and strike something'. Group 3 posits that there are innate concepts that guide the acquisition process, with domain-specific as opposed to domain-general learning mechanisms at the core of the ontogenetic process. This view is held by a number of developmental psychologists such as Carey (1996), Keil (1994), and Spelke (1994), as well as several evolutionary psychologists, including Cosmides and Tooby (1994) and Pinker (1997). Under this view, there is a system of core knowledge divided into domains such as folk physics, psychology, and biology, that guides how we experience and digest the world taken in by our sensory systems. This core knowledge is theory-like in that it is based on explanatory principles that are separate from the raw perceptual input, including such notions as agency and intentionality.

Group 1 and the Quinean version of Group 2 have relatively few supporters with respect to those pursuing the empirical evidence for concepts; we note, however, that Fodor's challenge is extremely important, and essential to the empirical research program we will defend. There is a slightly larger contingent supporting the Gibsonian version of Group 2, with interesting modifications on this view, especially with respect to how perceptual analyses may provide the necessary structure for building concepts (Mandler 2000). We take Group 3 to be the most serious contender (i.e. it's the one we believe and will defend; see also the chapter in this volume by Mahon and Caramazza), although there are disagreements concerning several pieces of the argument. Rather than debate these points here, we turn next to the target ontological problem of this essay—tools—and briefly discuss some of the relevant theoretical distinctions, especially as they bear on domain-general versus specific learning mechanisms.

2. USING TOOLS AND CONCEPTUALIZING THEM

When early anthropologists heralded our uniqueness by proclaiming us 'Man the toolmaker', they were referring to the hand-axes and cutting tools of some of the first hominids. Although relatively simple objects, these tools stood out on the comparative landscape as no other animal had, apparently, ever created or used a tool in nature. There were, of course, studies such as Kohler's showing that chimpanzees in captivity could use tools, including the famous observation of Sultan piling up boxes so that he could stand on top and then, with a stick, dislodging a banana hanging from the ceiling. These observations at least suggested that animals such as chimpanzees have the capacity to see one or more objects as a means to some end. When Jane Goodall famously described wild chimpanzees using sticks, stripped of their leaves, to extract termites from a termite mound, man the toolmaker no longer stood out from the landscape. Moreover, Goodall's observations opened the floodgates, and soon dozens of observations of tool-use in the wild emerged, spanning a wide range of species including other apes, monkeys, non-primate mammals, and birds. One could no longer claim that tool-use and manufacture were uniquely human characteristics (Griffin 2002; Hauser 1988; see also Gould, this volume), and recent studies on the New Caledonia crow suggest that the highest level of sophistication may not even rest with the primates (Chappell and Kacelnik 2002; Hunt 1996, 2004; Hunt and Gray 2003).

Until the 1990s no study of tool-use had bothered to ask either how animals recognize and represent tools (as opposed to other objects), or how these cognitive processes limit the range and qualities of the tools invented and used. As we discuss in section 3, work in the last ten years has begun to remedy this problem. Here, however, we would first like to sketch some of the relevant theoretical issues (for similar discussions, see the chapters in this volume by Kelemen and Carey, Mandler, and Mahon and Caramazza) underlying an empirical inquiry into tool-use in the animal kingdom.

As an attempt to simplify the theoretical landscape, we will discuss five views about the nature of tool representations (Fig. 15.1). The first of these views—the *Innateness* view—stems directly from the Group 1, Arch-Nativist stance on concept acquisition. Under this view, our concept of tools emerges in the same way as our other concepts: they are genetically endowed, appearing in the absence of experience or formal tutelage. If this characterization is correct, there should be continuity between the concepts of adults and infants, and this includes concepts of tools.

The next two hypotheses fall out of the Group 2 empiricist view of concept acquisition. The first is what we refer to as the *Affordances* perspective. Under this theoretical stance, humans represent artifacts only on the basis of their physical features. The properties of a hammer, its graspable shape and hard, pounding edge, are taken in by our perceptual systems and simply cry out for the action of hammering. Under this view, however, there is no HAMMER representation, no ontological category of an object with a particular shape that is used for a particular function that tends to be found in a toolbox, and certainly no organizing theoretical framework for organizing HAMMER into the more general concept of ARTIFACT. Our representation of a hammer-like object simply consists of a mapping between certain perceptual features (e.g. smoothness, hardness) and certain functional possibilities (e.g. graspability, poundability). As such, this view has a weak ontological structure.

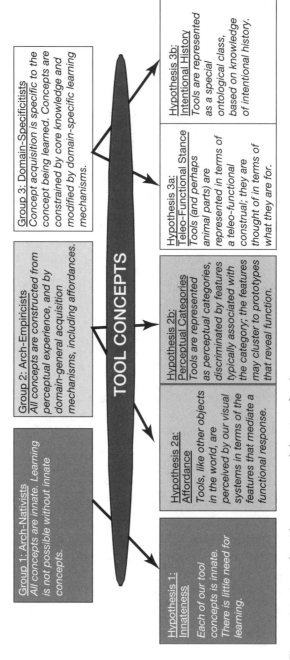

Figure 15.1. A rough guide to conceptual theories of tools

The other empiricist hypothesis of tools, what we call the *Perceptual Category*, is an ontologically richer proposal. Under this view, we possess ontological categories like HAMMER, CHAIR, and CLOCK that are distinguished from each other on the basis of different features. A HAMMER is distinguished from a CHAIR because the former has particular articulated parts (a rigid handle, a hard flat striking edge, etc.), whereas the latter does not. However, this difference is not definitional. Clearly, a hammer with a folding handle that locks into position before you strike something would still be a HAMMER. The prototype view, one variant of the Perceptual Category perspective, suggests that organisms represent different kinds of artifacts as constellations of features; an object with more hammer-like features will be considered a better HAMMER than objects with less hammer-like features. What is important about features from the perspective of distinguishing one object kind from another, however, is that some features are more salient when categorizing artifacts than others. For example, artifacts can readily change some of their perceptible properties without changing kinds; the hammer maintains its hammer-ness whether it is blue, red, green, or rainbow-colored. It can, however, lose its hammer-ness if it is a different shape. Similarly, a hammer must at least be harder than the object one wishes to strike, usually a nail. Clowns in a slapstick routine will, of course, use foam-rubber hammers in order to hit someone over the head. But this routine makes our point: it is because we expect a hammer to be harder than the object it strikes that we find humor in a clown striking a human over the head.

The last two hypotheses fit with a larger domain-specificity proposal. Again, the domain-specificity approach to conceptual knowledge posits that organisms are endowed with innate core knowledge that constrains how they divide up the world into ontological chunks and how experience modifies their ontologies. Each conceptual chunk or domain tends to reflect computational problems that are ecologically salient for a particular organism, both over developmental and evolutionary time. As many researchers have argued, a salient domain in human ecology is that of artifacts. As any new parent can attest, human infants are born into a world of artifacts that they quickly learn to use, categorize, and name. For these reasons, domain-specificists tend to agree that humans possess specialized mechanisms for representing and categorizing objects in the artifactual domain. What these mechanisms are and how they operate, however, is open to much speculation.

One way in which artifacts are distinguished from many, if not most, other kinds of objects is that they have a particular function. When we see a tool, even if we have never used it before, we tend to think or ask 'What is it for?', even though we would never formulate a similar question for a rock. This type of question is reserved for certain types of entities—those with the characteristics of functional design. The *Teleo-Functional* hypothesis proposes that humans reason about tools in line with just such a teleological mode of construal. This hypothesis was originally put forward by Keil (1994), and has been extended both theoretically and empirically by Kelemen (1999*c*). Importantly, the Teleo-Functional view of artifacts is domain-specific—for adults, it tends to apply only to objects that are created for a specific purpose. Interestingly, it is a view that is part of theology and evolutionary biology. Theologians' answer to the question of design is, clearly, some divine entity. Evolutionists' answer is natural selection; as Darwin articulated, natural selection is the only evolutionary process that can create non-random design features, suited to social and ecological problems. When it comes to artifacts, their design is solely due to the mind of their creator. Of course, it is also possible for an object to be used for a particular function even though it was not designed for this function; a shoe can be used as a hammer and a clock can be used as a paperweight. Nevertheless, it is important to note that a shoe used as a hammer does not necessarily become a HAMMER. Instead, it remains a SHOE because it was designed for the purpose of being used as a shoe.

The importance of a tool's history and intended design leads to the *Intentional History* perspective. This hypothesis, originally championed by Bloom (1996), builds on an argument originally developed by Levinson with respect to art. For Levinson (see this volume), the only way to understand art is by understanding the historical-intentional aspects of the product. In contrast to RED or LEMON, art can only be evaluated based on the intention of the artist (why she painted or sculpted the piece) at the particular time she created the piece. If it was intended as art then, it should be considered as art today, even if we don't like it. Bloom argues, symmetrically, that all artifacts are represented in terms of their intentional history—the reason why they were made and what they were made to do. Thus, we call something a HAMMER if its creator designed it with the intention of hammering things. An important consequence of this view is that even if the end-product fails to satisfy the designer's original intent (e.g. a broken hammer), we can nonetheless call it a HAMMER, albeit a bad one. Importantly for this view, one should not only be able to extract the intentional history of an artifact by seeing the artifact made or being told about it with language, but also by inferring intent from design. Thus, it is not the case that surface design is irrelevant in distinguishing hammers from screwdrivers. Rather, what their design invokes in human minds (at least adults) is an inference about what an intentional designer initially created them for.

If our rough sketch of the theories of tools, and artifacts more generally, is reasonable, then a research program designed to uncover how this conceptual domain evolved and develops must contend with these different positions. Critically, we believe, in thinking about either tool-use or creation in non-linguistic organisms (animals and human infants), it is essential to distinguish between recognition and perceptual discrimination on the one hand, and conceptual knowledge on the other. Although animals, for example, make and use a range of artifacts (e.g. tools, nests, dams), and discriminate among them using salient perceptual features, other evidence is required to show that these animals have a domain-specific theory about why tools are different from animals or trees, and that this theory guides conceptual change. To be clear, if animals lack an understanding of teleology or intentional design, then this does not take away from the significance of their tool-using abilities. It does, however, mean that they may represent tools in a fundamentally different way than human adults do.

We turn next to a review of some of the relevant literature on non-human primate tool-use, with a specific focus on both methodological issues and theoretical issues that relate to the hypotheses reviewed above and sketched in Fig. 15.1. Concerning the latter, we are particularly interested in exploring the extent to which tool-use relies on domain-specific as opposed to domain-general mechanisms. Consequently, we focus on the use of tools both by natural tool-users and by species that never spontaneously use tools in nature or in captivity. If performance on tool-related tasks depends on evolved specializations for tool use, then natural tool users should show greater proclivities than species that never spontaneously use tools.

3. HOW APES AND MONKEYS THINK ABOUT TOOLS

3.1. Wild chimpanzees

Any review of primate tool-use should begin with the most prolific non-human tool-user, the chimpanzee (Matsuzawa 1996; Matsuzawa and Yamakoshi 1996; McGrew 1992; Tomasello and Call 1997; Whiten *et al.* 1999). Chimpanzees use a variety of tools in a number of different situations, including twig sticks to probe termite mounds, stone hammers to crack nuts, crumpled leaves to sponge water, and bark sandals to climb up prickly trees (Alp 1997; Boesch and Boesch-Achermann 2000; Goodall 1986; Matsuzawa and Yamakoshi 1996; McGrew 1992). There is also much evidence to suggest that chimpanzees modify objects to create better tools; chimpanzees are known to chew leaves for better absorbency (Sugiyama 1995) and to bite the leaves off branches to allow them to fit in termite mounds more efficiently.

A number of recent observations suggest that in addition to using tools adeptly, chimpanzees may possess a sophisticated understanding of the functional properties of the objects they use. Studies by Boesch and colleagues (Boesch and Boesch-Achermann 2000) in Tai Forest, Ivory Coast, together with studies by Matsuzawa and colleagues (Matsuzawa and Yamakoshi 1996) in Bossou, Guinea, provide exquisitely detailed observations of nut-cracking behavior in chimpanzees. The Tai chimpanzees eat five different nut species, none of which can be opened with the bare hand. To crack them, chimpanzees secure the nuts using anvils (made of roots, branches, or rocks) and hit them with hammers (made of branches or stones). Boesch and colleagues suggest, based on their observations, that chimpanzees understand the properties that are necessary for an effective hammer. In particular, chimpanzees carry heavy stones further than wooden clubs (Boesch and Boesch 1984), suggesting that they understand the importance of the tool's material property; heavier hammers are more effective than lighter ones, and thus they are willing to carry them further. Matsuzawa's observations generally confirm the reports from Tai, but also demonstrate that chimpanzees appear to be sensitive to the physics of the tool-using task. In particular, and in contrast to juvenile chimpanzees, adults are sensitive to the stability of the anvil and its capacity to hold, in a stable position, the target nut. When adult chimpanzees find a suitable rock, one with a relatively flat surface or a depression that will envelop the nut, they assess whether the rock is level with the ground. If it is slanted, they will place a second rock under the first, in an attempt to provide a more level striking surface. Juveniles often place nuts on slanted surfaces, thereby leading to numerous failed attempts to crack the nut as it rolls off the anvil before they can strike. Suzuki *et al.* (1995) argue that chimpanzees in the Ndoki forest of Congo may possess a similar understanding of their probing tools. They report that chimpanzees use two different types of sticks while termite fishing: a perforating stick, a wide twig used for making deep holes into the termite nest, and a fishing probe, a thin stick, often with chewed-off, brush-like ends, that is used to extract the termites. That chimpanzees use two physically different objects as functionally different tools suggests that they are identifying different properties of objects and using those properties to choose which tools will be more effective for a given job.

The problem with the findings reviewed thus far is that we don't know how these chimpanzees developed an understanding of which tools are better than others. One possibility is that individual chimpanzees learn which tools are most effective through a process of trial and error. A Tai chimpanzee may try out many different kinds of objects as hammers, only to gradually learn that stones crack nuts most efficiently. If this is true, then an experienced chimpanzee only knows to carry a heavy stone further because his experiences with previous heavy stones taught him that these objects will crack nuts most effectively. Alternatively, chimpanzees may possess a richer understanding of the problem and may predict which features are important for a functional tool without trial-and-error learning. If this alternative is correct, then even inexperienced chimpanzees might know to carry stones long distances, having the foresight that stones are heavy and able to crack things better than softer objects like branches. Unfortunately, however, without data on an individual's previous experience with using a given tool, we cannot distinguish between these alternatives. And this point holds even when one considers the important developmental data collected by Matsuzawa and others, showing that it takes between eight and nine years before chimpanzees develop functionally appropriate, and problem-specific, tool-using techniques. Young animals could show sensitivity to some features but not others. These developmental data are thus mute with respect to this point.

3.2. Chimpanzees in the laboratory

Faced with the problems of assessing the depth of a wild non-human primate's understanding of tools, many researchers have taken to investigating what captive primates know about tools. In captivity, as opposed to the wild, experimenters can selectively vary an individual's experiences with an object and document the process by which an individual comes to learn about a particular object and its function. In a recent book, Povinelli (2000) presents the most recent of such studies, focusing on a group of chimpanzees. Across a wide variety of paradigms and conceptual problems, Povinelli consistently finds that chimpanzees lack a sophisticated understanding of the physics of tool-use, focusing instead on perceptual features that in some cases provide correct answers to the task at hand, but then fail to generalize to the more common, and functionally relevant, components of the problem. Here we discuss a few examples to highlight the relevant dimensions of Povinelli's approach, and the importance of distinguishing between having conceptual knowledge of tools that is sensitive to functional design features, and using perceptual features that are only sometimes predictive (associated with) of success.

Povinelli and colleagues tested seven chimpanzees. Subjects started the experiments as young juveniles and ended as sub-adults. Because different experiments were run at different ages, it is not possible to assess, with complete accuracy, whether differences in performance across experiments is due to differences in age, and whether performance on any given experiment might have been different with older chimpanzees; there are only a few cases where a young chimpanzee was re-tested on the same experiment at an older age. We mention this point here both because of the developmental studies on tamarins described below, and because of Matsuzawa's field studies which show that competent tool-use emerges after the age of 9–10 years old. Many of Povinelli's experiments were run on far younger chimpanzees.

In one experiment, Povinelli and colleagues examined whether or not chimpanzees understand that a tool's material often affects its function. They trained chimpanzees on a task in which subjects were allowed to use one of two T-shaped pulling tools to obtain an out-of-reach food reward (for similar tasks, see Brown 1990; Hauser 1997). During training, these pulling tools were made out of rigid materials (PVC tubing and plywood). Once subjects mastered the pulling task, however, they were presented with trials in which the top of one of the two tools was changed. The top of this new tool was made out of a flimsy material (a thin strip of rubber), and thus was no longer able to bring the food within reach. Povinelli and colleagues found that only one of their seven chimpanzees succeeded on the flimsy tool problem, consistently choosing the rigid tool over the flimsy tool during the test trials. The authors conclude that chimpanzees fail to spontaneously take into account a pulling tool's material when choosing between two potential tools.

Povinelli and colleagues also examined what these chimpanzees understand about a tool's three-dimensional orientation. They presented the same chimpanzees with a choice between two rake-shaped pulling tools. When these tools were oriented with their tines upward and their bases placed flat on the tray, they served as functional pulling tools; a flat base efficiently pulled the food within reach. However, when the rake was oriented with its tines facing downward, it no longer served as an effective pulling tool; with the tines down, pieces of food readily slipped under the base of the tool and thus could not be retrieved. Povinelli and colleagues found that chimpanzees did not distinguish between these two orientations. Chimpanzees were as likely to choose rakes oriented with tines up as rakes oriented with tines down. Chimpanzees also failed to attend to the substrate on which tools operated, pulling a tool that caused the reward to drop into a trap as often as a tool that brought the food within reach (Povinelli 2000, ch. 15.5). Povinelli's work suggests that, despite their skillful use of tools in the wild, chimpanzees do not understand the physics or functionality of tools, at least under the conditions tested.

3.3. Capuchins

Like chimpanzees, capuchins spontaneously use tools in the wild and in captivity (Phillips 1998; Visalberghi 1990; Westergaard et al. 1998). Visalberghi and her colleagues should be credited with the first systematic attempt to investigate what captive primates understand about the functional properties of different objects, using experiments on captive capuchins. Visalberghi and Trinca (1989) presented four tufted capuchins (*Cebus apella*) with a task in which a piece of food was placed out of reach inside a clear tube. Capuchins spontaneously solved the task by inserting a stick into the tube to obtain the food. Visalberghi and Trinca then explored what these subjects learned about the important aspects of their pushing tool by changing the properties of the available sticks. For example, they presented subjects with a bundle of sticks that was too wide to fit inside the tube and a series of broken sticks which together could be pushed inside the tube to obtain the reward. Although all subjects eventually solved the task with these new tools, none of the subjects solved the task spontaneously. Instead, subjects seemed to discover the correct solution only through a long series of trial-and-error attempts with different tools. Similarly, the capuchins failed to recognize the important aspects of the substrate on which their pushing tool operated. Specifically, Visalberghi and colleagues (1995) presented subjects with a modified version of the trap task in which the trajectory of the food reward was impeded by the trap in the bottom of the tube; if the food reward was pushed over this trap, it would fall inside and become unattainable. Only one of four capuchins was able to solve this trap problem, but only through a series of trial-and-error attempts. Subsequent transfer tests revealed that this subject failed to understand the trap:

she persisted with the same strategy even when the trap was positioned at the top of the tube, a position that had no impact on the movement of the food reward through the tube. These results, and others presented by Visalberghi and her colleagues, lead to the conclusion that although capuchins naturally use a variety of tools, they seem to lack an understanding of the functional properties of these tools. Like chimpanzees, they lack an understanding of the relevant physics.

3.4. Non-tool-user tool use

In contrast to the approach taken with captive capuchins and chimpanzees, we have focused on one species—the cotton-top tamarin—that never spontaneously uses tools in the wild or in captivity (Hauser 1997; Hauser, Kralik, and Botto-Mahan 1999; Hauser, Pearson, and Seelig 2002; Hauser *et al.* 2002; Santos, Miller, and Hauser 2003; Santos *et al.* 2006; Santos *et al.* 2005). As mentioned above, the primary goal of these studies has been to examine whether tool users are equipped with cognitive specializations for tool-use that non-tool-users lack. Said differently, can animals such as tamarins recognize the functionally relevant features of tools even if they never use such objects in captivity or in the wild?

In the first series of experiments, Hauser (1997) presented adult cotton-top tamarins with a task in which subjects had to pull one of two tools in order to obtain an out-of-reach food reward (Figure 15.2); this task was modeled on studies of human infants by Brown (1990). Subjects were initially presented with a tray holding two blue canes positioned near a small food reward. One of the two canes was hooked around the food reward, the other placed with the food reward outside the hook. With this set-up, only one cane was effective in pulling the out-of-reach food reward. Results showed that subjects with no prior experience with tools quickly learned to pull the correctly positioned cane. After subjects learned the initial task, Hauser tested subjects with a series of new canes that differed from the original on only a single dimension. For example, an experimenter presented subjects with a choice between a tool with a novel shape (e.g. a right-angled L-shape) and a tool with a novel texture (e.g. a bumpy cane). Similarly, subjects could choose between a tool with a new color (e.g. a red cane) and a tool with a new size (e.g. a cane that was twice as long). If tamarins rank-order the features with respect to their impact on the tool's functionality—how they affect the physics—then they should accept changes in color and texture, as these play no role in the tool's capacity to bring food forward; in contrast, changes in size and shape directly influence functionality, especially given the tamarins' dexterity, and capacity for altering the tool's properties. Subjects reliably chose differently colored and textured canes over differently shaped and sized canes, and did so on the first trial. These results suggest that tamarins spontaneously regard changes of a tool's form (its shape and size) to be more important to its function than changes to its surface features (color or texture).

Figure 15.2. Photographs of two non-tool-users—a cotton-top tamarin (left) and a ring-tailed lemur (right)—using simple pulling tools

Similar patterns emerged in a more recent series of experiments aimed at investigating what tamarins understand about a tool's material (Santos *et al.*, 2006). In this experiment, a different group of inexperienced tamarins were given a choice between a tool with a different color (e.g. a pink cane) and a tool made of a different material (e.g. a flimsy piece of blue yarn shaped in a cane shape). Subjects rejected canes made of yarn, indicating that even in the absence of direct experience (i.e. given the nature of the task, subjects evaluated their options on each trial based on visual information, and then selected a tool; under these conditions, they lacked the opportunity to try out tools), tamarins understand rigidity to be an important property of a pulling tool.

To further pursue the importance of experience, Hauser, Pearson, and Seelig (2002) extended the work on adult tamarins to infants. They found that infant tamarins, with no experimental experience of any kind, showed the same pattern of results as adults. Remarkably, in the absence of any relevant experience (e.g. there were no opportunities to manipulate freely moving objects), tamarins as young as 4 months understand which properties are functionally relevant to the effectiveness of a pulling tool.

After presenting subjects with these single-dimension changes, Hauser and colleagues went on to present adult and infant subjects with tools that differed from the original along many dimensions (e.g. a green V-shaped tool with large bumps; Hauser 1997; Hauser, Pearson, *et al.* 2002). Subjects received a final condition in which these novel tools were pitted against the original tool positioned in an incorrect orientation. Both infant and adult tamarins spontaneously chose the novel but functionally correct tool over the familiar yet now incorrect tool, suggesting that tamarins of all ages understand that orientation is an important aspect of a successful pulling tool. Hauser, Kralik, and Botto-Mahan (1999) reported similar success using a cloth pulling tool, one in which the functional or physical task was support (i.e. the food reward was either on the cloth or off it) as opposed to containment in the canes task; across a variety of manipulations to the size, shape, color, and material of the cloth, subjects invariably picked the cloth that provided continuous access to the reward; these preferences often emerged on the first trial of a new condition involving a new featural transformation.

Taken together, these findings suggest that tamarins, even infants with no task-relevant experience, take into account the relevant features of a pulling tool (e.g. shape, size, material, and orientation), and also disregard those features that are irrelevant for effective pulling (e.g. color, texture). Nevertheless, more recent evidence suggests that although they understand the relevant features of pulling tools, tamarins may lack a more sophisticated understanding of the pulling task.

We (Santos, Pearson, *et al.* 2006) have explored whether or not tamarins are able to solve the more difficult types of problems that chimpanzees and capuchins cannot solve. Specifically, we presented tamarins with a trap task like the one used to test chimpanzees and capuchins, and then examined whether or not tamarins spontaneously attend to the position of the trap. Subjects were as likely to pull a cane positioned over a trap as they were to pull a cane over a continuous surface. Like chimpanzees and capuchins, tamarins failed to understand the trap. Similarly, tamarins also failed a task involving rake-shaped tools. When an experimenter presented tamarins with a choice between one rake with tines up and one rake with tines down, subjects showed no preferences, even though the rake with tines up was functionally more efficient in bringing food forward. Like chimpanzees, the tamarins neglected to focus on this more subtle aspect of the pulling tool's orientation.

We have also recently completed a parallel sets of studies with other non-tool-using primates—vervet monkeys (Santos, Pearson, *et al.* 2006), rhesus macaques (Santos *et al.*, 2003), and lemurs (Santos, Mahajan, and Barnes 2006; Figure 15.2); these species rarely, if ever, use tools in the wild or in captivity (e.g. Hauser 1988). In one study, we showed free-ranging rhesus macaques a purple L-shaped tool sitting on a flat stage with a ramp. We then habituated subjects to a human experimenter using the L-shaped tool to push a grape down the ramp. After habituation, we changed the properties of the tool. In one test condition we changed the color of the tool, showing subjects a pink L-shaped tool. In the other condition, we changed the shape of the tool, showing subjects a purple I-shaped tool; this newly shaped cane lacked the base necessary for pushing the grape. We reasoned that if subjects perceived the change as relevant to the tool's function then they should dishabituate to the test trial, evidenced by an increase in looking time. Results showed that rhesus dishabituated only to the new shape condition. Like tamarins tested on a different paradigm, rhesus macaques spontaneously pay more attention to a tool's shape than its color.

We have now also tested vervet monkeys (Santos, Pearson, *et al.*, 2006) and lemurs (Santos, Mahajan and Barnes 2006) on the original canes task (Hauser 1997). Like tamarins, both vervets and lemurs show the same kinds of sensitivities to functionally relevant and irrelevant features. Thus, they attend to such features as size and orientation, while ignoring such features as color and texture. In contrast with tamarins, as well as chimpanzees and capuchins, vervets tested on a pulling/containment problem appeared more sensitive to other functional properties of the tool task. Specifically, a significant number of the vervets tested picked (1) a cane resting on a continuous surface over a cane resting on a trap; (2) a rake with tines up over a rake with tines down; and (3) a cane with the tip part of the hook broken (functionally irrelevant) over a cane with a break between the stem and hook (functionally relevant, as pulling the stem failed to advance the hook containing the food reward). These results are, of course, puzzling as they suggest that a non-tool-user—the vervet monkey—has a more sophisticated understanding of tools than two natural tool-users—chimpanzees and capuchins. Because there were some differences in the design of these experiments, as well as differences in the experimental histories of the test subjects, it is not possible at present to distinguish between significant differences among these species in their representation of tools and differences in testing procedures. Even with the reported differences, it must be further acknowledged that although the vervets performed above chance on these tasks, they made errors on approximately 30 per cent of all trials; whether this error rate is due to a relatively weak understanding of these functional problems or to something else (attention, motivation) is currently unclear.

4. HOW TO THINK ABOUT PRIMATES THINKING ABOUT TOOLS

In the last section we reviewed what non-human primates—both tool-users and non-tool-users—understand about tools based on observations of tool-use in five different primate species. Now we turn to the more pressing and difficult issue of how these animals represent tools. It is clear from the data reviewed that non-human primates represent tools in a fundamentally different way than they represent other kinds of objects. We base this claim on the observation that when monkeys and apes use an object as a tool they use different featural criteria than when they use an object as food or a landmark. As described above, a number of primates—tamarins, rhesus macaques, vervets, and lemurs—recognize that shape, size, material, and orientation are relevant featural dimensions for a functional tool, while color and texture are not. In contrast, when tamarins classify an object as a landmark, they use color and shape as relevant dimensions, but ignore orientation (deIpolyi, Santos, and Hauser 2001). Similarly, rhesus macaques, who also consider shape more important than color when reasoning about tools (Santos, Miller, and Hauser 2003), nevertheless pay attention to a different set of features when reasoning about food objects. When categorizing novel foods, rhesus from the same population pay more attention to surface features like color than form features like shape (Santos, Hauser, and Spelke 2001). More importantly, these results hold true for infant macaques who, though lacking experience with solid foods, also recognize that color is more important than shape for edible objects. At a general level, these findings lend support to the domain-specific view of concept acquisition. Even at very early ages and in the absence of task-relevant experience (Hauser, Pearson, and Seelig 2002; Santos *et al.* 2002), non-human primates seem to parse the objects in their world into meaningful global categories—tools, foods, landmarks, and animals (Santos, Hauser, and Spelke 2002). Such evidence suggests that non-human primates may have innate biases to interpret their world in domain-specific ways. In addition, non-human primates seem to reason about different domains in ways that make ontological sense; their recognition of which features matter for different domains seem to map onto those of conceptually sophisticated human adults. For these reasons, we side with the domain-specificists and argue that both tool-using and non-tool-using primates are biased to distinguish tool-like objects from other ontological categories, and that these biases facilitate experience-based learning about different kinds.

Although it is clear that many primate species distinguish tools from other kinds of things, we are still left with the question of how primates represent objects within the category of tools and, perhaps more importantly, whether or not non-human primates represent *tools as* TOOLS. The fact that tamarins, a species that never spontaneously uses tools in the wild or in captivity, categorize artifacts using the same featural criteria as do tool-users, and do so as experientially naive infants, suggests an innate bias, but one that cannot be interpreted as an innate concept of TOOL, *sensu strictu*. Given that tamarins do not naturally use tools, they simply can't have an innate understanding of tools. These data raise several significant methodological and theoretical issues. Methodologically, we argue that a description of featural biases is no longer sufficient for documenting how animals represent the tools that they use. Showing which features are relevant and which irrelevant is a first pass, but only that. Other experiments are necessary to show how non-linguistic animals think about tools. This methodological point leads to two theoretical points. If tamarins do not have a concept of TOOL, then how do they represent the objects they use in means–end tasks? And if it is not a concept of TOOL, then why, giving their lack of interest in tools under normal conditions, do they show such exquisite sensitivity to the functionally relevant and irrelevant features of tools when tested in the lab? At present, we don't have a satisfactory answer to the second question. Tamarins must face means–end problems in the wild: problems of connectivity in the canopy, problems involving the recognition of interconnected tree branches that must be used, and possibly tugged on, to get from one branch to another. These physical problems, involving means–end relationships, may fuel their capacity in captivity, tapping something like analogical reasoning: tree branch is to distant fruit as cane is to marshmallow. We leave this as a testable hypothesis, and turn next to the more general issue of how non-human primates represent tools, and how such representations may or may not differ from humans.

Another question that remains unanswered is whether tamarins represent objects in the domain of tools in the same way as conceptually sophisticated adult humans. Consider again the views of human tool representation that we put forth in Fig. 15.1. According to the Affordances view, for example, humans begin representing tools via their salient perceptual properties. Chair properties cry out to be sat on, whereas clock properties do not. As explained, this view of concept learning is ontologically weak; there are no theories of tools, how they function or what they are designed to do. Early concept learners simply perceive the salient affordances of different tool-like objects and use them accordingly. The current data on non-human animals are consistent with this type of categorization. From a very early age, tamarins recognize that a hard, cane-shaped object can be used as a pulling device. As such, they too seem to perceive tools in terms of salient, action-oriented properties like affordances.

Our data, however, are also consistent with the Perceptual Categories view. This perspective predicts that organisms learn about and classify things in the world on the basis of their perceptual features. A chair is considered a CHAIR because it possesses the type of features that CHAIRS tend to have: four legs, a flat seat, a back, and so on. These features are not definitional, but rather serve as a guide to classifying objects into particular categories. More importantly, however, the Perceptual Categories view is ontologically richer than the Affordances view. An animal with a capacity to form perceptual categories represents a tool as more than just the sum of its relevant features. A particular category of tool or artifact is represented as a kind. There are no sit-on-able objects and hammer-able objects, but CHAIRS and HAMMERS, meaningful ontological entities. Do non-human animals also represent tools as kinds? As reviewed earlier, non-human primates do take into account the types of features that a particular tool has. More importantly, they do not take into account any and all features; instead, they focus on only the particular features that are relevant for what a tool does (Hauser 1997; Hauser, Kralik, and Botto-Mahan 1999). This detail is important, as it implies that non-human primates might be doing more than just paying attention to features; they may instead understand tools in terms of their function, and therefore in terms of a rich theory of different kinds of things (Keil 1990, 1994).

This point brings us to the last two theories of tool concepts—those consistent with the domain-specificity position. In contrast to the domain-general empiricist position embodied in both the Affordances and Perceptual Category views, our tamarin data suggest that non-human primates may represent tool objects differently than other ontological kinds (e.g. landmarks), thereby implying that domain-specific learning mechanisms play a significant role in the acquisition of a tool concept. Unfortunately, however, the data we reviewed are silent on the question of whether tamarins and other primates reason about either the function of or intentions behind the objects they use in these tasks. For example, the data we reviewed could also be construed as consistent with the Teleo-Functional Concepts position. This perspective proposes that we represent tools as objects designed for a particular purpose. A chair is a CHAIR because it exists for the purpose of sitting. The Teleo-Functional perspective further posits that when we look at a chair, we infer the purpose of the object from the complexity of its features. If an object has many chair-like features, we assume that it is *for* a CHAIR-like purpose. Therefore, a teleological view of primate tool representations predicts that they should pay attention to the features of a tool that are relevant to its function, not because these properties are necessary and sufficient for their representation of the tool, but because these properties provide clues to the tool's purpose. Non-human primates clearly recognize the important features of tools. However, to date, the relevant data have been silent on whether or not primates use these features to infer some teleological origin.

A similar problem holds for the Intentional History position. Under this view, the intention of the designer determines its ontological kind. A chair is a CHAIR because it was made by a person who had the intention of turning several slabs of wood into a CHAIR. From this perspective, we would therefore expect primates to pay particular attention to a tool's causally relevant features because these features often serve as clues to the intentions of a designer. If an object has many chair-like features, we assume that the designer intended it to be a CHAIR. From the perspective of the Intentional History position, therefore, primates should pay attention to the features of a tool that are relevant to its function. This attentional focus should not arise because these are the necessary and sufficient properties for representing the tool, but because these properties provide clues about the designer's intentions. The data reviewed above are again silent on the question of whether non-human primates use these features to infer the intentions of a designer; no study has yet examined whether primates (or other animals) draw inferences about the intentions of a tool- or artifact-maker. Fortunately, a growing body of work in the field of primate social congnition suggests that it may be feasible to test the intentional history hypothesis. In contrast to what primate researchers thought a few years ago, primates (and other animals) appear to be capable of inferring the intentions of others under some conditions (for reviews, see Lyons and Santos 2006; Tomasello *et al.* 2005). Chimpanzees, for example, readily distinguish between the accidental and intentional actions of others (Call *et al.* 2004), particularly in tasks that involve competition (see Hare 2001, Lyons and Santos 2006). What is not yet known is whether this capacity translates to non-social domains, including especially the domain of artifacts, and whether primates use their intention-reading skills to attribute to others *an intent to create particular kinds of objects*, as the intentional history position might suggest. If primates do not use their intentional understanding when reasoning about tools, then this missing ingredient would make their use and thinking about tools quite different from our own. Taken together, the data reviewed here present a bit of a puzzle. Non-human primates seem to reason about tools as a specific domain of objects, but to date there is little direct evidence that they represent different tools as meaningful ontological entities. This lack of evidence is due in part to the fact that the ability to understand kinds is often defined by the capacity to label different types of objects with words. Since non-human primates lack the ability to use words, it is difficult to assess whether or not they have kind representations.

One move in the direction of establishing kinds in the absence of language comes from studies of property–kind individuation in human infants and non-human primates. The basic question is: How and when infants come to appreciate that there are different kinds of objects and that such kind distinctions play a role in object individuation? To explore this question, Xu, Carey, and their colleagues (Van de Walle *et al.* 2000; Xu and Carey 1996, 2000; Xu, Carey, and Welch 1999) have run a series of experiments with infants between the ages of 10 and 12 months; the methods entail both expectancy-violation looking-time procedures as well as search assays. In one condition, an experimenter presented an infant with an empty stage and then lowered a screen. Next, the infant watched as a toy duck emerged and then returned on one side of the screen, followed by a truck emerging and returning behind the opposite side of the screen. The experimenter then lowered the screen, allowing the infant to look at a stage with a duck and a truck, or a stage with just the duck or just the truck. If infants use property–kind differences to individuate the number of objects present, then they should look longer at the outcome of one object than at the outcome of two. Ten-month-olds look as long at outcomes of one and two objects, whereas 12-month-olds look longer at outcomes of one object. Ten-month-olds apparently fail to use property–kind distinctions to individuate the number of objects hidden behind the screen, while 12-month-olds use such distinctions. Importantly, especially for the Xu and Carey position, it is infants with comprehension of words for such objects (e.g. 'duck', 'truck') that show the differences in looking times. This leads to the hypothesis that language may be necessary for the acquisition of kind concepts. Although this hypothesis has been challenged by data from Needham and Baillargeon (2000) showing that younger infants can make these distinctions, but in the absence of language, an even stronger test would come from studies of non-linguistic primates. Using both the looking-time method (Uller, Carey, and Hauser 1997; Munakata *et al.* 2001), as well as the search procedure (Phillips and Santos, in press; Santos *et al.* 2002), we have now demonstrated parallel effects with rhesus monkeys. For example, using the expectancy-violation procedure with a piece of carrot and squash, rhesus monkeys look longer when shown an outcome of one object than when shown an outcome of two (Uller *et al.* 1997). Thus, language is clearly not necessary for kind distinctions of the kind described by Xu and Carey, although language may well play a role in changing the kind distinction. It is now essential that comparable studies be run with objects from other domains (i.e. not only food, but artifacts including tools) and other species, testing whether featural changes in some domains play a more significant role in individuation than do other features.

We have argued that non-human primates possess a domain-specific understanding of tools. They seem to understand which features are relevant to a tool's ability to function, and recognize that these features are different from those that are relevant for other objects including landmarks and food. Unfortunately, however, the data we have reviewed cannot determine the precise content of primate representations of tools. Consequently, we cannot yet say whether monkeys and apes simply use the affordances of tool-like objects (no representations at all), represent tools by highly associative perceptual features, or think about tools in a theory-laden fashion, considering either the function of a given artifact or the intentionality of the tool-maker. Nevertheless, the reader should certainly not come away feeling cynical. Over the past ten years primate researchers have gone beyond merely observing tool-use and have gained a much richer understanding of the way primates actually categorize the tools that they use. Such work has pushed us much closer to figuring out the representations that underlie primate tool-use. Perhaps more significantly, however, we have developed a suite of new empirical techniques that can be used to examine how primates represent both concrete objects such as tools, food, and landmarks as well as more abstract concepts such as number and mental states (Gallistel 1990; Hauser 2000; Heyes and Huber 2000; Shettleworth 1998; Tomasello and Call 1997; Tomasello *et al.* 2005). Some of these techniques, which directly parallel those used with human infants (Hauser and Carey 1998), require no training, can be used across different ages and species, and allow for direct comparisons with data on human conceptual acquisition. Such techniques promise a bright future for work investigating concepts in non-human primates and may reveal the evolutionary roots of our conceptual knowledge.

Although the parallels between human and non-human tool use are striking, at least in those areas where specific observations and experiments have been brought to bear on the hypotheses, we must not lose sight of some equally striking differences, summarized in Table 15.1. Some of these proclaimed differences

Table 15.1. *Comparisons between animal and human tools*

Trait	Animal tools	Human tools
Sensitivity to relevant design features	yes	yes
Use of multiple materials for different tools	yes	yes
Use of multiple materials for a single tool	no	yes
Tool consists of articulated parts	no	yes
Tool consists of parts with different functions	no	yes
Tool kept with user for more than one application	no	yes
Tool designed for one function is used for another	no	yes

may, of course, turn out to be wrong, based at present on insufficient data. Others, however, are most likely correct and, we believe, should point the way to a better understanding of how and why our representations of tools are different from those of the other tools-users on the planet. Consider, for example, the observation that no non-human animal has ever created a tool with multiple, functional parts and nor has any animal designed a tool for one function and then used this object for a different purpose; chimpanzees use sticks for termite fishing and for throwing, but a stick that has had its leaves removed *for* fishing is not then used for throwing. This may appear trivial, but we believe it actually represents a profound difference, one that may tap our capacity to entertain multiple representations of the same object, thereby leading to a combinatorial explosion of possible functions. For example, although we know that a screwdriver was designed for tightening screws, if we ask someone to write down other possible functions, they will generate a long list once they get into thinking about problems in this way; a screwdriver can be used to keep a window open, as a paperweight, to punch a hole in a piece of paper, as a fork, as a 'brush' to paint with, and so on. When this capacity evolved is currently unclear. Looking at the archaeological record might suggest that it is recently evolved. Most of the early tools were made of one material (stone), with one functional part (the point of a handaxe), and one functional role. This view is, in our opinion, misguided, as it is based solely on the fossilizable artifacts. The early hominids most likely created tools out of wood, and may well have used vines to bind one object to another, creating a tool with multiple parts. Independently of its phylogenetic origin, once this capacity evolved it opened the door to a different kind of tool technology and a different way of thinking about tools. And once this kind of representation evolved, it could be transformed and passed on by two other, uniquely human, capacities: imitation and teaching. The synergy between our concepts of tools and our ability to copy and teach provided the foundation for cultural innovations and change, from the simple Swiss army knife to a computer with megagigahertz processing speed. But that is another story.

16

Creations of Pre-Modern Human Minds: Stone Tool Manufacture and Use by *Homo habilis, heidelbergensis,* and *neanderthalensis*

Steven Mithen

1. THE ARTIFACTS OF MODERN HUMANS

Modern humans, *Homo sapiens*, first appear in the fossil record 130,000 years ago in East Africa. By 100,000 years ago their skeletal remains are found in Southern Africa and the Near East. During the next 60,000 years they colonize the Old World, seeming to reach Australia by 55,000 years ago and Europe by 40,000 years ago. Quite when they entered the Americas remains unclear; some archaeologists believe there is evidence for occupation at least 30,000 years ago, but others place colonization closer to 12,500 years ago. This remarkable dispersal of modern humans from their African origin is principally mapped by the artifacts they left behind at newly created settlements in Asia, Australasia, Europe, and the Americas. There are no written records, and skeletal remains are extremely scarce. And so archaeologists rely on the discovery and interpretation of artifacts such as stone tools, fireplaces, dwellings, and art objects.

These are used not only to document the dispersal of modern humans but to reconstruct their lifeways—the manner in which our Stone Age ancestors acquired their food, the way they organized their societies, their technology, and religious beliefs. Archaeologists also use artifacts to explore how societies change and culture evolves—addressing questions such as how people adapted to the last glacial maximum at 20,000 BC, how and why agriculture arose and the first civilizations developed. Archaeologists are able to use artifacts of modern humans in this manner because even the most mundane, such as slabs for grinding plants or stone blades for slicing meat, are potentially laden with information about the social, economic, and ideological worlds of past peoples.

It is normal for artifacts made in the modern world to be multi-purpose—to have a utilitarian function, to carry social information, and to have a symbolic meaning. The design of our clothes, cars, and mobile phones are obvious examples. Although some artifacts are merely passive reflections of inherited traditions and fashions, the majority are intentionally designed and used to mediate our social relationships. As the archaeologist Ian Hodder (1985) once described, they are 'symbols in action'.

This multi-purpose character of artifacts is a consequence of their having been made by modern humans, rather than a function of modern, industrial, or even agrarian-based society. When anthropologists have studied the artifacts of recent hunter-gatherers these are also found to have symbolic, social, and utilitarian functions layered upon each other. Polly Wiessner (1983), for instance, studied the arrowheads of the !Kung bushmen of Southern Africa and documented how their specific shapes are not only effective at killing game but define individual and social identity. The arrowheads play a critical role in economic exchange and are linked into the ideological beliefs of the !Kung. Similarly, we know that the rock paintings of recent Australian aboriginal groups have multiple meanings (Morphy 1989). A painting of a fish above a pool of water, for instance, can be a sign that this is a good fishing location, while also expressing the deeply held beliefs about the essence of life expressed through the 'rainbowness' that is seen in a fish's scales.

The fact that it is normal for the artifacts of modern humans to have multiple roles and meanings is of immense value to archaeologists. It means that when we find, for instance, the projectile points of prehistoric hunters, the potential exists to explore the social and symbolic lives of past peoples rather than just their hunting methods and manufacturing techniques. Consequently archaeologists have attempted to reconstruct territorial boundaries, ethnic groups, patterns of trade, and social relationships by the study of prehistoric stone tools (e.g. Gendel 1984; Petersen 1984). The same artifacts have been used to make detailed studies of manufacturing techniques and tool function, such as by using microwear techniques.

The propensity of modern humans to make artifacts that function simultaneously in multiple domains of behaviour is a consequence of 'cognitive fluidity' (Mithen 1996). Modern humans, and especially those in traditional societies, tend to have very fuzzy boundaries between those domains of behaviour that archaeologists, and social scientists in general, attempt to ring-fence, such as the 'social', technological', 'economic', and 'ideological'. Only in very rare circumstances can artifacts be described as functioning in just one behavioural domain alone. When archaeologists study pre-modern humans, species such as *Homo erectus* and *H. neanderthalensis*, they are unable to assume that such cognitive fluidity exists. As a consequence, they must approach early prehistoric artifacts quite differently. There is, for instance, no a priori reason to expect that a projectile point will necessarily carry social and symbolic information. In this regard, archaeologists face a far greater challenge than when they study modern humans; not only must they use artifacts to reconstruct past behaviour, but they must use the same artifacts, to understand the nature of past mentality. Fortunately, artifacts are rarely studied in isolation: skeletal remains can provide substantial behavioural information to supplement that from artifacts, while evidence from animal bones, plant remains, and sediments enables the reconstruction of past environments.

To explore the constraints and possibilities provided by the study of artifacts made by pre-modern humans, and to examine the changing nature of artifacts and mentality through the course of human evolution, I will examine those from three extinct species. First, the stone flakes made by *H. habilis* living in Africa about 2 million years ago; I will then leap through 1.5 million years and consider the handaxes made by *H. heidelbergensis* in southern England at 500,000 BP. Finally I will turn to the artifacts made by the Neanderthals, who lived in Western Asia and Europe between 200,000 and 28,000 BP. Each of these case studies will be considered within the broader context of human evolution, and will illustrate how the study of stone tools must be embedded within that of behaviour in general. Although each of the artifacts I consider are 'creations of the mind', the minds of *H. habilis*, *H. heidelbergensis*, and H. *neanderthalensis* appear to have been very different from each other as well as from that of modern humans.

2. THE AUSTRALOPITHECINES AND AN APE-LIKE TECHNOLOGY

Imagine yourself on the African savannah at around 2 million years ago. Although the landscape looks much as it does today, the animals that you must imagine squatting cautiously around a carcass are quite unlike anything in the modern world. Little over a meter tall, covered in body hair, and evidently adept on two legs, one moment they look like apes and the next like humans. Your interest is with the artifacts being used to slice through skin and tendons—stone flakes just struck from a nodule of basalt. These are used with considerable skill to dismember the carcass as quickly as possible. As the hominids work they look around warily for approaching carnivores; the flakes become greasy and lose their cutting edge. And so a nodule is picked from the ground, inspected carefully, and then struck with a hammerstone to remove a new flake. As soon as the carcass is divided the hominids flee the scene, taking the best bits and leaving the remnants for the scavengers that will soon arrive. A scatter of flakes and nodules remain at the site; one of the hominids carries the hammerstone and the recently struck flake as he runs to the trees.

This imaginative scene is how many archaeologists envisage the use of the first stone tools to appear in the archaeological record. The hominid concerned is conventionally thought to be *Homo habilis*, but it might have been any of numerous species known to have inhabited East and South Africa between 4.5 and 1.8 million years ago—a period known as the Plio-Pleistocene. Other than *H. habilis*, and the very earliest known hominid which is placed into its own genus as *Ardipithecus ramidus*, these are all known as australopithecines (Johanson and Edgar 1996). Wood and Collard (1999) believe that *H. habilis* should be redesignated as *Australopithecine habilis*.

2.1. A diversity of hominid species

The best-known australopithecine species is *A. afarensis*, appearing in the fossil record at 3.5 million years ago. The specimen known as Lucy has 50 per cent of the skeleton surviving from an individual that had once stood about 1 meter high (Johanson and Edgar 1996). Although clear indications of bipedalism are present, Lucy's long limbs and curved digits suggest that *A. afarensis* remained partly adapted to an arboreal lifestyle. Signs of knuckle-walking also exist, but these are most likely inherited traits reflecting an ancestral form of locomotion, one no longer used by *A. afarensis* (Collard and Aiello 2000).

The australopithecines come in a variety of anatomical forms suggesting a diversity of lifestyles, but they share common features of bipedalism and a brain size between 400 and 500 cc—essentially the same as a chimpanzee today. One group is known as the robust australopithecines, as they have particularly heavy and thick jawbones, massive molars, and, in some cases, saggital crests of bone for the attachment of large facial muscles. Such robust australopithecines had evidently evolved a highly specialized adaptation to grinding large quantities of grasses and other plant material.

The other australopithecines are known as gracile species and show a variety of cranial and post-cranial morphologies, with a mix of ape-like and more human-like characteristics. Other than *A. afarensis*, particularly notable species are *A. anamensis* from East Africa and *A. africanus* from South Africa. The specimens that have been designated as *H. habilis* are highly variable in size; some authorities suggest that more than one *Homo* species is represented (Wood 1992).

These hominids were living within savannah landscapes not dissimilar to those of East Africa today. As from 2.5 million years ago their fossilized remains are supplemented by stone artifacts. These are flakes struck from nodules of chert, basalt, quartz, and limestone by hammerstones, and the remnants of the nodules referred to as cores. Unmodified but transported stone nodules are frequently found with the flaked artifacts, along with fragmented animal bones. The latter come predominantly from animals such as zebra and bovids, although large species such as elephant and hippopotamus are also present (Potts 1988). The most important clusters of sites come from Olduvai Gorge, Tanzania, and

Koobi Fora, Kenya (the papers in Isaac B. (ed.) 1989 provide an archaeological review).

2.2. Hunters or scavengers?

Since the late 1970s there has been a vigorous debate amongst palaeoanthropologists about the interpretation of Plio-Pleistocene archaeological sites. Glynn Isaac (1978) began this by suggesting that those sites with both stone artifacts and animal bones were 'home bases' where hominids had shared meat and plant foods. He proposed an adaptation similar to that of recent African bushmen in which there was a division of labour, with men principally acquiring meat, either by hunting or primary scavenging (i.e. from freshly killed and largely intact animals), and women gathering plants. The home bases were believed to be the loci for child-care, and to have provided the context for the evolution of social complexity and language.

Isaac's home-base model was severely criticized by Lewis Binford (1981), on the grounds that it imposed too much of modern human behaviour into the distant past. He argued that the Plio-Pleistocene hominids had been no more than marginal scavengers who took tidbits from carnivore kills which were quite insufficient to enable food-sharing. Isaac (1983) modified his home-base model to one of central-place foraging—an attempt to characterize the adaptation as less like that of modern humans and to situate his model within the framework of community ecology. But he nevertheless maintained the notion of food-sharing as a key feature of Plio-Pleistocene hominid adaptation.

Neither Binford nor Isaac appear to have been entirely correct as, following two decades of meticulous study of the animal bones and stone artifacts, often in the context of acrimonious argument (e.g. Bunn and Kroll 1986; Binford 1986), it appears that the Plio-Pleistocene hominids were most likely opportunistic foragers. Some of the excavated animal bones have come from prime meat-bearing parts of a carcass and bear cut-marks that indicate the butchery of freshly killed animals; in other cases the type of marginal scavenging envisaged by Binford is the most appropriate interpretation, such as for collections of lower-limb bones that were smashed open to extract small morsels of marrow. It is evident, however, that in all cases stone artifacts were essential to this new lifestyle of meat-eating.

When chimpanzees are successful hunters they merely pull and bite their prey apart, this predominantly being small monkeys (Boesch and Boesch 1989). Hominids faced a more challenging problem in needing to remove limbs, meat, and fat from much larger prey. The sharp stone flakes and robust nodules were used for cutting through hide and tendons, smashing joints and bone itself (Schick and Toth 1993). We know that hominids themselves sometimes became the prey of carnivores, and suspect that there was substantial competition for animal carcasses on the savannah (Brain 1981; Blumenschine 1986). Speed in butchery is likely to have been essential, followed by a rapid retreat to a place of safety. We have evidence that hominids carried cores and flakes around the landscape, presumably in preparedness for scavenging or hunting opportunities. Richard Potts (1988) once suggested that caches of stone artifacts were made at selected locations to allow ready access should the need arise.

The association between stone tools and animal bones, together with the presence of cut and smash marks on the latter, clearly indicate that the artifacts were used in processing carcasses (Bunn 1981; Potts and Shipman 1981). It is likely that they would have also been used for digging roots, chopping plants, and perhaps sharpening sticks. We know that Oldowan tools were effective at such tasks by experimental work involving replicated artifacts (Schick and Toth 1993). But direct evidence remains elusive. Similarly, it would be surprising if hominids were not using a wide variety of tools made from organic materials. We know that chimpanzees use thin sticks to make termite sticks and ant probes, branches as hammers and anvils, and leaves as sponges (Boesch and Boesch 1990). It is reasonable to think that hominids were using a similar range of tools in a similar manner. Indeed, their lifestyle on the savannah may have led to an enlargement of this tool repertoire. Glynn Isaac proposed that hominids had used baskets for transporting raw materials and foodstuffs, suggesting some ready-made examples such as elephant foot-pads (Schick and Toth 1993, 174). But there is no direct evidence.

2.3. Cognitive implications of Oldowan tools

In the absence of tools made from organic materials, archaeologists have to concentrate their studies on the stone artifacts. Up until 1.5 million years ago these are all placed into the Oldowan Industry. This was first described by Mary Leakey in the 1970s on the basis of material excavated from Olduvai Gorge (Leakey 1971). She believed that hominids were intentionally making several distinct types of tools, giving these names such as 'choppers', 'polyhedrons', and 'spheroids', and implying that each tool type was made and used for a specific purpose. Few archaeologists now believe this to be the case; Leakey's tool types blend into each other as part of a continuum, and it appears likely that hominids were removing flakes from nodules without any intention of creating a specifically shaped artifact (Toth 1985; Potts 1988).

It is unclear as to which of the hominid species were making the stone artifacts. They were once all attributed to *H. habilis* and used as a means to distinguish that species from the australopithecines. But as several hominid species were contemporary with each other, and as there is no anatomical reason why australopithecines could not have manufactured stone artifacts (Susman 1991), we must be cautious about the identity of the tool-maker. This issue is of far less importance today than it was thirty or even just ten years ago, owing to the recognition of the extent and diversity of tool-use amongst chimpanzees.

Neither tool manufacture nor use can now be used as a genus-specific character of *Homo*, and consequently the recognition that australopithecines may have been flaking stone is no longer of great significance. The best guess is that several, if not all, of the australopithecine species were making and using stone tools.

One of the key archaeological debates has been whether Oldowan technology indicates that Plio-Pleistocene hominids were more intelligent than present-day African apes. Chimpanzees certainly manufacture tools in the sense of selecting twigs, stripping away the leaves, and biting them to an appropriate length to use as an ant probe or termite stick. Some chimpanzees use stone artifacts as hammers and anvils for cracking nuts and are known to transport these for up to 50 meters (Boesch and Boesch 1990). But there have been no observations of intentional modification of stone nodules before use by animals in the wild.

Thomas Wynn and Bill McGrew (1989) once argued that the manufacture of Oldowan tools required no greater technical skill or intelligence than that expressed by chimpanzees when making their termite sticks and other tools. But experiments using Kanzi, a bonobo that had already displayed good abilities at symbol use, suggested that Oldowan flaking techniques were beyond his comprehension (Toth *et al.* 1993). Hominids were systematically detaching flakes by locating 'platforms'—places on a nodule where two faces intersected at an acute angle—and then striking these with a hammerstone at an appropriate angle and with an appropriate amount of force to detach a flake. Kanzi was unable to acquire this technique, although he learnt how to detach flakes by smashing stone nodules against the floor.

One must be cautious when interpreting these results. Kanzi was already a mature adult by the time the experiments began, and this might have inhibited his learning abilities. A younger individual might have had more success, as might a chimpanzee rather than bonobo, as the latter are not known to make tools in the wild. Moreover, female chimpanzees appear more adept at tool-making and using than males (Boesch and Boesch 1990). Consequently, had Kanzi been a young, female chimpanzee rather than an old, male bonobo he might have had more success at acquiring Oldowan-like tool-making skills.

The absence of stone-flaking by chimpanzees and the other African apes in the wild may reflect no more than an absence of need for such artifacts. Alternatively, the production of sharp flakes may indeed be beyond their mental comprehension, as the Kanzi experiments suggest (Mithen 1996). If, therefore, the australopithecines had additional cognitive abilities to those possessed by modern apes, we must ask whether these had been acquired specifically for the manufacture of stone tools, whether they were part of a generalized intelligence, or whether they were the outcome of cognitive abilities whose primary purpose was in some unrelated area.

The first of these scenarios is more likely to be favoured by those who believe in strong degrees of mental modularity. Weaver *et al.* (2001) have, for instance, written about an 'object oriented' intelligence and distinguished this from social and conceptual intelligence, while in my own work (Mithen 1996) I have suggested a discrete 'technical intelligence' for pre-modern humans, although arguing that this is not fully evolved in Plio-Pleistocene hominids. The rationale for such arguments is that the knowledge and skills for flaking stone are very different to those required in other domains of activity, such as making decisions about food acquisition or social interaction. As such, hominids with dedicated mental modules for technology will have had greater success than those reliant on general-purpose capacities or those evolved for other tasks.

Such arguments, however, may be quite unnecessary to explain the emergence of Oldowan technology. *Homo* (or *Australopithecine*) *habilis* is likely to have been living in larger social groups than present-day chimpanzees, owing to its largely terrestrial lifestyle and the resulting predator risk (Aiello and Dunbar 1993). Larger social groups, and more intense relationships within those groups, may have resulted in greater opportunities for social learning about the use of tools than arise within chimpanzee groups today. Consequently, the knowledge and skills required to flake stone may have been a spin-off from increased social complexity.

Whatever the cognitive origin of the Oldowan technology, it is most unlikely that the appearance of such tools in the archaeological record marks a major technological threshold in human evolution. Oldowan tools were most likely made, used, and discarded much like those of chimpanzees—short-term aids to food acquisition. They may have been technically more demanding to make, and have been transported for greater distances around the landscape. But they have more in common with termite sticks and ant probes than the tools of either later hominids or modern humans.

3. EARLY HUMANS AND THE ENIGMA OF THE HANDAXE

Now imagine a hominid tool-maker living a mere 500,000 years ago, and far from the African savannah. Amidst a landscape of lagoons and a windswept coastal plain, imagine watching what is undisputedly a human being at a locality that will become known as Boxgrove in southern England. He is using a piece of deer antler to strike a nodule held firmly between his knees, approaching the completion of a stone artifact that had begun about fifteen minutes ago. Close by, another man and a women are also chipping at stone. Others are sitting or lying on the ground; one women is nursing an infant, a few children are playing with sticks.

These hominids are as large as modern humans; in fact their height, bulky muscles, and layers of fat make them larger than most. Hides and furs are draped around their shoulders, their hair is long and matted. The man we watch is evidently taking great care in his work. He had began by selecting a nodule of flint from the base of a nearby cliff and then shaped it into a rough oval by using a quartzite pebble as a hammerstone. He then switched tools to use the antler, as he knew that this would remove thinner flakes. The artifact is gradually shaped amid many pauses to assess where and how he should strike next. The result is an almost perfectly symmetrical ovate tool, one that he is pleased to show off to his companions. It had evidently given him a great deal of pleasure and pride to manufacture.

These hominids are known as *Homo heidelbergensis*, and the artifact being made is a handaxe, perhaps the most enigmatic type of artifact from the whole of human prehistory. To understand how both of these arise we must first return to Africa.

3.1. Out of Africa

At around 1.8 million years ago a new hominid species appears in the fossil record and marks a significant evolutionary transition from the australopithecines. Wood and Collard (1999) believe that it should be recognized as the first member of our genus—*Homo ergaster*. Some palaeoanthropologists prefer to designate this as *H. erectus*, while others restrict *H. erectus* to a descendant of *H. ergaster* that evolved in eastern Asia. *H. ergaster* is superbly represented by the Nariokotome Boy, the best preserved of all fossil skeletons and discovered in the vicinity of Lake Turkana (Walker and Leakey 1993). This is of a young male, aged between 11 and 15 years, which had already reached the stature of a modern adult. Its post-cranial skeleton shows that a fully modern and dedicated bipedalism had evolved, while its skull suggests that adult brain size remained below 1,000 cc.

Many archaeologists believe that *H. ergaster* was the first hominid species to disperse out of Africa. If so, it appears to have done so with great rapidity, as sites in Java with *H. erectus* fossils have been dated to 1.6–1.8 million years ago. Those dates remain contentious, but few archaeologists disagree with one of *c.*1.5 million years ago for 'Ubediya in Israel and 1.7 for Dmanisi, Georgia. Hominid remains have been claimed from Longuppo Cave in China at 1.9 million years ago and a similar date from Orce in southern Spain (Straus and Bar-Yosef 2001). While arguments remain over such dates, it is evident that the first dispersals from Africa were undertaken with Oldowan technology. The earliest sites in both Europe and Asia have no more than simple flakes and cores, indicating that the dispersal from Africa neither required nor instigated any technological development. The first hominids that occupied south-east Asia may have made no use of stone artifacts at all, perhaps utilizing bamboo as an alternative (Pope 1989).

3.2. Bifacial technology

The first substantial post-Oldowan technological development occurred in East Africa at around 1.4 million years ago (Asfaw *et al.* 1992). This is when the first handaxes appear. Hominids began to remove flakes from both sides of a nodule of stone, often in an alternate fashion by using the flake scar of one removal as the striking platform for the next. This is known as the 'bifacial' technique, and was frequently used to shape a nodule of stone into the shape of a teardrop about the size of one's palm—a handaxe.

After first appearing in Africa, handaxes become a pervasive element of the archaeological record for more than 1 million years. They dominate the archaeological remains from Africa, Europe, and Asia after 0.5 million years ago, often being found in extraordinary quantities, such as at Olorgesailie, Tanzania (Isaac 1977). The final handaxes were made in the late Pleistocene cultures of Europe a mere 50,000 years ago (Mellars 1996). As such, handaxes are also associated with the evolutionary descendants of *H. ergaster* and *H. erectus*. Perhaps the most significant of these is *H. heidelbergensis*, a species that evolved from *H. ergaster* in Africa and which dispersed into Europe. This may have been the common ancestor for *H. neanderthalensis* and *H. sapiens*, although the amount of morphological variation in those specimens assigned to *H. heidelbergensis* suggests that several species may be represented. By 200,000 years ago the Neanderthals had evolved in Europe and continued to make handaxes, although artifacts made from flakes become predominant. Handaxes are not known to have been made by anatomically modern humans whose fossilized remains first appear in Africa at 130,000 years ago.

Many handaxes have a strong aesthetic appeal on account of their symmetry. In some cases this is likely to be no more than an unintended by-product of the bifacial knapping technique used in their manufacture and the original shape of the nodule (Ashton and McNabb 1994). But in many specimens symmetry appears to have been deliberately imposed by the careful removal of flakes. Moreover, symmetry is often created in three dimensions with the same artifacts—in plan, in profile, and in section (Wynn 1989). The morphological aesthetic appeal of handaxes might be supplemented by the use of fine-grained raw materials, such as high-quality flint, and—in rare instances—the presence of fossils left intact within the stone of the artifact (Oakley 1981).

Archaeologists have frequently commented upon such aesthetic qualities, and even suggested that such artifacts might lie at the root of art and mathematics (e.g. Gowlett 1984). But little explanation has been offered with regard to why early humans invested time and effort in creating symmetrical handaxes to use in tasks such as animal butchery for which artifactual symmetry was quite unnecessary.

3.3. Social context of manufacture and use

Many thousands of handaxes have been excavated from sites in Africa, Europe, and Asia, and then subjected to detailed metrical studies (e.g. Isaac 1977; Roe 1981; Villa 1983; Wynn and Tierson 1990). They come in various shapes and sizes, sometimes being classified into discrete types. Archaeologists have undertaken microwear analysis, the refitting of debitage, and experimental studies concerned with manufacture and use (e.g. Keeley 1980; Jones 1980; Bergman and Roberts 1988; Austin 1994). Handaxes have also been at the centre of research regarding the evolution of human intelligence (e.g. Wynn 1979, 1989, 1993, 1995; Mithen 1996). Recent studies have challenged notions of chronological patterning for handaxe types, and placed emphasis on raw material and function, rather than culture and style, when explaining handaxe morphology (e.g. Ashton and McNabb 1994; Bosinski 1996). There has also been a greater recognition of the considerable variability in handaxes, ranging from the classic, highly symmetrical bifaces, to non-classic or atypical bifaces, which may lack a clearly imposed form (Ashton and McNabb 1994).

Handaxes are most likely to have been general-purpose artifacts, being used for the butchery of animals, cutting wood, slicing meat, and chopping vegetables. Direct evidence, however, is scarce. There are a few cases where microwear studies have been undertaken, such as on artifacts from Koobi Fora in Africa (Keeley and Toth 1981) and Hoxne in England (Keeley 1980). Both samples showed a range of wear traces, indicating that they had been used for a variety of tasks. Experimental work appears to confirm this, as handaxes are clearly effective for a range of activities (Jones 1980, 1981; Schick and Toth 1993). Handaxes may also have functioned as a source of flakes, having been carried around the landscape as curated artifacts (Hayden 1979), or as implements for throwing at game (Calvin 1993).

The dilemma archaeologists face is that, while the imposed symmetrical forms often allow the artifacts to sit comfortably in the hand, they do not appear to provide sufficient degrees of improvement over plain flakes or choppers to justify that extra investment: animals can be butchered, sticks sharpened, and plants chopped by tools requiring far less time and skill to make. The fine trimming flakes found on so many artifacts appear quite unnecessary for these activities. Resolution to this problem might be found, however, by considering the role of handaxes in social interaction.

As handaxes were made by a variety of hominid types in numerous different geographical areas with different resources, the social context of manufacture and use is likely to have been variable. Nevertheless, the two common characteristics of the hominid species involved—large brains and habitual bipedalism—imply some shared features. As Aiello and Dunbar (1993; Dunbar 1993) have argued, large brains imply large groups. These groups were likely to be highly competitive, requiring individuals to adopt a range of Machiavellian social tactics to survive and prosper (cf. Byrne and Whiten 1988; Whiten and Byrne 1997).

As large brains are metabolically expensive organs (Aiello and Wheeler 1995), the need for a high-quality diet most likely involved substantial meat consumption, which in turn required cooperation in its acquisition by either hunting or scavenging. This dependency on animal carcasses is also likely to have favoured large groups, due to the opportunities for food-sharing and/or tolerated theft.

Another factor would have been the risk from carnivore predation in Pleistocene environments. Owing to the spatial and temporal environmental variability during the Pleistocene, the extent of predator risk and meat consumption will have varied. Consequently hominid group size will have also varied, with larger groups being expected on open tundras and smaller groups within the wooded interglacial landscapes (Mithen 1994). The larger groups may have been essential in maintaining sufficient degrees of social learning for the transmission of handaxe-manufacturing techniques. The non-handaxe artifact collections, in which artifacts are Oldowan-like, such as those known as the Clactonian in southern England, may have been the product of hominids living in smaller, less complex social groups (Mithen 1994).

While handaxe-making hominids are likely to have lived in complex social environments, had considerable technical skill, and engaged in big-game hunting, it is unlikely that they had fully modern language and symbolic thought (Mithen 1996). The linguistic skills of human ancestors have been substantially discussed in recent publications (e.g. Mithen 1996; Bickerton 1996; Dunbar 1993, 1996; Deacon 1997), and remains open to much debate. Anatomical evidence suggests that there was a considerable development of vocal abilities between *Homo ergaster* and *H. neanderthalensis*; the encephalization between 600,000 and 250,000 years ago (Ruff, Trinkhaus, and Holliday 1997) is most likely related to the evolution of language ability. But as there are no traces of symbolic behaviour and thought in the archaeological record, it seems probable that fully modern language with a large lexicon and grammatical rules only evolved with modern humans at *c.*150,000 years ago.

With an absence of modern language abilities and symbolic thought, the hominid species that made handaxes were quite unlike modern humans. Consequently, analogies between the production of handaxes with that of similarly elaborate and aesthetic artifacts amongst cognitively fluid modern humans, which were then used for trade, in religious practices, or as items of prestige, are quite ill-founded. Those artifacts only functioned in such roles because they were invested with symbolic meanings, and we have no reason to believe that this was the case with handaxes. A more effective explanation for the aesthetic appeal of handaxes is found by focusing on the social and sexual relations within the hominid communities.

3.4. Handaxes as products of sexual selection

Kohn and Mithen (1999) suggested that the symmetry and fine workmanship of many handaxes were products of sexual selection—the hominid equivalent of a peacock's tail. Whether or not pair-bonding had arisen at this stage in human history, females are likely to have had considerable choice over which males to select as mating partners. Males would have needed to display to females, in much the same fashion as in those species which utilize handicapping traits such as extravagant tail-fans, antlers, or canines (Zahavi and Zahavi 1997). In this regard the time and skill required for handaxe manufacture, together with the imposed symmetry, may have acted as reliable indicators as to the fitness of the individual who made the handaxe. A highly symmetrical and skilfully made handaxe was a sign of 'good genes'. Those hominids—either male or female—who were able to make fine, symmetrical handaxes may have been preferentially chosen by the opposite sex as mating partners. Just as a peacock's tail may reliably indicate the ability of the peacock to fight off parasites, acquire a nutritious diet, and escape from predators, so might a handaxe have been a reliable indicator of an ability to secure food, find shelter, escape from predation, and successfully compete within the social group (Kohn and Mithen 1999).

Artifacts of a symmetrical form may have been particularly attractive to members of the opposite sex because of an evolved perceptual bias toward symmetry. Symmetry abounds in the morphology of living things, because single genes control the development of features on both sides of an organism. But high levels of symmetry are difficult to achieve owing to the impact of genetic mutations, pathogens, or stress during development which can lead to the presence of asymmetries in bilaterally distributed features (Parsons 1992). Consequently, the degree of symmetry is a good indicator of the degree of genetic and physical health of an individual, and many species use this to identify a mate that possesses 'good genes' (e.g. see Møller 1988 for swallows; Manning and Chamberlain 1993 for primates; Manning and Hartley 1991 for peacocks). Modern humans also appear to be attracted to symmetry when selecting partners (Thornhill and Gangestad 1994, 1996).

Owing to the pervasiveness of the symmetry cue among animal species, and its specific presence in modern humans, it seems very likely that the males and females of all hominid species would have also used symmetry as a cue when selecting mates. Kohn and Mithen (1999) argue that hominids were making use of a predisposed attraction to symmetry when manufacturing handaxes—although no conscious intentionality is implied. They use the sexual selection argument to explain several of the enigmatic features of the archaeological record, such as the particularly large number of handaxes at certain sites and the existence of specimens which are too large to be viable as butchery implements.

4. NEANDERTHAL ARTIFACTS: TECHNICAL SKILL AND TECHNOLOGICAL STASIS

Now imagine a women sitting in the entrance of a cave above a narrow wooded valley and below a natural pillar of rock. The date is 50,000 BP. One day the cave will be known as Amud and located in Israel—but quite what this Neanderthal calls her cave, if anything at all, we do not know. There is a smouldering fireplace by her side. A gaggle of children are approaching with fresh firewood. She holds a nodule of flint that she has been carefully shaping for the last twenty minutes. Each flake removal has left a scar on the nodule's surface—or core, as the worked piece of stone should be called. The women has skilfully created a pattern of scars that has two intersecting ridges. She now turns the core through 90 degrees and quickly removes a suite of tiny chips to prepare a platform for the final strike. With a single blow a particularly large flake is removed, its triangular shape defined by the pattern of ridges that had been created. The flake is in fact a point, one that is razor-sharp along both its sides. It will be hafted onto a wooden shaft and used for hunting gazelle.

Excavations in Amud Cave provided a rich collection of such points, which are known by archaeologists as 'levallois' points, as have excavations at many other sites in western Asia and Europe between 250,000 and 50,000 BP (for reviews of the evidence see Bar-Yosef 1994; Mellars 1996; Stringer and Gamble 1993). Amud has also provided a collection of Neanderthal skeletal remains, all of which are believed to date to around 50,000 BP (Hovers *et al.* 1995). This is towards the end of Neanderthal existence, as this species became extinct soon after 30,000 BP, the final Neanderthals being found in southern Spain and Gibraltar (Stringer and Gamble 1993). They were pushed into that corner of Europe by the modern humans that had dispersed from their African homeland.

4.1. Neanderthal evolution, anatomy, and behaviour

H. neanderthalensis gains its name from the 1856 discovery of a partial skeleton in a cave within the Neander Valley near Dusseldorf, Germany. The name was given by William King in 1864, who believed the specimen represented a new species of human, in contrast to those who thought it was either an ancient European or simply a degenerate recent individual (Trinkaus and Shipman 1992). As further discoveries were made, notably in France before the First World War, and in Israel and Italy between the wars, such disputes regarding the evolutionary status of the Neanderthals continued.

One of the most important discoveries was made in 1908 in the cave of La Chapelle-aux-Saints in south-west France. This is popularly known as the 'Old Man', even though the individual was probably no more than 35 years old when he died. The skeletal remains were described by the French anatomist Marcel Boule. He decided that the 'Old Man' had a stooped posture and no more than 'rudimentary intellectual faculties'. As such, it had to represent a quite separate species from *H. sapiens*. Some of Boule's contemporaries disagreed and were ready to see the Neanderthals as no more than a separate sub-species, calling them *H. sapiens neanderthalensis*.

It is from Boule's characterization of the Chapelle-aux-Saints specimen that the popular conception of Neanderthals as shambling brutes arose, one which modern studies have shown to be entirely inaccurate. The 'Neanderthal stoop', for instance, arose because Boule misinterpreted the arthritic condition of the

Old Man of Chapelle-aux-Saints as a general characteristic of the species. But Boule's view that *Homo neanderthalensis* was a quite separate species from *H. sapiens* has been vindicated, although for entirely different reasons than those of intellectual and physical inferiority.

Today we know that *Homo sapiens* shared a common ancestor with the Neanderthals about 500,000 years ago, this date having been estimated from the extent of difference between Neanderthal and modern human DNA (Ward and Stringer 1997). The common ancestor may have been *Homo heidelbergensis* or another—as yet—unidentified hominid species. Fossils are classified as *H. neanderthalensis* if they have a particular shape to their skull, arrangements to their teeth, and other recurrent physical traits (Stringer and Gamble 1993). Such fossils are only found in Europe and western Asia. Neanderthals were, on average, a little shorter than modern humans, with the same general differences in height and weight between males and females. They were more muscular than most of us today, perhaps similar to a modern athlete or boxer. Their chests were more barrel-shaped and their limbs shorter; they had larger noses, perhaps an adaptation for warming cold Ice Age air, prominent brow ridges, and rounded chins.

The Neanderthals lived through a period of considerable climatic and environmental change: 130,000 years ago marked a very cold and dry period in the planet's history, during which much of Europe was covered in tundra and western Asia in desert. Within 25,000 years the climate had become as warm and as wet as today, leading to the spread of woodland and forest, while large expanses of coastal plain were lost as the sea level rose owing to the melt-waters from glaciers. Although many more plant foods became available, it remains unclear whether or not Neanderthals made use of these to supplement a diet of large and small game.

After this warm period the climate began to get colder and drier once again as it approached the peak of the last Ice Age, that arrived at 20,000 years ago, almost ten millennia after the Neanderthals had become extinct. The Neanderthal anatomy shows us that they were adapted to the cold landscapes and that their lifestyle was rigorous (Churchill 1998). The Neanderthals built their muscular bodies through extensive physical exertion; broken limbs and other injuries appear to have been common in the adult population.

Hunting accidents are their most likely source, as the Neanderthals are thought to have relied upon short, stabbing spears which required that they got close to their prey, with the inevitable risk of injury. Some bone fractures show signs of healing, even when the individual concerned is likely to have been severely incapacitated (Trinkaus 1983). This suggests a degree of social care within their groups—the provision of food, protection, and perhaps the use of medicinal plants. But we have limited knowledge about Neanderthal social life. They most likely lived in small groups that periodically met to exchange news, food, raw materials, and members by marriage.

Young Neanderthal children required considerable parental care. Just like the infants of modern humans, they would have been quite helpless for several years after birth, having to be born when their brains required another year of foetal-rate expansion so that the babies could fit through the narrow pelvis that goes with fully bipedal hominids. The lactating and pregnant females would have required substantial support owing to the time and energy demands of motherhood. Some support is likely to have come from their own female relatives. This is the case for modern human hunter-gatherers, amongst whom 'grandmothers' play a critical role in supporting their daughters and granddaughters (Hawkes, O'Connell, and Blurton-Jones 1997). But whether there would have been sufficient grandmothers for such support is doubtful, as few Neanderthals appear to have survived beyond the age of 35 (Trinkaus 1995). Moreover, because the Neanderthal diet appears dependent on big-game hunting, 'grandmothers', and the elderly in general, would have had a limited contribution to food provisioning. Consequently adults males are likely to have played a key role in the provisioning of females and young children.

The excavation of Neanderthal occupation sites in Europe and western Asia adds further information to our picture of Neanderthal lifestyles. These have provided large collections of stone tools and the waste from their manufacture. Microscopic studies have told us what specific tools were used for, while patterns of movement around the landscape have been established by identifying the source of raw materials (Mellars 1996 reviews the evidence from western Europe). The animal bones at such sites have told us not only what species were hunted but indicate specific hunting methods, butchery techniques, and the seasonal patterns of resource use (e.g. Stiner 1994).

4.2. Neanderthal language and the brain

It is possible that cooperative hunting, social care, male provisioning, and the transmission of knowledge about tool-making, all occurred with minimal spoken language. A gestural language might have been used, or perhaps the nature of communication was so limited that 'language' is an inappropriate term. Alternatively, all of these activities might have been mediated by speech as sophisticated as our own. Philip Lieberman still clings to the idea that he and Ed Crelin proposed in 1971 that the Neanderthals were limited in the range of sounds they could make by a vocal anatomy that was more similar to that of an ape than a modern human (Lieberman and Crelin 1971; Lieberman 2001). But few anthropologists agree, as recent studies have argued that the Neanderthal vocal tract was not significantly different to that of modern humans (Houghton 1993; Arensburg *et al.* 1990). If so, then the physical apparatus for speech was present; but for spoken language to have existed the Neanderthal brain would have also required the relevant neural circuitry.

Very little can be said about the Neanderthal brain beyond its size as estimated by the volume of surviving crania. This shows little, if any, difference from the brain size of modern humans, averaging in the range 1,200–1,500 cc (Stringer and Gamble 1993). In fact, some Neanderthals had brains larger than those known in any modern human. The Amud I specimen for instance, dating to *c*.50,000 years BP, has a cranial capacity of 1750 cc. One must, however, also account for the relatively large Neanderthal body mass (Ruff, Trinkhaus, and Holliday 1997). When this is done the brains of modern humans might have a slight edge in relative size—but it is one that seems hardly significant in light of the variation found within both modern humans and Neanderthals.

The extent to which the outside surface and overall shape of the brain can be appreciated by looking at the inside of the skull is controversial, as is the utility of doing so. Casts of the inside of a cranium are known as endocasts, and have been examined to assess the similarities and differences between human and Neanderthal brains (Holloway 1985). But such evidence is limited and tells us nothing about how the billions of neurons inside are connected. Nevertheless, two observations suggest that the Neanderthal brain may have had the neural networks necessary for some type of spoken language.

We know from studies of modern humans that have suffered injury to the left hemisphere of their brain that this region is where key elements of the neural activity for language take place. This 'lateralization' of activity in modern humans appears to be reflected in the predominance of right-handedness in the population. The Neanderthals also appear to have been predominantly right-handed. This is indicated by the muscle attachments on the bones from their right side being larger, suggesting greater use, and by the direction of accidental cut marks from stone tools on their teeth. These show that meat, hide, and other materials had been predominantly cut by the right hand while being held in the teeth (Stringer and Gamble 1993). This right-handedness suggests that the Neanderthal brain might have been lateralized to the same extent as our's today. And that might suggest that the left hemisphere had become specialized for language.

In the 1850s Paul Broca identified one specific area of the left hemisphere as being vital to speech, this becoming named as Broca's area. This area can be identified on endocasts and appears prominent on those of *H. habilis*, leading some to argue that speech had begun to evolve 2 million years ago. Broca's area is as developed on Neanderthal endocasts as in those of modern humans (Holloway 1985). But we cannot take this as conclusive evidence for Neanderthal speech. By the use of brain-scanning technology, we now know that Broca's area is used for fine motor control—essential not only for speech but for tasks such as making stone tools. Moreover, the studies of brain activity have shown that the capacity for language is reliant on neural networks distributed throughout the brain (Lieberman 2001). Unfortunately, anthropologists have no opportunity to assess whether these networks were present in the Neanderthal brain from study of endocasts. But the mere size of the Neanderthal brain suggests some form of linguistic capacity is likely to have been present, even if one far less complex than that of modern humans.

4.3. Did the Neanderthals make and use visual symbols?

This is where a key problem with Neanderthal artifacts arises. The anatomical evidence indicates that they had the capacity for some type of spoken language—for the use of audible symbols. Should we not expect, therefore, that Neanderthals were also making and using visual symbols? Surely this must be a necessary consequence of possessing language. And yet, after more than 100 years of excavation and meticulous study, we have no convincing evidence that the Neanderthals made any visual symbols at all.

We have many, many thousands of stone artifacts, together with a few bone tools, fireplaces, and a great deal of food debris. All of these might have had symbolic meanings for the Neanderthals. But without any examples of representational or abstract art, it seems more likely that such meanings were completely absent. If so, it suggests that Neanderthals lacked a capacity for symbolism, and hence challenges the notion that they possessed spoken language.

Some archaeologists, such as Bednarik (1992, 1995), Mania and Mania (1998), and Marshack (1990, 1997) dispute the absence of representational and abstract art in the Neanderthal archaeological record, and indeed in that of *H. heidelbergensis* and earlier species. Several pieces of stone and bone have scratches on their surfaces which might have been deliberately made and which have no evident utilitarian function. But the lack of both unambiguous representational images and abstract patterns that are repeated so as to suggest the existence of a symbolic code leads most archaeologists to reject the idea of Neanderthal symbolism (Chase and Dibble 1987; Davidson 1992; Mithen 1998).

A Neanderthal capacity for symbolic thought has also been proposed on the basis of a small number of archaeological sites dating to the very end of the Neanderthal occupation in France, 35,000–30,000 years ago. These have stone tools and pieces of carved bone with similarities to those made by the incoming modern humans. These collections are know as the 'Châtelperronian culture' (Mellars 1996).

The Neanderthals and modern humans made their stone tools by using different techniques of knapping to produce flakes. They then turned the flakes into quite differently shaped tools by delicate chipping of their edges. Some of the final Neanderthals maintained their traditional methods of flake production but turned their flakes into the typical tool types made by modern humans. Moreover, they started carving animal bones into beads which, if known to have been made by a modern human, would unquestionably be attributed with having a symbolic meaning.

The most convincing interpretation of the 'Châtelperronian culture' is that the Neanderthals were imitating the behaviour of modern humans (Harrold 1989). The new arrivals in the valleys of south-west Europe must have been watched very closely by the indigenous population. One can readily imagine the Neanderthals visiting the abandoned campsites of modern humans and examining their discarded stone and bone tools. Similarly, the sight of the new arrivals wearing beads and pendants must have been striking. And so the Neanderthals might have copied what they saw, especially when they became aware that the modern humans were particularly effective hunters and gatherers. I suspect that the Neanderthals made and wore beads without appreciating that those worn by modern humans were imbued with social information and symbolic meanings.

While such acculturation is the most widely held viewpoint amongst archaeologists, some argue that the Neanderthals of Europe invented their new stone tools and began to make beads before the modern humans had appeared on the horizon. Francesco D'Errico and his colleagues are the main proponents of this view (D'Errico *et al.* 1998). They claim that all of the Châtelperronian sites date prior to the first appearance of modern humans in the region, and that the methods of carving bone are so distinctive that they cannot be explained by imitation of modern humans.

Their arguments are unconvincing (Mellars 1998, 2000) and slightly bizarre. The archaeological dating methods are simply insufficient to determine whether Châtelperronian tools were made just before or just after modern humans arrived. Archaeologists rely on the method of radiocarbon dating, which can only ever provide approximate dates. At around 30,000 years ago the most accurate date will still lie within a window of several hundreds, if not thousands, of years in scope.

In this light, it seems implausible that after 200,000 years in Europe the Neanderthals not only suddenly began to make beads and new types of tools just before the modern humans arrived, but chose the same designs that the modern humans would be using. Imitation is a far more reasonable argument. We should expect that the specific techniques used by Neanderthals will differ to those of the modern humans—the Neanderthals were imitating the idea of carving bone and wearing beads. I am sure that they did so while being quite unaware of the latent symbolic potency of body decoration.

4.4. Stasis in cultural evolution

The Neanderthals had immense technical skill, most evident from their manufacture of levallois points and handaxes. Both the levallois and bifacial techniques have been replicated by modern flint-knappers—people who have specialized in making prehistoric tools for museum displays and to aid academic research. Both techniques take several years of practice to perfect, the levallois method being particularly difficult to acquire, so that even the most experienced modern flint-knapper can struggle to make the type of flake that Neanderthals produced on a routine basis.

The Neanderthals employed a variety of additional stone-tool making methods, often adopting that most appropriate to the type of stone nodules available. When working relatively small pebbles they produced 'disc cores' by removing flakes sequentially around the circumference of the nodule (e.g. the Pontinian of Central Italy, Kuhn 1995). When large, fine-quality blocks of stone were available, the Neanderthals could make elegant long, thin flakes of stone known as blades. These look almost identical to those produced by modern humans who replaced the Neanderthals in Europe (Mellars 1996). But whereas such blades formed the basis for the whole technology of modern humans, Neanderthals made them on rare occasions. The pattern of Neanderthal tool-making is one in which several different techniques were used, but without any technological progress through time. The Neanderthals appear to have simply responded to the current environmental conditions with the most appropriate technology they could muster (Mithen 1996). The so-called 'ratchet effect', whereby one generation builds upon the technological achievements of the former (Tomasello, Kruger, and Ratner 1993), did not exist amongst the Neanderthals. So if we find a Neanderthal levallois flake, disc core, or handaxe without any supporting evidence, we have very little idea about when in the 200,000 years or more of Neanderthal existence it had been made.

This stasis in technology appears very odd if the Neanderthals were language-using people. If they used spoken language to pass on information about tool-making to their peers or the next generation we would expect there to be some directional change in their technology—a gradual improvement in tool-making and the introduction of new techniques. It is remarkable that, although the Neanderthals lived in harsh environments, suffered regular hunting injuries, and had large brains, they didn't invent the use of bows and arrows or spear-throwers. Both would have allowed hunting at a distance and protected Neanderthals from potential injury. If ever there was a population in need of some creative thought about technology it was the Neanderthals. And yet, just like their ancestors, they continued to use the same basic toolkit for almost a quarter-of-a-million years and through periods of immense environmental change.

During the warm period of Neanderthal existence around 115,000 years ago, when woodland spread across the landscape, we have no evidence for the use of grinding stones, pestles, and mortars for the efficient exploitation of plant foods. Modern humans were very quick to invent such tools when they found themselves in similar environments 10,000 years ago. Similarly, during the coldest periods of the Ice Age there is no evidence that the Neanderthals used bone needles to make better clothing, something that modern humans were quick to do. In summary, the Neanderthals appear to be astonishingly limited in their capacity to invent new technology, for a human species with such a large and expensive brain. How could they have continued for more than 200,000 years with the same repertoire of tools? Perhaps the absence of creative thought is a direct reflection of the absence of spoken language.

4.5. Language, thought, and the Neanderthal mind

The relationship between language and thought has been discussed by philosophers and psychologists for many years. A widespread view is that modern humans are only able to think creatively—enabling, amongst other things, the invention of new technology—because we have language. This implies the converse: the absence of creative thought implies the absence of language. The philosopher Daniel Dennett (1991) has explained how spoken language acts as 'self-stimulation'—it helps one to appreciate what one already knows and how to put that knowledge to good use. We see this most clearly with young children, who often talk themselves through tasks such as learning to tie their shoes. And we frequently do that ourselves, both out loud and 'in our heads' when facing particularly difficult problems. The Neanderthals certainly had the knowledge inside their heads to make an immense assortment of new tools; but they seem to have been unaware of their own knowledge, and that may have been because they lacked the words to express it.

Another means by which spoken language leads to creative thought is by the sharing of ideas—the linking of one mind to another. The philosopher Andy Clark has written eloquently about the impact that language makes in this regard: 'an idea that only Joe's prior experience could make available, but that can flourish only in the intellectual niche currently provided by the brain of Mary, can now realise its full potential by journeying between Joe and Mary as and when required. The path to a good idea can now criss-cross individual learning histories...' (Clark 1996, 206). It is difficult to reconcile this role of language with the stasis in Neanderthal culture. Imagine Neanderthals sitting around their fireplaces and talking about the tools they were making, hunts being prepared, social relationships, and so forth. New ideas would effortlessly arise, resulting in new and improved tools rather than the cultural stasis that archaeologists have found.

How, therefore, can we reconcile the evident technical skill, large brain, and evolved vocal tract of the Neanderthals with the lack of technological innovation? The only way is by invoking a strikingly different type of mind to that of modern humans. Rather than having a cognitively fluid mind, the Neanderthals appear to have had a domain-specific mentality. I have previously suggested that the Neanderthal mind had three core intelligences relating to social behaviour, the natural world, and technology (Mithen 1996). Each contained a store of knowledge and ways of thinking for addressing problems in its own particular domain; but these were unavailable for use by any other intelligence—quite unlike the cognitively fluid mind of modern humans.

This 'domain-specific' mentality explains why the Neanderthals appear so intelligent in some ways and so limited in others. The Neanderthals had, for instance, the same amount of technical skill for making stone artifacts as modern humans. Similarly, they knew just as much about animal behaviour—all hunter-gatherers have to be good zoologists. But unlike modern humans, they could not combine their knowledge about tool-making and animals together to design specialized hunting weapons. I used the same argument to explain why Neanderthals were unable to make beads, create art, or believe in supernatural beings. All of these required what I termed 'cognitive fluidity'—the mixing of knowledge and ways of thinking that had once been isolated in separate mental domains.

5. CREATIONS OF PRE-MODERN HUMAN MINDS

Oldowan flakes, handaxes, and levallois points are creations of three quite different types of pre-modern minds. *Homo habilis* is aptly described as a bipedal, meat-eating primate, a species whose technology is much closer to that of modern-day chimpanzees than modern humans. Although the techniques required to make Oldowan-like stone flakes may be beyond the mental capacities of present-day apes, *H. habilis* made sharp-edged flakes and robust chopping tools without any imposition of a preconceived form. Some were carried around the landscape, but they are all unlikely to have had any social or symbolic significance.

The handaxes made by *H. heidelbergensis*, and other pre-modern species such as *H. ergaster* and *H. neanderthalensis*, were markedly different from Oldowan artifacts because a specific form was frequently imposed onto the nodule of stone. They required more time and skill to manufacture, especially if one accounts for the acquisition of good-quality stone and preparation of hammers from a variety of materials. Handaxes are the first types of artifacts made by *Homo* to have an aesthetic quality. This may relate to their use in social strategies for acquiring mates. Yet, like Oldowan tools, handaxes appear to have been general-purpose artifacts with a predominant use in animal butchery. Of all the artifacts that archaeologists consider, these remain the most enigmatic—as does the type of mind that created them.

Although some Neanderthals made handaxes similar to those of *H. heidelbergensis*, their artifacts were predominantly made on flakes. These were produced by a variety of techniques, the most complex being the levallois method which required greater technical skill and forethought than the manufacture of handaxes that used the bifacial technique. On some occasions the levallois method was used to produce pointed artifacts to haft onto spears without requiring any further preparation. Unlike the projectile points of modern humans, there is no evidence that levallois points were imbued with social information or symbolic meanings. Neanderthal technology also differs from that of modern humans by its marked lack of directional change. For a quarter-of-a-million years the same range of techniques was used and artifacts produced, even though this was a period of substantial climatic change. Our experience of modern human technology suggests that technical skill and technological innovation go hand in hand with each other—if the first is present one expects to find the second. Neanderthal technology informs us that this was not always the case in human evolution.

With the appearance of modern humans at 130,000 years ago, technology begins to acquire new characteristics—a reflection of emergent cognitive fluidity (Mithen 1996). The first artifacts appear that can be confidently attributed with having social and symbolic significance (D'Errico, Henshilwood, and Nilssen 2001). Technological change begins to acquire a new dynamic. This remains limited until after 50,000 years ago, a date that many archaeologists recognize as a major threshold in human culture—the Middle/Upper Palaeolithic transition (Bar-Yosef 1998). This date most probably marks a demographic threshold after which population densities and the links between communities are sufficient for new innovations to arise, to become accepted, and to spread (Shennan 2001). The rate of innovation and technological change increases even more markedly after 20,000 years ago, as this marks the last major turnaround in global climate—the start of increasing warmth and rainfall after the last glacial maximum which peaks at around 10,000 years ago. That date marks the start of the Holocene and coincides with the start of farming (Bar-Yosef 1998). This provided the economic base for craft specialists and a further increase in the rate of technological innovation. The combination of cognitive fluidity, dense population, and the economic basis of farming created the type of artifacts and rates of technological change that we are familiar with in the modern world. As I have described in this chapter, these are quite peculiar for the genus *Homo*: human ancestors and relatives had spent 2 million years producing radically different types of artifacts, as epitomized by Oldowan flakes, handaxes, and levallois points.

References

ABBOTT, B. (1989). Nondescriptionality and natural kind terms. *Linguistics and Philosophy*, 12: 269–91.

——— (1997). A note on the nature of 'water'. *Mind*, 106: 311–19.

——— (2000). Water = H_2O. *Mind*, 108: 145–8.

AGUIAR, A. and BAILLARGEON, R. (1998). Eight-and-a-half-month-old infants' reasoning about containment events. *Child Development*, 69.3: 636–53.

AGUIRRE, G. K., ZARAHN, E., and D'ESPOSITO, M. (1998). An area within human ventral cortex sensitive to 'building' stimuli: Evidence and implications. *Neuron*, 21: 373–83.

AHN, W-K. (1998). Why are different features central for natural kinds and artifacts? *Cognition*, 69: 135–78.

——— (1999). The effect of causal structure on category construction. *Memory & Cognition*, 27: 1008–23.

——— and KIM, N. S. (2000). The causal status effect in categorization: an overview. In D. L. Medin (ed.), *The Psychology of Learning and Motivation: Advances in Research and Theory*, Vol. 40 (pp. 23–65). Academic Press.

——— and MEDIN, D. L. (1992). A two-stage model of category construction. *Cognitive Science*, 16: 81–121.

——— KIM, N. S., LASSALINE, M. E., and DENNIS, M. J. (2000). Causal status as a determinant of feature centrality. *Cognitive Psychology*, 41: 361–416.

——— KALISH, C. B., GELMAN, S. A., MEDIN, D. L., LUHMANN, C. A., ATRAN, S. E., COLEY, J. F., and SHAFTO, P. F. (2001). Why essences are essential in the psychology of concepts. *Cognition*, 82: 59–69.

AIELLO, L. C. and DUNBAR, R. I. M. (1993). Neocortex size, group size, and the evolution of language. *Current Anthropology*, 34: 184–93.

——— and WHEELER, P. (1995). The expensive-tissue hypothesis. *Current Anthropology*, 36: 199–220.

ALLEN, C., BEKOFF, M., and LAUDER, G. (1998). *Nature's Purposes: Analyses of Function and Design in Biology*. MIT Press.

ALLPORT, D. A. (1985). Distributed memory, modular subsystems and dysphasia. In S. Newman and R. Repstein (eds.), *Current Perspectives in Dysphasia*. Churchill Livingstone.

ALP, R. (1997). 'Stepping-sticks' and 'seat-sticks': New types of tools used by wild chimpanzees (*Pan troglodytes*) in Sierra Leone. *American Journal of Primatology*, 41: 45–52.

ANDERSON, R. C. and ORTONY, A. (1975). On putting apples into bottles: a problem of polysemy. *Cognitive Psychology*, 7: 167–80.

ARENSBURG, B., SCHEPARTZ, L. A., TILLER, A. M., VANDERMEERSCH, B., DUDAY, H., and RAK, Y. (1990). A reappraisal of the anatomical evidence for speech in Middle Palaeolithic hominids. *American Journal of Physical Anthropology*, 83: 137–46.

ARTERBERRY, M. E. and BORNSTEIN, M. H. (2001). Three-month-old infants' categorization of animals and vehicles based on static and dynamic attributes. *Journal of Experimental Child Psychology*, 80: 333–46.

ASFAW, B., BEYENE, Y., SUWA, G., WALTER, R. C., WHITE, T., WOLDEGABRIEL, G., and YEMANE, T. (1992). The earliest Acheulian from Konso-Gardula, Ethiopia. *Nature*, 360: 732–5.

ASHTON, N. M. and McNABB, J. (1994). Bifaces in perspective. In N. Ashton and A. David (eds.), *Stories in Stone* (pp. 182–91). *Lithics Studies Society Occasional Paper*, No. 4.

ASTUTI, R. (2001). Are we all natural dualists? A cognitive developmental approach. *The Malinowski Memorial Lecture. Journal of the Royal Anthropological Institute*, NS 7: 429–47.

—— SOLOMON, G., and CAREY, S. (2004). *Constraints on Conceptual Development: A Case Study of the Acquisition of Folkbiological and Folksociological Knowledge in Madagascar. Monograph of the Society for Research in Child Development*, 69.3.

ATRAN, S. (1990). *Cognitive Foundations of Natural History: Towards an Anthropology of Science*. Cambridge University Press.

—— (1998). Folk biology and the anthropology of science: cognitive universals and cultural particulars. *Behavioral and Brain Sciences*, 21: 547–609.

ATTENBOROUGH, D. (1998). *The Life of Birds*. Princeton University Press.

AUSTIN, L. (1994). The life and death of a Boxgrove biface. In N. Ashton and A. David (eds.), *Stories in Stone* (pp. 119–26). *Lithics Studies Society Occasional Paper No. 4*.

AYERS, M. (1997). Is *physical object* a sortal concept? A Reply to Xu. *Mind and Language*, 12.3/4: 393–405.

BAILLARGEON, R. (1993). The object concept revisited: new directions in the investigation of infant's physical knowledge. In C. Granrund (ed.), *Visual Perception and Cognition in Infancy* (pp. 265–315). Lawrence Erlbaum Associates.

—— (1998). Eight-and-a-half-month-old infants' reasoning about containment events. *Child Development*, 69: 636–53.

—— KOTOVSKY, L., and NEEDHAM, A. (1995). The acquisition of physical knowledge in infancy. In D. Sperber, D. Premack, and A. J. Premack (eds.), *Causal Cognition: A Multidisciplinary Debate*. Oxford University Press.

BALABAN, M. and WAXMAN, S. R. (1997). Do words facilitate object categorization in 9-month-old infants? *Journal of Experimental Child Psychology*, 64: 3–26.

BARBAROTTO, R., CAPITANI, E., and LAIACONA, M. (1996). Naming deficit in herpes simplex encephalitis. *Acta Neurologica Scandinavica*, 93.4: 272–80.

—— —— SPINNLER, H., and TRIVELLI, C. (1995). Slowly progressive semantic impairment with category specificity. *Neurocase*, 1: 107–19.

BARON-COHEN, S. (1995). *Mindblindness: An Essay on Autism and Theory of Mind*. MIT Press.

BARSALOU, L. W. (1982). Context-independent and context-dependent information in concepts. *Memory & Cognition*, 10: 82–93.

—— (1983). Ad hoc categories. *Memory & Cognition*, 11: 211–27.

—— (1987). The instability of graded structure: implications for the nature of concepts. In U. Neisser (ed.), *Concepts and Conceptual Development: Ecological and Intellectual Factors in Categorization* (pp. 101–40). Cambridge University Press.

BARSALOU, L. W. (1991). Deriving categories to achieve goals. In G. H. Bower (eds.), *The Psychology of Learning and Motivation: Advances in Research and Theory*, Vol. 27 (pp. 1–64). Academic Press.

BARSALOU, L. W. and MEDIN, D. L. (1986). Concepts: static definitions or context-dependent representations? *Cahiers de Psychology Cognitive*, 6: 187–202.

——— SLOMAN, S. A., and CHAIGNEAU, S. E. (2004). The HIPE Theory of Function. In L. Carlson and E. van der Zee (eds.), *Functional Features in Language and Space: Insights From Perception, Categorization, and Development* (pp. 131–48). Oxford University Press.

——— SIMMONS, W. K., BARBEY, A. K., and WILSON, C. D. (2003). Grounding conceptual knowledge in the modality-specific systems. *Trends in Cognitive Sciences*, 7: 84–91.

BAR-YOSEF, O. (1994). The contribution of S.W. Asia to the study of the origin of modern humans. In M. H. Nitecki and D. V.Nitecki (eds.), *Origin of Anatomically Modern Humans* (pp. 23–60). Plenum Press.

——— (1998). On the nature of transitions: the Middle to Upper Palaeolithic and the Neolithic revolution. *Cambridge Archaeological Journal*, 8: 141–63.

BASSO, A., CAPITANI, E., and LAIACONA, M. (1988). Progressive language impairment without dementia: a case study with isolated category-specific semantic defect. *Journal of Neurology, Neurosurgery, and Psychiatry*, 51: 1201–7.

BEAUCHAMP, M. S., LEE, K. E., HAXBY, J. V., and MARTIN, A. (2002). Parallel visual motion processing streams for manipulable objects and human movements. *Neuron*, 34: 149–59.

——— ——— ——— ——— (2003). FMRI responses to video and point-light displays of moving humans and manipulable objects. *Journal of Cognitive Neuroscience*, 15: 991–1001.

BEDNARIK, R. G. (1992). Palaeoart and archaeological myths. *Cambridge Archaeological Journal*, 2: 27–57.

——— (1995). Concept mediated marking in the Lower Palaeolithic. *Current Anthropology*, 36: 605–34.

BEHL-CHADHA, G. (1996). Superordinate-like categorical representations in early infancy. *Cognition*, 60: 104–41.

BERGMAN, C. A. and ROBERTS, M. B. (1988). Flaking technology at the Acheulian site of Boxgrove, West Sussex (England). *Revue Archeologique de Picardie*, 1–2: 105–13.

BERTENTHAL, B. (1993). Infants' perception of biomechanical motions: intrinsic image and knowledge-based constraints. In C. Granrud (ed.), *Visual Perception and Cognition in Infancy* (pp. 175–214). Lawrence Erlbaum Associates.

BICKERTON, D. (1996). *Language and Human Behaviour*. University College Press.

BINFORD, L. R. (1981). *Bones: Ancient Men and Modern Myths*. Academic Press.

——— (1986). Comment on 'Systematic butchery by Plio/Pleistocene hominids at Olduvai Gorge' by H. T. Bunn and E. M. Kroll. *Current Anthropology*, 27: 444–6.

BINKOFSKI, F., DOHLE, C., POSSE, S., STEPHAN, K., and HEFTER, H. (1998). Human anterior intraparietal area subserves prehension: a combined lesion-functional MRI activation study. *Neurology*, 50: 1253–9.

BLOCH, M., SOLOMON, G., and CAREY, S. (2001). Zafimaniry: an understanding of what is passed on from parents to children: a cross-cultural investigation. *Journal of Cognition and Culture*, 1: 43–68.

BLOCK, N. (1986). Advertisement for a semantics for psychology. In P. A. French, T. Uehling Jr., and H. Wettstein (eds.), *Midwest Studies in Philosophy, vol. 10: Studies in the Philosophy of Mind* (pp. 615–78). University of Minnesota Press.

—— (1997). Anti-reductionism slaps back. In J. Tomberlin (ed.), *Philosophical Perspectives 11: Mind, Causation and World* (pp. 107–31). Blackwell.

BLOOM, P. (1996). Intention, history, and artifact concepts. *Cognition*, 60: 1–29.

—— (1998). Theories of artifact categorization. *Cognition*, 66: 87–93.

—— (2000). *How Children Learn the Meanings of Words*. MIT Press.

—— (2004). *Descartes' Baby*. Basic Books.

—— and MARKSON, L. (1998). Intention and analogy in children's naming of pictorial representations. *Psychological Science*, 9: 200–4.

BLUMENSCHINE, R. J. (1986). *Early Hominid Scavenging Opportunities. British Archaeological Reports, International Series*, 283.

BOESCH, C. and BOESCH, H. (1984). Mental map in wild chimpanzees: an analysis of hammer transports for nut cracking. *Primates*, 25: 160–70.

—— —— (1989). Hunting behaviour of wild chimpanzees in the Taï National Park. *American Journal of Physical Anthropology*, 78: 547–73.

—— —— (1990). Tool-use and tool-making in wild chimpanzees. *Folia Primatologica*, 54: 86–99.

—— and BOESCH-ACHERMANN, H. (2000). *The Chimpanzees of the Tai Forest: Behavioural Ecology and Evolution*. Oxford University Press.

BOOKHEIMER, S. (2002). Functional MRI of language: new approaches to understanding the cortical organization of semantic processing. *Annual Review of Neuroscience*, 25: 151–88.

BORGO, F. and SHALLICE, T. (2001). When living things and other 'sensory-quality' categories behave in the same fashion: a novel category-specific effect. *Neurocase*, 7: 201–20.

BOSINSKI, G. (1996). Stone artefacts of the European Lower Palaeolithic. In W. Roebroeks and T. van Kolfschoten (eds.), *The Earliest Occupation of Europe* (pp. 263–7). *Analecta Praehistoria Leidensia, 27.*

BOYD, R. (1979). Metaphor and theory change: what is 'metaphor' a metaphor for? In A. Ortony (ed.), *Metaphor and Thought* (pp. 356–408). Cambridge University Press.

BRAIN, C. K. (1981). *The Hunters or the Hunted*. Chicago University Press.

BRAUER, M., CHATARD-PANNETIER, A., NIEDENTHAL, P., and CHAMBRES, P. (2003). The malleability of categories: influence of current goals on graded category structure and perceived typicality. Manuscript under review.

BREEDIN, S. D., MARTIN, N., and SAFFRAN, E. M. (1994). Category-specific semantic impairments: an infrequency occurrence? *Brain and Language*, 47: 383–6 (presented at the Academy of Aphasia conference, Cambridge, Mass., Oct. 1994).

BRENNAN, S. E. and CLARK, H. H. (1996). Conceptual pacts and lexical choice in conversation. *Journal of Experimental Psychology: Learning, Memory, and Cognition*, 22: 1482–93.

BROWN, A. (1990). Domain-specific principles affect learning and transfer in children. *Cognitive Science*, 14: 107–33.

BRUGMAN, C. (1983). *The Story of OVER*. Indiana University Linguistics Club.

BUDIANSKY, S. (2000). *The Truth About Dogs.* Penguin.

BUNN, H. T. (1981). Archaeological evidence for meat eating by Plio-Pleistocene hominids from Koobi Fora and Olduvai Gorge. *Nature,* 291: 574–7.

——and KROLL, E. M. (1986). Systematic butchery by Plio-Pleistocene hominids at Olduvai Gorge. *Current Anthropology,* 27: 431–52.

BURGE, T. (1979). Individualism and the mental. In P. French, T. Uehling Jr., and H. Wettstein (eds.), *Midwest Studies in Philosophy: Studies in Metaphysics* (pp. 73–122). University of Minnesota Press.

BUXBAUM, L. J. and SAFFRAN, E. M. (2002). Knowledge of object manipulation and object function: dissociations in apraxic and non-apraxic subjects. *Brain and Language,* 82: 179–99.

——VERAMONTI, T., and SCHWARTZ, M. F. (2000). Function and manipulation tool knowledge in apraxia: knowing 'what for' but not 'how'. *Neurocase,* 6: 83–97.

——SCHWARTZ, M. F., and CAREW, T. G. (1997). The role of semantic memory in object use. *Cognitive Neuropsychology,* 14.2: 219–54.

——SIRIGU, A., SCHWARTZ, M. F., and KLATZKY, R. (2003). Cognitive representations of hand posture in ideomotor apraxia. *Neuropsychologia,* 41: 1091–113.

BYRNE, A. and PRYOR, J. (2004). Bad Intensions. In M. García-Carpintero and J. Macià (eds.), *Two-Dimensional Semantics* (pp. 38–54). Oxford University Press.

BYRNE, R. and WHITEN, A. (1988). *Machiavellian Intelligence: Social Expertise and the Evolution of Intellect in Monkeys, Apes and Humans.* Clarendon Press.

CALVIN, W. (1993). The unitary hypothesis: a common neural circuitry for novel manipulations, language, plan-ahead and throwing. In K. R. Gibson and T. Ingold (eds.), *Tools, Language and Cognition in Human Evolution* (pp. 230–50). Cambridge University Press.

CAPITANI, E., LAIACONA, M., and BARBAROTTO, R. (1993). Dissociazioni Semantiche Intercategoriali. Parte II: Procedura Automatica di Analisi di una Batteria Standardizzata. *Archivio di Psicologia, Neurologia e Psichiatria,* 54: 457–76.

——————MAHON, B., and CARAMAZZA, A. (2003). What are the facts of category-specific deficits? A critical review of the clinical evidence. *Cognitive Neuropsychology,* 20: 213–62.

CARAMAZZA, A. and SHELTON, J. R. (1998). Domain specific knowledge systems in the brain: the animate–inanimate distinction. *Journal of Cognitive Neuroscience,* 10: 1–34.

——and MAHON, B. Z. (2003). The organization of conceptual knowledge: the evidence from category-specific semantic deficits. *Trends in Cognitive Sciences,* 7: 325–74.

——————(2006). The organization of conceptual knowledge in the brain: the future's past and some future directions. *Cognitive Neuropsychology,* 23: 13–38.

——HILLIS, A. E., RAPP, B. C., and ROMANI, C. (1990). The multiple semantics hypothesis: multiple confusions? *Cognitive Neuropsychology,* 7: 161–89.

CAREY, S. (1985). *Conceptual Change in Childhood.* MIT Press.

——(1988). Conceptual differences between children and adults. *Mind and Language,* 3: 167–81.

——Knowledge acquisition: enrichment or conceptual change. In S. Carey and R. Gelman (eds.), *The Epigenesis of Mind: Essays on Biology and Cognition* (pp. 257–69). Lawrence Erlbaum Associates.

___ (1994). Does learning a language require the child to reconceptualize the world? *Lingua*, 92: 143–67.

___ (1995). The growth of causal understandings of natural kinds. In D. Sperber, D. Premack, and A. J. Premack (eds.), *Causal Cognition: A Multidisciplinary Debate* (pp. 263–91). Oxford University Press.

___ (1996). Cognitive domains as modes of thought. In D. R. Olson and N. Torrance (eds.), *Modes of Thought: Explorations in Cognition and Culture* (pp. 187–215). Cambridge University Press.

___ (2000). The origins of concepts. *Journal of Cognition and Development*, 1.1: 37–41.

___ and SPELKE, E. (1994). Domain-specific knowledge and conceptual change. In L. A. Hirschfeld and S. A. Gelman (eds.), *Mapping the Mind: Domain Specificity in Cognition and Culture* (pp. 169–200). Cambridge University Press.

___ and MARKMAN, E. M. (1999). Cognitive development. In B. Bly and D. Rumelhart (eds.), *Cognitive Science: Handbook of Perception and Cognition*, 2nd edn. (pp. 201–54). Academic Press.

CARON, A. J., CARON, R. F., and ANTELL, S. E. (1988). Infant understanding of containment: an affordance perceived or a relationship conceived? *Developmental Psychology*, 24: 620–7.

CARPENTER, M., CALL, J., and TOMASELLO, M. (2002). Understanding 'prior intentions' enables 2-year-olds to imitatively learn a complex task. *Child Development*, 73: 1431–41.

___ NAGELL, K., and TOMASELLO, M. (1998). *Social Cognition, Joint Attention, and Communicative Competence from 9- to 15-Months of Age. Monographs of the Society for Research in Child Development*, 63.

CARTWRIGHT, R. (1975). Scattered objects. In id., *Philosophical Essays* (pp. 171–86). MIT Press.

CARVER, L. J., and BAUER, P. J. (2001). The dawning of a past: the emergence of long-term explicit memory in infancy. *Journal of Experimental Psychology: General*, 130: 726–45.

CASLER, K. and KELEMEN, D. (2005). Young children's rapid learning about artifacts. *Developmental Science*, 8: 472–80.

___ ___ (2006). Reasoning about artifacts at 24 months: the developing teleofunctional stance. *Cognition* (in press).

CASTELLI, F., HAPPÉ, F., FRITH, U., and FRITH, C. (2000). Movement and mind: a functional imaging study of perception and interpretation of complex intentional movement patterns. *NeuroImage*, 12: 314–25.

___ FRITH, C., HAPPÉ, F., and FRITH, U. (2002). Autism, Asperger Syndrome and brain mechanisms for the attribution of mental states to animated shapes. *Brain*, 125: 1839–49.

CHANDLER, M., FRITZ, A. S., and HALA, S. (1989). Small-scale deceit: deception as a marker of two-, three-, and four-year-olds' early theories of mind. *Child Development*, 60: 1263–77.

CHAO, L. L. and MARTIN, A. (2000). Representation of manipulable man-made objects in the dorsal stream. *NeuroImage*, 12: 478–84.

___ HAXBY, J. V., and MARTIN, A. (1999). Attribute-based neural substrates in posterior temporal cortex for perceiving and knowing about objects. *Nature Neuroscience*, 2: 913–19.

CHAO, L. L., MARTIN, A., and HAXBY, J. V. (1999). Are face-responsive regions selective only for faces? *Neuroreport*, 10: 2945–50.

——WEISBERG, J., and MARTIN, A. (2002). Experience-dependent modulation of category-related cortical activity. *Cerebral Cortex*, 12: 545–51.

CHAPPELL, J., and KACELNIK, A. (2002). Tool selectivity in a non-primate, the New Caledonian crow (*Corvus moneduloides*). *Animal Cognition*, 5: 71–8.

CHASE, P. and DIBBLE, H. (1987). Middle Palaeolithic symbolism: a review of current evidence and interpretations. *Journal of Anthropological Archaeology*, 6: 263–93.

CHENEY, D. L. and SEYFARTH, R. M. (1990). *How Monkeys See the World: Inside the Mind of Another Species*. Chicago University Press.

CHIARA, M. L. D. and DI FRANCIA, G. T. (1995). Quine on physical objects. In P. Leonardi and M. Santambrogio (eds.), *On Quine: New Essays* (pp. 104–12). Cambridge University Press.

CHI, M., GLASER, R., and REES, E. (1982). Expertise in problem solving. In R. Sternberg (ed.), *Advances in the Psychology of Human Intelligence*. Lawrence Erlbaum Associates.

CHOMSKY, N. (1995). Language and nature. *Mind*, 104: 1–61.

CHURCHILL, S. (1998). Adaptation, heterochrony and Neanderthals. *Evolutionary Anthropology*, 7: 46–61.

CLARK, A. (1996). *Being There: Putting Brain, Body and World Together Again*. MIT Press.

CLARK, H. H. and WILKES-GIBBS, D. (1986). Referring as a collaborative process. *Cognition*, 22: 1–39.

COLLARD, M. and AIELLO, L. C. (2000). From forelimbs to two legs. *Nature*, 404: 339–40.

COLLIAS, N. and COLLIAS, E. (1984). *Nest Building and Bird Behavior*. Princeton University Press.

COLLINGWOOD, R. G. (1938). *The Principles of Art*. Oxford University Press.

COMSTOCK, J. H. (1940). *The Spiders*. Cornell University Press.

CORBETTA, M., MIEZIN, F. M., DOBMEYER, S., SHULMAN, G. L., and PETERSEN, S. E. (1990). Attentional modulation of neural processing of shape, color, and velocity in humans. *Science*, 248: 1556–9.

COSMIDES, L. and TOOBY, J. (1994). Origins of domain specificity: the evolution of functional organization. In L. A. Hirschfeld and S. A. Gelman (eds.), *Mapping the Mind: Domain Specificity in Cognition and Culture* (pp. 85–116). Cambridge University Press.

CREE, G. S. and McRAE, K. (2003). Analyzing the factors underlying the structure and computation of the meaning of Chipmunk, Cherry, Chisel, Cheese, and Cello (and many other such concrete nouns). *Journal of Experimental Psychology: General*, 132.2: 163–201.

CRUTCH, S. J. and WARRINGTON, E. K. (2003). The selective impairment of fruit and vegetable knowledge: a multiple processing channels account of fine-grain category specificity. *Cognitive Neuropsychology*, 20: 355–73.

CSIBRA, G. and GERGELY, G. (1998). The teleological origins of mentalistic action explanations: a developmental hypothesis. *Developmental Science*, 1: 255–59.

——BÍRÓ, S., KOÓS, O., and GERGELY, G. (2003). One-year-old infants use teleological representations of actions productively. *Cognitive Science*, 27: 111–33.

_____ GERGELY, G., BÍRÓ, S., KOÓS, O., and BROCKBANK, M. (1999). Goal attribution without agency cues: the perception of 'pure reason' in infancy. *Cognition*, 72: 237–67.

CUBELLI, R., MARCHETTI, C., BOSCOLO, G., and DELLA SALA, S. (2000). Cognition in action: testing a model of limb apraxia. *Brain and Cognition*, 44: 144–65.

DARWIN, C. (1872). *The Origin of Species*, 6th edn. John Murray.

DAVIDSON, I. (1992). There's no art—to find the mind's construction—in offence (reply to R. Bednarik). *Cambridge Archaeological Journal*, 2: 52–7.

DAVIDSON, N. S. and GELMAN, S. A. (1990). Inductions from novel categories: the role of language and conceptual structure. *Cognitive Development*, 5: 151–76.

DAWKINS, R. (1976). *The Selfish Gene*. Oxford University Press.

_____ (1982). *The Extended Phenotype*. Oxford University Press.

DEACON, T. (1997). *The Symbolic Species*. Allen Lane.

DECETY, J., PERANI, G., JEANNEROD, M., BETTINARDI, V., TADARY, B., WOODS, R., MAZZIOTTA, J. C., and FAZIO, F. (1994). Mapping motor representations with positron emission tomography. *Nature*, 371: 600–2.

DEFEYTER, M. (2003). Acquiring an understanding of design: evidence from functional fixedness problems and verbal fluency tasks. Unpublished doctoral dissertation. University of Essex.

_____ and GERMAN, T. (2003). Acquiring an understanding of design: evidence from children's insight problem-solving. *Cognition*, 89: 133–55.

DEIPOLYI, A., SANTOS, L., and HAUSER, M. D. (1999). The role of landmarks in cotton-top tamarin spatial foraging: evidence for geometric and non-geometric features. *Animal Cognition*, 4: 99–108.

DENNETT, D. (1987). *The Intentional Stance*. MIT Press.

_____ (1990). The interpretation of texts, people and other artifacts. *Philosophy and Phenomenological Research*, 50: 177–94.

_____ (1991). *Consciousness Explained*. Penguin.

D'ERRICO, F., HENSHILWOOD, C., and NILSSEN, P. (2001). An engraved bone fragment from ca. 75 kyr Middle Stone Age levels at Blombos Cave, South Africa: implications for the origin of symbolism and language. *Antiquity*, 75: 309–18.

_____ ZILHAO, J., JULIEN, M., BAFFIER, D., and PELEGIN, J. (1998). Neanderthal acculturation in Western Europe? A critical review of the evidence and its interpretation. *Current Anthropology*, 39: 1–44.

Devitt, M. (1991). *Realism and Truth*, 2nd edn. Princeton University Press.

_____ and STERELNY, K. (1999). *Language and Reality*, 2nd edn. MIT Press.

DEVLIN, J. T., GONNERMAN, L. M., ANDERSON, E. S., and SEIDENBERG, M. S. (1998). Category-specific semantic deficits in focal and widespread brain damage: a computational account. *Journal of Cognitive Neuroscience*, 10.1: 77–94.

_____ RUSSELL, R. P., DAVIES, M. H., PRICE, C. J., MOSS, H. E., FADILI, M. J., and TYLER, L. K. (2002). Is there an anatomical basis for category-specificity? Semantic memory studies in PET and fMRI. *Neuropsychologia*, 40: 54–75.

DEWEY, J. (1934). *Art as Experience*. G. P. Putnam.

DIESENDRUCK, G. and GELMAN, S. (1999). Domain difference in absolute judgments of category membership: evidence for an essentialist account of categorization. *Psychonomic Bulletin and Review*, 6: 338–46.

DIESENDRUCK, G., MARKSON, L., and BLOOM, P. (2003). Children's reliance on creator's intent in extending names for artifacts. *Psychological Science*, 14: 164–8.

DIXON, M. J., PISKOPOS, K., and SCHWEIZER, T. A. (2000). Musical instrument naming impairments: the crucial exception to the living/nonliving dichotomy in category specific agnosia. *Brain and Cognition*, 43: 158–64.

DIYANNI, C. and KELEMAN, D. (2005). Time to get a new mountain: the role of function in children's conceptions of natural kinds. *Cognition*, 97.3: 327–35.

DIYANNI, C. (2006). Using a bad tool with good intention: how preschoolers weigh physical and intentional cues when learning about artifacts. Unpublished doctoral dissertation. Boston University.

DIYANNI, C. and KELEMEN, D. (2006). Using a bad tool with good intention: how preschoolers weigh physical and intentional cues when learning about artifacts. Manuscript in submission.

DONNELLAN, K. (1966). Reference and definite descriptions. *Philosophical Review*, 75: 281–304.

DUMONT, C., SKA, B., and JOANETTE, Y. (2000). Conceptual apraxia and semantic memory deficit in Alzheimer's disease: two sides of the same coin? *Journal of International Neuropsychological Society*, 6: 693–703.

DUNBAR, R. I. M. (1993). Coevolution of neocortical size, group size and language in primates. *Behavioral and Brain Sciences*, 16: 681–735.

——— (1996). *Grooming, Gossip and the Evolution of Language*. Faber & Faber.

DUPRÉ, J. (1993). *The Disorder of Things: Metaphysical Foundations of the Disunity of Science*. Harvard University Press.

ELDER, C. (1983). The case against irrealism. *American Philosophical Quarterly*, 20: 239–53.

——— (1986). Why the attacks on the way the world is entail there is a way the world is. *Philosophia*, 16: 191–202.

——— (1989). Realism, naturalism, and culturally generated kinds. *Philosophical Quarterly*, 39: 425–44.

——— (1992). An epistemological defense of realism about necessity. *Philosophical Quarterly*, 42: 317–36.

——— (1994). Laws, natures, and contingent necessities. *Philosophy and Phenomenological Research*, 54: 649–67.

——— (1995). A different kind of natural kind. *Australasian Journal of Philosophy*, 73: 516–31.

——— (1996). On the reality of medium-sized objects. *Philosophical Studies*, 83: 191–211.

——— (1998). Essential properties and coinciding objects. *Philosophy and Phenomenological Research*, 58: 317–31.

——— (2003). Kripkean externalism versus conceptual analysis. *Facta Philosophica*, 5.1: 75–86.

——— (2004). *Real Natures and Familiar Objects*. MIT Press.

EPSTEIN, R. and KANWISHER, N. (1998). A cortical representation of the local visual environment. *Nature*, 392: 598–601.

ERESHEFSKY, M. (2001). *The Poverty of the Linnaean Hierarchy: A Philosophical Study of Biological Taxonomy*. Cambridge University Press.

—— (2006). Species. In E. Zalta (ed.), *The Stanford Encyclopedia of Philosophy* (Fall 2006 edn.). http://plato.stanford.edu/entries/species.

EVANS, E. M. (2000). Beyond scopes: why creationism is here to stay. In K. S. Rosengren, C. N. Johnson, and P. L. Harris (eds.), *Imagining the Impossible: Magical, Scientific, and Religious Thinking in Children* (pp. 305–33). Cambridge University Press.

—— (2001). Cognitive and contextual factors in the emergence of diverse belief systems: creation versus evolution. *Cognitive Psychology*, 42: 217–66.

EVANS, G. (1973). The causal theory of names. *Aristotelian Society Supplementary Volume*, 47: 187–208.

FABRE, J. H. (1916). *Life of the Caterpillar.* Dodd, Mead, & Co.

FARAH, M. J. and WALLACE, M. A. (1992). Semantically bounded anomia: implication for the neural implementation of naming. *Neuropsychologia*, 30: 609–21.

—— and RABINOWITZ, C. (2003). Genetic and environmental influences on the organization of semantic memory in the brain: is 'living things' an innate category? *Cognitive Neuropsychology*, 20: 401–8.

—— RANEY, G. E., and BOYER, M. E. (1992). Knowledge, concepts, and inferences in childhood. *Child Development*, 63: 673–91.

—— HAMMOND, K. M., MEHTA, Z., and RATCLIFF, G. (1989). Category-specificity and modality-specificity in semantic memory. *Neuropsychologia*, 27: 193–200.

FODOR, J. A. (1990). A theory of content. In id., *A Theory of Content and Other Essays.* MIT Press.

—— (1991). Information and representation. In P. Hanson (ed.), *Information, Language and Cognition* (pp. 175–90). Oxford University Press.

—— (1998). *Concepts: Where Cognitive Science Went Wrong.* Oxford University Press.

—— and PYLYSHYN, Z. (1988). Connectionism and cognitive architecture: a critical reanalysis. *Cognition*, 28: 3–71.

FRANKS, F. (1982). *Polywater.* MIT Press.

FRISCH, K. v. (1967). *The Dance Language and Orientation of Honey Bees.* Harvard University Press.

—— (1974). *Animal Architecture.* Harcourt Brace Jovanovich.

FRYE, D., RAWLING, P., MOORE, C., and MYERS, I. (1983). Object–person discrimination and communication at 3 and 10 months. *Developmental Psychology*, 19: 303–9.

FUNNELL, E. and SHERIDAN, J. (1992). Categories of knowledge? Unfamiliar aspects of living and nonliving things. *Cognitive Neuropsychology*, 9: 135–53.

GAILLARD, M. J., AUZOU, P., MIRET, M., OZSANCAK, C., and HANNEQUIN, D. (1998). Trouble de la dénomination pour les objets manufacturés dans un cas d'encéphalite herpétique. *Révue Neurologique*, 154: 683–9.

GALLESE, V. and GOLDMAN, A. (1998). Mirror neurons and the simulation theory of mind reading. *Trends in Cognitive Sciences*, 2: 493–501.

GALLISTEL, C. R. (1990). *The Organization of Learning.* MIT Press.

GARRARD, P., LAMBON-RALPH, M. A., HODGES, J. R., and PATTERSON, K. (2001). Prototypicality, distinctiveness and intercorrelation: analyses of semantic attributes of living and nonliving concepts. *Cognitive Neuropsychology*, 18: 125–74.

GELMAN, R., DURGIN, F., and KAUFMAN, L. (1995). Distinguishing between animates and inanimates: not by motion alone. In D. Sperber, D. Premack, and A. Premack (eds.), *Causal Cognition: A Multidisciplinary Debate* (pp. 150–84). Clarendon Press.

GELMAN, S. A. (1988). The development of induction within natural kind and artifact categories. *Cognitive Psychology*, 20: 65–95.

—— (2003). *The Essential Child*. Oxford University Press.

—— and MARKMAN, E. M. (1986). Categories and induction in young children. *Cognition*, 23: 183–209.

—— and O'REILLY, A. W. (1988). Children's inductive inferences within superordinate categories: the role of language and category structure. *Child Development*, 59: 876–87.

—— and KREMER, K. E. (1991). Understanding natural cause: Children's explanations of how objects and their properties originate. *Child Development*, 62: 396–414.

—— and EBELING, K. (1998). Shape and representational status in children's early naming. *Cognition*, 66: 835–47.

—— and HIRSCHFELD, L. A. (1999). How biological is essentialism? In S. Atran and D. Medin (eds.), *Folkbiology* (pp. 403–46). MIT Press.

—— and BLOOM, P. (2000). Young children are sensitive to how an object was created when deciding what to name it. *Cognition*, 76: 91–103.

—— COLEY, J. D., and GOTTFRIED, G. M. (1994). Essentialist beliefs in children: the acquisition of concepts and theories. In L. A. Hirschfeld and S. A. Gelman (eds.), *Mapping the Mind: Domain Specificity in Cognition and Culture* (pp. 341–65). Cambridge University Press.

—— COLLMAN, P., and MACCOBY, E. E. (1986). Inferring properties from categories versus inferring categories from properties: the case of gender. *Child Development*, 57: 396–404.

—— COLEY, J., ROSENGREN, K. S., HARTMAN, E., and PAPPAS, A. (1998). *Beyond Labeling: The Role of Maternal Input in the Acquisition of Richly Structured Categories. Monographs of the Society for Research in Child Development*, 63.

GENDEL, P. A. (1984). *Mesolithic Social Territories in North-Western Europe. British Archaeological Reports, International Series*, 218.

GENTNER, D. (1978). A study of early word meaning using artificial objects: what looks like a jiggy but acts like a zimbo? *Papers and Reports on Child Language Development*, 15, 1–6 (Repr. in J. Gardner (1982). *Readings in Developmental Psychology*, 2nd edn. (pp. 137–42) Little, Brown & Co.).

—— (1982). Why nouns are learned before verbs: linguistic relativity versus natural partitioning. In S. A. Kuczaj II (ed.), *Language Development, Vol. 2. Language, Thought, and Culture* (pp. 301–34). Lawrence Erlbaum Associates.

GERGELY, G., BEKKERING, H., and KIRÁLY, I. (2002). Rational imitation in preverbal infants. *Nature*, 415: 755.

—— NADASDY, Z., CSIBRA, G., and BIRO, S. (1995). Taking the intentional stance at 12 months of age. *Cognition*, 56: 165–93.

GERLACH, C., LAW, I., GADE, A., and PAULSON, O. B. (2000). Categorization and category-effects in normal object recognition: a PET study. *Neuropsychologia*, 38: 1693–703.

—— —— —— (2002). The role of action knowledge in the comprehension of artifacts—a PET study. *NeuroImage*, 15: 143–52.

GERMAN, T. and JOHNSON, S. (2002). Function and the origins of the design stance. *Journal of Cognition and Development*, 3: 279–300.

_____ and DEFEYTER, M. A. (2000). Immunity to functional fixedness in young children. *Psychonomic Bulletin and Review*, 7: 707–12.

GHISELIN, M. T. (1974). A radical solution to the species problem. *Systematic Zoology*, 23: 536–44.

GIBSON, E. J. and ADOLPH, K. (1999). Affordances. In R. A. Wilson and F. C. Keil (eds.), *The MIT Encyclopedia of the Cognitive Sciences* (pp. 4–6). MIT Press.

_____ RICCIO, G., SCHMUCKLER, M. A., STOFFREGEN, T. A., ROSENBERG, D., and TAROMINA, J. (1987). Detection of the traversibility of surfaces by crawling and walking infants. *Journal of Experimental Psychology: Human Perception and Performance*, 13: 533–44.

GIBSON, J. J. (1950). *The Perception of the Visual World*. Houghton Mifflin.

_____ (1979). *The Ecological Approach to Visual Perception*. Houghton Mifflin.

GILBERT, S. F. (2000). *Developmental Biology*, 6th edn. Sinauer Associates, Inc.

GILLIARD, E. T. (1969). *Birds of Paradise and Bower Birds*. Weidenfeld & Nicolson.

GOLDENBERG, G. and HAGMANN, S. (1998) Tool use and mechanical problem solving in apraxia. *Neuropsychologia*, 36.7: 581–9.

GOLDMAN, A. (1970). *A Theory of Human Action*. Princeton University Press.

GONNERMAN, L., ANDERSEN, E. S., DEVLIN, J. T. KEMPLER, D., and SEIDENBERG, M. (1997). Double dissociation of semantic categories in Alzheimer's disease. *Brain and Language*, 57.2: 254–79.

GOODALL, J. (1986). *The Chimpanzees of Gombe: Patterns of Behavior*. Harvard University Press.

GOODFELLOW, P. (1977). *Birds as Builders*. David & Charles.

GOULD, J. L. and GOULD, C. G. (1995). *The Honey Bee*, 2nd edn. W. H. Freeman.

_____ _____ (1997). *Sexual Selection*, 2nd edn. W. H. Freeman.

_____ _____ (1999). *The Animal Mind*, 2nd edn. W. H. Freeman.

_____ _____ (2007). *Animal Architects: Building and the Evolution of Intelligence*. Basic Books.

GOULD, S. J. (1997). Darwinian fundamentalism. *New York Review of Books*, 27–30.

_____ and LEWONTIN, R. C. (1979). The spandrels of San Marco and the Panglossian paradigm: a critique of the adaptationist programme. *Proceedings of the Royal Society of London, B*, 205: 581–98.

GOWLETT, J. (1984). Mental abilities of early man: a look at some hard evidence. In R. Foley (ed.), *Hominid Evolution and Community Ecology* (pp. 167–92). Academic Press.

GRABOWSKI, T. J., DAMASIO, H., and DAMASIO, A. R. (1998). Premotor and prefrontal correlates of category-related lexical retrieval. *NeuroImage*, 7: 232–43.

GRAHAM, S. A., WILLIAMS, L. D., and HUBER, J. F. (1999). Preschoolers' and adults' reliance on object shape and object function for lexical extension. *Journal of Experimental Child Psychology*, 74: 128–51.

GRANT, P. R. (1986). *The Ecology and Evolution of Darwin's Finches*. Princeton University Press.

GREIF, M. L. (2004). Developing a concept of function: children's knowledge of tools and their properties. Poster presented at the *Annual Meeting of the Jean Piaget Society*, Toronto, Ontario.

GREIF, M. L., KEIL, F., and GUTIERREZ, F. (2003). Developing a notion of tool function: evidence from a video task. Poster presented at the *Biennial Meeting of the Cognitive Development Society*, Park City, Utan.

_____ KEMLER NELSON, D. G., KEIL, F. C., and GUTIERREZ, F. (2006). What do children want to know about animals and artifacts? Domain-specific requests for information. *Psychological Science*, 17: 455–9.

GRÈZES, J. and DECETY, J. (2001). Functional anatomy of execution, mental simulation, observation, and verb generation of actions: a meta-analysis. *Human Brain Mapping*, 12: 1–19.

GRIFFIN, D. R. (1992). *Animal Minds*. University of Chicago Press.

_____ (2002). *Animal Minds: Beyond Cognition to Consciousness*, revd. and expanded edn. University of Chicago Press.

GROSSMAN, E. D. and BLAKE, R. (2002). Brain areas active during visual motion perception of biological motion. *Neuron*, 35: 1167–75.

_____ DONNELLY, M., PRICE, R., PICKENS, D., MORGAN, V., NEIGHBOR, G., and BLAKE, R. (2000). Brain areas involved in perception of biological motion. *Journal of Cognitive Neuroscience*, 12: 711–20.

HALL, D. G. (1993). Basic-level individuals. *Cognition*, 48: 199–221.

_____ (1995). Artifacts and origins. Unpublished manuscript, University of British Columbia.

HANLEY, J. R., YOUNG, A. W., and PEARSON, N. A. (1989). Defective recognition of familiar people. *Cognitive Neuropsychology*, 6: 179–210.

HANNA, E. and MELTZOFF, A. (1993). Peer imitation by toddlers in laboratory, home and day-care contexts: implications for social learning and memory. *Developmental Psychology*, 29: 701–10.

HANSELL, M. (2000). *Bird Nests and Construction Behaviour*. Cambridge University Press.

HARE, B. (2001). Can competitive paradigms increase the validity of social cognitive experiments on primates? *Animal Cognition*, 4: 269–80.

_____ CALL, J., and TOMASELLO, M. (2001). Do chimpanzees know what conspecifics know? *Animal Behaviour*, 61: 139–51.

_____ _____ AGNETTA, B., and TOMASELLO, M. (2000). Chimpanzees know what conspecifics do and do not see. *Animal Behaviour*, 59: 771–85.

HARMAN, G. (1987). (Non-solipsistic) Conceptual Role Semantics. In E. Lepore (ed.), *New Directions in Semantics* (pp. 55–81). Academic Press.

HARROLD, F. J. (1989). Mousterian, Chatelperronian and early Aurignacian in Western Europe: continuity or discontinuity? In P. A. Mellars and C. Stringer (eds.), *The Human Revolution: Behavioural and Biological Perspectives on the Origins of Modern Humans* (pp. 677–713). Edinburgh University Press.

HART, J. and GORDON, B. (1992). Neural subsystems for object knowledge. *Nature*, 359: 60–4.

_____ BERNDT, R. S., and CARAMAZZA, A. (1985). Category-specific naming deficit following cerebral infarction. *Nature*, 316: 439–40.

HATANO, G. and INAGAKI, K. (1996). Young children's recognition of commonalities between animals and plants. *Child Development*, 67: 2823–40.

_____ _____ (1999). A developmental perspective on informal biology. In D. L. Medin and S. Atran (eds.), *Folkbiology* (pp. 321–54). MIT Press.

HAUSER, M. D. (1988). Invention and social transmission: new data from wild vervet monkeys. In R. W. Byrne and A. Whiten (eds.), *Machiavellian Intelligence: Social Expertise and the Evolution of Intellect in Monkeys, Apes, and Humans* (pp. 327–43). Oxford University Press.

—— (1997). Artifactual kinds and functional design features: what a primate understands without language. *Cognition*, 64: 285–308.

—— (2000). *Wild Minds: What Animals Really Think.* Henry Holt.

—— and CAREY, S. (1998). Building a cognitive creature from a set of primitives: evolutionary and developmental insights. In D. Cummins and C. Allen (eds.), *The Evolution of Mind* (pp. 51–106). Oxford University Press.

—— KRALIK, J., and BOTTO-MAHAN, C. (1999). Problem solving and functional design features: experiments with cotton-top tamarins. *Animal Behaviour*, 57: 565–82.

—— PEARSON, H. E., and SEELIG, D. (2002). Ontogeny of tool use in cotton-top tamarins *Saguinus oedipus*: innate recognition of functionally relevant features. *Animal Behaviour*, 64: 299–311.

—— SANTOS, L., SPAEPEN, G., and PEARSON, H. E. (2002). Problem solving, inhibition, and domain-specific experience: experiments on cotton-top tamarins (*Saguinus oedipus*). *Animal Behaviour*, 64: 387–96.

—— TSAO, F., GARCIA, P., and SPELKE, E. S. *et al.* (2003). Evolutionary foundations of number: spontaneous representation of numerical magnitudes by cotton-top tamarins. *Proceedings of the Royal Society, London, B*, 270: 1441–6.

HAWKES, K., O'CONNELL, J. F., and BLURTON-JONES, N. G. (1997). Hadza women's time allocation, offspring provisioning and the evolution of long, post-menopausal lifespans. *Current Anthropology*, 38: 551–77.

HAXBY, J. V., UNGERLEIDER, L. G., CLARK, V. P., SCHOUTEN, J. L., HOFFMAN, E. A., and MARTIN, A. (1999). The effect of face inversion on activity in human neural systems for face and object perception. *Neuron*, 22: 189–99.

—— GOBBINI, M. I., FUREY, M. L., ISHAI, A., SCHOUTEN, J. L., and PIETRINI, P. (2001). Distributed and overlapping representations of faces and objects in ventral temporal cortex. *Science*, 293: 2425–30.

HAYDEN, B. (1979). *Palaeolithic Reflections.* Humanities Press.

HEIDER, F. and SIMMEL, M. (1944). An experimental study of apparent behavior. *American Journal of Psychology*, 57: 243–59.

HENSCHEL, J. R. (1995). Tool use by spiders. *Ethology*, 101: 187–99.

HESPOS, S. and BAILLARGEON, R. (2001). Reasoning about containment events in very young infants. *Cognition*, 78: 207–45.

HEYES, C. M. and HUBER, F. (2000). *The Evolution of Cognition.* MIT Press.

HILLIS, A. E. and CARAMAZZA, A. (1991). Category-specific naming and comprehension impairment: a double dissociation. *Brain*, 114: 2081–94.

HILPINEN, R. (1992). On artifacts and works of art. *Theoria*, 58: 58–82.

—— (1993). Authors and artifacts. *Proceedings of the Aristotelian Society*, 93: 155–78.

—— (1999). Artifact. *The Stanford Encyclopedia of Philosophy* (Spring 1999 edition). Retrieved from http://plato.stanford.edu/archives/spr1999/entries/artifact/.

—— (2004). Artifact. *The Stanford Encyclopedia of Philosophy* (Fall 2004 edn.). Retrieved from http://plato.stanford.edu/archives/fall2004/entries/artifact.

HIRSCH, E. (1997). Basic objects: a reply to Xu. *Mind and Language*, 12.3/4: 406–12.

Hobbes, Thomas (1994). Elements of philosophy. In *The Collected Works of Thomas Hobbes*, V.1 ed. William Molesworth. Routledge.

Hodder, I. (1985). *Symbols in Action*. Cambridge University Press.

Hodges, J. R., Graham, N., and Patterson, K. (1995). Charting the progression of semantic dementia: implications for the organisation of semantic memory. *Memory*, 3: 463–95.

——— Spatt, J., and Patterson, K. (1999). 'What' and 'how': evidence for the dissociation of object knowledge and mechanical problem-solving skills in the human brain. *Proceedings of the National Academy of Sciences, USA*, 96: 9444–8.

——— Bozeat, S., Lambon-Ralph, M., Patterson, K., and Spatt, J. (2000). The role of conceptual knowledge in object use. Evidence from semantic dementia. *Brain*, 123: 1913–25.

Hoffman, E. A. and Haxby, J. V. (2000). Distinct representations of eye gaze and identity in the distributed human neural system for face perception. *Nature Neuroscience*, 3: 80–4.

Hölldobler, B. and Wilson, E. O. (1990). *The Ants*. Harvard University Press.

Holloway, R. L. (1985). The poor brain of *Homo sapiens neanderthalensis*: see what you please. In E. Delson (ed.), *Ancestors: The Hard Evidence* (pp. 319–24). Alan R. Liss.

Houghton, P. (1993). Neanderthal supralaryngeal vocal tract. *American Journal of Physical Anthropology*, 90: 139–46.

Hovers, E., Rak, Y. Lavi, R., and Kimbel, W. H. (1995). Hominid remains from Amud Cave in the context of the Levantine Middle Palaeolithic. *Paléorient*, 21: 47–61.

Hubbell, S. (2001). *Shrinking the Cat: Genetic Engineering Before We Knew about Genes*. Houghton Mifflin.

Hull, D. (1965). The effect of essentialism on taxonomy: two thousand years of stasis. *British Journal for the Philosophy of Science*, 15: 314–26 and 16: 1–18.

Humphreys, G. W. and Forde, E. M. (2001). Hierarchies, similarity, and interactivity in object recognition: 'Category-specific' neuropsychological deficits. *Behavioral and Brain Sciences*, 24: 453–509.

Hunt, G. R. (1996). Manufacture and use of hook-tools by New Caledonian crows. *Nature*, 379: 249–51.

——— (2004). The crafting of hook tools by wild New Caledonian crows. *Proceedings of the Royal Society, London, B*, 271: S88–S90.

——— and Gray, R. D. (2003). Diversification and cumulative evolution in New Caledonian crow tool manufacture. *Proceedings of the Royal Society, London, B*, 270: 867–4.

Huntley-Fenner, G., Carey, S., and Solimando, A. (2002). Objects are individuals but stuff doesn't count: perceived rigidity and cohesiveness influence infants' representations of small groups of discrete entities. *Cognition*, 85: 203–21.

Isaac, B. (ed.) (1989). *The Archaeology of Human Origins: Papers by Glynn Isaac*. Cambridge University Press.

Isaac, G. (1977). *Olorgesailie*. Chicago University Press.

——— (1978). The food-sharing behaviour of proto-human hominids. *Scientific American*, 238: 90–108.

——— (1983). Bones in contention: competing explanations for the juxtaposition of Early Pleistocene artefacts and faunal remains. In J. Clutton-Brock and C. Grigson (eds.),

Animals and Archaeology: Hunters and Their Prey (pp. 3–19). *British Archaeological Reports, International Series* 163.

ISHAI, A., UNGERLEIDER, L. G., MARTIN, A., SCHOUTEN, J. L., and HAXBY, J. V. (1999). Distributed representation of objects in the human ventral visual pathway. *Proceedings of the National Academy of Sciences USA*, 96: 9379–84.

JASWAL, V. (2006). Preschoolers favor the creator's label when reasoning about an artifact's function. *Cognition*, 99: B83–B92.

JOHANSON, D. and EDGAR, B. (1996). *From Lucy to Language*. Weidenfeld & Nicolson.

JOHNSON, M. (1987). *The Body in the Mind*. University of Chicago Press.

JOHNSON, P., FERRAINA, S., BIANCHI, L., and CAMINITI, R. (1996). Cortical networks for visual reaching: physiological and anatomical organization of frontal and parietal lobe arm regions. *Cerebral Cortex*, 6: 102–99.

JOHNSON, S. C. (2000). The recognition of mentalistic agents in infancy. *Trends in Cognitive Sciences*, 4: 22–8.

—— and SOLOMON, G. E. A. (1997). Why dogs have puppies and cats have kittens: the role of birth in young children's understanding of biological origins. *Child Development*, 68: 404–19.

—— BOOTH, A., and O' HEARN, K. (2001). Inferring the goals of a nonhuman agent. *Cognitive Development*, 16: 637–56.

JOHNSON-FREY, S. H. (2004). The neural basis of complex tool use in humans. *Trends in Cognitive Sciences*, 8.2: 71–8.

—— MALOOF, F. R., NEWMAN-NORLUND, R., FARRER, C., INATI, S., and GRAFTON, S. T. (2003). Actions or hand object interactions: human inferior frontal cortex and action observation. *Neuron*, 39: 1053.

JONES, P. (1980). Experimental butchery with modern stone tools and its relevance for Palaeolithic archaeology. *World Archaeology*, 12: 153–65.

—— (1981). Experiment implement manufacture and use: a case study from Olduvai Gorge. *Philosophical Transactions of the Royal Society of London, B*, 292: 189–95.

JOSEPH, J. E. (2001). Functional neuroimaging studies of category specificity in object recognition: a critical review and meta-analysis. *Cognitive, Affective and Behavioral Neuroscience*, 1.2: 119–36.

JUBIEN, M. (1997). *Contemporary Metaphysics*. Blackwell.

KANWISHER, N. (2000). Domain specificity in face perception. *Nature*, 3: 759–63.

—— McDERMOTT, J., and CHUN, M. M. (1997) The fusiform face area: a module in human extrastriate cortex specialized for face perception. *Journal of Neuroscience*, 17.11: 4302–11.

—— STANLEY, D., and HARRIS, A. (1999). The fusiform face area is selective for faces not animals. *Neuroreport*, 10: 183–7.

KAPLAN, A. and MURPHY, G. L. (1999). The acquisition of category structure in unsupervised learning. *Memory & Cognition*, 27: 699–712.

—— —— (2000). Category learning with minimal prior knowledge. *Journal of Experimental Psychology: Learning, Memory, and Cognition*, 26: 829–46.

KAPLAN, D. (1979). Dthat. In P. French, T. Uehling, Jr., and H. Wettstein (eds.), *Contemporary Perspectives in the Philosophy of Language* (pp. 383–400). University of Minnesota Press.

KARMILOFF-SMITH, A. (1992). *Beyond Modularity*. MIT Press.

Katz, J. J. (1972). *Semantic Theory*. Harper & Row.

Keeley, L. (1980). *Experimental Determination of Stone Tool Uses: A Microwear Analysis*. Chicago University Press.

—— and Toth, N. (1981). Microwear polishes on early stone tools from Koobi Fora, Kenya. *Nature*, 203: 464–65.

Keil, F. C. (1979). *Semantic and Conceptual Development*. Harvard University Press.

—— (1989). *Concepts, Kinds, and Cognitive Development*. MIT Press.

—— (1990). Constraints on constraints: surveying the epigenetic landscape. *Cognitive Science*, 14: 135–68.

—— (1992). The origins of an autonomous biology. In M. R. Gunnar and M. Maratsos (eds.), *Minnesota Symposia on Child Psychology: Vol.25. Modularity and Constraints in Language and Cognition* (pp. 103–37). Lawrence Erlbaum Associates.

—— (1994). The birth and nurturance of concepts by domains: the origins of concepts of living things. In L. A. Hirschfield and S. A. Gelman (eds.), *Mapping the Mind: Domain Specificity in Cognition and Culture* (pp. 234–54). Cambridge University Press.

—— and Smith, W. C. (1996). Is there a different 'basic' level for cause? Paper presented at the 1996 meeting of the *Psychonomics Society*, Chicago.

—— —— Simons, D., and Levin, D. (1998). Two dogmas of conceptual empiricism. *Cognition*, 65: 103–35.

Kelemen, D. (1999*a*). The scope of teleological thinking in preschool children. *Cognition*, 70: 241–272.

—— (1999*b*). Why are rocks pointy? Children's preference for teleological explanations of the natural world. *Developmental Psychology*, 35: 1440–53.

—— (1999*c*). Beliefs about purpose: on the origins of teleological thought. In M. Corballis and S. Lea (eds.), *The Descent of Mind: Psychological Perspectives on Hominid Evolution* (pp. 278–94). Oxford University Press.

Kelemen, D. (1999*d*). Functions, goals and intentions: children's teleological reasoning about objects. *Trends in Cognitive Sciences*, 12: 461–8.

—— (2001). Intention in children's understanding of artifact function. Paper presented at the *Biennial Meeting of the Society for Research in Child Development*, Minnesota, MN (April).

—— (2003). British and American children's preferences for teleo-functional explanations of the natural world. *Cognition*, 88: 201–21.

—— (2004). Are children 'intuitive theists'? Reasoning about purpose and design in nature. *Psychological Science*, 15: 295–301.

—— (2006). Tool use, artifact concepts, and the development of the human function compunction. Manuscript in preparation.

—— and DiYanni, C. (2005). Intuitions about origins: purpose and intelligent design in children's reasoning about nature. *Journal of Cognition and Development*, 6.1: 3–31.

—— Widdowson, D., Posner, T., Brown, A., and Casler, K. (2003). Teleo-functional constraints on preschool children's reasoning about living things. *Developmental Science*, 6: 329–45.

Kellenbach, M. L., Brett, M., and Patterson, K. (2003). Actions speak louder than functions: the importance of manipulability and action in tool representation. *Journal of Cognitive Neuroscience*, 15: 30–46.

KELLMAN, P. J. (1993). Kinematic foundations of infant visual perception. In C. E. Granrud (ed.), *Visual Perception and Cognition in Infancy* (pp. 121–73). Lawrence Erlbaum Associates.

KEMLER NELSON, D. (1999). Attention to functional properties in toddlers' naming and problem-solving. *Cognitive Development*, 14: 77–100.

——— and 11 Swarthmore College Students (1995). Principle-based inferences in young children's categorization: revisiting the impact of function on the naming of artifacts. *Cognitive Development*, 10: 347–80.

——— HERRON, L., and MORRIS, C. (2002). How children and adults name broken objects: inferences and reasoning about design intentions in the categorization of artifacts. *Journal of Cognition and Development*, 3: 279–300.

——— FRANKENFIELD, A., MORRIS, C., and BLAIR, E. (2000). Young children's use of functional information to categorize artifacts: three factors that matter. *Cognition*, 77: 133–68.

——— RUSSELL, R., DUKE, NELL, and JONES, K. (2000). Two-year-olds will name artifacts by their functions. *Child Development*, 71: 1271–88.

KERNER, R. and KEIL, F. (2003). Promiscuous teleology and children's preferences for different types of teleological explanations. Poster presented at the *Biennial Meeting of the Society for Research in Child Development*, Tampa, Fla.

KITCHER, P. (1984). Species. *Philosophy of Science*, 51: 308–33.

——— (1988). The child as parent of the scientist. *Mind and Language*, 3: 217–28.

KOFFKA, K. (1935). *Principles of Gestalt Psychology*. Harcourt Brace.

KÖHLER, W. (1927). *The Mentality of Apes*. Harcourt Brace.

KOHN, M. and MITHEN, S. (1999). Handaxes: products of sexual selection? *Antiquity*, 73: 518–26.

KORNBLITH, H. (1980). Referring to artifacts. *Philosophical Review*, 89.1: 109–14.

KOURTZI, Z. and KANWISHER, N. (2000). Activation in human MT/MST by static images with implied motion. *Journal of Cognitive Neuroscience*, 12: 48–55.

KRIPKE, S. (1972/1980). *Naming and Necessity*. Harvard University Press.

KRONENFELD, D. B., ARMSTRONG, J. D., and WILMOTH, S. (1985). Exploring the internal structure of linguistic categories: An extensionist semantic view. In J. W. D. Dougherty (ed.), *Directions in Cognitive Anthropology* (pp. 91–113). University of Illinois Press.

KUHN, S. (1995). *Mousterian Lithic Technology*. Princeton University Press.

KUHN, T. S. (1962). *The Structure of Scientific Revolutions*. University of Chicago Press.

——— (1983). Commensurability, comparability, communicability. In P. D. Asquith and T. Nickles (eds.), *Proceedings of the 1982 Biennial Meeting of the Philosophy of Science Association* (pp. 669–88). Philosophy of Science Association.

LAIACONA, M. and CAPITANI, E. (2001). A case of prevailing deficit for non-living categories or a case of prevailing sparing of living categories? *Cognitive Neuropsychology*, 18: 39–70.

——— BARBAROTTO R., and CAPITANI, E. (1993). Perceptual and associative knowledge in category specific impairment of semantic memory: a study of two cases. *Cortex*, 29: 727–40.

——— CAPITANI, E., and BARBAROTTO, R. (1997). Semantic category dissociations: a longitudinal study of two cases. *Cortex*, 33: 441–61.

LAIACONA, M., CAPITANI, E., and CARAMAZZA, A. (2003). Category-specific semantic deficits do not reflect the sensory-functional organization of the brain: a test of the 'sensory-quality' hypothesis. *Neurocase*, 9: 221–31.

LAKOFF, G. (1987). *Women, Fire and Dangerous Things.* University of Chicago Press.

LAMBON-RALPH M. A., HOWARD, D., NIGHTINGALE, G., and ELLIS, A. W. (1998). Are living and non-living category-specific deficits causally linked to impaired perceptual or associative knowledge? Evidence from a category-specific double dissociation. *Neurocase*, 4: 311–38.

LANDAU, B., SMITH, L., and JONES, S. (1992). Syntactic context and the shape bias in children's and adults' lexical learning. *Journal of Memory and Language*, 31: 807–25.

_____ SMITH, LINDA B., and JONES, S. (1998). Object shape, object function, and object name. *Journal of Memory and Language*, 38: 1–27.

LANGACKER, R. (1987). *Foundations of Cognitive Grammar (Vol. 1).* Stanford University Press.

LAPORTE, J. (1998). Living water. *Mind*, 107: 451–5.

LASSALINE, M. E. and MURPHY, G. L. (1996). Induction and category coherence. *Psychonomic Bulletin and Review*, 3: 95–9.

LAZARIS, A., ARCIDIACONO, S., HUANG, Y., ZHOU, J.-F., DUGUAY, F., CHRETIEN, N., WELSH, E. A., SOARES, J. W., and KARATZAS, C. N. (2002). Spider silk fibers spun from soluble recombinant silk produced in mammalian cells. *Science*, 295: 472–6.

LEAKEY, M. (1971). *Olduvai Gorge, Volume 3. Excavations in Beds I and II, 1960–1963.* Cambridge University Press.

LESLIE, A. M. (1988). The necessity of illusion: perception and thought in infancy. In L. Weiskrantz (ed.), *Thought without Language* (pp. 185–210). Oxford Science Publications.

_____ (1994). ToMM, ToBY, and Agency: core architecture and domain specificity. In L. A. Hirschfeld and S. A. Gelman (eds.), *Mapping the Mind: Domain Specificity in Cognition and Culture* (pp. 119–48). Cambridge University Press.

_____ and KEEBLE, S. (1987). Do six-month-old infants perceive causality? *Cognition*, 25: 265–88.

LEVIN, D. T., TAKARAE, Y., MINER, A. C., and KEIL, F. (2001). Efficient visual search by category: specifying the features that mark the difference between artifacts and animals in preattentive vision. *Perception and Psychophysics*, 63: 676–97.

LEVINSON, J. (1979). Defining art historically. *British Journal of Aesthetics*, 19: 232–50. [Reprinted in id., *Music, Art, and Metaphysics.* Cornell University Press, 1990.]

_____ (1983). Refining art historically. *Journal of Aesthetics and Art Criticism*, 47: 21–33. [Reprinted in id., *Music, Art, and Metaphysics.* Cornell University Press, 1990.]

_____ (1988). Extending art historically. *Journal of Aesthetics and Art Criticism*, 51: 411–23. [Reprinted in id., *The Pleasures of Aesthetics.* Cornell University Press, 1996.]

_____ (2002). The irreducible historicality of the concept of art. *British Journal of Aesthetics*, 42: 367–79.

LEVY, I., HASSON, U., AVIDAN, G., HENDLER, T., and MALACH, R. (2001). Center–periphery organization of human object areas. *Nature Neuroscience*, 4: 533–9.

LEWIS, D. (1993). Many, but almost one. In J. Bacon, K. Campbell, and L. Reinhardt (eds.), *Ontology, Causality and Mind: Essays in Honour of D. M. Armstrong* (pp. 23–38). Cambridge University Press.

LHERMITTE, F. and BEAUVOIS, M.-F. (1973). A visual speech disconnection syndrome: report of a case with optic aphasia, agnosic alexia and color agnosia. *Brain*, 96: 695–714.

LIBERMAN, A. M., COOPER, F. S., SHANKWEILER, D. P., and STUDDERT-KENNEDY, M. (1967). Perception of the speech code. *Psychological Review*, 74: 431–61.

LIEBERMAN, P. (2001). On the neural basis of spoken language. In A. Nowell (ed.), *In the Mind's Eye: Multidisciplinary Approaches to the Evolution of Human Cognition* (pp. 172–86). International Monographs in Prehistory.

_____ and CRELIN, E. S. (1971). On the speech of Neanderthal man. *Linguistic Inquiry*, 2: 203–22.

LIN, E. L. and MURPHY, G. L. (1997). Effects of background knowledge on object categorization and part detection. *Journal of Experimental Psychology: Human Perception and Performance*, 23: 1153–69.

_____ _____ (2001). Thematic relations in adults' concepts. *Journal of Experimental Psychology: General*, 130: 3–28.

LOCKE, J. (1690/1975). *An Essay Concerning Human Understanding*. P. Nidditch (ed.). Clarendon Press.

LOPEZ, A., ATRAN, S., and COLEY, J. D. (1997). The tree of life: universal and cultural features of folkbiological taxonomies and inductions. *Cognitive Psychology*, 32.3: 251–95.

LOWE, E. J. (1991). Substance and selfhood. *Philosophy*, 66: 81–99.

McCARRELL, N. S. and CALLANAN, M. A. (1995). Form–function correspondences in children's inference. *Child Development*, 66: 532–46.

McCARTHY, C., PUCE, A., GORE, J. C., and ALLISON, T. (1997). Face-specific processing in the human fusiform gyrus. *Journal of Cognitive Neuroscience*, 9: 605–10.

McDONOUGH, L. and MANDLER, J. M. (1994). Very long-term recall in infants: infantile amnesia reconsidered. *Memory*, 2: 339–52.

_____ _____ (1998). Inductive generalization in 9- and 11-month olds. *Developmental Science*, 1: 227–32.

_____ CHOI, S., and MANDLER, J. M. (2003). Understanding spatial relations: Flexible infants, lexical adults. *Cognitive Psychology*, 46: 229–59.

McGREW, W. C. (1992). *Chimpanzee Material Culture*. Cambridge University Press.

MACNAMARA, J. (1986). *A Border Dispute: The Place of Logic in Psychology*. MIT Press.

McRAE, K. and CREE, G. S. (2002). Factors underlying category-specific semantic impairments. In E. M. E. Forde and G. W. Humphreys (eds.), *Category-Specificity in the Brain and Mind* (pp. 211–48). Psychology Press.

MADOLE, K. L. and COHEN, L. B. (1995). The role of object parts in infants' attention to form–function relations. *Developmental Psychology*, 31: 637–48.

_____ OAKES, L. M., and COHEN, L. B. (1993). Developmental changes in infants' attention to function and form-function correlations. *Cognitive Development*, 8: 189–209.

MAHON, B. Z. and CARAMAZZA, A. (2001). The sensory/functional assumption or the data: which do we keep? *Behavioral and Brain Sciences*, 24: 488–9.

_____ _____ (2003). Constraining questions about the organization and representation of conceptual knowledge. *Cognitive Neuropsychology*, 20: 433–50.

_____ _____ (in prep). Features, modalities, and domains as explanations of category-specific deficits: the last shall be the first.

MALT, B. C. (1991). Word meaning and word use. In P. Schwanenflugel (ed.), *The Psychology of Word Meanings* (pp. 37–70). Lawrence Erlbaum Associates.

——(1994). Water is not H_2O. *Cognitive Psychology*, 27: 41–70.

——and JOHNSON, E. C. (1992). Do artifact concepts have cores. *Journal of Memory and Language*, 31: 195–217.

——and SLOMAN, S. A. (2003). Linguistic diversity and object naming by non-native speakers of English. *Bilingualism: Language and Cognition*, 6: 47–67.

—— —— (2004). Conversation and convention: enduring influences on name choice for common objects. *Memory & Cognition*, 32.8: 1346–54.

—— —— and GENNARI, S. (2003*a*). Speaking vs. thinking about objects and actions. In D. Gentner and S. Goldin-Meadow (eds.), *Language in Mind: Advances in the Study of Language and Thought* (pp. 81–111). MIT Press.

—— —— —— (2003*b*). Universality and linguistic specificity in object naming. *Journal of Memory and Language*, 49: 20–42.

—— —— —— SHI, M., and WANG, Y. (1999). Knowing versus naming: similarity and the linguistic categorization of artifacts. *Journal of Memory and Language*, 40: 230–62.

MANDLER, J. M. (1990). Recall of events by preverbal children. In A. Diamond (ed.), *The Development and Neural Bases of Higher Cognitive Functions* (pp. 485–516). New York Academy of Sciences.

——(1992). How to build a baby II: conceptual primitives. *Psychological Review*, 99: 587–604.

——(1994). Precursors of linguistic knowledge. *Philosophical Transactions of the Royal Society*, 346: 63–9.

——(1996). Preverbal representation and language. In P. Bloom, M. Peterson, L. Nadel, and M. Garrett (eds.), *Language and Space* (pp. 365–84). MIT Press.

——(1998). The rise and fall of semantic memory. In M. Conway, S. Gathercole, and C. Cornoldi (eds.), *Theories of Memory II* (pp. 147–69). Psychology Press.

MANDLER, J. M. (2000). Perceptual and conceptual processes in infancy. *Journal of Cognition and Development*, 1: 3–36.

——(2002). On the foundations of the semantic system. In E. Forde and G. Humphreys (eds.), *Category-Specificity in Brain and Mind* (pp. 315–40). Psychology Press.

——(2004). *The Foundations of Mind: Origins of Conceptual Thought*. Oxford University Press.

——(2006). Actions organize the infant's world. In K. Hirsch-Pasek and R. M. Golinkoff (eds.), *Action Meets Word: How Children Learn Verbs*. Oxford University Press.

——and MCDONOUGH, L. (1993). Concept formation in infancy. *Cognitive Development*, 8: 291–318.

—— —— (1996). Drinking and driving don't mix: inductive generalization in infancy. *Cognition*, 59: 307–35.

—— —— (1998*a*). On developing a knowledge base in infancy. *Developmental Psychology*, 34: 1274–88.

—— —— (1998*b*). Studies in inductive inference in infancy. *Cognitive Psychology*, 37: 60–96.

—— —— (2000). Advancing downward to the basic level. *Journal of Cognition and Development*, 1: 379–403.

_____ Bauer, P. J., and McDonough, L. (1991). Separating the sheep from the goats: differentiating global categories. *Cognitive Psychology*, 23: 263–98.

_____ Fivush, R., and Reznick, J. S. (1987). The development of contextual categories. *Cognitive Development*, 2: 339–54.

Mania, D. and Mania, U. (1988). Deliberate engravings on bone artefacts by *Homo erectus*. *Rock Art Research*, 5: 91–107.

Manning, J. T. and Hartley, M. A. (1991). Symmetry and ornamentation are correlated in the peacock's train. *Animal Behaviour*, 42: 1020–1.

_____ and Chamberlain, A. T. (1993). Fluctuating asymmetry, sexual selection and canine teeth in primates. *Proceedings of the Royal Society of London, Series B*, 251: 83–7.

Margolis, E. (1998). How to acquire a concept. In E. Margolis and S. Laurence (eds.), *Concepts: Core Readings* (pp. 549–67). MIT Press.

Markson, L. M. (2001). Developing understanding of artifact function. Paper presented at the *Biennial Meeting of the Society for Research in Child Development*, Minnesota, MN (April).

Marshack, A. (1990). Early hominid symbol and the evolution of human capacity. In P. Mellars (ed.), *The Emergence of Modern Humans* (pp. 457–98). Edinburgh University Press.

_____ (1997). The Berekhat Ram figurine: a late Acheulian carving from the Middle East. *Antiquity*, 71: 327–37.

Marshall, A. J. (1954). *Bowerbirds*. Oxford University Press.

Martin, A. (1998). Organization of semantic knowledge and the origin of words in the brain. In N. G. Jablonski and L. C. Aiello (eds.), *The Origin and Diversification of Language* (pp. 69–88). *Memoirs of the California Academy of Sciences*, No. 24.

_____ and Chao, L. L. (2001). Semantic memory and the brain: structure and processes. *Current Opinion in Neurobiology*, 11.2: 194–201.

_____ and Weisberg, J. (2003). Neural foundations for understanding social and mechanical concepts. *Cognitive Neuropsychology*, 20: 575–87.

_____ Ungerleider, L. G., and Haxby, J. V. (2000). Category specificity and the brain: the sensory/motor model of semantic representations of objects. In M. Gazzaniga (ed.), *The New Cognitive Neurosciences* (pp. 1023–36). MIT Press.

_____ Wiggs, C. L., Ungerleider, L. G., and Haxby, J. V. (1996). Neural correlates of category-specific knowledge. *Nature*, 379: 649–52.

_____ Haxby, J. V., Lalonde, F. M., Wiggs, C. L., and Ungerleider, L. G. (1995). Discrete cortical regions associated with knowledge of color and knowledge of action. *Science*, 270: 102–5.

Matan, A. and Carey, S. (2001). Developmental changes within the core of artifact concepts. *Cognition*, 78: 1–26.

Matsuzawa, T. (1996). Chimpanzee intelligence in nature and in captivity: isomorphism of symbol use and tool use. In W. C. McGrew, L. F. Marchant, and T. Nishida (eds.), *Great Ape Societies* (pp. 196–209). Cambridge University Press.

_____ and Yamakoshi, G. (1996). Comparison of chimpanzee material culture between Bossou and Nimba, West Africa. In A. E. Russon, K. A. Bard, and S. T. Parker (eds.), *Reaching into Thought: The Minds of the Great Apes* (pp. 211–34). Cambridge University Press.

MEDIN, D. L., and ORTONY, A. (1989). Psychological essentialism. In S. Vosniadou and A. Ortony (eds.), *Similarity and Analogical Reasoning* (pp. 179–95). Cambridge University Press.

——— WATTENMAKER, W. D., and HAMPSON, S. E. (1987). Family resemblance, conceptual cohesiveness, and category construction. *Cognitive Psychology*, 19: 242–80.

——— GOLDSTONE, R. L., and GENTNER, D. (1993). Respects for similarity. *Psychological Review*, 100: 254–78.

——— ROSS, N., ATRAN, S., BURNETT, R., and BLOK, S. (2002). Categorization and reasoning in relation to culture and expertise. In B. Ross (ed.), *Psychology of Learning and Motivation*, Vol. 41 (pp. 1–41). Academic Press.

MELLARS, P. A. (1996). *The Neanderthal Legacy*. Princeton University Press.

——— (1998). Reply to D'Errico *et al*. 1998. Neanderthal acculturation in Western Europe? A critical review of the evidence and its interpretation. *Current Anthropology*, 39: 25–6.

——— (2000). Chatelperronian chronology and the case for Neanderthal/modern human acculturation in Western Europe. In C. B. Stringer, R. N. E. Barton, and J. C. Finlayson (eds.), *Neanderthals on the Edge* (pp. 27–33). Oxbow Books.

MELTZOFF, A. (1990). Toward a developmental cognitive science: the implications of cross-modal matching and imitation for the development of representation and memory in infancy. In A. Diamond (ed.), *The Development and Neural Bases of Higher Cognitive Functions* (pp. 1–31). New York Academy of Sciences.

——— (1995). Understanding the intentions of others: re-enactment of intended acts by 18-month-old children. *Developmental Psychology*, 31: 838–50.

MERRIAM, G. and MERRIAM, C. (1981). *Webster's New Collegiate Dictionary*. Merriam.

Merriam–Webster online dictionary (2005). Retrieved from http://www.m-w.com.

MERRIMAN, W. E., SCOTT, P. D., and MARAZITA, J. (1993). An appearance-function shift in children's naming. *Journal of Child Language*, 20: 101–18.

MICELI, G., FOUCH, E., CAPASSO, R., SHELTON, J. R., TAMAIUOLO, F., and CARAMAZZA, A. (2001). The dissociation of color from form and function knowledge. *Nature Neuroscience*, 4: 662–7.

MICHOTTE, A. (1963). *The Perception of Causality*. Basic Books.

MILLIKAN, R. (1984). *Language, Thought, and Other Biological Categories: New Foundations for Realism*. MIT Press.

——— (1993). *White Queen Psychology and Other Essays for Alice*. MIT Press.

——— (1998). Language conventions made simple. *Journal of Philosophy*, 95: 161–80.

——— (1999*a*). Historical kinds and the special sciences. *Philosophical Studies*, 95: 45–65.

——— (1999*b*). Wings, spoons, pills and quills: a pluralist theory of function. *Journal of Philosophy*, 96.4: 191–206.

——— (2000). *On Clear and Confused Ideas*. Cambridge University Press.

——— (2002). Biofunctions: two paradigms. In R. Cummins, A. Ariew, and M. Perlman (eds.), *Functions: New Readings in Philosophy of Biology and Philosophy of Psychology* (pp. 113–43). Oxford University Press.

——— (2003). In defense of public language. L. Antony and N. Hornstein (eds.), *Chomsky and His Critics* (pp. 215–37). Blackwell.

MITHEN, S. (1994). Technology and society during the Middle Pleistocene. *Cambridge Archaeological Journal*, 4: 3–33.

_____ (1996). *The Prehistory of the Mind*. Thames & Hudson.

_____ (1998). A creative explosion? Theory of mind, language and the disembodied mind of the Upper Palaeolithic. In id. (ed.), *Creativity in Human Evolution and Prehistory*, (pp. 165–91). Routledge.

MØLLER, A. P. (1988). Female choice selects for male sexual tail ornaments in the monogamous swallow. *Nature*, 332: 640–2.

MONTOMURA, N. and YAMADORI, A. (1994). A case of ideational apraxia with impairment of object use and preservation of object pantomime. *Cortex*, 30: 167–70.

MOORE, C. J. and PRICE, C. J. (1999). A functional neuroimaging study of the variables that generate category-specific object processing differences. *Brain*, 122: 943–62.

MOREAUD, O., CHARNALLET, A., and PELLAT, J. (1998). Identification without manipulation: a study of the relations between object use and semantic memory. *Neuropsychologia*, 36: 1295–301.

MORGAN, L. H. (1886). *The American Beaver and his Works*. Lippincott.

MORPHY, H. (1989). On representing Ancestral Beings. In H. Morphy (ed.), *Animals into Art* (pp. 144–60). Unwin Hyman.

MOSCOVITCH, M., WINOCUR, G., and BEHRMANN, M. (1997). What is special about face recognition? Nineteen experiments on a person with visual object agnosia and dyslexia but normal face recognition. *Journal of Cognitive Neuroscience*, 9: 555–604.

MOSS, H. E. and TYLER, L. K. (1997). A category-specific semantic deficit for nonliving things in a case of progressive aphasia. *Brain and Language*, 60: 55–8.

_____ _____ (2000). A progressive category-specific semantic deficit for non-living things. *Neuropsychologia*, 38: 60–82.

_____ _____ (2003). Weighing up the facts of category-specific semantic deficits: a reply to Caramazza and Mahon (August 2003). *Trends in Cognitive Sciences*, 7.11: 480–1.

_____ _____ DURRANT-PEATFIELD, M., and BUNN, E. M. (1998). Two eyes of a see-through: impaired and intact semantic knowledge in a case of selective deficit for living things. *Neurocase*, 4: 291–310.

MULLEN, A. M. and ASLIN, R. N. (1978). Visual tracking as an index of the object concept. *Infant Behavior and Development*, 1: 309–19.

MUMMERY, C. J., PATTERSON, K., HODGES, J. R., and PRICE, C. J. (1998). Functional neuroanatomy of the semantic system: divisible by what? *Journal of Cognitive Neuroscience*, 10.6: 766–77.

MUNAKATA, Y., SANTOS, L. R., SPELKE, E. S., HAUSER, M. D., and O'REILLY, R. C. (2001). Visual representation in the wild: how rhesus monkeys parse objects. *Journal of Cognitive Neuroscience*, 13: 44–58.

MURPHY, G. L. and MEDIN, D. (1985). The role of theories in conceptual coherence. *Psychological Review*, 92: 289–316.

NEANDER, K. (1991). Functions as selected effects: the conceptual analyst defence. *Philosophy of Science*, 58: 168–84.

NEEDHAM, A. and BAILLARGEON, R. (2000). Infants' use of featural and experiential information in segregating and individuating objects: a reply to Xu, Carey, and Welch. *Cognition*, 74: 255–84.

NELSON, J. (1982). Schwartz on reference. *Southern Journal of Philosophy*, 20: 359–65.

NEWCOMBE, F., MEHTA, Z., and DE HANN, E. H. F. (1994). Category specificity in visual recognition. In M. Farah and G. Ratcliff (eds.), *The Neuropsychology of High-Level Vision* (pp. 103–32). Lawrence Erlbaum Associates.

OAKES, L. M. and COHEN, L. B. (1990). Infant perception of a causal event. *Cognitive Development*, 5: 193–207.

——— COPPAGE, D. J., and DINGEL, A. (1997). By land or by sea: the role of perceptual similarity in infants' categorization of animals. *Developmental Psychology*, 33: 396–407.

OAKLEY, K. P. (1981). The emergence of higher thought. *Philosophical Transactions of the Royal Society, B*, 29: 205–11.

OCHIPA, C., ROTHI, L. J. G., and HEILMAN, K. M., (1989). Ideational apraxia: a deficit in tool selection and use. *Annals of Neurology*, 25: 190–3.

ONISHI, K. and BAILLARGEON, R. (2005). Do 15-month-old infants understand false beliefs? *Science*, 308: 255–8.

ORIGGI, G. and SPERBER, D. (2000). Evolution, communication, and the proper function of language. In P. Carruthers and A. Chamberlain (eds.), *Evolution and the Human Mind: Language, Modularity and Social Cognition* (pp. 140–69). Cambridge University Press.

Oxford English Dictionary, 2nd edn. (1989). Oxford University Press.

PARSONS, P. A. (1992). Fluctuating asymmetry: a biological monitor of environmental and genomic stress. *Heredity*, 68: 361–4.

PATTERSON, K. and HODGES, J. R. (1995). Disorders of semantic memory. In A. D. Baddeley, B. A. Wilson, and F. N. Watts (eds.), *Handbook of Memory Disorders* (pp. 167–86). Wiley.

PAUEN, S. (2000). Early differentiation within the animate domain: are humans something special? *Journal of Experimental Child Psychology*, 75: 134–51.

——— (2002). Evidence for knowledge-based category discrimination in infancy. *Child Development*, 73: 1016–33.

PERANI, D., SCHNUR, T., TETTAMANTI, M., GORNO-TEMPINI, M., CAPPA, S. F., and FAZIO, F. (1999). Word and picture matching: a PET study of semantic category effects. *Neuropsychologia*, 37: 293–306.

——— CAPPA, S. F., BETTINARDI, V., BRESSI, S., GORNO-TEMPINI, M., MATARRESE, M., and FAZIO, F. (1995). Different neural systems for the recognition of animals and man-made tools. *Neuroreport*, 6: 1637–41.

PERNER, J., and WIMMER, H. (1985). 'John thinks that Mary thinks that…': Attribution of second order beliefs by 5- to 10-year-old children. *Journal of Experimental Child Psychology*, 39: 437–71.

PETERSEN, P. V. (1984). Chronological and regional variation in the Late Mesolithic of Eastern Denmark. *Journal of Danish Archaeology*, 3: 7–18.

PETROSKI, H. (1992). *The Evolution of Useful Things*. Vintage Books.

PETROVICH, O. (1997). Understanding of non-natural causality in children and adults: a case against artificialism. *Psyche and Geloof*, 8: 151–65.

PHILLIPS, J. A., NOPPENEY, U., HUMPHREYS, G. W., and PRICE, C. J. (2002). Can segregation within the semantic system account for category-specific deficits? *Brain*, 125: 2067–80.

PHILLIPS, K. A. (1998). Tool use in wild capuchin monkeys (*Cebus albifrons trinitatis*). *American Journal of Primatology*, 46: 259–61.

PHILLIPS, W. and SANTOS, L. R. (in press). Evidence for kind representations in the absence of language: experiments with rhesus monkeys (*Macaca mulatta*). *Cognition*.

PIAGET, J. (1951). *Play, Dreams, and Imitation in Childhood*. W. W. Norton.

_____ (1952). *The Origins of Intelligence in the Child*. International Universities Press.

PINKER, S. (1997). *How the Mind Works*. Norton.

PLANTINGA, A. (1993). *Warrant and Proper Function*. Oxford University Press.

PLAUT, D. C. (2002). Graded modality-specific specialization in semantics: a computational account of optic aphasia. *Cognitive Neuropsychology*, 19: 603–39.

POLLAN, M. (2001). *The Botany of Desire: A Plant's-Eye View of the World*. Random House.

POPE, G. (1989). Bamboo and human evolution. *Natural History*, 10: 49–56.

POTTS, R. (1988). *Early Hominid Activities at Olduvai Gorge*. Aldine de Gruyter.

_____ and SHIPMAN, P. (1981). Cutmarks made by stone tools on bones from Olduvai Gorge, Tanzania. *Nature*, 29: 577–80.

POULIN-DUBOIS, D., LEPAGE, A., and FERLAND, D. (1996). Infants' concept of animacy. *Cognitive Development*, 11: 19–36.

POVINELLI, D. (2000). *Folk Physics for Apes*. Oxford University Press.

_____ and EDDY, T. (1996). *What Young Chimpanzees Know About Seeing. Monographs of the Society for Research in Child Development*, 61.

PUTNAM, D. (1982). Natural kinds and human artifacts. *Mind*, 91: 418–19.

PUTNAM, H. (1970). Is semantics possible? Repr. in id., *Mind, Language and Reality* (pp. 139–52). Cambridge University Press.

_____ (1973). Meaning and reference. *Journal of Philosophy*, 70: 699–711.

_____ (1975). The meaning of 'meaning'. Repr. in id., *Mind, Language and Reality: Philosophical Papers vol. 2* (pp. 215–271). Cambridge University Press.

QUINE, W. V. O. (1960). *Word and Object*. MIT Press.

_____ (1969). Natural kinds. In S. P. Schwartz (ed.), *Naming, Necessity, and Natural Kinds* (pp. 155–75). Cornell University Press. Reprinted in Quine, *Ontological Relativity and Other Essays* (pp. 114–38).

_____ (1981). Things and their place in theory. In his *Theories and Things* (pp. 1–23). Harvard University Press.

QUINN, P. C. and EIMAS, P. D. (1997). A reexamination of the perceptual-to-conceptual shift in mental representations. *Review of General Psychology*, 1: 271–87.

_____ _____ (1998). Evidence for a global categorical representation of humans by young infants. *Journal of Experimental Child Psychology*, 69: 151–74.

_____ _____ and ROSENKRANTZ, S. L. (1993). Evidence for representations of perceptual similar natural categories by 3-month-old and 4-month-old infants. *Perception*, 22: 463–75.

REA, M. (1997). *Material Constitution: A Reader*. Rowman & Littlefield.

REGEHR, G. and BROOKS, L. R. (1995). Category organization in free classification: the organizing effect of an array of stimuli. *Journal of Experimental Psychology: Learning, Memory, and Cognition*, 21: 347–63.

REHDER, B. and HASTIE, R. (2001). Causal knowledge and categories: the effects of causal beliefs on categorization, induction, and similarity. *Journal of Experimental Psychology: General*, 130: 323–60.

RICHARDS, D. D., GOLDFARB, J., RICHARDS, A. L., and HASSEN, P. (1989). The role of the functionality rule in categorization of well-defined concepts. *Journal of Child Experimental Psychology*, 47: 97–115.

RIDDOCH, M. J. and HUMPHREYS, G. W. (1987a). A case of integrative visual agnosia. *Brain*, 110: 1431–62.

RIDDOCH, M. J. and HUMPHREYS, G. W. (1987*b*). Visual object processing in optic aphasia: a case of semantic access agnosia. *Cognitive Neuropsychology*, 4: 131–85.

———— COLTHEART, M., and FUNNELL, E. (1988). Semantic systems or system? Neuropsychological evidence re-examined. *Cognitive Neuropsychology*, 5.1: 3–25.

RIPS, L. J. (1989). Similarity, typicality and categorization. In S. Vosniadou and A. Ortony (eds.), *Similarity and Analogical Reasoning* (pp. 21–59). Cambridge University Press.

———— (2001). Necessity and natural categories. *Psychological Bulletin*, 127: 827–52.

ROCA, A. L., GEORGIADIS, N., PECON-SLATTERY, J., and O'BRIEN, S. J. (2001). Genetic evidence for two species of elephant in Africa. *Science*, 293: 1473–7.

ROCHAT, P., MORGAN, R., and CARPENTER, M. (1997). Young infants' sensitivity to movement information specifying social causality. *Cognitive Development*, 12: 537–61.

ROE, D. (1981). *The Lower and Middle Palaeolithic Periods in Britain*. Routledge & Kegan Paul.

ROSCH, E., MERVIS, C. B., GRAY, W. D., JOHNSON, D. M., and BOYES-BRAEM, P. (1976). Basic objects in natural categories. *Cognitive Psychology*, 8: 382–439.

ROSCI, C., VALENTINA, C., LAIACONA, M., and CAPITANI, E. (2003). Apraxia is not associated to a disproportionate naming impairment for manipulable objects. *Brain and Cognition*, 53: 412–15.

ROSS, B. H. and MURPHY, G. L. (1999). Food for thought: cross-classification and category organization in a complex real-world domain. *Cognitive Psychology*, 38: 495–553.

ROTHI, L. J. G., OCHIPA, C., and HEILMAN, K. M. (1991). A cognitive neuropsychological model of limb praxis. *Cognitive Neuropsychology*, 8.6: 443–58.

RUFF, C. B., TRINKAUS, E., and HOLLIDAY, T. W. (1997). Body mass and encaphalization in Pleistocene Homo. *Nature*, 387: 173–6.

RUMIATI, R. I., ZANINI, S., VORANO, L., and SHALLICE, T. (2001). A form of ideational apraxia as a selective deficit of contention scheduling. *Cognitive Neuropsychology*, 18.7: 617–42.

SACCHETT, C. and HUMPHREYS, G. W. (1992). Calling a squirrel a squirrel but a canoe a wigwam: a category-specific deficit for artefactual objects and body parts. *Cognitive Neuropsychology*, 9: 73–86.

SAMSON, D. and PILLON, A. (2003). A case of impaired knowledge for fruit and vegetables. *Cognitive Neuropsychology*, 20: 373–401.

———— and DE WILDE, V. (1998). Impaired knowledge of visual and non-visual attributes in a patient with a semantic impairment for living entities: a case of a true category-specific deficit. *Neurocase*, 4: 273–90.

SANTOS, L. R. and CARAMAZZA, A. (2002). The domain-specific hypothesis: a developmental and comparative perspective on category-specific deficits. In E. M. E. Forde and G. W. Humphreys (eds.), *Category-Specificity in the Brain and Mind* (pp. 1–24). Psychology Press.

———— HAUSER, M. D., and SPELKE, E. S. (2002) Domain-specific knowledge in human children and non-human primates: artifacts and foods. In M. Bekoff, C. Allen, and G. M. Burghardt (eds.), *The Cognitive Animal: Empirical and Theoretical Perspectives on Animal Cognition* (pp. 205–16). MIT Press.

———— ———— (2001). Recognition and categorization of biologically significant objects by rhesus monkeys (*Macaca mulatta*): the domain of food. *Cognition*, 82: 127–55.

_____ MAHAJAN, N., and BARNES, J. (2005). How prosimian primates represent tools: experiments with two lemur species (*Eulemur fulvus and Lemur catta*). *Journal of Comparative Psychology*, 119: 394–403.

_____ MILLER, C. T., and HAUSER, M. (2003). Representing tools: how two nonhuman primates species distinguish between functionally relevant and irrelevant features of a tool. *Animal Cognition*, 6: 269–81.

_____ PEARSON, H. M., SPAEPEN, G. M., TSAO, F., and HAUSER, M. D. (2006). Probing the limits of tool competence: experiments with two non-tool-using species (*Cercopithecus aethiops* and *Saguinus Oedipus*). *Animal Cognition*, 9: 94–109.

_____ SULKOWSKI, G. M., SPAEPEN, G., and HAUSER, M. D. (2002). Object individuation using property/kind information in rhesus macaques (*Macaca mulatta*). *Cognition*, 83: 241–64.

_____ ROSATI, A., SPROUL, C., SPAULDING, B., and HAUSER. M. D. (2005). Means–end tool choice in cotton-top tamarins (*Saguinus oedipus*): finding the limits on primates' knowledge of tools. *Animal Cognition*, 8: 236–46.

SARTORI, G. and JOB, R. (1988). The oyster with four legs: A neuropsychological study on the interaction between vision and semantic information. *Cognitive Neuropsychology*, 5: 105–32.

_____ MIOZZO, M., and JOB, R. (1993). Category-specific naming impairments? Yes. *Quarterly Journal of Experimental Psychology*, 46(A): 489–504.

_____ COLTHEART, M., MIOZZO, M., and JOB, R. (1994). Category specificity and informational specificity in neuropsychological impairment of semantic memory. In C. A. Umiltà and M. Moscovitch (eds.), *Attention and Performance*, 15 (pp. 537–50). MIT Press.

_____ JOB, R., MIOZZO, M., ZAGO, S., and MARCHIORI, G. (1993). Category-specific form-knowledge deficit in a patient with herpes simplex virus encephalitis. *Journal of Clinical and Experimental Neuropsychology*, 15: 280–99.

SCHICK, K. D. and TOTH, N. (1993). *Making Silent Stones Speak: Human Evolution and the Dawn of Technology*. Simon & Schuster.

SCHLESINGER, M. and LANGER, J. (1999). Infants' developing expectations of possible and impossible tool-use events between ages 8 and 12 months. *Developmental Science*, 2: 195–205.

SCHOLL, B. J. and TREMOULET, P. D. (2000). Perceptual causality and animacy. *Trends in Cognitive Sciences*, 4: 299–308.

SCHWARTZ, S. (1977). Introduction. In id. (ed.), *Naming, Necessity, and Natural Kinds* (pp. 13–41). Cornell University Press.

_____ (1978). Putnam on artifacts. *Philosophical Review*, 87.4: 566–74.

_____ (1979). Natural kind terms. *Cognition*, 7: 301–15.

_____ (1980). Natural kinds and nominal kinds. *Mind*, 89: 182–95.

_____ (1983). Reply to Kornblith and Nelson. *Southern Journal of Philosophy*, 21: 475–9.

SEARLE, J. (1995). *The Construction of Social Reality*. Free Press.

_____ (2005). What is an institution? *Journal of Institutional Economics*, 1: 1–22.

_____ (2006). Social Ontology: some basic Principles. *Anthopological Theory*, 6: 12–29.

SELLARS, W. (1963). Philosophy and the scientific image of man. In id., *Science, Perception and Reality* (pp. 1–40). Routledge & Kegan Paul.

SENIOR, C., BARNES, J., GIAMPIETRO, V., SIMMONS, A., BULLMORE, E. T., BRAMMER, M., and DAVID, A. S. (2000). The functional neuroanatomy of implicit-motion perception or representational momentum. *Current Biology*, 10: 16–22.

SHELTON, J. R., FOUCH, E., and CARAMAZZA, A. (1998). The selective sparing of body part knowledge: a case study. *Neurocase*, 4: 339–51.

SHENNAN, S. (2001). Demography and cultural innovation: a model and its implications for the emergence of modern human culture. *Cambridge Archaeological Journal*, 11: 5–16.

SHERIDAN, J. and HUMPHREYS, G. W. (1993). A verbal-semantic category-specific recognition impairment. *Cognitive Neuropsychology*, 10.2: 143–84.

SHETTLEWORTH, S. (1998). *Cognition, Evolution and Behavior*. Oxford University Press.

SIDELLE, A. (1989). *Necessity, Essence, and Individuation*. Cornell University Press.

—— (1998). A sweater unraveled: following one thread of thought for avoiding coincident entities. *Noûs*, 32: 423–48.

SIEGAL, M. and BEATTIE, K. (1991). Where to look first for children's knowledge of false beliefs. *Cognition*, 38: 1–12.

SILVERI, M. C. and GAINOTTI, G. (1988). Interaction between vision and language in category-specific semantic impairment. *Cognitive Neuropsychology*, 5.6: 677–709.

—— —— PERANI, D., CAPPELLETTI, J. Y. CARBONE, G., and FAZIO, F. (1997). Naming deficit for non-living items: neuropsychological and PET study. *Neuropsychologia*, 35: 359–67.

SIMONS, D. J. and KEIL, F. C. (1995). An abstract to concrete shift in the development of biological thought: the insides story. *Cognition*, 56: 129–63.

SIRIGU, A., DUHAMEL, J., and PONCET, M. (1991). The role of sensorimotor experience in object recognition. *Brain*, 114: 2555–73.

SLOMAN, S. A. (1998). Categorical inference is not a tree: the myth of inheritance hierarchies. *Cognitive Psychology*, 35: 1–33.

—— HARRISON, M., and MALT, B. C. (2002). Recent exposure affects artifact naming. *Memory & Cognition*, 30: 687–95.

—— LOVE, B., and AHN, W.-K. (1998). Feature Centrality and Conceptual Coherence. *Cognitive Science*, 22: 189–228.

—— and LAGNADO, D. (2005). The Problem of Induction. In K. Holyoak and R. Morrison (eds.), *Cambridge Handbook of Thinking and Reasoning* (pp. 95–116). Cambridge University Press.

—— and MALT, B. C. (2003). Artifacts are not ascribed essences, nor are they treated as belonging to kinds. *Language and Cognitive Processes* (Special Issue: Conceptual Representation), 18: 563–82.

—— MALT, B.C., and FRIDMAN, A. (2001). Categorization versus similarity: the case of container names. In U. Hahn and M. Ramscar (eds.), *Similarity and Categorization* (pp. 73–86). Oxford University Press.

SMITH, A. W. (1978). Investigation of the mechanisms underlying nest construction in the mud wasp. *Animal Behaviour*, 26: 232–40.

SMITH, L., JONES, S., and LANDAU, B. (1996). Naming in young children: a dumb attentional mechanism? *Cognition*, 60: 143–71.

SOLOMON, G. E. A., JOHNSON, S. C., ZAITCHIK, D., and CAREY, S. (1996). Like father, like son: young children's understanding of how and why offspring resemble their parents. *Child Development*, 67: 151–71.

SPALDING, T. L. and MURPHY, G. L. (1996). Effects of background knowledge on category construction. *Journal of Experimental Psychology: Learning, Memory, and Cognition*, 22: 525–38.

SPARKS, J. (1982). *The Discovery of Animal Behavior*. Little, Brown & Co.

SPELKE, E. S. (1985). Perception of unity, persistence, and identity: thoughts on infants' conception of objects. In J. Mehler and R. Fox (eds.), *Neonate Cognition* (pp. 89–113). Lawrence Erlbaum Associates.

—— (1990). Principles of object perception. *Cognitive Science*, 14: 29–56.

—— (1991). Physical knowledge in infancy: reflections on Piaget's theory. In S. Carey and R. Gelman (eds.), *The Epigenesis of Mind: Essays on Biology and Cognition* (pp. 133–69). Lawrence Erlbaum Associates.

—— (1994). Initial knowledge: six suggestions. *Cognition*, 50: 431–45.

—— PHILLIPS, A., and WOODWARD, A. (1995). Infants, knowledge of object motion and human action. In D. Sperber, D. Premack, and A. Premack (eds.), *Causal Cognition: A Multidisciplinary Debate* (pp. 44–78). Oxford University Press.

—— BREINLINGER. K., MACOMBER, J., and JACOBSON, K. (1992). Origins of knowledge. *Psychological Review*, 99: 605–32.

SPERBER, D. (1996). *Explaining Culture: A Naturalistic Approach*. Blackwell.

—— (2000). An objection to the memetic approach to culture. In R. Aunger (ed.), *Darwinizing Culture: The Status of Memetics as a Science* (pp. 163–73). Oxford University Press.

SPRADBERY, J. P. (1973). *Wasps*. University of Washington Press.

SPRINGER, K. and KEIL, F. C. (1989). On the development of biologically specific beliefs: the case of inheritance. *Child Development*, 60: 637–48.

STALNAKER, R. (1997). Reference and necessity. Reprinted in id., *Ways a World Might Be: Metaphysical and Anti-Metaphysical Essays* (pp. 165–87). Oxford University Press.

STEWART, F., PARKIN, A. J., and HUNKIN, N. M. (1992). Naming impairments following recovery from herpes simplex encephalitis. *Quarterly Journal of Experimental Psychology*, 44A: 261–84.

STEWART, J. (1984). Object motion and the perception of animacy. Paper presented at the meeting of the *Psychonomic Society*, San Antonio, Tex. November.

STINER, M. (1994). *Honor Among Thieves: A Zoological Study of Neanderthal Ecology*. Princeton University Press.

STRAUS, L. G. and BAR-YOSEF, O. (eds.) (2001). *Out of Africa in the Pleistocene. Quaternary International*, 75.

STREVENS, M. (2000). The essentialist aspect of naïve theories. *Cognition*, 74: 149–75.

STRINGER, C. and GAMBLE, C. (1993). *In Search of the Neanderthals*. Thames & Hudson.

STRUHSAKER, T. T. (1967). Auditory communication among vervet monkeys (*Cercopithecus aethiops*). In S. A. Altmann (ed.), *Social Communication Among Primates* (pp. 281–324). Chicago University Press.

SUGIYAMA, Y. (1995). Drinking tools of wild chimpanzees at Bossou. *American Journal of Primatology*, 37/1: 263–9.

SULKOWSKI, G. and HAUSER, M. D. (2001). Can rhesus monkeys spontaneously subtract? *Cognition*, 79: 239–62.

SULLIVAN, K., ZAITCHIK, D., and TAGER-FLUSBERG, H. (1994). Preschoolers can attribute second-order beliefs. *Developmental Psychology*, 30: 395–402.

SUSMAN, R. L. (1991). Who made the Oldowan tools? Fossil evidence for tool behaviour in Plio-Pleistocene hominids. *Journal of Anthropological Research*, 47: 129–51.

SUZUKI, S., KURODA, S., and NISHIHARA, T. (1995). Tool-set for termite-fishing by chimpanzees in the Ndoki Forest, Congo. *Behaviour*, 132/3–4: 219–35.

TALMY, L. (1988). Force dynamics in language and cognition. *Cognitive Science*, 12: 49–100.

TARR, M. J. and GAUTHIER, I. (2000). FFA: a flexible fusiform area for subordinate-level visual processing automatized by expertise. *Nature Neuroscience*, 3: 764–69.

TARSITANO, M. S. and JACKSON, R. R. (1994). Jumping spiders make predatory detours requiring movement away from prey. *Behaviour*, 131: 65–73.

TAYLOR, J. R. (1995). *Linguistic Categorization: Prototypes in Linguistic Theory*. Oxford University Press.

THAGARD, P. (1992). *Conceptual Revolutions*. Princeton University Press.

THOMASSON, A. (1999). *Fiction and Metaphysics*. Cambridge University Press.

—— (2001). Geographic objects and the science of geography. *Topoi*, 20.2: 149–59.

—— (2003). Realism and human kinds. *Philosophy and Phenomenological Research*, 67.3: 580–609.

—— (2005). The ontology of art and knowledge in aesthetics. *Journal of Aesthetics and Art Criticism*, 63.3: 221–9.

—— (2007). *Ordinary Objects*. Oxford University Press.

THOMPSON, S. A., GRAHAM, K. S., WILLIAMS, G., PATTERSON, K., KAPUR, N., and HODGES, J. R. (2004). Dissociating person-specific from general semantic knowledge: roles of the left and right temporal lobes. *Neuropsychologia*, 42: 359–70.

THOMPSON-SCHILL, S. L. (2003). Neuroimaging studies of semantic memory: inferring 'how' from 'where'. *Neuropsychologia*, 41: 280–92.

THORNHILL, R. and GANGESTAD, S. (1994). Human fluctuating asymmetry and sexual behaviour. *Psychological Science*, 5: 297–302.

—— —— (1996). The evolution of human sexuality. *Trends in Ecology and Evolution*, 11: 98–102.

TINBERGEN, N. (1952). The curious behavior of sticklebacks. *Scientific American*, 187.6: 22–6.

TOMASELLO, M. (1999). The cultural ecology of young children's interactions with objects and artifacts. In E. Winograd, R. Fivush, and W. Hirst (eds.), *Ecological Approaches to Cognition: Essays in Honor of Ulric Neisser* (pp. 153–70). Lawrence Erlbaum Associates.

—— and CALL, J. (1997). *Primate Cognition*. Oxford University Press.

—— KRUGER, A. C., and RATNER, H. H. (1993). Cultural Learning. *Behaviour and Brain Sciences*, 16: 495–552.

—— CARPENTER, M., CALL, J., BEHNE, T., and MOLL, H. (2005). Understanding and sharing intentions: the origins of cultural cognition. *Behavioural and Brain Sciences*, 8: 675–91.

TOMIKAWA, S. A. and DODD, D. H. (1980). Early word meanings. Perceptually or functionally-based? *Child Development*, 51: 1103–9.

TOTH, N. (1985). The Oldowan re-assessed: a close look at early stone artefacts. *Journal of Archaeological Science*, 12: 101–20.

—— SCHICK, K. D., SAVAGE-RUMBAUGH, E. S., SEVCIK, R. A., and RUMBAUGH, D. M. (1993). Pan the tool-maker: investigations into the stone tool-making and tool-using capabilities of a bonobo (*Pan paniscus*). *Journal of Archaeological Science*, 20: 81–91.

TRÄUBLE, B. and PAUEN, S. (in press). The role of functional information for infant categorization. *Cognition*.

TRINKAUS, E. (1983). *The Shanidar Neanderthals*. Academic Press.

—— (1995). Neanderthal mortality patterns. *Journal of Archaeological Science*, 22: 121–42.

—— and SHIPMAN, P. (1992). *The Neanderthals*. Knopf.

TRUXAW, D., KRASNOW, M., WOODS, C., and GERMAN, T. (2006). Conditions under which function information attenuates name extension via shape. *Psychological Science*, 17: 367–71.

TYLER, L. K. and MOSS, H. E. (2001). Towards a distributed account of conceptual knowledge. *Trends Cognitive Science*, 5: 244–52.

TYLER, L. K., BRIGHT, P., DICK, E., TAVARES, P., PILGRIM, L., FLETCHER, P., GREER, M., and MOSS, H. (2003). Do semantic categories activate distinct cortical regions? PET studies of picture processing. *Cognitive Neuropsychology*, 20: 541–61.

ULLER, C., CAREY, S., and HAUSER, M. (1997). Is language needed for constructing sortal concepts? A study with nonhuman primates. *Proceedings of the 21st Annual Boston University Conference on Language Development*, 21: 665–77.

—— HAUSER, M. D., and CAREY, S. (2001). Spontaneous representation of number in cotton-top tamarins. *Journal of Comparative Psychology*, 115: 248–57.

UNGER, P. (1979*a*). There are no ordinary things. *Synthese*, 41: 117–54.

—— (1979*b*). I do not exist. In G. Macdonald (ed.), *Perception and Identity* (pp. 235–51). Cornell University Press.

VAN DE WALLE, G. A., CAREY, S., and PREVOR, M. (2000). Bases for object individuation in infancy: evidence from manual search. *Journal of Cognition and Development*, 1.3: 249–80.

VAN INWAGEN, P. (1990). *Material Beings*. Cornell University Press.

VILLA, P. (1983). *Terra Amata and the Middle Pleistocene Record from Southern France*. University of California Press.

VINSON, D. P., VIGLIOCCO, G., CAPPA, S., and SIRI, S. (2003). The breakdown of semantic knowledge: insights from a statistical model of meaning representation. *Brain and Language*, 86: 347–65.

VISALBERGHI, E. (1990). Tool use in Cebus. *Folia primatologica*, 54: 146–54.

—— and TRINCA, L. (1989). Tool use in capuchin monkeys: distinguishing between performance and understanding. *Primates*, 30: 511–21.

—— FRAGASZY, D. M., and SAVAGE-RUMBAUGH, E. S. (1995). Performance in a tool-using task by common chimpanzees (*Pan troglodytes*), bonobos (*Pan paniscus*), an orangutan (*Pongo pygmaeus*), and capuchin monkeys (*Cebus apella*). *Journal of Comparative Psychology*, 109: 52–60.

WALKER, A. and LEAKEY, R. (eds.) (1993). *The Nariokotome Homo erectus Skeleton*. Springer Verlag.

WALLACE, J. B. and SHERBERGER, F. F. (1975). The larval dwelling and feeding structure of *Macronema transversum*. *Animal Behaviour*, 23: 192–96.

WARD, R. and STRINGER, C. (1997). A molecular handle on the Neanderthals. *Nature*, 388: 225–6.

WARRINGTON, E. K. (1975). The selective impairment of semantic memory. *Quarterly Journal of Experimental Psychology*, 27: 635–57.

WARRINGTON, E. K., and McCARTHY, R. (1983). Category specific access dysphasia. *Brain*, 106: 859–78.

———— (1987). Categories of knowledge: further fractionations and an attempted integration. *Brain*, 110: 1273–96.

———— (1994). Multiple meaning systems in the brain: a case for visual semantics. *Neuropsychologia*, 32.12: 1465–73.

——and SHALLICE, T. (1984). Category-specific semantic impairment. *Brain*, 107: 829–54.

WATSON, J. (1972). Smiling, cooing, and 'the game'. *Merrill-Palmer Quarterly*, 18: 323–40.

WATSON, J. S. (1979). Perception of contingency as a determinant of social responsiveness. In E. Thoman (ed.), *The Origins of Social Responsiveness* (pp. 33–64). Lawrence Erlbaum Associates.

—— (1985). Contingency perception in early social development. In T. M. Field and N. A. Fox (eds.), *Social Perception in Infants* (pp. 157–76). Ablex.

WATTENMAKER, W. D. (1992). Relational properties and memory-based category construction. *Journal of Experimental Psychology: Learning, Memory, and Cognition*, 18: 1125–38.

WAXMAN, S. and MARKOW, D. B. (1995). Words as invitations to form categories. Evidence from 12- to 13-month-old infants. *Cognitive Psychology*, 29: 257–302.

WEAVER, A., HOLIDAY, T. W., RUFF, C. B., and TRINKAUS, E. (2001). The fossil evidence for the evolution of human intelligence in Pleistocene Homo. In A. Nowell (ed.), *In the Mind's Eye: Multidisciplinary Approaches to the Evolution of Human Cognition* (pp. 154–71). International Monographs in Prehistory.

WEIR, A., CHAPPEL, J., and KACELNIK, A. (2002). Shaping of hooks in New Caledonian crows. *Science*, 297: 981.

WELLMAN, H. M. and GELMAN, S. A. (1992). Cognitive development: foundational theories of core domains. *Annual Review of Psychology*, 43: 337–75.

WESTERGAARD, G. C., LUNDQUIST, A. L., HAYNIE, M. K., KUHN, H. E., and SUOMI, S. J. (1998). Why some capuchin monkeys use probing tools (and others do not). *Journal of Comparative Psychology*, 112: 207–11.

WHITE, P. A. (1988). Causal processing: origins and development. *Psychological Bulletin*, 104: 36–52.

WHITEN, A. and BYRNE, R. (1997). *Machiavellian Intelligence II: Extensions and Evaluations.* Cambridge University Press.

—— GOODALL, J., McGREW, W. C., NISHIDA, T., REYNOLDS, V., SUGIYAMA, Y., TUTIN, C. E. G., WRANGHAM, R. W., and BOESCH, C. (1999). Cultures in chimpanzees. *Nature*, 399: 682–85.

WIESSNER, P. (1983). Style and social information in Kalahari San projectile points. *American Antiquity*, 48: 253–7.

WIGGINS, D. (1997). Sortal concepts: a reply to Xu. *Mind and Language*, 12.3/4: 413–21.

WIGGINS, G. B. (1977). *Larvae of North American Caddisflies.* University of Toronto Press.

WILLATTS, P. (1999). Development of means–end behavior in young infants: pulling a support to retrieve a distant object. *Developmental Psychology*, 35: 651–67.

WILSON, E. O. (1971). *The Insect Societies.* Harvard University Press.

WILSON, N. J. (1986). An implementation and perceptual test of a principled model of biological motion. Unpublished master's thesis, University of Pennsylvania.

WOOD, B. (1992). Origin and evolution of the genus Homo. *Nature*, 355: 783–90.

—— and COLLARD, M. (1999). The Human genus. *Science*, 284: 65–71.

WOODWARD, A. L. (1998). Infants selectively encode the goal object of an actor's reach. *Cognition*, 69: 1–34.

WRIGHT, L. (1973). Functions. *Philosophical Review*, 82: 139–69.

WYNN, T. (1979). The intelligence of later Acheulian hominids. *Man*, ns 14: 371–91.

—— (1989). *The Evolution of Spatial Competence*. University of Illinois Press.

—— (1993). Two developments in the mind of early Homo. *Journal of Anthropological Research*, 12: 299–322.

—— (1995). Handaxe enigmas. *World Archaeology*, 27: 10–23.

—— and MCGREW, W. C. (1989). An ape's view of the Oldowan. *Man*, 24: 383–98.

—— and TIERSON, F. (1990). Regional comparison of the shapes of later Acheulian handaxes. *American Anthropologist*, 92: 73–84.

XU, F. (1997). From Lot's wife to a pillar of salt: evidence that *physical object* is a sortal concept. *Mind and Language*, 12.3/4: 365–92.

—— and CAREY, S. (1996). Infants' metaphysics: the case of numerical identity. *Cognitive Psychology*, 30: 111–53.

—— —— (2000). The emergence of kind concepts: a rejoinder to Needham and Baillargeon. *Cognition*, 74: 285–301.

—— —— and WELCH, J. (1999). Infants' ability to use object kind information for object individuation. *Cognition*, 70: 137–66.

ZAHAVI, A. and ZAHAVI, A. (1997). *The Handicap Principle*. Oxford University Press.

ZIMMERMAN, D. (1995). Theories of masses and problems of constitution. *Philosophical Review*, 104: 53–110.

Index